Enrique Martino

Touts

Recruiting Indentured Labor in the Gulf of Guinea

DE GRUYTER
OLDENBOURG

ISBN 978-3-11-075464-3
e-ISBN (PDF) 978-3-11-075592-3
e-ISBN (EPUB) 978-3-11-075596-1
ISSN 2509-8861

Library of Congress Control Number: 2022937455

Bibliographic information published by the Deutsche Nationalbibliothek
The Deutsche Nationalbibliothek lists this publication in the Deutsche Nationalbibliografie; detailed bibliographic data are available on the internet at http://dnb.dnb.de.

Cover image: Canoe smugglers arriving in Santa Isabel, May 1944. Reproduced with permission of The National Archive of the UK (TNA, CO 554/139/5).
Printing and binding: CPI books GmbH, Leck

www.degruyter.com

Enrique Martino
Touts

Work in Global and Historical Perspective

Edited by
Andreas Eckert, Sidney Chalhoub, Mahua Sarkar,
Dmitri van den Bersselaar, Christian G. De Vito

Work in Global and Historical Perspective is an interdisciplinary series that welcomes scholarship on work/labor that engages a historical perspective in and from any part of the world. The series advocates a definition of work/labor that is broad, and specially encourages contributions that explore interconnections across political and geographic frontiers, time frames, disciplinary boundaries, as well as conceptual divisions among various forms of commodified work, and between work and 'non-work.'

Volume 14

Acknowledgements

This book is partly based on my doctoral thesis which began in 2010 at the Institute of African Studies of the Humboldt University in Berlin. In the summer of 2011, I joined the research group "Forced Labour Africa: An Afro-European Heritage in Sub-Saharan Africa (1930 – 1975)" as a PhD research fellow with funding from the ERC Starting Grant no. 240898 under Framework Programme 7 of the European Commission. This grant, secured and led by the Principal Investigator Alexander Keese, provided an unusual amount of support, and made all the field work possible. My gratitude goes first to my supervisor, Andreas Eckert who took me in at the beginning even though I only possessed a vague plan and little motion; being around the scholarly activities of The International Research Centre "Work and Human Lifecycle in Global History" (Re:work) was a real boon and provided a constant beam of insight for my investigations. At the Institute of African Studies of the Humboldt, I am also forever grateful to Joël Glasman for telling me to go to the archive before anything else, an important lesson, and to Michael Pesek and Ineke Phaf-Rheinberger for their welcoming orientations into the Institute.

The thesis was completed in November 2015 and defended in April 2016. I had to spend much of 2016 resolving an issue with my website, www.opensourceguinea.org, where I had started sharing the archival sources of my research, to which one member of the dissertation committee raised considerable objections. The still-live website displays the empirical and evidentiary substratum of the entire dissertation and book. As there was little earlier research on my area and topic and as I was reporting on surprising findings, I considered it prudent to open my entire source base to enrich any disbelief and disputes of interpretation. I had dedicated much time and resources to the website itself and then worked to put it on a long-term footing after securing agreements from different archives and grounding the legal parameters of my initially free-wheeling initiative. In addition, I compiled and published key sources on the Humboldt University library's open access "edoc-server" in late 2016, as part of wider scientific research data sharing directives. As recommended by the dissertation examiners I also reduced the original sprawling 650-page manuscript by removing the more elaborate comparative elements, the discussion of the early post-colonial period, and the dedicated chapters on areas outside of Nigeria, such as Liberia, Cameroon, Gabon, and Río Muni, which formed part of the investigation and are now partly published elsewhere. The final dissertation, in its cut late-2016 state, was published open access by the Humboldt University library as "Touts

https://doi.org/10.1515/9783110755923-001

and Despots: Recruiting Assemblages of Contract Labour in Fernando Pó and the Gulf of Guinea, 1858–1979."

I was on my way out of academia, but then an energizing and fresh relief came. Therefore, it is my great pleasure to acknowledge my gratitude to Ravi Ahuja and the 2017 postdoctoral fellowship at the Centre for Modern Indian Studies of the University of Göttingen in the Volkswagenstiftung-funded research group "A Global Network for Global History." My stay in Göttingen allowed me to conduct new research into conceptual considerations with which I revised the book manuscript again. I want to thank everyone in the exceptionally enriching intellectual milieu of Göttingen, and especially Anna Sailer, David Mayer, Ritesh Kumar Jaiswal, and Aditya Sarkar. The opportunity to join such a cohort of colleagues, whose research approaches are all uniquely brilliant and distinctively their own but working in a recognizable tradition and style, very much inspired me to advance my own agenda for the revised book and to refocus my interests around new themes, such as money and the contract. I hope they forgive my attempt at seriously revisiting the concept of the lumpenproletariat, the usual disclaimer, "all faults are mine," applies particularly in this case.

Starting in 2018 I have also benefited from a Juan de la Cierva postdoctoral fellowship, financed by the Spanish State Research Agency, with the treasured support of Gonzalo Álvarez Chillida and Javier Moreno Luzón and my new colleagues at the *Departamento de Historia, Teorías y Geografía Políticas* of the Complutense University of Madrid. During the first half of 2021 I also very much enjoyed a junior fellowship at the Freiburg Institute for Advanced Studies (FRIAS), University of Freiburg, where I was doing research for my second book, but my new focused studies on money and monetary transformations also nourished the final revisions of this book. Therefore, the research leading to these results have also received funding from the Balzan Prize for Global History awarded to Jürgen Osterhammel by the Fondazione Internazionale Premio Balzan, which financed my particular FRIAS fellowship, and I am more than grateful to Jürgen Osterhammel for making pensiveness possible, if only by example. At the final stage I would also like to thank the superb editorial guidance of Rabea Rittgerodt and the editors and the two anonymous reviewers of the series, who also thankfully advised against the haphazard title that I, semi-seriously, wanted to give the book in honor of the centennial of the publication of Bronisław Malinowski's *Argonauts*, with a play on its full title: *Lumpen-touts of the Eastern Gulf of Guinea: An Account of African Enterprise and Adventure in the Archipelago of Biafrian Spanish Guinea.*

For being there from the early stages and throughout all other key parts, I thank Benita Sampedro, Dmitri van den Bersselaar, William Clarence-Smith, and Anton Nikolotov; a big wholehearted thank you. For providing the encouraging and critical comments that jolted me into transforming the dissertation into a better book, I am also forever grateful to Frederick Cooper, Adam McKeown, and Joseph C. Miller who generously shared their attention in exciting emails that helped resolve some of the conceptual and empirical problems that still plagued me after my PhD and I hope to have cleared up in the present book. I was deeply saddened by the passing of Adam McKeown in 2017 and Joseph Miller in 2019 and I wish to academically dedicate this book to them and their rare courage in advancing arguments, insights, and broad scopes.

I would need to thank many people at the two dozen different archives and research libraries I consulted for my research, so I best send out a general note of thank you to all archivists of the world, with great respect for their patience and knowledge of the archive as catalogue. In Equatorial Guinea I would also like to thank many people, but I should only publicly acknowledge the official institutions: the *Biblioteca Nacional de Malabo*, the *Universidad Nacional de Guinea Ecuatorial*, and the Spanish Cultural Centre in Bata, without which getting the visas would have been close to impossible. Similarly, for helping me to get to know and travel to the Nigerian archives, I thank Simon Heap, David Aworawo, Axel Harneit-Sievers, Chima Korieh, Gloria Chuku, Ute Röschenthaler, David Imbua, Nnanna Onuoha Arukwe, and Edlyne Anugwom.

For different archives in France, Germany, Sierra Leone, Liberia, Ghana and Cameroon, I also depended on and continue to endlessly appreciate the small community of African history doctoral students who had mostly gathered around Andreas Eckert, and the associated Re:work summer schools on global labor history, such as Kerstin Stubenvoll, Romain Tiquet, Tristan Oestermann, Christine Whyte, Caroline Authaler, William Lyon, and especially Sara Katz. They generously shared or looked into specific files related to Fernando Po which they or I had found referenced in old publications or in archival catalogues. Ideally, I should include these informal networks in the methods section of the introduction to underline the fact that this was a key part of the method of leaving no stone unturned to reach in-depth results for the Gulf of Guinea as a whole.

At the writing stage, two chapters, revised and each almost doubled for this book, were originally prepared for publication in journals; specifically the articles "*Panya:* Economies of Deception and the Discontinuities of Indentured Labour Recruitment and the Slave Trade, Nigeria and Fernando Pó, 1890s–1940s," published in *African Economic History*, and "*Dash*-Peonage: The Contradictions of Debt Bondage on the Colonial Plantations of Fernando Pó," published in *Africa: Journal of the International African Institute*, and so I wish to thank the original convenors and editors of the special issues, Zachary Kagan Guthrie, Stefano Bellucci, and the late Bill Freund, as well as the reviewers and others who commented on drafts of the developing book either directly or as part of workshops and panels, including especially Dmitri van den Bersselaar, Cassandra Mark-Thiesen, Ugo Nwokeji, Paul Lovejoy, David Pratten, Chika Onyenezi, Prabhu Mohapatra, Keith Breckenridge, Jelmer Vos, Barbara Cooper, Cheikh Babou, Benoît Henriet and Evelyn P. Jennings, Christian De Vito, Adam Jones, Ruma Chopra, Alex Lichtenstein, and Marcel van der Linden. I wish to also thank especially Cassandra Mark-Thiesen again for the interesting panel we co-organized on "Recruiters, Agencies, Brokers and Transport Workers" at the European Conference on African Studies, held in Basel in 2017, and Rana Behal, Prabhu Mohapatra and Rossana Barragán and the other organizers of the conference "XI International Conference on Labour History" of The Association of Indian Labour Historians, held in India in 2016, and the Latin American Labor Congress, held in Bolivia in 2017, where I presented some of the new ideas to prepare the book with more encompassing themes and hopefully with a wider audience in mind.

Finally, and in awe, there is in me simply infinite appreciation for the singular ethos of unconditional mutual intellectual and empirical enrichment that was characteristic of the annual two-week workshops held at the UNED in Madrid between 2013 and 2018, organized by the research project "*Lo que sabemos, ignoramos, inventamos y deformamos acerca del pasado y el presente de Guinea Ecuatorial. Revisión crítica multidisciplinar nuevas vías de investigación*" (HAR2012–34599) funded by the Spanish Ministry of Economy and led, heart and soul, by the inimitable Juan Aranzadi. These great gatherings, regularly attended by Benita Sampedro, Enrique Okenve, Gustau Nerín, Gonzalo Álvarez Chillida, Alba Valenciano, Celeste Muñoz Martínez, Mayka de Castro Rodríguez, and others, directly led to a most profound range of salutary tips, advice, discussions, and source sharing. My investigations and this book have benefited immeasurably from that collective and energetic "epic" research revival of the history of Equatorial Guinea. On a final and personal note, I thank, as ever, Sabine, for being there every step of the way, and I wish to dedicate this book to our twin children, Carmen and Esther, who joined us on that fateful day in early 2019.

Contents

Abbreviations

ILO	International Labour Organization, Geneva.
DGMC	Colonial Office, Madrid (*Ministerio de Ultramar*, 1863–1899; *Sección Colonial del Ministerio de Estado*, 1901–1925; *Dirección General de Marruecos y Colonias* within *Presidencia del Gobierno*, 1925–1931; *Inspección General de Colonias* within *Presidencia del Consejo de Ministros*, 1931–1935; Suppressed, 1934–1936; *Servicio Nacional de Marruecos y Colonias* within *Vicepresidencia del Gobierno*, 1938–1939; *Dirección General de Marruecos y Colonias* within *Ministerio de Asuntos Exteriores* [MAE], 1939–1942; within *Presidencia del Gobierno*, 1942–1956; *Dirección General de Plazas y Provincias Africanas* within *Presidencia del Gobierno*, 1956–1969).
GG	Governor, Santa Isabel (*Gobernador General de Fernando Póo y sus Dependencias*, 1859–1885; *Gobernador General de los Territorios Españoles del Golfo de Guinea*, 1885–1956; *Gobernador General de la Provincia del Golfo de Guinea* then *Region Ecuatorial*, 1957–1963; *Comisario General de la Region Ecuatorial*, 1963–1968).
SubGG	Lieutenant Governor, Bata (*Subgobernador General de la Guinea Continental*; subdivided between Bata y Elobey, 1909–1935, then unified in Bata).
Curaduría	Labor Office, Santa Isabel (*Curaduría Colonial*, 1901–1941; *Delegación de Trabajo*, 1941–1968; The Labor Officer was called *Curador*).
Cámara	Agricultural Chambers of Commerce, Santa Isabel (*Cámara Agrícola de Fernando Póo*, 1906–1976).
AT	District Offices in Spanish Guinea (*Administración Territorial* in each *Demarcación*; Fernando Pó was divided into Santa Isabel, San Carlos, and Concepción, then Este and Oeste).
Policía	Police, Santa Isabel (*Comisario Jefe de la Policía Gubernativa de Santa Isabel*).
CO	Colonial Office, London.
FO	Foreign Office, London.
British VC	British Vice-Consul, Santa Isabel (between 1912–1940 the position was honorary and run part-time by a resident merchant from one of the various British firms).
British LO	British Labour Officer, Santa Isabel (established between 1941–1945, then duties were subsumed into the position of Vice-Consul, with most of the work being done by Nigerian Assistant Labour Officers in the Consulate who remained uncredited as authors or compilers of archival reports).
DO	District Officer of Nigerian divisions (the most relevant Eastern Provinces were Calabar and Owerri, each was headed by a so-called "Resident." Provinces were in turn subdivided into districts or divisions).

https://doi.org/10.1515/9783110755923-002

List of Maps and Illustrations

https://doi.org/10.1515/9783110755923-003

Introduction: Smugglers and Strangers

> Touting is not a job. It is a way of being in the world, a distillate of pure attitude: the chest puffed out, the body limber, the jaw set to brook no opposition. There is in every tout the same no-nonsense attitude, the quick temper, the willingness to get into a fight over any and all conflicts. There is a strut they do, a swagger. These are the original wiseguys of Lagos; some of them are as young as fourteen. They do not go home in the evening and stop being touts. The thing is bound to their souls.
>
> – Teju Cole, *Every Day is for the Thief*

There is an interesting figure in colonial and even post-colonial labor markets that has escaped the systematic attention and prolonged reflection of historians. In contrast, their equivalent in the precolonial period, the slave trader, has always been a central concern, especially in the African history literature. This subject is the recruiter: the labor broker or agent, the labor contractor or subcontractor, the runners, the touts, the "hooks," etc., those who not only provided access to work, but vice versa, found workers for jobs, and exerted a tremendous influence in setting the actual conditions of paid work, including its location and rate of renumeration. They chaotically coordinated the social and financial dimensions of emerging labor markets.

The opening of the wide window onto the original African composition of coastal and regional trading confederacies, and of specific "middlemen" groups and their volatile and waning fortunes, has been one of the great achievements of African social and economic history.[1] While the continuities between the slave traders of the precolonial period and their new commercial intermediary activity in the produce trades, the so-called transition to "legitimate" trade, have been

1 For southern Nigeria see Kenneth O. Dike, *Trade and Politics in the Niger Delta: 1830–1885* (Oxford: Clarendon Press, 1956); David Northrup, *Trade without Rulers: Pre-Colonial Economic Development in South-Eastern Nigeria* (Oxford: Clarendon Press, 1978); Paul E. Lovejoy, *Transformations in Slavery: A History of Slavery in Africa* (Cambridge: Cambridge University Press, 2011); Kenneth O. Dike and Felicia Ifeoma Ekejiuba, *The Aro of South-Eastern Nigeria, 1650–1980: A Study of Socio-Economic Formation and Transformation in Nigeria* (Ibadan: University Press, 1990); Adiele E. Afigbo, *The Abolition of the Slave Trade in Southeastern Nigeria, 1885–1950* (Rochester: University Rochester Press, 2006); G. Ugo Nwokeji, *The Slave Trade and Culture in the Bight of Biafra: An African Society in the Atlantic World* (New York: Cambridge University Press, 2010). For more continental or oceanic edited collections see: Suzanne Miers and Igor Kopytoff, eds., *Slavery in Africa: Historical and Anthropological Perspectives* (Madison: University of Wisconsin Press, 1979); Suzanne Miers and Richard Roberts, eds., *The End of Slavery in Africa* (Madison: University of Wisconsin Press, 1988); Paul E. Lovejoy and Nicholas Rogers, eds., *Unfree Labour in the Development of the Atlantic World* (London: Frank Cass, 1994); Suzanne Miers and Martin A. Klein, eds., *Slavery and Colonial Rule in Africa* (London: Routledge, 1999).

https://doi.org/10.1515/9783110755923-004

amply examined, the agents involved in the formation of the colonial labor market have been very much overlooked, especially in West Africa. Studies of concrete market-based mediations of labor migrations during what the eminent economic historian of West Africa Anthony Hopkins long ago called "this event," "namely the decline of internal slavery and the rise of a free (wage) labour force," only started to materialize this century, earlier of course in the South African historiography.[2]

The most interesting aspect about the recruiter in African history is that they do not of course appear as purified market agents devoid of culture or local networks, but as internal transformations of repertoires of Afro-European exchange practices with many precursors in precolonial commercial societies and slave trading networks. In Eric Wolf's chapter on the slave trade in his *Europe and the People without History* he refers to it as "new trade" "engrafted" upon "kin-organized lineage" societies, which became "fused" with long-distance commercial elites and networks, principally because the debts arising from the domestic economy such as bridewealth became denominated and only payable in currencies provided by slave traders such as cowries, copper, and brass.[3] This is also the insight of Joseph Miller's *Way of Death: Merchant Capitalism and the Angolan Slave Trade:* how did externally injected European credit transform African societies from within, so that slave supply routes opened in between the splits of their societies.[4] Miller followed these merchants as they reordered as

2 Anthony G. Hopkins, *An Economic History of West Africa* (London: Longman, 1973), 225; see also David Northrup, *Beyond the Bend in the River: African Labor in Eastern Zaire, 1865–1940* (Athens: Ohio University Center for International Studies, 1988); for British West Africa, see Ibrahim Abdullah, "Rethinking African Labour and Working-Class History: The Artisan Origins of the Sierra Leonean Working Class," *Social History* 23, no. 1 (1998): 80; Ayodeji Olukoju, "Beyond a Footnote: Indigenous Scholars and the Writing of West African Economic History," in *Routledge Handbook of Global Economic History*, eds. Francesco Boldizzoni and Pat Hudson (London: Routledge, 2015), 385; Anne Phillips, *The Enigma of Colonialism: British Policy in West Africa* (London: James Currey, 1989); Carolyn A. Brown, *"We Were All Slaves": African Miners, Culture, and Resistance at the Enugu Government Colliery* (Portsmouth: Heinemann, 2003); Gareth Austin, *Labour, Land, and Capital in Ghana: From Slavery to Free Labour in Asante, 1807–1956* (Rochester: University of Rochester Press, 2005). For Africa see Stefano Bellucci and Andreas Eckert, eds., *General Labour History of Africa: Workers, Employers and Governments, 20th–21st Centuries* (Rochester: Boydell & Brewer, 2019), and especially the chapters by Eckert on wage labor, and by Fall and Roberts on forced labor. For the Southern Africa literature see footnote 29.

3 Eric Wolf, *Europe and the People Without History* (Berkeley: University of California Press, 1982), 204.

4 Joseph C. Miller, *Way of Death: Merchant Capitalism and the Angolan Slave Trade, 1740–1830* (Madison: University of Wisconsin Press, 1988); Steven Feierman, "African Histories and the Dissolution of World History," in *Africa and the Disciplines: The Contributions of Research in Africa to*

many territories as they could drift and unfold themselves onto, with unprecedented, conceptually guided reconstructive detail.

The aim of this book is to partake in and recuperate the tradition of studying the commercial form in African social and economic history, by centering the character of labor mobilization under colonial conditions. In West and Central African history, labor markets based on colonial contracts were relatively small in comparison to local or state arrangements based on kin or kin-like affiliations and labor tributes and punitive sanctions. The specific techniques and energies needed to impersonally and semi-anonymously mobilize the commodity "labor" in an imperial economy that outlawed slavery remain unclarified, subsumed into broad portrayals of the commercial instability and transformed structural conditions of the colonial countryside, or channeled within the rise of colonial-era political intermediaries or "chiefs" and post-slavery patronage networks, or, most commonly, analogized to new types of slaveries and conflated with the alien imposition of coercive state-mandated forced labor.[5]

One of the long-standing strengths and recent original contributions of African history to the thematics of global economic and labor history has been the focus on regions and periods where a labor market failed to take off or was simply supplanted by forced labor. Colonial states either prepared such schemes for the benefit of their own public works or for a small number of colonial employers or alternatively permitted state-like monopoly and concessionary companies and their subsidiaries to do likewise. This pre-emptive and impatient relapse to a non-commercial and often permanent and veiled mode of sourcing labor through state directives and imperial regulations such as labor taxes and draconian anti-vagrancy laws lasted throughout the entire colonial period.[6] Viewing the structure of colonization this way has the analytical and methodological effect of bringing into focus blunt designs and permanent terrors, with responsible agents arranged hierarchically. This simplified foundation of the history of imperialism has made it difficult to approach the expansion and transformation of

---

the Social Sciences and Humanities, eds. Robert Bates and Valentin Y. Mudimbe (Chicago: University of Chicago Press, 1993).

5 Frederick Cooper, *Decolonization and African Society: The Labor Question in French and British Africa* (Cambridge: Cambridge University Press, 1996); Richard Rathbone, "West Africa, 1874–1948: Employment Legislation in a Nonsettler Peasant Economy," in *Masters, Servants, and Magistrates in Britain and the Empire, 1562–1955*, eds. Douglas Hay and Paul Craven (Chapel Hill: University of North Carolina Press, 2004).

6 There is fresh and much recent book-length work in this vein, see in the bibliography the books by Zachary K. Guthrie, Opolot Okia, Romain Tiquet, and Benoît Henriet. For a more interdisciplinary collection see Darshan Vigneswaran and Joel Quirk, eds., *Mobility Makes States: Migration and Power in Africa* (Pittsburgh: University of Pennsylvania Press, 2015).

political economy in African societies and to follow the intricate colonial economic interventions and parameters, such as currency regimes and types of labor contracts, which underpinned the transformation of the productive and reproductive basis of colonized societies.

Even in straightforwardly empirical accounts of constellations of labor mobility and mobilization where recruiters regularly appear in and out of view as they seek out future workers, they are named but then left unpacked. Usually they retain the classifiers and descriptors that colonial-era sources made for them, or worse, become shrouded in even more layers of hearsay and amoral archetypes. Where a distinct broker or intermediary was highlighted in the study of African labor migrations, the overly sociological frames of ethnicity and kinship have come to guide the research of the last few decades. I consider these trends a theoretical impasse, a non-confrontation with the conduits of money and alienation, and a refusal of the paradoxes of "free" and "forced" movements. The embracing of the moral, rather than theoretical, language of a sequence of meaningful and voluntary "choices," is a way to bypass the deep structural transformations that arise when looking at the specific category of relationships between workers and colonial society that have little to do with "embeddedness" or obvious pressures and everything to do with highly commercialized exchange.[7]

In contrast to a well-established line of reasoning in migration studies, the bulk trajectories of migrant labor in the Gulf of Guinea cannot be said to have been "channeled" through an "independent networks of friends, family and villagers." People in these corners of the world were also "on the move, flowing into factories, construction projects, mines, plantations, agricultural frontiers, and commercial networks across the globe,"[8] and almost all of them were

---

7 For a cross-section of these two trends, I suspect the following collection will be a good reflection of the state of the current art: Ewout Frankema and Michiel de Haas, eds., *Migration in Africa: Shifting Patterns of Mobility from the 19th to the 21st Century* (London: Routledge, 2022). Unfortunately, I completed this book before this interesting, and I am sure revealing, edited collection goes to print. For short and clear reviews of more recent historical literature, see Pérez Niño, "Labour Migration," and Ralph Callebert, "African Mobility and Labor in Global History," *History Compass* 14, no. 3 (2016). There is of course a colossal literature on African migrations, but I always recommend, at least to myself, to always keep returning to the 1970s, Samir Amin and Daryll Forde, *Modern Migrations in Western Africa* (Oxford: Oxford University Press, 1974); Segun Osoba, "The Phenomenon of Labour Migration in the Era of British Colonial Rule: A Neglected Aspect of Nigeria's Social History," *Journal of the Historical Society of Nigeria* 4, no. 4 (1969).

8 Adam Mckeown, "Global Migration, 1846–1940," *Journal of World History* 15, no. 2 (2004): 167. See also Philip D. Curtin, *Why People Move: Migration in African History* (Waco: Markham Press

being brought into colonial workplaces by recruiters. Micro-historical strands in global history have tried to plunge the networks of commercial capitalism into the social networks of workers themselves.[9] The "friends and relatives" vogue, or as the case may be, "chiefs" or "patrons," popularized in the American post-war social sciences and injected into the study of migration and labor market dynamics, is obviously true for many periods and sectors, as it is a self-sustaining "feedback" loop in "normal" times. However, and this is the key to my argument, such a framework does not help understand the turbulent beginnings of labor markets or their crisis ridden turning points, or their sudden halts and contradictory implosions.

As I endeavor to point out, the effectivity of recruiter techniques was based on their "strangerhood," as both a type of creditor or commercial relay and a strictly impersonal and partly amoral marketing agent. The recurring but unsystematic presence of an uncle, friend or community leader, weather as a sincere helpful guide and sponsor or as a disingenuous receiver of commissions, does not advance the inquiry; because it was mostly recruiters who were creating the financial logistics, and what could be called the "hermeneutics" of movements or the depiction and creation of expectations; while others set the parameters for the conditions of exploitation both during transit and arrival.[10] If anything, the model of "friends and family" could be successfully applied to the social network of how brokers recruited other brokers, or how employers came to entrust them within their network of affinities. However, apart from a chance quasi-biography, the colonial archive does not reach that deep; these were after all largely informal and criminal enterprises.

The original theoretical findings by sociologists and economists around the abstract "weak ties" that seemed to weave labor markets and lead to the successful placing of new hirelings hold up extremely well, even in colonial situations which they never considered, precisely because they defined such "ties" as aleatory and serendipitous – or "chance acquaintances," i.e. people found jobs

---

Fund, 1995); Dennis D. Cordell, Joel W. Gregory, and Victor Piché, *Hoe and Wage: A Social History of a Circular Migration System in West Africa* (Boulder: Westview Press, 1996).

9 For this critique see Prabhu Mohapatra, "Eurocentrism, Forced Labour, and Global Migration: A Critical Assessment," *International Review of Social History* 52, no. 1 (2007): 113; Fred Krissman, "Sin Coyote ni Patrón: Why the 'Migrant Network' Fails to Explain International Migration," *International Migration Review* 39, no. 1 (2005).

10 For an analysis of recruitment where all these parameters and dimensions appear especially clearly see Ravi Ahuja, "Networks of Subordination–Networks of the Subordinated: The Ordered Spaces of South Asian Maritime Labour in an Age of Imperialism (c.1890 – 1947)," in *The Limits of British Colonial Control in South Asia: Spaces of Disorder in the Indian Ocean Region*, eds. Ashwini Tambe and Harald Fischer-Tiné (London: Routledge, 2009).

through others they did "not know" "well," in the words of Mark Granovetter in his classic *Getting a Job: A Study of Contacts and Careers.*[11] Yet apart from the obvious distortions to this theory of "social networks" arising from not sampling the more volatile and impermanent labor markets of the colonial world or informal and underground labor markets more generally, what was paradoxically missing in their extremely influential dyadic chain frameworks was the autonomous economic figure of the broker as a kind of "false friend."

The main paradigms of labor market economics – micro, behavioral, sociological, institutional, etc. – have never considered applying the insights of their own, likewise Nobel-laureate winning, colleagues' writings on financial brokerage, speculation, manias, and world-historical swindles, onto the labor market. I propose to combine these in a non-orthodox way.[12] Just like the mythical or deductive theories of modern money in classical and neo-classical political economy but also Marxist thought are obviously not actually real histories of money, theories of work retroactively based on the ideal of free labor cannot provide a guide to a historical account of labor markets. There is a mostly valid impression that it is mainly patent or covert Marxists or critics of economics coming from more historically oriented intellectual traditions who always shift the focus to the destructive creation of markets and especially their brutal and continuous "beginnings." Undoubtedly, no other tradition has generated so many enduring concepts around capital's birth in "blood and dirt," notably Engels' own *The Condition of the Working Class in England*. An immersion in this tradition is indispensable because it provides for the reordering of research attention, and the connection to unique and unmoralizing concerns with class formation, economic composition, and analysis of longer-term structural transformations.

The idea behind combining a study of the formation of labor markets with the "financial science of the lumpenproletariat," under the rule of merchant and colonial rather than industrial capital, is to find the conceptual contours of a commercial equivalent to Marx's mostly state-centered "theory of coloniza-

---

11 Mark Granovetter, *Getting a Job: A Study of Contacts and Careers* (Chicago: University of Chicago press, 1974), x, 51; Mark Granovetter, "The Strength of Weak Ties," *American Journal of Sociology* 78, no. 6 (1973); Charles Tilly, "Transplanted Networks," in *Immigration Reconsidered: History, Sociology, and Politics*, ed. Virginia Yans-McLaughlin (Oxford: Oxford University Press, 1990); James D. Montgomery, "Social Networks and Labor-Market Outcomes: Toward an Economic Analysis," *The American Economic Review* 81, no. 5 (1991).

12 George A. Akerlof and Robert J. Shiller, *Phishing for Phools: The Economics of Manipulation and Deception* (Princeton: Princeton University Press, 2015). For a review of this literature see my short article "Irrationality and Speculation in Finance," *HAU: Journal of Ethnographic Theory* 8, no. 3 (2018).

tion" and "originary," *ursprüngliche*, "primitive accumulation." Such state-centric theories of colonization, involving predation and tribute primarily, have a long history of being reinvigorated conceptually through African history and anthropology.[13] Yet it was overwhelmingly financial and mercantile agents of colonization who forged autonomous labor markets. It was these forces who, as Engels originally observed in his supplementary contributions to *Capital* Volume III, drove the new "colonisation. Today this is purely a subsidiary of the stock exchange, in whose interests the European powers divided Africa a few years ago."[14] However, rather than following the monopolistic joint-stock companies or the concessionary corporate patchwork in the footsteps of the classical early twentieth-century literature on imperialism and its revival in the 1960s, I propose that the key agents, in pursuit of this methodological and conceptual alternative, are those emissaries and mediators who at a local level actually managed to establish new colonial relations, and who were often labor recruiters or otherwise concerned with the mobilization of a new labor force.

The results of this study are specific to the surge of stomping grounds for various kinds of massive labor recruitment operations linked to a generalization of contract and indentured labor in the colonial world, roughly between the 1840s and World War I, and in seemingly exceptional cases into the late colonial period. Indeed, most of the concerns and terms around recruiting, even the term "labour recruiter," were formed in a flurry of British colonial reports on the "irregularities" of recruitment in eastern India for plantations in Mauritius, the Caribbean, and elsewhere. In the case of South Africa, this is where the British coined the term "labour touts" to refer to the new types of informal brokers linked to contract labor, and from there the label spread to the Nigerian recruiters who illegally brought workers to the planters in the Spanish cacao plantation island of Fernando Po.

---

13 Samir Amin, "Modes of Production and Social Formations," *Ufahamu: A Journal of African Studies* 4, no. 3 (1974): 60; Catherine Coquery-Vidrovitch, "Research on an African Mode of Production," *Critique of Anthropology* 2, no. 4/5 (1975); Pierre-Philippe Rey, *Colonialisme, néo-colonialisme et transition au capitalisme: exemple de la Comilog au Congo-Brazzaville* (Paris: F. Maspero, 1971); Peter Gutkind, Robin Cohen, and Jean Copans, eds., *African Labor History* (Beverly Hills, London: Sage Publications, 1978); John Lonsdale and Bruce Berman, "Coping with the Contradictions: The Development of the Colonial State in Kenya, 1895–1914," *The Journal of African History* 20, no. 4 (1979): 503; Georges Dupré and Pierre-Philippe Rey, "Reflections on the Pertinence of a Theory of the History of Exchange," in *The Articulation of Modes of Production*, ed. Harold Wolpe (London: Routledge, 1980).

14 Friedrich Engels, "Supplement to Capital, Volume Three," in *MECW*, vol. 37 (London: Lawrence & Wishart, 1975), 897.

My research led me to focus only on this last constellation, but from here I bring the specific recruiting techniques I found dominating this region into relation with the comparative study of indentured labor, which has always been a great strength of the older and more recent regional and global labor histories, especially of South Asia and the Americas. These attempts to trace the global connections of recruiting techniques become more interesting because while many recruiters were Nigerian and operating in British West Africa, the plantation island that was their destination was Spanish, and Spanish Guinea had its own genealogies of contract labor acquired via its initially direct administration from Cuba. Notably, in Cuba the British had supplied the planters there with contract templates and even recruiting grounds in southern China in the 1850s.[15] The analytical circle I will tie together takes all these routes but reaches into the second half of twentieth-century West Africa, and dwells on them from there.

Cross-border migration following on the heels of certain job offers or promises of contracts of course continues, in entirely new geographies but, as I will hope to show, with only faintly altered recruiting techniques. While I cover only on the "classical" colonial period of indentured labor, there are important direct precedents between Europe and the British and French colonial Americas. Nevertheless what could be called the contract-recruiter nexus only became a global pattern and paradigm after the abolition of slavery and the slave trade in the mid-nineteenth century, and followed the boom of world trade which quintupled in these same decades, including in Africa.[16] These new labor recruiters spread out ahead and reached many more places than early colonial administrators or the previous generation of slave traders to which they were often retroactively compared to. Indeed colonial-era recruiters seemed to work most

15 In June 1847 the first *culíes* landed in Havana on eight-year contracts, at a cost of 170 pesos each, with a large subsidy provided by the government's *Junta de Fomento* and paid over to Zulueta and Company, a London-based undertaking set up to recruit coolies in the recently conquered British treaty port city of Amoy or Xiamen. Until 1874 about 125,000 Chinese workers landed on the island, another 100,000 were taken to Peru. Lisa Yun, *The Coolie Speaks: Chinese Indentured Laborers and African Slaves in Cuba* (Philadelphia: Temple University Press, 2008), 15; Mònica Ginés-Blasi, "Exploiting Chinese Labour Emigration in Treaty Ports: The Role of Spanish Consulates in the 'Coolie Trade,'" *International Review of Social History* 66, no. 1 (2021): 3.

16 Jairus Banaji, *A Brief History of Commercial Capitalism* (Chicago: Haymarket Books, 2020), 30. According to British data, "trade volumes between Africa and the Atlantic World may well have quintupled between the 1820s and 1860s," David Eltis and Lawrence C. Jennings, "Trade between Western Africa and the Atlantic World in the Pre-Colonial Era," *The American Historical Review* 93, no. 4 (1988): 942; Niklas Frykman, "Indentured Contracts," in *The Princeton Companion to Atlantic History*, ed. Joseph C. Miller (Princeton: Princeton University Press, 2015).

effectively in remoter areas beyond the strict control of colonial states, weather in "tribal" and highland India and Southeast Asia, or various islands in Oceania, or in the marginalized semi- or non-peasant societies of Africa and South and Central America.[17]

Recruiters necessarily operated in areas "external" to the European capitalist world-economy or, rather, outside the conduits of its shipping routes and the narrow "peripheral" zones of production. Their sole area of operation was the "field" – to constantly bring in batches of new recruits. A detailed analysis of how a buyer of labor power is put in contact with its possessor, via a market, that is money, with its distinct carriers and messengers, reveals a stark contrast to the slave trade or state-organized forced labor schemes. These steps, always present, before the axiomatic "face to face" "contact" between workers and employers of free labor, provides new locations for a serious reconsideration of how global labor markets were created outside of the simple expansion of the paradigmatic case studies of early modern Europe.[18] A focus on recruiters also helps overcome what Karl Polanyi called the "abandonment" by political economy of the ultra-periphery deemed "irrelevant to an understanding of the problems of our age," even though, as he notes and contrary to more popular interpretations, the "differences" between this ultra-periphery and the capitalist core "have been vastly exaggerated, especially in the economic sphere."[19]

A sustained focus on such recruiters provides for what Jarius Banaji has called an "inquiry" into the formation of a labor market, into "the forms in which employers recruited labour," "wherever labour was recruited through con-

---

17 Christopher A. Bayly, *The Birth of the Modern World, 1780–1914: Global Connections and Comparisons* (Oxford: Blackwell, 2004), 408; see especially Gopalan Balachandran, "Making Coolies, (Un)Making Workers: 'Globalizing' Labour in the Late-19th and Early-20th Centuries," *Journal of Historical Sociology* 24, no. 3 (2011); Adrian Graves, "Truck and Gifts: Melanesian Immigrants and the Trade Box System in Colonial Queensland," *Past & Present* 101 (1983); David McCreery, "Debt Servitude in Rural Guatemala, 1876–1936," *The Hispanic American Historical Review* 63, no. 4 (1983); Kaushik Ghosh, "A Market for Aboriginality: Primitivism and Race Classification in the Indentured Labour Market of Colonial India," in *Subaltern Studies X: Writings on South Asian History and Society*, eds. Gautam Bhadra et al. (New Delhi: Oxford University Press, 1999); Richard B. Allen, "Re-Conceptualizing the 'New System of Slavery,'" *Man in India* 92, no. 2 (2012).

18 Louis Althusser and Etienne Balibar, *Reading Capital* (London: Verso, 1998), 208. The literature here is of course wide-ranging and monumental, so I will simply refer to an excellent "overview of the literature" study which also provides a focused reinterpretation of the "origins" of labor markets, partly in the lagoons and seas off Venice, John Milios, *The Origins of Capitalism as a Social System: The Prevalence of an Aleatory Encounter* (New York: Routledge, 2019).

19 Karl Polanyi, *The Great Transformation: The Political and Economic Origins of Our Time* (Boston: Beacon Press, 1957), 47.

tracts, regardless of the nature of those contracts or the terms and conditions of employment," as distinct from the realms of both the general tendencies of its long-term availability and localized labor control at sites of production.[20] It is common for the operations and influence of the recruiter to be ubiquitously abbreviated in labor history, and even sometimes to be conflated with "taskmasters," "headmen," or "boss-boys" who were themselves contracted to supervise workers on their journey and at the worksite itself.[21] However, recruiters in their role as recruiters were only present at the inception and expiration of contracts. This is what gave them the power to set the price of labor, often speculatively and in advance. They did not play any role in "productive" exploitation during the working day, which is the main reason recruiters have rarely been an object of systematic interest in labor history: they are not involved in production and are categorially not laborers, or what the contemporary Nigerian literature called "manpower" and the Spanish called "hands" or "arms," *braceros*.

Recruiters did not often appear in the statutes of labor departments, labor codes, labor movements or labor theories of value; they themselves did not force labor, nor were they imagined to form part of the desirable and functional division of labor, but they partly created it – with the "effort, skill, imagination,

20 Jairus Banaji, *Agrarian Change in Late Antiquity: Gold, Labour, and Aristocratic Dominance* (Oxford: Oxford University Press, 2007), 197.

21 The term recruiter does not even appear even once – except when conflated with authoritarian "labor bosses" who were "recruiters and managers of labor" in China, and as state-run agencies for exporting domestic workers in Indonesia executing a management function – in the almost thousand-page volumes of Jan Lucassen, ed., *Global Labour History: A State of the Art* (Bern: Peter Lang, 2008), 381, 502; Jan Lucassen and Leo Lucassen, *Migration, Migration History, History: Old Paradigms and New Perspectives* (Bern: Peter Lang, 1997). Similarly, the role, beyond an undifferentiated name for a process, "recruitment," is not present in Marcel van der Linden and Magaly Rodriguez Garcia, eds., *On Coerced Labor: Work and Compulsion After Chattel Slavery* (Leiden: Brill, 2016), nor in Marcel van der Linden and Karin Hofmeester, eds., *Handbook Global History of Work* (Berlin: De Gruyter, 2017), 474, 366, though the chapter by Rosemarijn Hoefte on indenture does say: "the role of recruiters was crucial"; "It is hard to gauge individual motives for signing a contract of indenture, but the army of recruiters played a crucial role in this decision." This tendency was only reversed with a special issue put together by Ulbe Bosma, Elise van Nederveen Meerkerk, and Aditya Sarkar, eds., *Mediating Labour: Worldwide Labour Intermediation in the Nineteenth and Twentieth Centuries* (Cambridge: Cambridge University Press, 2012). See also the European-centric collection, with the only extended discussion of recruiter-brokers in the chapter by Amit Kumar Mishra, in Sigrid Wadauer, Thomas Buchner, and Alexander Mejstrik, eds., *The History of Labour Intermediation: Institutions and Finding Employment in the Nineteenth and Early Twentieth Centuries* (New York: Berghahn Books, 2015).

collaboration, and so on" of their own recruiting techniques.[22] They pocketed commissions as market agents and not as delegates or representatives of employers or states. They prepared the tracks leading to workplaces on their own initiative and by molding their own concepts, arming themselves primarily with enthusiastic promises about fictitious places and still fictitious payment. Yet even though they remained at a distance, they could almost completely shape the experience of labor migrants, including the quality and type of work they ended up in.[23]

Recruitment Works

The revival of labor history in a global comparative frame opened vast research fields on neglected labor relations that did not neatly fall under the headings of either slave, forced or free labor. The endless combinations of this tripartite schema led to what can even be called the "discovery" of their world-historical simultaneity, and the study of their even more overlapping recruiting techniques which were supposed to belong to each mode separately.[24] The regional historiographies had understood these constitutively messy features at the same time or earlier. Distinct sets of recruiters had only come into more sustained focus in isolated instances of national or bi-national labor or maritime histories. In this regard the literature around South Asia and the recruitment of mariners or lascars and plantation coolies is field-defining, and as the footnotes in the later chapters show, I have prioritized this literature in order to attain maximum insights for my own study, which has benefited from trying to emulate their distinct patience and creativity with the archive and a salutary air of not being beholden

---

22 Jane Guyer, "Labor," in *Critical Terms for the Study of Africa*, eds. Gaurav Desai and Adeline Masquelier (Chicago: University of Chicago Press, 2018), 199.

23 For an elaboration of this insight for nineteenth-century South Asia see Tirthankar Roy, "Labour-Intensity and Industrialization in Colonial India," in *Labour-Intensive Industrialization in Global History*, eds. Gareth Austin and Kaoru Sugihara (London: Routledge, 2013), 115–117.

24 Shahid Amin and Marcel van der Linden, eds., *Peripheral Labour: Studies in the History of Partial Proletarianization* (Cambridge: Cambridge University Press, 1997); Pepijn Brandon and Aditya Sarkar, "Labour History and the case against Colonialism," *International Review of Social History* 61 (2019). For a more recent and more analytical synthesis see also Christian De Vito, Juliane Schiel, and Matthias van Rossum, "From Bondage to Precariousness? New perspectives on Labor and Social History," *Journal of Social History* 54, no. 2 (2020); Damir-Geilsdorf et al., *Bonded Labour.* A foundational comparative work is by Willemina Kloosterboer, *Involuntary Labour since the Abolition of Slavery: A Survey of Compulsory Labour throughout the World* (Leiden: Brill, 1960).

to careless paradigms reified by ideological premises.[25] The older literature from the Americas has generated a continuous Andean-like range of formidable studies on recruiting systems, with unique book-length treatments of them, such as Gunther Peck's *Reinventing Free Labor* and Jose Moya's *Cousins and Strangers*, and articles, from Chiapas and Belize to Chile, about the so-called *enganche* system, which in many ways is precisely what the Spanish implanted in the Gulf of Guinea.[26]

In African history there are rare and extremely valuable studies that have offered "a rare glimpse into the actual mechanics of the labor market" where a wide range of "intermediaries and interlopers" necessarily appear. Such "interlopers" were sometimes affiliated but formally and clearly outside of the statist or licensed-monopoly recruitment drives and agencies that have been the most common focus of the social and economic literature studying the colonial peri-

---

25 Gopalan Balachandran, "Searching for the Sardar: The State, Pre-Capitalist Institutions, and Human Agency in the Maritime Labour Market, Calcutta, 1880–1935," in *Institutions and Economic Change in South Asia*, eds. Burton Stein and Sanjay Subrahmanyam (Delhi: Oxford University Press, 1996); Tirthankar Roy, "Sardars, Jobbers, Kanganies: The Labour Contractor and Indian Economic History," *Modern Asian Studies* 42, no. 5 (2008); Ravi Ahuja, "Mobility and Containment: The Voyages of South Asian Seamen, c. 1900–1960," *International Review of Social History* 51, S14 (2006); Samita Sen, "Commercial Recruiting and Informal Intermediation: Debate Over the Sardari System in Assam Tea Plantations, 1860–1900," *Modern Asian Studies* 44, no. 1 (2010). In the past decade this literature has blossomed, remarkably without any reduction in quality. For the early modern period see Mathias van Rossum, "Changing Tides: Maritime Labor Relations in Europe and Asia," in *Colonialism, Institutional Change, and Shifts in Global Labour Relations*, eds. Karin Hofmeester and Pim Zwart (Amsterdam: Amsterdam University Press, 2018). For more contemporary studies see especially Geert De Neve, "Entrapped Entrepreneurship: Labour Contractors in the South Indian Garment Industry," *Modern Asian Studies* 48, no. 5 (2014); Filippo Osella, "The (Im)Morality of Mediation and Patronage in South India and the Gulf," in *Patronage as Politics in South Asia*, ed. Anastasia Piliavsky (Cambridge: Cambridge University Press, 2014).

26 Gunther Peck, *Reinventing Free Labor: Padrones and Immigrant Workers in the North American West, 1880–1930* (Cambridge: Cambridge University Press, 2000); Jose C. Moya, *Cousins and Strangers: Spanish Immigrants in Buenos Aires, 1850–1930* (Los Angeles: University of California Press, 1998); O. Nigel Bolland, "Systems of Domination after Slavery: The Control of Land and Labor in the British West Indies after 1838," *Comparative Studies in Society and History* 23 (1981); Michael Monteon, "The *Enganche* in the Chilean Nitrate Sector, 1880–1930," *Latin American Perspectives* 6, no. 3 (1979); Peter Blanchard, "Recruitment of Workers in the Peruvian Sierra at the Turn of the Century: *The Enganche* System," *Inter-American Economic Affairs* 33, no. 3 (1979); Sarah Washbrook, "*Enganche* and Exports in Chiapas, Mexico: A Comparison of Plantation Labour in the Districts of Soconusco and Palenque, 1876–1911," *Journal of Latin American Studies* 39, no. 4 (2007).

od.[27] The "role played by the recruitment of extra-territorial African workers" was never left unemphasized, even in the founding and original works of Giovanni Arrighi, developed during his time as an economics lecturer in Harare and resulting in his first book. His account of the "development of capitalist agriculture" and its labor market in Southern Rhodesia in the 1970 article "Labor Supplies in Historical Perspective: A Study of the Proletarianization of the African Peasantry of Rhodesia" details various attempts to "eliminate the labor shortage" during what he called a "transitional period" where the role of recruiters could "hardly be exaggerated."[28] During the golden age of South African labor history between the 1970s and early 1990s there were certainly notable dedicated pursuits of the enigmatic recruitment networks that brought hundreds of thousands of migrant laborers to the plantation and mining epicenters – those by Charles van Onselen and Patrick Harries loom large.

More recently there has been a distinct regional revival of this traditionally strong South African focus by Andrew MacDonald, Maxim Bolt, and Francis Musoni.[29] There are a growing range of inquiries dedicated to recruitment in West, East, and more neglected parts of Central and Southern African history, including works in progress, unpublished doctoral theses or smaller stand-alone pieces by Kletus Likuwa, Anusa Daimon, Walter Nkwi, William Lyon, Michael Rösser, Carlos Fallas Santamaria, Nidhi Mahajan, Fahad Bishara, Tara Weinberg, Trina Leah Hogg, and others, as well as the excellent recent books *Margins of the Market: Trafficking and Capitalism across the Arabian Sea* by Johan Mathew, and Cas-

---

27 Martin J. Murray, "'Blackbirding' at 'Crooks Corner': Illicit Labour Recruiting in the Northeastern Transvaal, 1910 – 1940," *Journal of Southern African Studies* 21 (1995): 376.

28 Giovanni Arrighi, "Labour Supplies in Historical Perspective: A Study of the Proletarianization of the African Peasantry in Rhodesia," *Journal of Development Studies* 6, no. 3 (1970): 209. As Alan Jeeves says for Southern Africa, when "attempting to explain this sudden and dramatic increase in the black labour supply, which resulted in a massive expansion of the migrant labour system," historians tended to speak in terms of "structural changes" without looking "in any detailed way at the recruiting policies and mechanisms of the mining industry itself." Alan Jeeves, "Over-Reach: The South African Gold Mines and the Struggle for the Labour of Zambesia, 1890 – 1920," *Canadian Journal of African Studies* 17, no. 3 (1983): 395.

29 See especially Alan Jeeves and Jonathan Crush, eds., *White Farms, Black Labor: The State and Agrarian Change in Southern Africa, 1910 – 50* (Oxford: James Currey, 1997); Alan Jeeves, *Migrant Labour in South Africa's Mining Economy: The Struggle for the Gold Mines' Labour Supply, 1890 – 1920* (Kingston: McGill-Queen's University Press, 1985), 3 – 34, 239 – 264; Andrew MacDonald, "Colonial Trespassers in the Making of South Africa's International Borders 1900 to C. 1950" (PhD diss., Cambridge University, 2012), 242 – 290; Maxim Bolt, *Zimbabwe's Migrants and South Africa's Border Farms: The Roots of Impermanence* (Cambridge: Cambridge University Press, 2015), 70 – 90; Francis Musoni, *Border Jumping and the Control of Migration in Southern Africa* (Bloomington: Indiana University Press, 2020), 38 – 82.

sandra Mark-Thiesen's *Mediators, Contract Men, and Colonial Capital* on Liberian workers in Ghana.[30]

The past decade has seen a blossoming of studies on recruitment in anthropology and sociology, seemingly burst open by the 2012 collection edited by Johan Lindquist, Biao Xiang, and Brenda Yeoh, specific to Asia.[31] The only historical piece in the issue was an extraordinary reflective essay by the late Adam McKeown, "How the Box Became Black: Brokers and the Creation of the Free Migrant," based on his extensive research into South Asian and Chinese contract labor migrations. In a series of short paragraphs, he makes a most lucid critique of the bulk of the histography on indentured labor and the small industry of mainstream contemporary migration research that until recently looked at the irregularity and opacity of labor recruiters to provide "explanations for the inequities and exploitation surrounding migration." With this insight, and with his milestone pieces, *Melancholy Order* and "Global Migration, 1846–1940," we can firmly delimit the influential legacy of the twentieth-century classics on indenture: David Northrup's *Indentured Labor in the Age of Imperialism* and Hugh Tinker's *A New System of Slavery.*

The "Northrupian" and "Tinkerian" paradigms were politically opposed, yet both were conceptually fully immersed in the liberal commitments of an imperial self-modeling with almost permanent distortionary and even damaging effects for the study of contract labor, and in particular recruitment. McKeown notes that the "stark dichotomy" of free and unfree forms of labor movement emerged alongside the abolition of the African slave trade to encourage and then suppress yet again the "new types of 'slave-traders' who were being mobilized to informally recruit indentured labour." New generations of brokers were initially unleashed as viable substitutes but then became actively "excluded from the

30 Johan Mathew, *Margins of the Market: Trafficking and Capitalism across the Arabian Sea* (Los Angeles: University of California Press, 2016); Cassandra Mark-Thiesen, *Mediators, Contract Men, and Colonial Capital: Mechanized Gold Mining in the Gold Coast Colony, 1879–1909* (Melton: Boydell & Brewer, 2018); Kletus Likuwa, *Voices from the Kavango: A Study of the Contract Labour System in Namibia, 1925–1972* (Basel: Basler Afrika Bibliographien, 2020), 56–59; Anusa Daimon, "Settling in Motion as Consciousness: Nyasa (Malawian) Informal Transit across Southern Rhodesia towards South Africa from the 1910s to the 1950s," *African Studies* 80, no. 1 (2021); Michiel de Haas, "Moving Beyond Colonial Control? Economic Forces and Shifting Migration from Ruanda-Urundi to Buganda, 1920–60," *The Journal of African History* 60, no. 3 (2019), 379–406.

31 Johan Lindquist, Biao Xiang, and Brenda S.A. Yeoh, "Opening the Black Box of Migration: Brokers, the Organization of Transnational Mobility and the Changing Political Economy in Asia," *Pacific Affairs* 85, no. 1 (2012). See also Biao Xiang and Johan Lindquist, "Migration Infrastructure," *International Migration Review* 48, no. 1 (2014).

management of mobility" by booming imperial political economies. They had to found and improvise niches and techniques between and beyond "legal jurisdictions and frameworks."[32]

Even Spanish colonial scandalized contemporaries talked of uncontainable contagions, of "veritable slave-traders resurging in the twentieth century, we call them *reclutadores*."[33] French officials across the border of Spanish Guinea spoke of its "employers, using methods of the slave-trade rather than '*recrutement*'."[34] Historians too have observed, often disconcertingly, what Catherine Coquery-Vidrovitch called the "plague of recruiters," who forged the distant gateways to the mines and railways in Central and Southern Africa, with regressive methods that were, as Frederick Cooper notes, "sometimes closer to kidnapping."[35] Residing in what seemed to be a separate and uncontrollable new underground, producing, or taking advantage of the commercial turbulence brought on by phases of colonial expansion, recruiters were always morally and even economically placed both outside the new order of ideal colonizers (administrators, limited liability companies, missionaries, etc.) and of the shifting imaginary of the colonized (traditional rulers, peasant villages, assimilating elites, urban workers, etc.). Recruiters were associated with vectors of uprooting and disease as well as exacerbators of internal tensions and dysphoria in what Georges Balandier called the "collective circumstances" of the "colonial situation" – the term he coined to designate the "dislocation of traditional groupings, the appearance of social classes, the nature and role of the proletariat, etc."[36]

In southern Nigeria many recruiters were descendants of the aristocratic and specialized diasporic merchant groups who just a few generations prior had

---

32 Adam McKeown, "How the Box Became Black: Brokers and the Creation of the Free Migrant," *Pacific Affairs* 85, no. 1 (2012): 22. David Northrup, *Indentured Labor in the Age of Imperialism, 1834–1922* (Cambridge: Cambridge University Press, 1995); Hugh Tinker, *A New System of Slavery: The Export of Indian Labour Overseas, 1830–1920* (London: Oxford University Press, 1974).

33 Angel Yglesias de la Riva, *Politica indígena en Guinea* (Madrid: Instituto de Estudios Africanos, 1947), 219.

34 Chef de la Subdivision Ambam to Chef de Circonscription, Ebolowa, September 21, 1931, ANC, APA, 10165/A.

35 Catherine Coquery-Vidrovitch, "The Colonial Economy of the Former French, Belgian and Portuguese Zones," in *General History of Africa, Volume VII: Africa Under Colonial Domination 1880–1935*, ed. A. Adu Boahen (Paris: UNESCO, 1985), 363; Cooper, *Decolonization*, 44. John Higginson, "The Making of an African Working Class: The Union Minière du Haut Katanga and the African Mine Workers, 1907–1945" (PhD diss., University of Michigan, 1979), 290–310.

36 Georges Balandier, "The Colonial Situation: A Theoretical Approach," in *Social Change: The Colonial Situation*, ed. Immanuel Wallerstein (New York: John Wiley & Sons, 1966[1951]), 60.

been partially or fully dedicated to supplying the external and internal slave trades. The paradox is that while they were described as a new type of slave trader, they were nothing of the sort. Recruiters did not use arms or physical binds. They did not need such violence to operate successfully, only errant representations and errant payments. They engaged potential workers in a drawn-out and usually negotiated set of purposefully uncertain illustrations and transactions. There were never more than 50 to 200 of these recruiters at a time; they could each mobilize dozens of new recruits every year. They did this through different means, sometimes they conducted a type of fraud that amounted to a non-violent kidnapping, other times, more commonly, all that they needed to do was make the fictitious promise of a large wage advance or a well-placed job, whether in Fernando Po or elsewhere. Recruiters peddled in small gifts and big promises, but their principal way of being effective came from their handling and relaying of unofficial wage advances underpinned by the contract form.

To get laborers onto the Iberian colonial plantation islands in the Gulf of Guinea, Fernando Po and São Tomé and Príncipe, William Clarence-Smith says, "every formula was tried. Slavery, indentured labor, forced labor, tax-induced migration, and free-wage labour," sometimes in no particular order and even simultaneously. The sheer dimension of indentured labor in this particular Gulf, and the techniques that brought them about, requires an exclusive analytical commitment.[37] The number of Nigerian contract laborers in Spanish Guinea in 1939, around 25,000, was equivalent to over ten per cent of Nigeria's entire wage-employed population – and practically all had arrived in the 1930s through the clandestine routes set up by the labor touts operating out of Calabar in southeastern Nigeria. This number was about half of those employed in the entire Nigerian civil service – by far the biggest employer in British West Africa.[38] In the 1950s, more Nigerians were working Spanish Guinea than in the entirety of Nigeria's medium to large scale agriculture, forestry, and fishing sectors.[39] Cumu-

---

37 William G. Clarence-Smith, "Cocoa Plantations and Coerced Labor in the Gulf of Guinea, 1870–1914," in *Breaking the Chains: Slavery, Bondage and Emancipation in Africa and Asia*, ed. Martin A. Klein (Madison: University of Wisconsin Press, 1993), 153.

38 Heinrich A. Wieschhoff, *Colonial Policies in Africa* (Philadelphia: University of Pennsylvania Press, 1944), 38. The figures for Nigeria in 1938 for those employed for wages was 182,600, of which 50,000 each in mines and government, in a Nigerian population of twenty-one million. Granville St. J. Orde-Browne, *Labour Conditions in West Africa* (London: H. M. Stationary Office, 1941), 79.

39 Central Office of Information, December 1959, TNA, LAB 43/357, "Fact Sheets on the U.K. Dependencies, The Federation of Nigeria." Of the "principal wage-earning occupation" in 1957, in "undertakings employing ten or more persons" were "Agriculture, Forestry and Fishing, 42,680; Mining, Quarrying, 53, 640; Government, 120,000."

latively, for the colonial twentieth century, there were at least a quarter of a million indentured Nigerian workers in Spanish Guinea; about half the number of Indians who went to Mauritius, the "largest recipient of indentured labor" in the British Empire, and twice the number of all the Chinese "coolies" brought to Peru and Cuba in a similar time frame of around half a century.[40] Until recently there was little awareness, even amongst the regional specialists, that this was one of the largest inter-colonial African labor migrations, and certainly the largest that was still being explicitly called "indenture" by the British in Nigeria. There is only one line on the matter in the *Cambridge History of Africa*, by Clarence-Smith: "The main source of labour came to be Ibo smuggled in African canoes from Nigeria. The British rather reluctantly made this current of labour migration legal in 1942, in order to control it."[41]

---

40 Allen, *Slaves, Freedmen and Indentured Laborers*, 59. For reference: 63,695 Chinese coolies were brought on three-year contracts to the Witwatersrand gold mines between 1904 and 1907, and 152,000 from the Bay of Bengal to the sugar plantations in Natal over a 50-year period until 1911, on 384 ships from Madras and Calcutta. Goolam Vahed, "Power and Resistance: Indentured Labour in Colonial Natal, 1860 – 1911," in *Resistance and Indian Indenture Experience. Comparative Perspectives*, eds. Brij V. Lal et al. (Delhi: Manohar, 2014), 106; Peter Richardson, *Chinese Mine Labour in the Transvaal* (London: Macmillan Press, 1982), 204.

41 William G. Clarence-Smith, "Spanish Equatorial Guinea, 1898 – 1940," in *The Cambridge History of Africa: From 1905 to 1940*, eds. Arthur D. Roberts et al. (Cambridge: Cambridge University Press, 1986), 540. In the next volume when the complete shift to Nigerian labor occurs by the 1940s, Equatorial Guinea appears as an appendix to Basil Davidson's chapter on Portuguese Africa, written by himself, and less than a half a line mentions Nigerian "contract laborers." Basil Davidson, "Appendix Equatorial Guinea, c.1940 to 1975," in *The Cambridge History of Africa: From c. 1940 to c. 1975*, ed. Michael Crowder (Cambridge: Cambridge University Press, 1984), 807. In the most authoritative Spanish and French texts, there were similarly only a few lines, necessarily based on readings of the published compendium of colonial legislation and colonial-era publications because the Francoist colonial archive was still closed off. Max Liniger-Goumaz, *La Guinée Équatoriale: Un pays méconnu* (Paris: L'Harmattan, 1979), 361; Mariano L. de Castro Antolín and Donato Ndongo-Bidyogo, *España en Guinea. Construcción del desencuentro: 1778 – 1968* (Toledo: Sequitur, 1998), 139, 151. For the most updated and thorough new overviews, which now include the Nigerian dimension, see Enrique N. Okenve, "An Island in the Middle of Everywhere: Bioko under Colonial Domination," in *African Islands: Leading Edges of Empire and Globalization*, eds. Toyin Falola et al. (Rochester: University of Rochester Press, 2019), 129; and both introductory "chapters," in reality small books, by Juan Aranzadi, "Estudio introductorio. Hacia un replanteamiento radical de los estudios sobre Guinea Ecuatorial," and Gonzalo Álvarez Chillida, "Claves de la historia colonial española de la Guinea Ecuatorial," in *Guinea Ecuatorial (des)conocida: lo que sabemos, ignoramos, inventamos y deformamos acerca de su pasado y su presente*, eds. Juan Aranzadi and Gonzalo Álvarez Chillida, vol. 1, (Madrid: UNED, 2020), 210 – 243, 271 – 400.

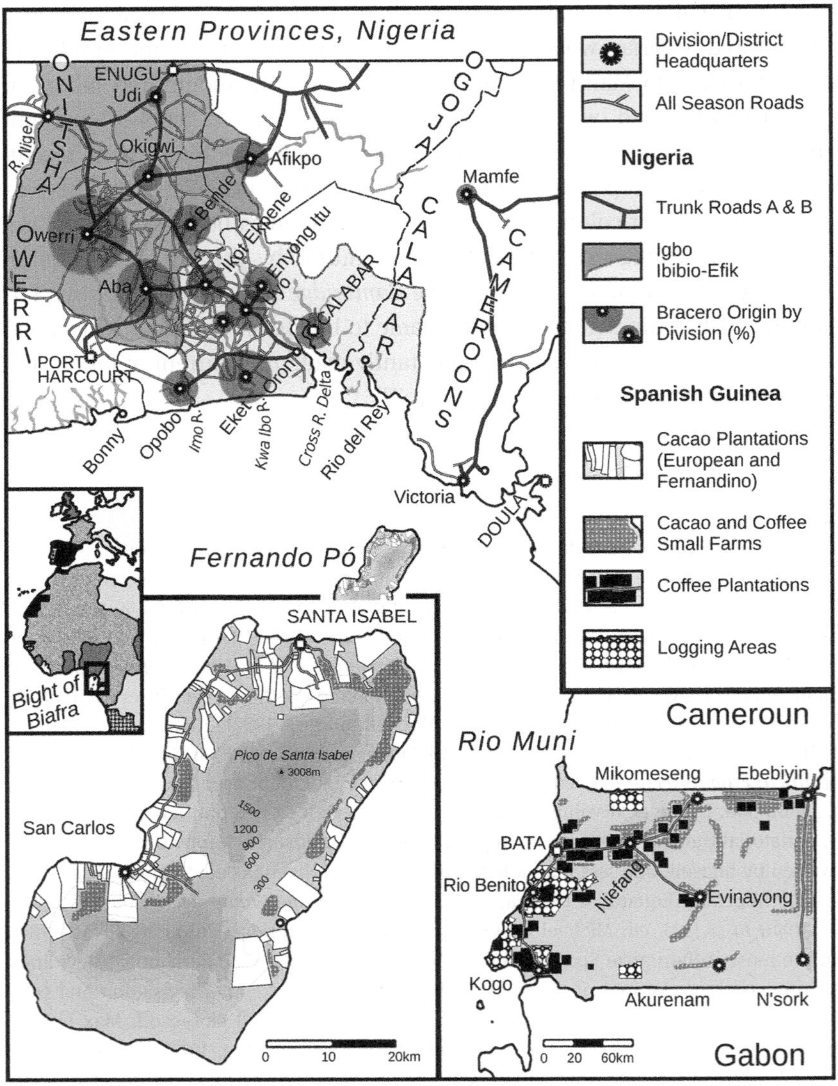

Figure 1: Map of the Bight of Biafra in 1940. Map by Author.

From the distant existing literature, the movement of people from south eastern Nigeria onto Fernando Po's plantations has been painted as a short wide pipe, with two phases. On one end, during the first phase, for about a decade after the beginning of the Spanish Civil War in 1936, was the distinct explosion of *braceros* being smuggled over on canoes from the Cross River delta. The second phase, starting in 1943, was an "indentured labour treaty" that supposedly represented the "efforts of the Nigerian Government [to] control and regulate on a sound humanitarian basis a [canoe-based] traffic which existed on a slave basis."[42] However this "legal" recruitment took until the late 1950s to consolidate itself. Between the 1930s and the 1950s the main source of labor was being recruited by touts with the informal techniques that I spend much of the book describing and conceptualizing at length, supported with an abundance of archival and other sources.

The first of three distinct types of recruited workers that populated the ranks of plantation labor in post-civil war Fernando Po were those "recruited by deceit and shoved into the plantation by force, who did not want this work and are therefore more prone to wreak *palabras,*" palavers or disputes. The second, according to Bona Ekatem, a Nigerian journalist from the *West African Pilot* who had lived on the island, are those "that are voluntary, the good ones, the *bien conformados,*" which means those who have acquiesced, have resigned themselves or been knocked into shape – partly a provisional category and largely a figment hovering over the canvas of any planter's idyll. After listing the first two classes, Ekatem outlines a "third class" whom he calls "the *vagos,*" the vagrants: in "one word, the *maleteros,*" the "suitcasers" "who have until now have dedicated themselves to trying to carry the suitcases of passing passengers in Calabar to live off the tips and in this way to spend life in 'dolce far niente'" in "delicious idleness." "These types have gone to Fernando Poo following the scent of the *regalo* [gift or wage advance] which the recruiters then swindled them out of."[43] Importantly, these third "types," joined partly by the ranks of the first two and even of those who were recruited legally via the labor treaty with Nigeria and were supposed to be repatriated after one contract, stayed on the island for further contracts, because of the dynamic of the informal wage advances. Touts single-handedly illegally recruited well over 100,000 people to Fer-

42 British VC (Lewis) to British Embassy, Barcelona, July 5, 1946, NAE, CALPROF 17/1/278. The only detailed treatment are the long articles by Akinjide Osuntokun, *Equatorial Guinea Nigerian Relations: The Diplomacy of Labour* (Lagos: Oxford University Press, 1978), a brief study which relies solely on the archive in London, and by Henderson M. Tapela, "Nigerian Labour for Fernando Po," *The Calabar Historical Journal* 3, no. 1 (1985), using great sources from the archives in Calabar. See also their other publications in the bibliography, as well as the shorter pieces by Nkparom C. Ejituwu and David Aworawo, and the master's thesis and dissertation coursework which recovered new archival, newspaper, and oral sources by Anthony C. Oham, "Labor Migration from Southeastern Nigeria to Spanish Fernando Po, 1900 – 1968" (MA Thesis, Central Michigan University, 2006); Samuel Fury Childs Daly, "Dropped Subjects: Igbo Labor Migration to Fernando Po, 1940 – 1974," *Igbo Studies Review* 1, no. 1 (2013).

43 J.E. Bona Ekatem, "El trabajo en Fernando Poo," *La Guinea Española*, Santa Isabel, September 3, 1939.

nando Po from Nigeria, yet they also worked on the island by redirecting the *braceros* who were already there. This intervention accounts for the movement of another 100,000 people who found themselves between contracts. They could travel hundreds or thousands of kilometers on foot, trucks, and steamers or, principally, on canoes or they could stay put on the island and still arrange for vast reconfigurations. The idea behind the book is to describe their arena of operation in so much detail so as to distil in a crystallized way the specific techniques of the recruiters who after the abolition of the slave trade made it possible to bring laborers to the rising plantations run on indenture right off the West African coast.

The historical and etymological differentiation of the labor "broker" from other "middlemen" figures of commerce is complex. I will keep in mind these distinctions and overlaps to the extent that it allows a better delineation of the most preponderant and powerful type of recruiter that appeared in the colonial Gulf of Guinea. The complex social constellations of the agents who actively filled the expanding division of labor through money and agreements, separate from but still underpinned by formal contracts, also leads to a longer examination of the broad milieu which they emerged from and belonged to: the *lumpenproletariat*. This well-worn and sometimes eyebrow-raising concept, which I closely define later, unlocks the most important finding of the book: the recruiters' frenzied, volatile, and loosely coordinated nature which was essential for their effectivity as "mediators."[44] They brought with them distinctly erratic, shifting and escalating techniques, which systematically emerged too in many widening and deep pockets of global social and economic history. The formation of the colonial labor market was of course not uniform and varied greatly across empires. However, the surging pan-colonial and independent economic force of recruiters cannot be made sense of in a strictly socio-cultural milieu or within the limited frontiers of a particular empire.

Without this characteristic and built-in volatility recruiting techniques would not have worked, or much less effectively. Certainly, if conditions of work had been described accurately and transparently and pay was predictably constant with no possibility for advances, a fraction of those eventually recruited

44 "Mediators" here and in this book are defined in opposition to reliable and faithful "intermediaries," following Bruno Latour's paradigmatic distinction recovered from Gabriel Tarde's turn away from the mechanistic concept of the quasi-automatic "social" towards the "sociology of associations" or the "discovery of the ingredients necessary to the extension of any practice whatsoever." Bruno Latour, *An Inquiry into Modes of Existence: An Anthropology of the Moderns* (Harvard: Harvard University Press, 2013), 33; Bruno Latour, *Reassembling the Social: An Introduction to Actor-Network-Theory* (Oxford: Oxford University Press, 2005), 42–64.

would have ended up at these new worksites. An austere, painfully slow, and staged instance of contract making, imposed or opted into without an excess of language or advance money, with only the low official wage and the most economical communication exchanged would not have generated movements. Only recruiters and their techniques allowed for the constant appearance of plantation workers on Fernando Po. In this historical world, which this book heavily leans into, there was no such thing as non-distorted information or price, which given enough time would shed its elements of extra-exploitative coercion and revert to a fixed and balanced point of transparent decisions and un-political value distribution. The complex financial dynamics of the commodity labor cannot be captured by axioms of game-theoretical bargaining power or stable power asymmetries, nor of course as a naturally arising correct number which approximates the "substance" of value. Adopting such vocabulary impedes the tracing of historically emergent labor markets because it conceptually creates shadows, an "imperfect," "distorted," "extra-exploitative" "extra-economics."

The Chapters

The first chapter provides a straightforward account of the labor economics and politics of the Spanish colonial territories in the Gulf of Guinea, including the changing composition of the *braceros*, planters, and traders, told through the almost century-long preoccupation with resolving the "labor scarcity" or the so-called "labor question." However, to begin to outline the logical emergence of the recruiters, this first chapter is also devoted to examining the paradigm of indentured labor as it was implanted in Spain's last plantation colony in the second half of the nineteenth century from Cuba and initially applied to the first generation of *braceros*, primarily Kru from Liberia. The chapter ends with a close examination, almost a dissection, of the labor contract itself: a many-paged and -sided booklet ruling the complete social and economic existence of *braceros* and containing everything from the labor code to an identification sheet, to a sprawling double-entry bookkeeping table of lumped wage payments and variable deductions.

The title of the second chapter, "Take or Give," alludes to the translation of two pidgin terms, *panya* and *dash*, which condense and precisely denominate the recruiting methods I explore at length in the book. This brief chapter proposes a schema of these two original African or Afro-European exchange relations for a global history of recruiting techniques. The historical transformation of the meaning of the pidgin term *panya* (and *panyarring*) provides for comparative insights into the patterns of kidnapping within the recruitment systems of indentured labor that followed the abolition of the slave trade: the abductions known as "black-birding" or "shanghaiing." The meaning of the term *dash*, which became the pidgin equivalent of wage advances, is traced back as a vital component of the trade practices in precolonial West Africa with its own complex economics and conceptual genealogies. I then contrast this necessary "giving" of the *dash* with the cognate concepts of advances, peonage, and debt bondage across various islands and enclaves of indenture in global history to highlight the closely related question of incentives for desertion.

The third and fourth chapters are entirely archival and empirical accounts of these two recruiting techniques, *panya* and *dash*. I define *panya* in its twentieth century southern Nigerian sense of the word as being "taken," or the "removal to the unknown." *Panya* operated through an inversion of the kidnapping techniques of the slave trade, without the political violence of raids or the sanctioned violence of creditors. Touts did not create capitalist labor markets through slaving violence but by applying a hermeneutical skill set and supplying misinformation about destinations and type of work. Tens of thousands of Nigerians, particularly in the turbulent decade until the end of World War II, responded to the call of touts and ended up contracted to Fernando Po's planters. They considered their temporary fate to be a type of slavery and the recruiters' high commission as the price of their sale. This operation only worked because once on the island signing a contract was obligatory. Touts created *panya* autonomously by deploying their indispensable know-how which allowed them to bypass imperial bureaucracies, as the unauthorized emigration to Fernando Po was being repressed by the British in Nigeria, while in Fernando Po the authorities tried to limit and even eliminate the touts' commissions and the wage advances.

The second technique revolves around the *dash*, whose elementary structure is an "ancillary to an exchange," as Jane Guyer defines it. *Dash* in Fernando Po's *pichinglis*, as in many of the Pidgins spoken on the West African coast, meant the "gift-money" that comes before but, like a supplement, is constitutive of the exchange.[45] The *dash* was and is used in precolonial and postcolonial contexts to facilitate, mediate, and stabilize distinct types of exchanges, such as bribes, obligatory commissions, and informal advances. The *dash* that emerged in relation to Fernando Po's contract was a type of wage advance that by most accounts engendered a type of debt peonage. Increasingly from the 1940s on, workers stayed on in Fernando Po for a second contract, because the advances they were often

45 Jane Guyer, *Marginal Gains: Monetary Transactions in Atlantic Africa* (Chicago: University of Chicago Press, 2004), 20, 59.

promised, and which constituted the bulk of earnings had gone to the recruiter. This time the re-contracted workers demanded their own very substantial *dash* before they entered a further contract. The *dash* effectively increased total wages for a fixed contract, and even guaranteed that one would be paid at all, as planters could go bankrupt or withhold and deduct wages at the end of the contract. Planters kept deploying the arguments of outstanding debts to justify the forced recontracting of their laborers for a third or fourth contract, with reference to the large *dash* that quickly exceeded the total official wages. Yet this wage advance did not only generate domination and immobility; exactly the opposite, it produced unprecedented waves of further escalation and higher rates of desertions, aided by touts. Together they turned this linchpin of indentured labor and debt peonage into a counter-practice that almost led to the collapse of the plantations in the 1950s.

The last chapter and the conclusion delve into the conceptual character of the post-slavery labor broker in the context of class formation and the history of labor markets, money, and trade. I elaborate on these financial and mercantile agents of colonization by exploring and combining the umbrella terms of the "lumpenproletariat" and the "broker," or the recruiter as *lumpen-brokers*. No other concept even comes close to capturing the full details of recruitment and how volatile colonial labor markets were made. The commercial techniques of recruiters squarely belong to the lumpenproletariat, a category unique to the Marxist social imaginary of class composition. This element distinctly springs forth and multiplies during booms or the "gold rush" phase as Marx called it and can come to span and underpin new markets entirely. While the *lumpen* concept has partial parallels in other theoretical traditions, it is unique because Marx specifies its "financial science", or the promises of "gifts and loans," as he says in *The Eighteenth Brumaire of Louis Bonaparte*.

As the lumpenproletariat label is difficult to define and often misapplied, and to justify this conceptual import, I also enter into the intellectual moment of its original coinage in the 1840s. I then revisit the early but failed post-colonial attempts to revive it, in particular through Peter Worsley's 1972 essay "Fanon and the Lumpenproletariat" and the study of "rogues of vagabonds" in the African and labor history of that period.[46] The argument in this final chapter on lumpen-brokers shows how the concept contains a unique analytic for understanding the historical emergence and transformations of labor markets. This combination goes beyond the socio-economic aspect of the broker as a mediator of

46 Peter Worsley, "Frantz Fanon and the 'Lumpenproletariat,'" in *Socialist Register* (New York: Monthly Review Press, 1972).

simple exchange or circulation or the lumpen as a semi-criminal or outcast object of social opprobrium and invisibility. Certainly, almost all the steps the recruiters took were dubious and technically illegal in both Nigeria and Spanish Guinea, even though many of these were effectively permitted as they were not pursuable in courts or could continue after the payment of a bribe or fine, an added cost of business. However, merely positing "transactional crime" as a kind of mirror image of the firm does not lend itself to capturing volatile structure-creating historical realities, as if their motley and brazen techniques simply followed universal and automatic market dictates, but on the illegal or demoralizing side of a world split into the regulated and the "underground," where the latter only adds transaction costs or socially undesirable outcomes or externalities.

In the conclusion I return to the recruiters as an autonomous phenomenon which cannot analytically be reduced to any pre-existing order or cause, while still being posited by imperial instruments and ruling economic orders. It is this very autonomy, free to improvise but also to break away, that reveals the breadth of recruiting techniques in all their subtlety, but also their more fundamental production of colonial "contradictions": the formal contracting of informally enslaved people, and the payment of demanded unofficial advances leading to stunning reevaluations of power relations.

The Archives

Studying recruiters is difficult, not because of a lack of sources – as sources about them are abundant – but because of existing conceptualizations of the figure of the recruiter. Recruiters, in their own voice, make rare guest appearances in the colonial archive, even less than the subaltern laborers themselves. I prioritized following the recruiters themselves, and asking who they were, where they organized their deployments, what changed hands, what information and misinformation did they channel, who saw whom in which light. Following the trajectories of the formal and informal figures who organized or guided labor migration in colonial Africa involves a discontinuous tour through the social organization and transactional economy of ports of call and points of contact which workers necessarily passed through. To start and sustain movement, recruiters had to relay credits and forge scripts; and every cent and sentence should be accounted for if the question of why and how people moved is to be answered.

The different steps and passages of recruitment had many components: transport infrastructures and navigable geographies, paperwork and surveillance mechanisms, an underground economy of forgeries, briberies, promises, credits, guarantees, and differently divided commissions, as well as the entire hermeneutical construction of visions and expectations. In African history there are only rare investigations into this quotidian organization of workers' migration by "recruiters, smugglers, shipping companies, bankers, moneylenders, and local officials," enmeshed in "enticement, pressure and debt" as Jürgen Osterhammel observed, so I consider this to be my principal empirical contribution to both regional and comparative histories of labor, trade, and mobility.[47] A particularly difficult but important to research dimension is the crux of "petty financiers, and speculators" that "worked together with—and, at times, against—the colonial state and European planters," as Sunil Amrith says in his account of indenture and debt-based Tamil labor migrations to Malaya across the Bay of Bengal.[48]

The archive for this sort of investigation is always dispersed, and most of the key clues were found in small snippets of detail in the regular correspondence between officials and the non-serialized data-rich appendices of their standardized reports. I looked through almost every type of government department and non-governmental files touching on labor and trade, but the "singular" items always proved most valuable, from police interrogations of workers and recruiters, to intrepid self-propelling journalists, to astute planters, to foreign consuls keenly reporting on incidents and new tendencies, who all relied on observant and even participating informants.

Tracing the Nigerian migrants and traders who already from the 1930s on, and for the next half century, constituted, by far, most of the population of Fernando Po, required an extra effort because of the structure of the Spanish archive itself – minimal, fragmented, partial, and non-digital inventories, and even the absence of such catalogues for whole sub-collections and entire decades, in particular for the key Francoist period (1936–1968). Archival journeys can be both short and long. At the *Archivo General de la Administración* in Alcalá de Henares I consulted around 250 boxes, each about a fist wide, several complete shelves worth, or more than six months of daily archival work and photocopying – primarily of the Spanish Guinea sub-series of the archive's *África* sec-

47 Jürgen Osterhammel, "Hierarchies and Connections: Aspects of a Global Social History," in *An Emerging Modern World, 1750–1870*, eds. Sebastian Conrad and Jürgen Osterhammel (Cambridge: Harvard University Press, 2018), 859.

48 Sunil S. Amrith, *Crossing the Bay of Bengal: The Furies of Nature and the Fortunes of Migrants* (Cambridge: Harvard University Press, 2013), 114.

tion, which houses all colonial-era records.[49] I would eventually go on to transcribe many sources for my website, https://www.opensourceguinea.org; indeed, any archival source I cite here in this book is available to see there, either transcribed or as a downloadable file. I conducted a type of self-imposed pre-hermeneutic monastic exercise which took well over a year or three, I cannot remember. In retrospect, the compiling of tens of thousands of images into files, and the clunky use of optical character recognition software to help transcribe over three million words for my website, created a quite salutary cognitive seep: it was necessary to get a sense of the archives of a defunct empire and the realities it indexed and produced. This growing sense, in turn, allowed me to locate in this and other archives more precise information I was looking for once the research focus crystallized.

In all the archives, recruiters appear indirectly spread heterogeneously along colonial bureaucratic debris, excisions from longer correspondences, samples of serial files produced by the courts and the labor office, one-off interrogations, depositions of workers, an occasional outpouring of the press, specimens of bureaucratic logging systems, lumps of colonial regulations, single tissues from uninterrupted military dispatches, batches of statistics, and so on; even though this list is not that much longer. I consider the archive a residue of a praxis – prescription, description, anticipation, and surprise – a very messy index of what the colonial economy was like.

49 The AGA holds all the colonial "layers," the Foreign Ministry and the Colonial Office files produced in Madrid, as well as the colonial government files produced in the colony, practically all of it without any gaps or discarded or "re-ordered" elements. The AGA thus is a comparatively unique colonial archive, but the paper-based catalogues are fragmented and very imperfectly described. The different Equatorial Guinean, British, Nigerian, and German state and missionary archives and research libraries required another few months of in situ work and they were usually conveniently catalogued with clear and granular file names relating to Spanish Guinea. In Equatorial Guinea, colonial records are held at the Archivo General, Presidencia del Gobierno, but they were and are still not accessible to outsiders. Through an old inventory from 1985 the archive is known to contain material from the 1950s and the 1960s related to local or municipal administration, as well as a considerable part of the public works department and the forestry industry files for this period. Constantino Ocha'a Mve, *Fuentes archivísticas y bibliotecarias de Guinea Ecuatorial: guía general del administrativo, del investigador y del estudiante* (Madrid: Anzos, 1985).

Figure 2: Screenshot of www.opensourceguinea.org. Accessed May 2021.

Notes on Touts

Recruiters primarily appeared in a modality I describe and theorize as "touts". I use this term without hesitation, even though this was the label used by British colonial authorities. It is a historical irony that the term "tout" in Nigeria, which was such a significant economic force in the colonial economy, has today been demoted to the lowest rung of brokerage, denoting either merely someone who helps "navigate bureaucracy" without any guarantees after taking payment, giving them a reputation for being "excessively venal and unscrupulous in their dealings with the public," or otherwise designating the "urban urchins who populate lorry parks and bus stations trying to make a few cents shepherding people onto public transportation."[50] The word still perfectly implies their two techniques at different points of the recruiting trajectories between Nigeria and Spanish Guinea. Importantly, this "archival" concept is also abstract enough to allow for the fact that touts were a wide, open, and shifting category, composed at times of equal parts men and women, and Europeans and Africans. The terms in other colonial sources for this type of labor broker, *rabatteur* in French, translated as touts and connoting a predatory hunt of clients, or *gancho* in Spanish, translated as runners or hooks with a similarly predatory connotation of hardened and crooked rope, are the ones I would use consistently if I had written this book in another language.

In English, the term "tout" was coined in so-called "rogues' cant" or "peddler's French" by eighteenth-century street thieves and meant "to act as a lookout, spy on." Tout as a verb, touting, acquired its most well-known meaning, "to look out for jobs, votes, customers, etc., to try to get them," by the 1730s. Only with the consumer revolution in the 1920s does a new meaning of embellishment appear: "praise highly in an attempt to sell." Today it lives on in British English, in an opposite way, to primarily designate "ticket touts" or scalpers who corner some scarce good in great demand and so have guaranteed but overcharged customers. The economy of "touts," of ruthlessly bidding up prices to find the highest bidder, is not socially accurate, as it is not a rationalized economic activity, but is mediated through relationships of marginality, distance, and illegality. They are a type of inversion of the auctioneer as through their informal dispersal in a messily coordinated space they can easily add complications to exchange with their own rules and parameters. A more appropriate genealogy is another urban argot, "crimp" or "spirit," as the recruiter-tout who "decoys or entraps men into the military or naval service" and eventually other long term and dangerous contract labor was called in eighteenth-century England. Crimp is related to "crook," whose specialty was not only deviating from the regulations they were generated by, but also to deploy manipulative capacities that folded or twisted wills, a structurally forceful knavery.[51] "By hook or by crook," an expres-

50 Daniel Jordan Smith, *A Culture of Corruption: Everyday Deception and Popular Discontent in Nigeria* (New Jersey: Princeton University Press, 2007), 95.

51 "Tout," last modified May 14, 2021, https://www.etymonline.com/word/tout; Hensleigh Wedgwood, *A Dictionary of English Etymology* (London: Macmillan, 1878), 183. The common

sion still common in Nigeria, and still meaning "by any means necessary," captures well the recruiters' techniques and the philosophy of the migration enterprise. As various British colonial observers noted: "The growing sums of capital invested in the island made it increasingly necessary, however, for the Spaniards to obtain labour at all costs." The "farmers are glad to get boys no matter how obtained, or within reason, at any cost."[52]

In German, the term *Anwerber*, recruiter or scout, speaks to both the acquisition and extolling in the economic process of securing or "turning" an interested party, and can be subsumed under the general term for broker: *Makler*. The etymology of this term is unclear, but is related to *maken*, or to "make," and entered the language via Dutch traders in the Hanseatic league as a distinct subcategory of the general commercial act of *Vermittlung*, mediation, because they were positioned both between and under buyers and sellers. They were and are commonly associated with fraud, double-dealing, deception, and swindle. Interestingly, the word swindle comes from the German for giddy or dizzy, imported to London by Yiddish speakers in the eighteenth century, from the term *Schwindler*, "a cheat," onomatopoetically denoting excitement mixed with disorientation, or the wooziness, or worse, felt by the duped party once the deception was realized.

This always potentially present moment in an exchange is a core characteristic that I wish to keep very closely in mind as the various recruiting journeys involved many ruses and traps, for both workers and employers. Yet "knavery" in the negative sense of cheating or stealing is to be located within the more ambiguous subcategory of dishonesty and deception, rather than the destructive category of violence. Fakery, forgery, fiction, as well as the verb "to feign" stem from Latin verbs referring to the "productive, creative, and inventive" activity of shaping, *facere*, *fabricare*, and "cannot be clearly distinguished from poetic and poietic activity."[53]

In a great book on the extensive Nigerian history and sociology of dissimulation and "organised crime, including document fraud, embezzlement, and large scale smuggling," Stephen Ellis proposes the sensible idea that many well-documented and "bizarre" economies of fraud speak to new "possibilities

---

nineteenth-century meaning of "tout" as in a type of trumpet or the sound of a blaring trumpet was used only in literary contexts.

52 Nigerian Secretariat, Lagos, August 1953, RHL, 600.18 s. 21/XI (10), "Memorandum on the labour connection between Nigeria and the Spanish territories in the Gulf of Guinea"; British VC (Twigge-Molecey) to Resident, Calabar Province, November 30, 1938, NAE, CALPROF 5/1/194.

53 "Swindle," last modified May 14, 2021, https://www.etymonline.com/word/swindle; Giovanni Da Col, preface to *Fake: Anthropological Keywords*, eds. Jacob Copeman and Giovanni Da Col (Chicago: HAU, 2020), x.

for self-advancement" or "new realms of risk, destiny and self-fashioning." He argues that such a tendency was particularly accentuated in historically stateless societies, such as those of south eastern Nigeria, where social and economic studies of Igbo areas have emphasized the ease and regularity with which the limits of colonial law were traversed – "itself poorly known, and not generally seen as legitimate."[54] There was an element not just of fraud, of faulty information, of crucial omissions, but also of active molding. In local terms the recruiter was associated with what in late colonial Nigeria was already called the *wayo-man* or "con-man." The term, in colloquial lower-class diction especially in the Southern Nigerian English dialects, connotes "cleverness" and "craftiness," and in the Igbo language in particular the *wayo* is distinctively a swindler, "a cheat and someone who is cunning."[55]

In a valuable and exceptional study of contemporary migration brokers in Anglophone Cameroon, Maybritt Jill Alpes distinguishes three types of brokers according to the vernacular categories which aspiring migrants themselves use: *dokimen*, *feymen*, and "big men." *Feymen* is the Cameroonian equivalent of *wayoman*, the term for successful urban tricksters, defined as those who use "the scarcity of legal avenues for international travel to swindle and make money," while *dokimen* or "document-men" sell "travel documents for travel purposes without further guarantees about success or other follow-up services," and "big men" are public figures who use their social networks to act as patrons for others who are less well placed.[56] Her study suggests, as does this book, that it is such middling and meddling figures that produced and continue to create labor markets through promises and money, rather than the "consumers" or employers of labor.

The range of informal labor brokers that exist today are often subsumed under the labels "traffickers" and "people smugglers," who are, more often than not, touts who have the means and know-how to "assist" and navigate the unauthorized emigration to destinations with a viable labor market – a

---

54 Stephen Ellis, *This Present Darkness: A History of Nigerian Organized Crime* (Oxford: Oxford University Press, 2016), 30; see also Samuel Fury Childs Daly, *A History of the Republic of Biafra: Law, Crime, and the Nigerian Civil War* (Cambridge: Cambridge University Press, 2020), 111–151.
55 Akinlolu Ake, "In Nigeria Parents warn your Children" [newspaper unknown], September 11, 1954, in RHL, MSS. Brit. Emp. S.24 J.50; "Wayo," last modified January 23, 2021, http://naijalingo.com/words/wayo.
56 Maybritt Jill Alpes, "Why Aspiring Migrants Trust Migration Brokers: The Moral Economy of Departure in Anglophone Cameroon," *Africa* 87, no. 2 (2017): 305; on *feymania*, see Basile Ndjio, "Mokoagne Moni: Sorcery and New Forms of Wealth in Cameroon," *Past & Present* 199, no. 3 (2008); see also Maybritt Jill Alpes, *Brokering High-Risk Migration and Illegality in West Africa: Abroad at Any Cost* (New York: Taylor & Francis, 2016), 65.

route made possible by their opaque and unpredictable logistics.[57] When they are thematized or scapegoated by the media, politicians, and activists, the pitch involves a direct but forgotten link to colonial-era debates over indentured recruitment, including the wholesale importation of condemnatory imagery and its original vocabulary of misplaced concern. Present on Fernando Po was a link or discontinuity between the abolition of the slave trade and the range of new techniques often found in what would today be called "modern slavery." However, even in the extremely clarifying works of the political scientist Joel Quirk who expertly follows the juridical and definitional turns of "modern slavery" starting from the crucial inter-war League of Nations period, there is little sense for how the different techniques and figures of post-abolition colonial labor recruitment were the direct predecessor of practically all varieties of "modern slavery."

The foundational definition in the International Labour Organization's 1936 *The Recruiting of Indigenous Workers Convention*, as the orchestrating of an influx of those who did "not spontaneously offer their services at the place of employment," has never been taken as distinct or even highlighted apart from the conventions on slavery (1926) and forced labor (1930) which have been the focus of "modern slavery" academic and policy discourses.[58] I suggest this blind spot is because recruiters, or rather the underlying dynamics of labor migrations, generate massive grey areas that reveal a whole range of paradoxes, ambivalences and collusions. Under these conditions recruiters could not be considered or thought through to the same extent as the uncontroversial and even unanimous interest in and suppression of slavery and forced labor proper. When recruiters do appear and in order to repress the insights they provide, they become collapsed into or equated with slavery or slavery by another name. To this end, I problematize the "contract" of contract labor, to argue that it was a sovereign category or political relationship, that – much like the categories of citizenship and variegated non-citizenship today – constituted the underlying dynamics of regional and global labor recruitment and migration and its permissible economies of exploitation.

---

57 Julia O'Connell Davidson, *Modern Slavery: The Margins of Freedom* (London: Palgrave Macmillan, 2015); Bruno Lamas, *When Looms Begin to Weave by Themselves: The Decomposition of Capitalism, Automation and the Problem of "Modern Slavery"* (Berlin: EB Verlag, 2021).

58 Joel Quirk, *The Anti-Slavery Project: From the Slave Trade to Human Trafficking* (Pittsburgh: University of Pennsylvania Press, 2011), 107; Darshan Vigneswaran and Joel Quirk, eds., *Slavery, Migration and Contemporary Bondage in Africa* (Trenton: Africa World Press, 2013); John Donoghue, "Kidnappers and Subcontractors: Historical Perspectives on Human Trafficking," in *Human Bondage and Abolition: New Histories of Past and Present Slaveries*, eds. Elizabeth Swanson and James B. Stewart (Cambridge: Cambridge University Press, 2018). Definition from *The Recruiting of Indigenous Workers Convention*, no. 50 (Geneva, International Labor Office, 1936), art. 2.

1 Indentured Contract Labor

> Wherever seen it has been an object of intense curiosity, to all persons who think. Yet the question of its *modus operandi* is still undetermined. Nothing has been written on this topic which can be considered as decisive – and accordingly we find everywhere men of mechanical genius, of great general acuteness, and discriminative understanding, who make no scruple in pronouncing the Automaton a *pure machine*, unconnected with human agency in its movements, and consequently, beyond all comparison, the most astonishing of the inventions of mankind. And such it would undoubtedly be, were they right in their supposition.
>
> – Edgar Allan Poe, *Maelzel's Chess-Player*

The contract in Spanish Guinea, and the closely associated *enganche* system, sprung from its own peculiar vortex laterally connected to the Spanish Antilles. The entire vocabulary related to the economy, such as the peculiar words for worker and recruiter and recruitment – *bracero*, *gancho*, and *enganche* – were derived from Cuban Spanish. These were not terms commonly employed in Spain, except in the marginal provinces such as in the Canary Islands where recruiters for Cuban planters operated in the late nineteenth century.[1] The most important and uniquely Guinean colonial institution, the *Curaduría Colonial*, broadly the "labor office", and its head, the *Curador*, was also derived from post-abolition Cuba. This figure or institution did not exist in any equivalent way in the Spanish governmental and legal system. It connotes a "tutelary" and "educational" scope and function. In Cuba it was used to refer only to the individual *Curadores* or "tutors" or "guardians" of manumitted or freed slaves, who would act as their sponsors, advocates, and keepers in official proceedings.[2] In Spanish Guinea the *Curador* became a centralized entity that regulated all facets of the social and economic existence of *braceros*, including contract-making. This chapter explores its apparatus in detail with the aim of showing how it was at the root of the entire recruitment system and of the structure of the colonial economy itself.

The *Curaduría Colonial* was founded in 1901 to take over the work of registering contracts from the Governor's secretary and streamline the charging of a small two peseta tax for each *bracero*. It was given its own statute in 1904 as part of the creation of the *Patronato de Indigenas*, which envisioned the full reg-

1 José Antonio Piqueras, ed., *Azucar y esclavitud en el final del trabajo forzado. Homenaje a M. Moreno Fraginals* (Madrid: Fondo de Cultura Economica, 2002); on Spanish *braceros* see Francisco J. Macías Martín, *Cuba: Crisis política, crisis económica y emigración* (Tegueste: Ediciones de Baile del Sol, 2002).

2 Francisco de Armas y Céspedes, *De la esclavitud en Cuba* (Madrid: T. Fortanet, 1866), 150–168.

https://doi.org/10.1515/9783110755923-005

ulation of the legal, matrimonial, religious, and commercial aspects of "indigenous" life. The *Curaduría* split off to become exclusively dedicated to the "labor question" with the inaugural 1906 labor code, the *Reglamento de Trabajo Indígena.* This first labor code was not entirely new, as it adopted many precepts of the individual labor-related decrees issued by previous governors-general who drew mainly on the Cuban colonial legal corpus, but in a fragmented way. Publications by the British Foreign Office in the early twentieth century praised this new "Native Labour ordinance" regulating "all classes of indentured labour," as "well-drafted and beneficent." Its first article was the provision "that all unemployed residents in Fernando Po who cannot show means of subsistence or are not registered in the books of the District Council must perform such work as the *Curaduría* may assign to them, whether for the State or for private employers."[3] The code also contained the nucleus of a new range of "anti-vagrancy" laws, elaborated and more closely defined in later decades, targeting "socially dangerous undesirables, under diverse laws of public order and *vagos y maleantes* [vagrants and miscreants]."[4] The labor code remained largely intact for the next half-century, with modifications altering mainly the quantitative elements regulated therein, and even when a new and final colonial labor code was passed in 1953 its first article was repeated wholesale: "every resident of the Spanish Territories of the Gulf of Guinea has the social duty to work, the compliance of which may be required by the authorities."[5] The entire imperial century of Spanish Fernando Po was marked by the constant repetition of this contradictory new labor regime: contractual but obligatory. Such a political economic order was relatively unique in African history because of its early imperial unfolding and late colonial intactness, but it is precisely because of this imperially imposed "iron law" that a characteristic and perduring form of a labor market emerged.

The legal peg to colonial Cuba forces a reconsideration of the traditional study of the contract "unit" as dominantly framed in studies of indenture. My main disagreement with the literature based on genealogies of the British Empire is that it uses two distinctively British thresholds to mark the beginning and end of indenture in a sequential phase-like way: the abolition of slave labor in its plantation colonies in the 1840s brings about indenture as a substitute and rupture; and the period around the 1910s sees it being reformed out of existence by colonial officials experiencing and implementing new visions of the nature of

---

3 Great Britain, *Spanish Guinea* (London: H.M. Stationery Office, 1920), 31.

4 José María Cordero Torres, *Política colonial* (Madrid: Cultura Hispánica, 1953), 543.

5 Spain, *Reglamentación del Trabajo de 9 de Noviembre de 1953,* art. 1.

labor markets. In addition, the most orthodox of these "British" works on indenture always insist on definitions that involve "inter-continental" long-distances organized as wholesale passages by colonial states, with contracts finalized at the ports of embarkation – "indenture at the point of departure."[6] This does not seem correct, since a migrant that signs on nearby or *in situ* to an indentured contract is still indentured, no matter how or when they arrived. Divides and thresholds in imperial measures or metrics cannot be made; what is conceptually significant is the social form of the contract itself and the specific recruiting relations that it could found and prefigure. As Prabhu Mohapatra says, "even in the absence of (and after the abolition of) a formal indenture system" in the British Empire, indenture "acted as a template for the 'contract' and debt-bonded migration of free labourers" that followed the formalized colonial "export" of emigrants to the plantation colonies following abolition.[7] In Spanish Guinea the contract only existed and was valid on site. As I argue in this chapter it was the form of the *contrato* itself, at the foundation of the imperial order, that allowed for highly commercialized labor recruitment across the Gulf of Guinea.

Unlike the heavily state-subsidized indentures in the British or French empires arrayed intra or inter-imperially, recruitment in the Gulf of Guinea ended up being primarily a private affair, arranged on private steamship companies and sailing and rowing vessels. The constellations in the Gulf of Guinea were thus more akin to the contract labor migrations in Southern Africa between the 1870s and 1940s or to much of the "non-oceanic" Chinese labor migration in Southeast Asia and South Asian colonial migrations around the Bay of Bengal, or to the Haitian labor movements in the Caribbean in the early twentieth century.[8] Fernando Po has often been conceptually placed alongside the chain of volcanic slopes also covered in colonial plantations, stretching between São

6 Northrup, *Indentured Labor*, 13; David Northrup, "Free and Unfree Labor Migration, 1600–1900: An Introduction," *Journal of World History* 14, no. 2 (2003).

7 Mohapatra, "Eurocentrism, Forced Labour, and Global Migration," 111.

8 Adam McKeown, "Conceptualizing Chinese Diasporas, 1842 to 1949," *The Journal of Asian Studies* 58, no. 2 (1999); Donna Gabaccia, "Migration and Globalization: Bridging Three Eras in Modern World History," in *Connecting Seas and Connected Ocean Rims: Indian, Atlantic, and Pacific Oceans and China Seas Migrations from the 1830s to the 1930s*, eds. Dirk Hoerder and Donna R. Gabaccia (Leiden: Brill, 2017); Mònica Ginés-Blasi, "A Philippine 'Coolie Trade': Trade and Exploitation of Chinese Labour in Spanish Colonial Philippines, 1850–98," *Journal of Southeast Asian Studies* 51, no. 3 (2020); Samuel Martínez, "From Hidden Hand to Heavy Hand: Sugar, the State, and Migrant Labor in Haiti and the Dominican Republic," *Latin American Research Review* 34, no. 1 (1999); Philip A. Howard, *Black Labor, White Sugar: Caribbean Braceros and their Struggle for Power in the Cuban Sugar Industry* (Baton Rouge: Louisiana State University Press, 2015), 21–61.

Tomé and Príncipe and the German lands around Mount Cameroon. Recruiting was quite different in each, sometimes worlds apart, primarily, because of the distinct types of contracts reigning in each territory. In addition, what distinguished Fernando Po from São Tomé was its commercially active class of Fernandino Creoles, who had personal and other connections to all the main ports on the Gulf of Guinea with similar Creole communities and who initiated much of the initial independent recruitment. Santa Isabel was a stop on most of the main West African steamer routes, and the island was also reachable by ocean-going canoes from the coast.

Fernando Po was in no way analogous to São Tomé, where up until the early twentieth century those enslaved on the Bié plateau in northern Angola "continued to be imported, bought, and sold under the guise of contract labour" and kept in perpetuity on the plantations, under post-abolition eight-year *serviçais* contracts out of which there was no escape.[9] Only during World War I did the slaving caravan routes finally collapse. The modalities of recruitment quickly switched to a type of militarized in situ levy from Angola, Mozambique, and Cape Verde, where the drafting and squeezing of entire resident populations for colonial infrastructure and agriculture in the first half of the twentieth century was widespread.[10] Because of the absence of an extensive hinterland, excluding the small Spanish territory of Río Muni, Fernando Po was also very unlike the large state-supported German plantations in Cameroon whose labor control and supply was underpinned by the effective military conquest of much of the interior by the 1890s. In comparison, such designs were only belatedly imposed in Spanish Guinea to drive indigenous workers into plantations, in

9 Miers and Roberts, "The End of Slavery," 20, 54; Clarence-Smith, "Labour Conditions in the Plantations," 149.

10 Augusto Nascimento, "Escravatura, trabalho forçado e contrato em S. Tomé e Príncipe nos séculos XIX e XX: sujeição e ética laboral," *Africana Studia* 7 (2004); Michel Cahen, "*Indigenato* before Race? Some proposals on Portuguese Forced Labour Law in Mozambique and the African Empire (1926–62)," in *Racism and Ethnic Relations in the Portuguese-Speaking World*, eds. Francisco Bethencourt and Adrian Pearce (Oxford: Oxford University Press, 2012); Michel Cahen, "Slavery, Enslaved Labour and Forced Labour in Mozambique," *Portuguese Studies Review* 21, no. 1 (2013). In 1909 there were some 35,544 *serviçais* on about 200 *roças* or plantations, the year São Tomé became the world's largest producer of cocoa, 18% of the world total. Between 1928 and 1958 another 85,000 *serviçais* arrived on São Tomé. The previous quarter between 1902 and 1928 almost 100,000 *serviçais* were dispatched to São Tomé. Their numbers remained high before declining in the post-World War II period to some 20,000 *serviçais*, by which time the island's primary residents outnumbered them, the creole *forros*, many of whom were *libertos*, who had always disdained the idea of "farm work for wages" and rejected plantation labour.

short bursts and numerically overall less effectively.[11] Fernando Po, surrounded by recruiting prohibitions and labor migration embargoes from the British, French and German colonies along the Gulf of Guinea, was forced to pursue indirect and unregulated channels outside of its territory.

From Cuba and Liberia, 1850s–1890s

Fernando Po was located in a gap between the northeast and southeast trade winds at the inner margins of the West African and South Atlantic slaving and circulation systems, and was spared involvement in the transatlantic slave trade for this and various other reasons, including the resolute isolationism of its indigenous Bubi inhabitants, and because from the 1820s to the 1850s, armed with steamships and a lease from the Spanish crown, various naval, merchant, and missionary British abolitionists set up base on the island's shores. In the mid-nineteenth century the British naval base and subsequent trading and refueling station of Clarence in Fernando Po – the eventual Santa Isabel of Spanish Guinea and Malabo of Equatorial Guinea – became a staging ground for the colonization of the Niger Delta and was used to track down European slave traders, set fire to coastal barracoons, and sign treaties with monarchs and rulers along the Bight of Biafra. The naval station was even briefly the site of one of the Mixed Commission Courts set up to prosecute the staff on board slave ships – a "horde of miscreants, the refuse of all nations." About a thousand "liberated captives" from Freetown in Sierra Leone had been hired to the island to work as clerks and staff. They remained once the British merchants who were in effective control of the island handed it over to the Spanish navy in 1858. The Spanish navy arrived to reclaim what a 1778 land-and-sea-swapping-treaty with the Portuguese had made technically theirs.[12] Immediately, Fernando Po became a dependency or "sub-colony" of the Captaincy General of Cuba – its budg-

11 Enrique Martino, *How to Create a Labour Market in Colonial Situations: Spanish Guinea, Southern Cameroon, and Northern Gabon, 1890s–1940s* (Berlin: EB Verlag, 2021). Spanish and Guinean scholars have also paid close attention to the destructive and often short-lived despotic recruitment of the indigenous Bubi of the island and of the Fang in Río Muni in the first third of the twentieth century. See in the bibliography the works by Gonzal Sanz Casas, Valentin Oyono Sa Abegue, Gustau Nerín, Dolores García Cantús, and José Fernando Siale Djangany.

12 Sundiata, *From Slaving to Neoslavery*, 22, 31; citing Nichols to Hay, March 31, 1831, TNA, CO 82/4; Martin Lynn, "Commerce, Christianity and the Origins of the 'Creoles' of Fernando Po," *The Journal of African History* 25, no. 3 (1984): 261; Jeff Pardue, "Antislavery and Imperialism: The British Suppression of the Slave Trade and the Opening of Fernando Po, 1827–1829," *Itinerario* 44, no. 1 (2020).

et, officers, and legislation came directly from across the Atlantic. It was a small colony's colony: the profits gained from selling a hundred people from a slave ship in Cuba was the same as the entire annual administrative budget, about half a million *reales*. In the remaining nineteenth century this budget was squandered on organizing various projects aiming to bring several hundred Spanish *colonos* (subsidized land-owning settlers, including from Oran in Algeria) and Spanish, Cuban and even Filipino *deportados* (convicts and exiles), all of which ended in many deaths and repatriations.[13]

In Santa Isabel, the former captives from Freetown were joined by deserting slaves from São Tomé and littoral African slaving towns such as Bimbia who rowed themselves onto the island on canoes. Within a year of the first permanent Spanish government sponsored expedition, the Spanish Governor, Carlos Chacón, declared slavery abolished, even though it was already non-existent, and practically non-existent in previous centuries: "all people of whatever class and provenance are necessarily considered to be free."[14] This 1859 decree came early, decades before final abolition in Puerto Rico and Cuba (1873 and 1886), and half a century before other European colonial powers had managed to colonize most neighboring African territories and abolish slavery, in the primary sense of not being a legal position recognized in the courts (for example Southern Nigeria in 1901 or French West Africa in 1903).

Fernando Po was to Cuba as Freetown was to the British Caribbean, or Monrovia was to the United States, in that the contradictions of abolition in the Americas were made clear in the "emancipation" crucibles created by these empires on the West African coast. Fernando Po's labor question was founded on an island without a slave system in place, through the combination of what Michael Zeuske has characterized as the two most significant "blurs" to the boundaries of slavery in Cuba during the early phase of abolition: the *emancipado* (apprenticed recaptives from slave ships) and coolie contracts, both appearing when the

---

13 Benita Sampedro, "¡Aquella mansión de desconsuelo y de horror!," in *Guinea Ecuatorial (des)conocida: lo que sabemos, ignoramos, inventamos y deformamos acerca de su pasado y su presente*, eds. Juan Aranzadi and Gonzalo Álvarez Chillida, vol. 1, (Madrid: UNED, 2020); Enrique Martino, "Money, Indenture, and Neo-Slavery in the Spanish Gulf of Guinea, 1820s to 1890s," *Comparativ* 30, no. 5/6 (2020).

14 Miranda, *Leyes coloniales*, 28. Two Royal Orders came on the same day, one was issued in response to a merchant from São Tomé asking for "their fugitive slaves" who had found "refuge" to be returned, and the other was to assuage a British navy commander who was worried that some residents of the island had "illegally obtained on the nearby coast some blacks, who they then have treated as veritable slaves on the island."

Figure 3: Map of Fernando Póo, 1850. Inset of "Posesiones de África: Islas del Golfo de Guinea en la costa occidental de África" (IGN, 913/MAP42, CC-BY 4.0, ign.es).

illegal slave trade of the Iberian Atlantic was reaching its final peak.[15] It was these two forms, *emancipado* and coolie contracts, that were quickly poured into the last Spanish plantation colony in the early 1860s, during the termination shock internal to the Cuban slaving system anticipating corrosions and crises.

15 Michael Zeuske, *Handbuch Geschichte der Sklaverei: Eine Globalgeschichte von den Anfängen bis zur Gegenwart* (Berlin: Walter de Gruyter, 2013), 24, 214; Franklin W. Knight, *Slave Society in Cuba during the Nineteenth Century* (Madison: University of Wisconsin Press, 1970), 10; Josep M. Fradera and Christopher Schmidt-Nowara, eds., *Slavery and Antislavery in Spain's Atlantic Empire* (New York: Berghahn Books, 2013).

The *emancipado* status was introduced in Cuba and Puerto Rico in the 1850s as an explicit equivalent of the British "apprenticeship" scheme imposed on "liberated captives" in Sierra Leone and elsewhere. In cases where those freed by the British navy had been intercepted in Spanish territorial waters the "human cargo" disembarked in Cuba according to the terms of the Spanish-British treaty to abolish the slave trade. The *emancipado* regime gave the governor of Cuba the position of protector and guardian or *patron*, analogous to reassigning the custody of orphans in Spanish family law. Cuban policy usually involved consigning them to private plantation estates, but at various moments in the early 1860s, newly arriving *emancipados* in Havana were offered a chance to offer themselves "spontaneously and voluntarily" for emigration and join the official Fernando Po expeditions. Only in 1862 did a group of 200 *emancipados* arrive – recent captives who had been purchased at various barracoons on the Congo estuary by Spanish, Portuguese and other slave traders.[16] In Santa Isabel the *emancipados* worked on government land clearing and urban infrastructure projects on what became the foundation of all subsequent Spanish imperial labor law.

Soon after their arrival in 1862 the *emancipados* lodged a collective complaint, bordering on a peaceful uprising, arising from their "strange surprise that they were being forced to work" at almost non-existent wage rates as set by the contract. While the costs of food, housing, and transport were covered by the employer as per the terms of the contract, the wages being paid out were the lowest calculable and largely symbolic unit, one *real* a day. Officially the wage was 50 *reales* a month (the governor's salary was 8,000 *reales* a month), but almost half of it was paid out only at the completion of the contract. The *emancipados* could expect to earn around £4 per year if they completed their contract, in contrast, even the free Kru workers on the island at the same time received at least £1 a month in addition to rations, while *libertos* or free ex-slaves in Havana could bid up their wage rates and earn up to 400 *reales* or around £3 a month. After the complaint, the governor wondered "where did they conceive of these dreamy [*songeras*] ideas in the course of the journey from Havana," and "every Sunday" took to gathering all the *emancipados* in the "Congo-town" part of Santa Isabel to give them a sermon "on the conditions of the contracts that they had entered into." The governor, Pantaleón López Ayllón (1862–1865), a colonel who had been expelled from Cuba after being accused on two occasions

16 Inés Roldán de Montaud, "On the Blurred Boundaries of Freedom: Liberated Africans in Cuba, 1817–1870," in *New Frontiers of Slavery*, ed. Dale W. Tomich (Albany: SUNY Press, 2016), 147; Ibrahim Sundiata, "'Cuba Africana': Cuba and Spain in the Bight of Biafra, 1839–1869," *The Americas* 34, no. 1 (1977); Mariano L. de Castro Antolín, "Fernando Poo y los emancipados de La Habana," *Estudios Africanos* 8 (1994): 13. See also AGA, C-81/7209 and C-81/6944.

of complicity in the clandestine importation of new slaves, "made them understand their obligations and the regime to which they will be subject" – and not only because in this case the administration and public works department also happened to be their employer, but because the "regime" was the counterparty of every labor contract.[17]

A major part of the early social composition of Santa Isabel were the between 400 and up to 1,000 "transient" Kru workers who lived in their own peri-urban "Kru-Town." The Kru were an agglomerate group of eventual Liberians, who lived around Maryland and Cape Palmes. A British naval officer on Fernando Po, writing in 1850, observed with dismay that it was "cheaper to transport these men" from the Kru coast "nearly two thousand miles to perform this work, than it was to employ the liberated Africans residing on the spot." The Creole population "had learned to read" and even "hired the Kroomen to work their farms for them."[18] Cape Palmes was sucked into one of the centers of British imperial labor recruitment. Kru were described by colonial employers, during the peak of indenture, as "the Chinese of West Africa." Over 50,000 were recruited to the British and French Caribbean in the mid-nineteenth century. Europeans were recruiting as many as 20,000 workers from the Kru Coast each year from the 1860s on to work as factors or agents in coastal British and German trading outposts, and increasingly for work with almost all colonial shipping and public works departments, especially in the Oil Rivers Protectorate in the 1890s and for the building of the Lagos Port and railroad north of Lagos in the early 1900s. They were paid around £1 a month, which in comparison to local labor markets on the West African coast seemed like a "bargain."[19]

---

17 GG (López Ayllón) to Ministro de Ultramar, October 18, 1862, AGA, C-81/6941; Dolores García Cantús, "Fernando Poo: una aventura colonial española en el África Occidental (1778–1900)" (PhD diss., Universitat de València, 2004), 437, 515; Sampedro, "¡Aquella mansión de desconsuelo y de horror!," 450–454. The 150 emancipados who survived by 1869 made up an important nucleus of the *Fernandinos*.

18 Henry V. Huntley, *Seven Years' Service on the Slave Coast of Western Africa* (London: T.C. Newby, 1850), 167; Ibrahim Sundiata, "The Rise and Decline of Kru Power: Fernando Po in the 19th Century," *Liberian Studies Journal* 6, no. 1 (1975): 28.

19 Jane Martin, "Krumen 'Down the Coast': Liberian Migrants on the West African Coast in the 19th and early 20th Centuries," *The International Journal of African Historical Studies* 18, no. 3 (1985): 402; Diane Frost, *Work and Community among West African Migrant Workers since the Nineteenth Century* (Liverpool: Liverpool University Press, 1999), 20; Lovejoy, *Transformations in Slavery*, 146; Clarence-Smith, "Emigration from Western Africa," 45–48.

The Spanish navy had initially joined this circuit and turned to the "*crumanes* whom we are forced to go looking for on the coast."[20] Spanish steamers would go to Cape Palmes, armed with a manual, a "guide for commercial transactions" on the West African coast, in which the author advises how to handle negotiations with "a good dose of diplomacy" and the delicate steps required to recruit Kru labor – the amount and denomination of advances and gifts, the currency exchange rates in different areas, and the not so obvious rates of equivalence of the "objects of value that represent money" such as gunpowder, rum, tobacco, manillas, and linen.[21] In 1867 Spanish recruiters dispatched to Cape Palmes were told that the Kru were "by nature suspicious and mistrustful" and were instructed not to emphasize Spanish sovereignty over Fernando Po and to "especially not mention the island of Cuba or Havana, well these names are odious to them, otherwise they might think that they were being misled."[22] In addition, in 1881 the colonial office in Madrid had to remind them "not to hand over excessively extravagant commissions to their intermediary interlopers, in light of the repugnance with which the English are beginning to see the matter."[23]

The Spanish had initially adopted a uniform contract duration of eight years, following the indentured contracts for Chinese coolies in Cuba, but the Kru had negotiated down the terms of service to two years. A recruiter on board a Spanish navy ship in 1864 set a precedent by "contracting 24 Kruman in Cape Palmes for a stay of only two years at 4 pesos a month," and the Spanish "colonial government had no choice but to assuage the conditions of contract."[24] This duration

20 Presidencia (O'Donnell) to Consejo de Ministros, November 9, 1858, AGA, C-81/7060, also cited in García Cantús, "Fernando Poo," 370; Sundiata, *From Slaving to Neoslavery*, 51.

21 Joaquín J. Navarro, *Apuntes sobre el estado de la costa occidental de Africa y principalmente de las posesiones españoles en el Golfo de Guinea* (Madrid: Impr. Nacional, 1859), 133.

22 Miranda, *Leyes coloniales*, 57.

23 Ministro de Estado, Madrid to GG (Montes de Oca y Aceñero), May 1881, AGA, C-81/7123, also cited in García Cantús, "Fernando Poo," 426. The Baptist Minister John Clarke, based in Fernando Po in the 1840s, in a meeting of the Anti-Slavery Society responded to a misunderstanding when he explained he witnessed people being "purchased on the Kroo coast" claiming: "I did not say they were positively purchased. I said a price was paid for them." To which Laird, a navy official who had also been based in Fernando Po, interceded ironically from the audience: "That is a nice distinction." British and Foreign Anti-slavery Society, *Proceedings of the General Anti-Slavery Convention, called by the Committee of the British and Foreign Anti-Slavery Society, and Held in London, from Tuesday, June 13th, to Tuesday, June 20th, 1843* (London: J. Snow, 1843), 261.

24 GG (Ayllón) to DGMC, May 21, 1864, AGA, C-81/6941; García Cantús, "Fernando Poo," 439, 515. For the previous 1862 ordinance, "Proyecto de reglamento para el regimen de los trabajadores

was in the upper limits of the existing expectations on the Kru coast, where residents had become used to being "detached without force from land and lineage to rotate [usually in intervals of less than one year] in and out of European overseas export enclaves under a system with low, fixed wages."[25]

However, it is precisely because of the contractual compromises and dynamics set in motion by the Kru that Spanish Guinea cannot be compared with the early so-called "under the guise of contracts" neo-slavery initiatives of the British, French, or Portuguese empires across the African coast. These state-sanctioned indentures, apprenticeships or *engagé* schemes in the post-abolition mid-nineteenth century, saw many tens of thousands of recently enslaved freed captives become signed up for "contracts."[26] The only equivalent in Spanish Guinea were the Cuban or Congolese *emancipados* of the 1860s. However most of Fernando Po's *braceros*, even in the nineteenth century, were strictly temporary immigrants; they were considered statutory strangers, *alienígenas*, who usually intended and could return home, and were in general uninterested in becoming residents or landowners on the island. Unlike with the slave trade or an entrenching debt bondage, most *braceros* permanently returned home or left to elsewhere after a period of one or more contracts. Unlike wage-laborers they rarely re-settled nearby enclaves of contract labor and so the pool of workers would diminish after each round of contract expirations. A Methodist missionary on the island in the 1870s noted that the Kru in Fernando Po would

> engage themselves to do all sorts of toil, such as rowing boats, paddling canoes, cutting forest wood, carrying water, clearing ground, cooking food, and, in fact, anything their masters dictate. They could never be forced into slavery, and say they would rather be kil-

que lleguen a esta Isla, bien sean contratados en la Costa Vecina, bien procedentes de aprehensiones hechas a los buques negreros por nuestra marina de guerra," see AGA, C-81/7124.

25 Schuler, "Kru Emigration to British and French Guiana," 180.

26 Clarence-Smith, "Emigration from Western Africa," 46–50; Johnson U. J. Asiegbu, "British Slave Emancipation and 'Free' Labour Recruitment from West Africa, 1840–1861," *Sierra Leone Studies* 26 (1970). For French efforts to supply Martinique and Guadeloupe as well as Reunion and Mayotte with *engagé* labor from Dahomey, Senegal, Gabon, and Mozambique, see François Renault, *Libération d'esclaves et nouvelle servitude: les rachats de captifs africains pour le compte des colonies françaises après l'abolition de l'esclavage* (Abidjan: Les Nouvelles Éditions Africaines, 1976); Jelmer Vos, "'Without the Slave Trade, No Recruitment': From Slave Trading to 'Migrant Recruitment' in the Lower Congo, 1830–90," in *Trafficking in Slavery's Wake: Law and the Experience of Women and Children in Africa*, eds. Benjamin N. Lawrance and Richard L. Roberts (Athens: Ohio University Press, 2012); Mathew, *Margins of the Market*, 52–81.

> led, or kill themselves than be slaves; yet they will cheerfully do all manner of drudgery – even the most slavish work – so long as they are free, and fed and paid.[27]

The Kru considered themselves to be drawn into a labor market freely in the sense of securing wages, in the form of large advances and bulk payments sustained by long contracts, to reproduce not themselves, as rations and housing were part of the contract, but for their own collective reproduction in their societies. The Kru valued the ability to be paid in gold pounds which was the currency that could secure the best rates along the mostly British coastal merchant shops near their home areas. In Fernando Po they were paid in silver pesos which would be immediately cashed in for goods at the factories on the island at a high mark-up – the main complaint by the Kru in this period as it drastically reduced their earning power. Employers on the island were forced to pay a part of the wage in pounds as demanded by workers and this was formalized in the contract in the late 1860s too, to attract new workers in the first place.

Recruiters could only operate in certain areas once colonial money and its equivalence in a variety of imported goods, such as alcohol, tobacco, and cloth, became indispensable components of key social obligations such as ceremonial marriage payments. These are the arenas where recruiters appear and in this way they became the vectors for how the bulk of colonial money and imported commodities were being deposited and incorporated into "traditional" non-peasant and not fully colonized societies. Recruiters devised, negotiated, and provided the rate and proportion and type of goods needed to link up with the "internal" economies of societies with a high bridewealth. While I cannot delve into the ethnography here, it is worth noting that the Kru shared a similar characteristically high bridewealth with the primary workforce in the twentieth century, the Fang of central Africa, and the Igbo of Nigeria. However, in the case of the Kru their self-produced copper-bracelet currencies used for "social transactions" such as bridewealth had already been almost fully replaced by imported trade currencies in the nineteenth century.[28]

---

27 Roe, *West African Scenes*, 44.

28 Frost, *Work and Community*, 10 – 12, 160; Sundiata, *Brothers and Strangers*, 65. It is also worth noting that this is not only the case for African indentured workers: "efforts by European agents to acquire Chinese women for indentured labourers in Cuba had resulted in the sale of women by their families at the point of embarkation and their purchase by indentured labourers in Cuba. 'The Chinese, in every station of life, buy their wives', the article [in The Anti-Slavery Reporter of 1859], concluded. The hyper-capitalistic qualities that made Chinese labourers so attractive as short-term agents of social engineering also made them wife-buyers and a liability

Scarce Money

On hearing another instance of the planters' eternal lament, the labor scarcity, an early twentieth-century *Gobernador* of Fernando Po, who previously held an administrative post in Cuba, was "reminded of the Cuban planters" who "screeched and screamed into the heavens, arguing that the abolition of slavery will paralyze and cause the total ruin of the island."[29] After the complete abolition of slavery in Cuba in the 1880s, as Rebecca Scott notes, "planters seeking subsidized immigration or laws restricting workers' rights tended to speak in terms of a 'scarcity' of workers."[30] The Spanish in Fernando Po looked to new Cuban post-abolition labor recruitment strategies and observed how in the first decades of the twentieth century Cuban planters were still "employing many thousands of blacks during the sugar harvest; they are free to recruit *indigenas* wherever they find them, inside or outside their territory. They fork out wages and commissions at whatever price can be negotiated," either to recruiters or to workers themselves.[31] In the first half of the twentieth century Fernando Po threw a new generation of informal recruiters at their own *problema* – a self-generated labor "scarcity," an "impediment" or "disequilibrium" term in the language of a neo-classical economics that naturalizes capitalism and turns the political contexts behind the transformation of an entire volcanic island into a

as long-term residents." Christopher Bischof, "Chinese Labourers, Free Blacks, and Social Engineering in the Post-Emancipation British West Indies," *Past & Present* 231, no. 1 (2016): 161.

29 Ramos-Izquierdo, *Descripción geográfica*, 262.

30 Scott, *Slave Emancipation in Cuba*, 239; Imilcy Balboa Navarro, "Libertos, vagos y bandoleros: La reglamentación del trabajo tras la abolición de la esclavitud (Cuba 1886–1895)," *Relaciones* 32, no. 127 (2011).

31 DGMC (Jordana) to GG (Núñez de Prado), September 19, 1927, AGA, C-81/6415, E-13. The smuggling of undocumented labor into Cuba was common in the early 1900s, including of *braceros* from Korea and Japan via other Central American territories. The American United Fruit Company in 1913 was granted the first-ever government permit to bring a large "contingent of *braceros*" from "neighbouring islands." Soon "another law was signed that authorized private parties to introduce *braceros*, although certain restrictions were imposed, and the government reserved the right to repatriate them when necessary." Cuban planters had managed to bring 40,000 "Haitian *braceros*" annually to the eastern provinces between 1913 and the early 1930s, whom Fidel Castro described as having suffered in "new and even worse forms, the slavery that had just been abolished in 1886." Margarita Cervantes-Rodriguez, *International Migration in Cuba: Accumulation, Imperial Designs, and Transnational Social Fields* (University Park: Pennsylvania State University Press, 2011), 127; Oscar Z. Lecuona, "La United Fruit Company en Cuba: organización del trabajo y resistencia obrera," *Clío América* 2, no. 4 (2008): 246. The Fidel quote in Matthew Casey, "From Haiti to Cuba and Back: Haitians' Experiences of Migration, Labor, and Return, 1900–1940" (PhD diss., University of Pittsburgh, 2012), 15.

settler-run mono-agriculture into the logical "necessity" of "coercive" recruitment.[32]

I adopt the supposition put forward by Tom Brass and Henry Bernstein that the concept of "scarcity" is strictly a product of power relations, applied "to situations where market forces or political consciousness permit free workers to act as (and reap the benefits from being) proletarians."[33] This reframing contrasts with the most powerful trend in African economic history that in the past decades has revived and selectively reapplied the conceptual apparatus of neoclassical economic theory to the economics of colonial labor. This orthodox approach has strengths and weakness, but the main critique I wish to highlight is methodological: it is impossible to determine "wage levels" and what they mean based on data from official statistical yearbooks or "blue-books." These cannot lead to an appropriate, that is accurate, understanding of colonial labor market dynamics, because the effective bulk of payments, channeled through recruiters, were unstandardized informal advances.[34] In addition effective "wages" and ad-

---

32 Anthony G. Hopkins, "The New Economic History of Africa," *The Journal of African History* 50, no. 2 (2009); Gareth Austin and Stephen Broadberry, "Introduction: The Renaissance of African Economic History," *The Economic History Review* 67, no. 4 (2014).

33 Tom Brass and Henry Bernstein, "Proletarianisation and Deproletarianisation on the Colonial Plantation," *The Journal of Peasant Studies* 19, no. 3/4 (1992): 17.

34 See for example Dácil Juif and Ewout Frankema, "From Coercion to Compensation: Institutional Responses to Labour Scarcity in the Central African Copperbelt," *Journal of Institutional Economics* 14, no. 2 (2018). The "Nieboer-Domar hypothesis" is straightforward enough, where land and employers made themselves abundant through colonization – and made labor "scarce" – forms of violence or force in labor relations predictably followed. Gareth Austin, "Factor Markets in Nieboer Conditions: Pre-Colonial West Africa, c.1500–c.1900," *Continuity and Change* 24, no. 1 (2009): 25; Erik Green, "The Economics of Slavery in the Eighteenth-Century Cape Colony: Revising the Nieboer-Domar Hypothesis," *International Review of Social History* 59, no. 1 (2014). Nieboer was a late nineteenth-century wide-ranging comparative ethnologist of slavery proposing all sorts of analytical patterns, the unidimensional hypothesis only came with Evsey D. Domar, "The Causes of Slavery or Serfdom: A Hypothesis," *The Journal of Economic History* 30, no. 1 (1970). The "Domar," at the expense of the "Nieboer" part of the hypothesis is the result of funding dynamics and inequalities in university endowments, and much of the economic history of unfree labor literature is most useful to the hiring committees of economics departments. To take one example: "coercion" or "guns" "is mainly about forcing workers to accept employment, or terms of employment, that they would otherwise reject," which can be expressed in historically meaningless formalities: "we assume that c(0) = 0 and that c(·) is strictly increasing, strictly convex, and twice differentiable, with derivative denoted by c', and we also impose that lima→1 c(a) = ∞ to ensure interior solutions. Suppose that the market price for the output of the producer is P. Thus when the agent accepts contract (wy, py) and chooses effort a, guns are equal to g, and output realization is y, the producer's payoff is Pywy [...] {g}." Daron

vances were often constituted by a panoply of currencies and denominations, with various premiums or discounts and shifting exchange rates, that make any straightforward assumptions about comparative costs, competitive advantage, balance of trade, and purchasing power meaningless.

Labor disputes and recruitment techniques took place on a terrain of "monetary" struggles, and so it is crucial to understand that fragmented currency and payment regimes were never unified or smoothed over by an imaginary universalization of accounting whereby wealth and exchange could be tabulated on one balance sheet. The hegemonic analytic which presents money as an initially arbitrary but then neutral and homogenous numéraire equivalent to the metric measuring system, is especially catastrophic for the study of imperialism (and neo-imperialism). Looking at concrete currencies, whether the imported commodity currencies "floating" without any parity whatsoever and loosely correlated to the local export of other commodities, or starting in the interwar period, the bills issued by semi-autonomous colonial currency boards with revisable but non-convertible "pegs" to metropolitan currencies, should provide important insights into the monetary instabilities and power relations that underpinned the labor market.[35] The extreme divergence of exchange rates or inflation vis-a-vis an external currency, and the spectacular unearned monetary premiums unrelated to production or carrying costs shows clearly that the powers of seigniorage, credit creation and the financial system were in the hands of the colonial state and para-state trading monopolies. Recruiting could only occur downstream of this commercial power arrangement, whose intricacies I cannot explore here, but it worth underlining that recruiters systematically appeared, offering "credit," at precisely such convulsive monetary "conjunctures" – transitions, splits, demonetizations, wholesale substitutions and extreme devaluations.

Only by situating economic history in its properly "imperial," or expansive and hierarchical, context, within a geopolitical horizon and various in-built one-way asymmetries, together with localized and reconstructive research can one even hope to begin to start measuring prices dynamically rather than through one-dimensional and aggregate calculations. Indeed, the most glaring

---

Acemoglu and Alexander Wolitzky, "The Economics of Labor Coercion," *Econometrica* 79, no. 2 (2011): 557, 561.

35 See for example the valuable studies by Karin Pallaver, "Paying in Cents, Paying in Rupees: Colonial Currencies, Labour Relations, and the Payment of Wages in Early Colonial Kenya," in *Colonialism, Institutional Change, and Shifts in Global Labor Relations*, eds. Karin Hofmeester and Pim Zwart (NL Amsterdam: Amsterdam University Press, 2018), and the new edited collection Karin Pallaver, ed., *Monetary Transitions: Currencies, Colonialism and African Societies* (Basingstoke: Palgrave Macmillan, 2022).

omission in the new African economic history is the most important insight of that tradition: the subjective "acceptance" of certain moneys and payment intervals according to socially and culturally determined "preferences," which are a derivative of variable local estimations of "assets" and strategies for their accumulation. Recruiters were experts in those highly localized and Guyer-esque domains of translation, conversion, and making equivalent. An economic history that does not include them empirically and theoretically cannot answer the larger questions that it sets itself, such as on the origin and hierarchy of the world market.

Scarce Labor

Recruiters orchestrated the obscure groundwork of the so-called "labor question" – an endemic obsession pervading the African colonial archive but also many other colonial capitalist archives elsewhere.[36] In Fernando Po the shortage and compulsive recruitment of labor was unusually pronounced: "There exist here the *problema de braceros*. It is said 'we lack *braceros*' and this is the principal and almost sole obsession of the planters." Apart from the rhythms and discipline of plantation cultivation, "recruitment is the principal activity of plantation businesses." A Spanish colonial administrator noted truthfully: "*de la recluta cuenta se y no se acaba*," "once talk of recruitment starts it cannot stop."[37] The sources are unanimous: "Speaking in terms unequivocal and without the slightest fear of contradiction the labour problem in Fernando Poo is of paramount importance."[38] The "so-called *problema* is principal and decisive," it

36 Cooper, *Decolonization*; Jeff Crisp, "The Labour Question in the Gold Coast, 1870–1906," in *Proletarianisation in the Third World: Studies in the Creation of a Labour Force under Dependent Capitalism*, eds. Barry Munslow and Martin H. J. Finch (London: Croom Helm, 1984). Post-abolition Latin America, for example Brazil, was also plagued by the "*falta de braços*," though here it was over-coded with a racial imaginary of trying to "whiten" the country with European labor. Lucia Lamounier, "Between Slavery and Free Labour: Early Experiments with Free Labour and Patterns of Slave Emancipation in Brazil and Cuba," in *From Chattel Slaves to Wage Slaves: The Dynamics of Labour Bargaining in the Americas*, ed. Mary Turner (Bloomington: Indiana University Press, 1995), 195.

37 Perpiñá, *De colonización y economía en la Guinea española*, 118; Ángel Miguel Pozanco, *Guinea mártir: narraciones, notas y comentarios de un condenado a muerte* (Barcelona: Colección Actualidad, 1937), 86.

38 Kicks-Dadzie to Resident, Calabar Province, September 1939, NAE, CALPROF 5/1/195, "Confidential Report: Labour in Fernando Poo."

was said to be the "*principalisimo* of all colonial policies."[39] The archive of Equatorial Guinea "seems to be only about el *problema bracero*," the historian Enrique Okenve told me in 2014.[40] As the long-running Francoist *Curador*, Sebastian Llompart Aulet, observed:

> The *problema* of the labor scarcity has produced a flood of decrees and provisions; well, it is of transcendental importance. Except through divine intervention – and this I insist upon this point – we will never find a definitive solution. Those in the colony, before 1909 were already complaining of the scarcity of *brazos* when there were only 5000 contract workers, today [in 1945] with 27,000 contracts we are still lamenting the lack of *brazos*."[41]

Over the course of its colonial century, Fernando Po's recruiters spread to almost every corner of the Gulf of Guinea, and very intensively in the Fang areas of Río Muni, Cameroon, and Gabon between the 1910s and early 1930s – mainly driven by unrelated sets of recruiters, who however deployed exactly the same techniques. To sharpen and advance the conceptual questions of this book I focus on one area and set of recruiters: the Nigerian touts who were the principal labor suppliers between the 1930s and 1950s. Already at the beginning of the Spanish Civil War, from 1936 on, most *braceros* on the island were Nigerian. With thousands of new settlers and a spree of corporate-backed plantations rushing in during the Francoist period (1936–1968), colonial hopes that labor needs could be met were perpetually thwarted. By the 1950s, Fernando Po became draped in a patchwork of ever-larger plantations. "Two thirds of the surface" cascading down West Africa's largest island, which Livingstone had called an "unpolished jewel," had been studded with an agro-capitalist crown, "transformed into an immense square," its shape on older maps, "where every square meter has been put to use."[42]

The problem of labor scarcity and the associated recruitment campaigns is *the* running theme across Fernando Po's colonial history. Fernando Po is one of the most understudied territories in African and Atlantic history, even though

39 Román Perpiñá Grau, "Mano de obra africana, factor de coste colonial: investigación sobre el peso de los braceros contratados en Fernando Poo," *Cuadernos de Estudios Africanos* 3 (1947): 127.

40 The "'manpower crisis' obsessively preoccupied colonial officers and settlers alike. In fact, one only needs to look at the colonial archives to realize that, in addition to government personnel, the bulk of the documentation deals with labour matters." Enrique N. Okenve, "Equatorial Guinea 1927–1979: A New African Tradition" (PhD diss., SOAS, 2007), 174; Sanz Casas, "Política colonial y organización del trabajo," 222.

41 Sebastian Llompart Aulet, *Legislación del trabajo de los territorios españoles del Golfo de Guinea* (Madrid: Dirección General de Marruecos y Colonias, 1946), 15.

42 [Untitled newspaper clipping from Cameroon], June 18, 1957, AGA, C-81/8221, E-1.

it generated some of the most significant colonial labor migrations: cumulatively an estimated 300,000 Nigerians worked in Spanish Guinea, heavily concentrated in the Francoist period.[43] Starting in 1908, cacao became lavishly subsidized by Spanish consumers, a premium that was hiked in the 1920s when planters and commercial houses on the island exporting via the chocolate "syndicate" in Barcelona, the *Sindicato Agrícola*, could rely on an assured buyout by Spanish chocolate manufacturers at almost thrice and later twice the global market rate.[44] From just a few hundred – largely Fernandino – planters at the turn of the century, by the final decade of colonial rule there were about 2,000 planters. In the 1920s the island's cacao plantations exported 15,000 tonnes of cacao and employed about 15,000 *braceros*, while by the early 1960s there were well over 30,000 *braceros* on the island producing about 30–40,000 tonnes of cacao for export.[45]

In 1940, 26,340 hectares or 71% of land under cultivation was under the control of Europeans, and 10,600 hectares or 29% by Africans, around half of the latter, did not employ migrant labor. In the 1950s about 400 Bubi and smaller Fernandino farmers were hiring, as a mean, about one *bracero* each.[46] The "number of plantations and farms is unclear, there are a few thousand for

---

43 Around half were recruited through the 1942 "labor treaty" or agreement between the colonial governments of Nigeria and Spanish Guinea. The other half were clandestinely recruited on what were later called "*contratos libres*", or those signed on the island itself. It is difficult to estimate because of the confused statistics on "recontracted" laborers and their origin – which included deserters from the treaty and new illegal migrants posing as locally recontracted labourers, etc. – but at least 100,000 to 200,000 *braceros* were recruited outside of the "treaty," which is known to have brought 103,881 new recruits in the first 20 years of its operation (1943–1962). The tabulation of the individual records for the 1962 to 1968 period, or beyond up to 1975 is also complicated. The revised 1963 Treaty with the Nigerian state doubled the minimum length of the contract to three years (and four and half in total). A reliable figure for 1964 says that under this revised treaty some "40,000 Nigerians" were under contract in Fernando Pó, in addition to "10,000" in Río Muni. Comisión para el Desarrollo Económico de Fernando Poo y Río Muni, *Plan de desarrollo económico de la Guinea Ecuatorial: 1964–1967* (Madrid: Presidencia del Gobierno, 1963), 37–48; United States Department of Labor, *Labor Digests on Countries in Africa* (Washington: Bureau of Labor Statistics, 1966), xxxiii; Sebastian Llompart Aulet, "Nigerianos en las provincias ecuatoriales," *Estadística española: revista del Instituto Nacional de Estadística* 10 (1961): 66.

44 Clarence-Smith, "The Impact of the Spanish Civil War," 309; Sant Gisbert, "El negocio del cacao," 156–163.

45 GG (Núñez), March 17, 1962, AGA, C-81/11846; see also Campos Serrano, *De colonia a Estado*, 171.

46 Wolff, "Wirtschaft von Fernando Poo," 93; Curaduría, 1957, AGA, C-81/8667, "Relacion de trabajadores nigerianos actualmente contratados."

sure. These are diverse, from the 10,000 hectares of INASA [a Spanish corporate plantation with numerous patios] to ones with only 3 or 4 hectares belonging to [African] farmers." By 1950 the island had about 50,000 hectares under cultivation and in the final years of colonial rule around 90,000 – 97% of the island's arable surface covered overwhelmingly with labor intensive cacao trees, and only a few hundred hectares of other crops such as coffee, oil palms and cassava. With "approximately 60 to 80 *braceros* required for every 100 hectares" of planted cacao there were necessarily around 50–60,000 workers. This figure of contract labor "is reliable for it is known that farmers cannot operate with less men per hectare."[47]

The 1960 census picked up around 14,000 Nigerian resident traders, smugglers, artisans, administrative workers, and so-called *libres* – "free" or non-treaty workers on local contracts – in addition to the 32,000 (plus 15,000 family members) "indentured treaty labourers," brought in, regulated and repatriated according to the revised terms of the 1942 Spanish Guinean-Nigerian labor treaty.[48] Recruiting dynamics were significantly reconfigured by the 1960s because of the high numbers of workers, up to 15,000 a year, coming through this treaty. At independence in 1968, the island had a population of 100,000 souls and plantation "agriculture employed 82%" of the labor force, "out of which 90% [were] Nigerian immigrants under *peonaje* contracts."[49] There was "probably no other territory in the world" that at this point was "so completely dependent on immigrant labour."[50] Even then, Spanish colonialists were still clamoring: "the total solution of the *problema* will never be found. Alas, we will need to find partial solutions by further intensifying our work of *captación de braceros*," the capturing or recruitment of *braceros*.[51]

The polarized and unidimensional productive colonial structure of the plantation island of Fernando Po gave it certain Caribbean-like qualities and sharply distinguishes it from neighboring "trade" colonies run on indirect-rule, such as Nigeria, or the concessionary regimes of Central Africa. Spanish Guinea only had about 0.1% of Africa's land and population, but accounted for 1% of total ex-

47 MAE, March 10, 1962, "Desarollo de la economía en Fernando Poo," AGA, C-81/13039, E-392; British VC (Spencer-Cooke) to Commissioner of Labor, Lagos, October 10, 1950, TNA, FO 371/89597.

48 British Consul, Yaounde, May 4, 1961, TNA, CO 554/2502.

49 Armin Kobel, "La République de Guinée Equatoriale: ses ressources potentielles et virtuelles et les possibilités de son développement" (PhD diss., Université de Neuchâtel, 1976), 494; Sandinot, "Guinea ecuatorial (española)," 104.

50 "Nigeria over the Water," *West Africa*, London, January 1, 1958.

51 Ruiz, "Guinea española," 50.

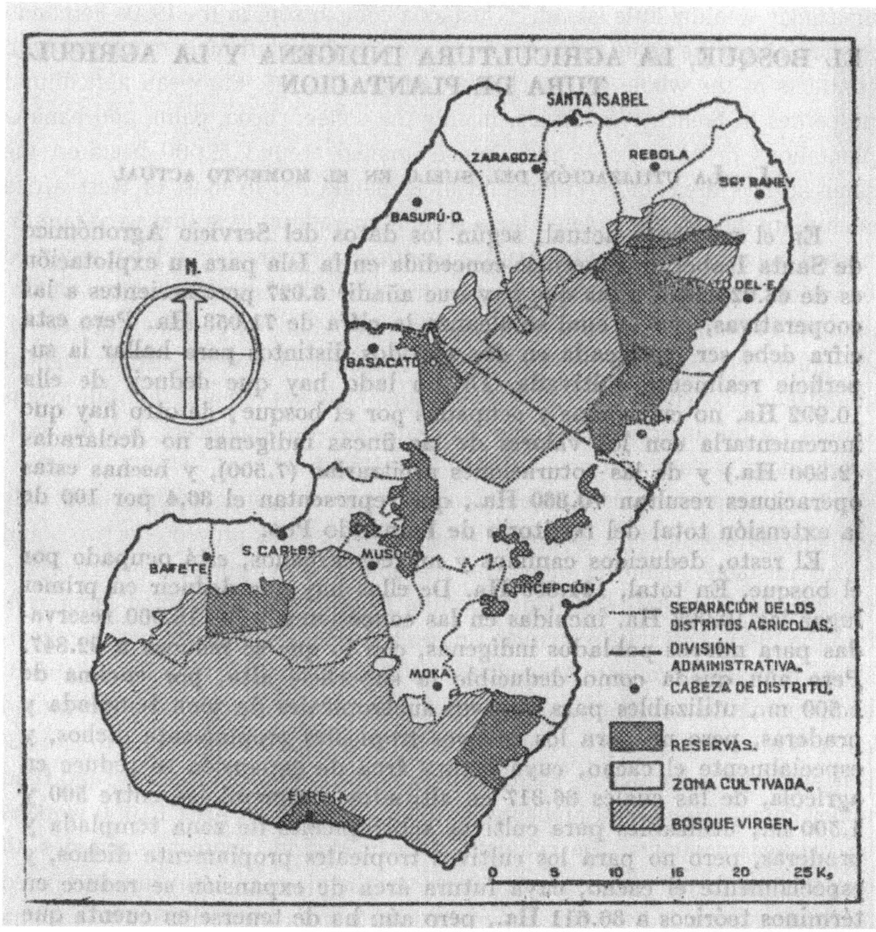

Figure 4: Map of area under cultivation; shaded area is steep mountain scrub (Terán 1962, 82).

ports from Africa in 1960, ten times its weight or size.[52] In 1960, its GDP per capita of was around $135, $500 only for Fernando Poo excluding Río Muni; in contrast, in Nigeria it was around $12.[53] A British missionary on the island observed in 1938 that it was "so different form anywhere else in West Africa [...] it is an

52 Pélissier, *Los territorios españoles de Africa*, 44, 62; DGMC, 1960, "Repercusiones en la Regional Ecuatorial española de la situación general en África," AGA, C-81/11852, E-4.

53 US dollar value in 1960. The GDP of Fernando Po in the 1960s was 14,737 pesetas, higher than 29 Spanish provinces, that is, almost all of them. Ballano, *Aquel*, 548.

amazingly wealthy little island."[54] Just as a comparison, in the 1930s Fernando Po had about the same number of *braceros* as those privately employed with contracts in the whole of French West Africa. In 1945, European agricultural properties in French West Africa, mainly the coffee, cocoa, palm, and banana plantations in Ivory Coast and Guinea, totaled around 75,000 hectares, the same surface area under cultivation in Fernando Po. In most of West Africa such plantations were isolated large-scale corporate projects that were far surpassed in terms by output by peasant producers who drew on a labor recruited by various means, including debt pawnship, through shifting definitions of kinship, and informal and short-term wage labor.[55] As an early Francoist *Gobernador* briefly reflected: "the *problema* is kind of our fault for we chose the system of colonization based on propertied Europeans. I always thought that Europeans should be the intermediaries and the *indígenas* the producers, but oh well, what's done is done and now we have to deal with it."[56]

There were hundreds of different initiatives to try to import workers, but only the informal recruiting techniques I analyze in this book proved effective – and highly unstable. Spanish Guinea was the only imperial power in Africa trying persistently to re-start state-led exporting facilities for indentured labor well into the 1960s. Officials in Spanish Guinea were desperate to disentangle themselves from their complete dependency on Nigeria, particularly as its independence approached in 1960. Spanish diplomats continued to propose indentured labor treaties in parts of the world under dictatorships with affinities to Francoism, such as the Portuguese Estado Novo and the Dominican Republic and Haiti under Rafael Trujillo and François Duvalier, asking for at least 10,000 workers on five-year contracts. The colonial office in Madrid, Spanish embassies all over the world, and well-connected friends of the planters' lobby initiated failed agreements intended to bring indentured labor from India (1928, 1947), China (1928), Indonesia, Malaysia and the Philippines (1928), Morocco (1929–1930), Romania (1929), São Tomé (1929, 1931), Cameroon (1934–1936), Congo (1945),

54 Dodds, July 1939, "Notes on Visit to West African District, February to June 1939," SOAS, MMS/Special Series/Notes and Transcripts/FBN 1 (fiche 15–17).

55 Cooper, *Decolonization*, 51. Figures for French West Africa are from 1935, total private contracts: 22,785; total employed without contract: 117,803. There is a certain dearth of literature on plantations in AOF, but see Meillassoux, *Anthropologie économique des Gouro*, chap. 12; Asiwaju, "Migrations as Revolt." On different types of local recruitment in West African "peasant" plantations, see E. Adeniyi Oroge, "Iwofa: An Historical Survey of the Yoruba Institution of Indenture," *African Economic History* 14 (1985); B. A. Agiri, "The Development of Wage Labour in Agriculture in Southern Yorubaland 1900–1940," *Journal of the Historical Society of Nigeria* 12, no. 1/2 (1983); Austin, "Cash Crops and Freedom"; Berry, *No Condition is Permanent*.

56 GG (Suances) to SubGG (Cabrera), October 1, 1939, AGA, C-81/8195, E-2.

Cape Verde (1951), Upper Volta (1962), El Salvador (1958), Haiti (1934, 1949, 1959), from Liberia again (1949), and persistently Mozambique (1927, 1933, 1952) and Angola (1930, 1939, 1945, 1952): "Oh the lengthy list of hopes and the aborted plans: Romanian workers, Muslim *braceros*, and even Chinese coolies!"[57] Most of these far-fetched plans were false starts, while others crumbled after being signed (Cameroon) or after the first group of laborers was sent (Morocco). Treaties offered a constantly thwarted hope for "the agriculture of the island, as recruitment costs made up the highest share of planter expenditure." The reasoning was always rooted in an ideal and impractical argument about the costs of recruitment, i.e. the commissions and the inflating advances, both of which "could be almost eliminated [through a labor treaty] and so we will have finally resolved the *problema de brazos*."[58]

Contract Forms

The labor contract is a shared template across colonial archives, and a closer examination of it allows for a consistent conceptualization of the historical dynamics of indentured labor in and around the labor-demanding imperial peripheries of the post-abolition era. As I will endeavor to show, accounting for the form of the contract makes the parallels and unifying themes of recruitment, debt peonage, and desertion across a variety of times and regions appear more clearly as a dynamic contradiction of the colonial economy. No other medium or presupposition sustained and underpinned the entire reach of recruitment and its techniques. There was no labor mobility without contracts and associated anti-vagrancy ordinances, or to put it generally: there was no exchange and circulation without meditation and inscription. These recruiting "assemblages" were extrapolated and premised on the contract's stamp.[59] To see this analytical shift, one needs to turn away from a concern with external form and formal procedure towards its actual mode of operation.

57 Llompart, *Legislación del trabajo*, 12; "Los braceros chinos," *España Colonial*, Santa Isabel, February 1, 1929. See AMAE, R887, E-52; R3215, E-56; AGA, C-81/8095; C-81/8147; C-81/12373; and Max Liniger-Goumaz, "La cuestion bracera: 150 años de busqueda de mano de obra en Guinea Equatorial," *Estudios de Asia y Africa* 22, no. 74 (1987): 502.

58 GG (Lluesma) to DGMC (Alvarez-Buylla), September 18, 1933, AGA, C-81/06867, E-5.

59 I use the concept of assemblage in this Deleuzian sense of how circulation is "inscribed" through different "devices," etc.; though Serres and Latour have done much to reinvigorate the concept and make it methodologically concrete, see Michel Serres and Bruno Latour, *Conversations on Science, Culture, and Time* (Ann Arbor: University of Michigan Press, 1995), 141–143.

The colonial contract is the conduit which led to the new growth of plantations through recruitment. The two features which made up the consistent core of indenture were its "fixed length" of at least a couple of years and its "irrevocability" until expiration. The *bracero* contract on Fernando Po was between two to five years long. While the numbers shifted through different reforms and agreements and the lower bound 12-month limit was allowed for in the 1906 Labor Code, the 24-month standard was the most common duration for all *bracero* contracts between 1862 until 1968. These two units or even simply "calendrical" features, I argue, were the motor behind consistent recruiting techniques, since it was the "irrevocability" that made possible *panya*, and the "duration" that yielded the *dash*. Touts could only turn recruiters if they, in the final instance, appeared through channels structured by the destination, the "contract, legal and binding; it is an artefact of action and connection."[60] The legal and historical ensemble of the contract forms unique constellations whose elements should not be disentangled if one is to understand its dynamic local and regional effects.

The contract could only work by being contiguous with the internal organization of sovereign power, a foundational asymmetry. An entry into its territory marked an automatic acceptance of what economists call "state supplied defaults"; being in place was a "consent to jurisdiction."[61] In this sense, as Caroline Pateman surmised, the language of contracts "perpetuated and presented" itself as a "free institution" in order to uphold the background unfreedom of unconditional "state power" which is thereby made to appear to stand outside individual market relations.[62] It was a non-negotiated device imposed from above, with an

---

60 Catherine Alexander, "Legal and Binding: Time, Change and Long-Term Transactions," *Journal of the Royal Anthropological Institute* 7, no. 3 (2001): 482.

61 Don Herzog, *Happy Slaves: A Critique of Consent Theory* (Chicago: University of Chicago Press, 1989), 161–163. Randy E. Barnett, "The Sound of Silence: Default Rules and Contractual Consent," *Virginia Law Review* 78 (1992); Patrick Atiyah, *The Rise and Fall of Freedom of Contract* (Oxford: Oxford University Press, 1979); Victoria Kahn, *Wayward Contracts: The Crisis of Political Obligation in England, 1640–1674* (Princeton: Princeton University Press, 2009). As the jurist Friedrich Kessler already reasoned in the inter-war period: when all employers "use the same clauses" or deploy contracts under a "monopoly" – under an "artificial" "sovereignty" – then the contract becomes by definition "but a subjection more or less voluntary to terms dictated by the stronger part." Friedrich Kessler, "Contracts of Adhesion: Some Thoughts About Freedom of Contract," *Columbia Law Review* 43 (1943): 632; see also Banaji, "Fictions of Free Labour," 74–77, and his main critique against Brass: even if free labour should be "based on the 'consent' of the individual worker and the free bargain that embodies that 'consent'," to oppose it to "unfree labour" ignores "contract law's role in making actual domination appear free, natural, and rational."

62 Carole Pateman, *The Sexual Contract* (Stanford: Stanford University Press, 1988), 70, 20.

elaborate code pre-set by the state's printing press, yet it could introduce volatile and unpredictable effects. Within its borders the contract was imposed in its most complete and uncompromising shape: long, obligatory, and irrevocable which gave both indenture and recruitment its primary qualities. This was achieved through the closely associated implanting of anti-vagrancy laws from Europe and other colonies, without which, as Alessandro Stanziani has already noted, "indenture would have been impossible."[63]

The contract's logical operations and local realities cannot be made sense of as a dyadic or two-way power relationship between employer and employee, or genealogically by situating it within a history of the transfer of templates, formulated and reformulated ideally in Europe, then "spread" and partially or imperfectly applied.[64] Even the initial British staff of palm oil merchants on Fernando Po were there on three year indentures, "young fellows" recruited in Liverpool, who after "their initiating term of servitude" and with the ability to dabble in trading activities would usually be able to take £10,000 "home with them" – thus it makes little to no sense to subsume contracts into a single category or stage or history or even region.[65] The interpretative frame can thus neither be strictly transactional nor genealogical, but needs to include, as Joseph Miller suggests, an empirically "comprehensive" context at an "analytically comprehending scale." This requires a rejection of strict temporal lines or geographic demarcations according to different imperial powers, a traditional "comparative" method that has served to present "an unintegrated set of separate regional narratives" rather than a "coherent sequence of incremental historical adaptations that they in fact formed."[66]

The indentured contracts' primary and explicit economic purpose was to hold down the potential of freely negotiated wages to make hiring and paying labor workable for employers – to work this way contracts had to be a "default" and encompass a large share of laborers classified and targeted as immigrants from certain origins or occupying a specific place in the division of labor. This "default" underlying quality gives the contract a structural economic reality

63 Alessandro Stanziani, "Beyond Colonialism: Servants, Wage Earners and Indentured Migrants in Rural France and on Reunion Island (c. 1750–1900)," *Labor History* 54, no. 1 (2013): 71.
64 Stanziani, "Local Bondage in Global Economies"; Stanziani, *Labor on the Fringes of Empire*, 137–176; see also Douglas Hay and Paul Craven, eds., *Masters, Servants, and Magistrates in Britain and the Empire, 1562–1955* (Chapel Hill: University of North Carolina Press, 2004); Anderson, "Master and Servant in Colonial Kenya."
65 John Holt, *The diary of John Holt with the voyage of the "Maria"* (Liverpool: Henry Young, 1948), 18.
66 Miller, *Slavery as History*, 40, 132.

and an ability to function as a parameter in the entire social field. At first sight the amortization of displacement or the high costs of long-distance recruitment seems to be the underlying reason of why the contract was so stubbornly long and irrevocable. The planters themselves always started form this inverted logic: only "long contracts" could offset the "repayment of the onerous initial expenses," primarily the recruiters' commission.[67] Throughout the twentieth century planters thought of the two-year minimum as a "tradition"; "it has always been this way on the island." Even at moments of potential reform, the planter lobby always lamented that "shorter-term contracts" would be "detrimental rather than favorable, well after six months *el problema*" of needing to find new workers "would rear its head again." All the necessary formalities would eat into the time of "short-term contracts," with the resulting "loss" of the labor time of "their *braceros*" to "time-consuming tasks, like registration, medical check-ups, etc."[68] Logically, the historically planted circuitry inside the work contract itself comes first: the consistent core of indenture, which produced the appearance of the recruiter and made possible the wealth built by recruited labor.

Contract Contents

I do not spend much time finding conceptual importance in the contract's "surface" or self-referential criteria, nor do I try to dissect the admixture of discreet free and unfree elements in it to reveal a semantic ideological obfuscation, a "mask" of "neo-slavery." This can only lead to truncated critiques of incorrect procedure, as a Francoist functionary said worryingly in 1936: the "terms of the contract," the need for "attestation," etc., "are all merely poetics ably written on paper, but none of it occurs in our colony."[69] As I will detail at length in the *panya* chapter, the colonial state, in particular the *Curador*, did not put any emphasis on the supposedly crucial moment where workers who entered contracts were ritually screened for consent and determined to be unencumbered by undue influence to draw a "boundary between compulsion and free will." This

67 Union de Agricultores de la Guinea Española (Rodriguez Barrera), Barcelona to DGMC (Canovas), October 9, 1931, AGA, C-81/8095, L-2, E-21.

68 Cámara to GG (Fontán), April 13, 1938, AGA, C-81/8126, E-1. For actual contracts see AGA, C-81/6730, C-81/8081.

69 Antonio Babiloni Navarro, January 1937, "Los territorios españoles del Golfo de Guinea vistos por un 22 colono al terminar el año 1936, Libro Segundo," AGA, C-81/12427.

divide as elsewhere was "neither distinct nor of any great interest".[70] I have already outlined the bundle of parameters and regulations to the extent these generated recruitment. Nevertheless, I will briefly dwell and describe the "instrument" itself, so that its enveloping reaches become clearer. The *bracero* contract was not as a simple device to fix expectations, determine payment schedules and the acceptable bounds of concrete working conditions. It produced the legal and economic identity, and the appearance, of *braceros*.

The contract on Fernando Po objectified the very person it generated; it was a "type of contract called '*bracero*' to which all who are *braceros* are subject."[71] It allotted the *bracero* a place within the island's division of labor where almost everyone had a contract, including managers, overseers, and functionaries. The *bracero* was of course the most preponderant, as in proportion there were not many foremen, guards, bricklayers, carpenters, drivers, nurses, and domestic workers, etc. who each had their own modified contractual conditions and thus different recruitment logics. The *Curador*, Sebastian Llompart, noted its most immediate and flexible features: "for the *indígena*, the contract is a *document vivo*", a "living document," wherein "all incidents and relations with his employers are inscribed, whether it be for contracting debts," or "for annotating the loss of working days due to sickness, desertion and leave permission, etc."[72] A "copy of the contract" was of course put into "the hands of the carrier" "free of charge" in order to "serve as the document supporting the 'identity' for all procedures that need this effect," while losing or hiding the copy of the contract would incur a 100 peseta fine or about three months' wages.[73] The *bracero* contract was what Weber would call variously a "political," "feudal," or a "status contract" that "temporarily or permanently" changes a person's "total legal situation (the universal position) and the social status of the person involved."[74]

70 Ulrich Herbert, *Hitler's Foreign Workers: Enforced Foreign Labor in Germany Under the Third Reich* (Cambridge: Cambridge University Press, 1997), 59, also Banaji, "Fictions of Free Labour," 79.

71 Curaduría (Carrillo) to GG (Núñez de Prado), December 9, 1926, AGA, C-81/7720, E-1.

72 Llompart, *Anuario estadistico*, 192. In 1936 the *Curador* looked at the booklet of one labourer who had "been detained for 138 days in addition to being *fugado* for 58 days" with a "contract booklet full of annotated punishments," and concluded that the labourer had "*fugado* several times. He is wayward and rebellious towards the authorities, the ones who give orders." Curaduría (Guixeres) to GG (Serrano), November 30, 1936, AGA, C-81/8153.

73 Curaduría (Carrillo) to Farley Smith, n.d. [1940], AGA, C-81/8131, E-3.

74 Weber, *Economy and Society*, 672. This transformation not only naturalized alienation and the labor discipline expected to arise from wage payments, but stripped people previously considered free or freed to legally reconstitute them in bondage. In the Chinese coolie contract in Cuba this subsumption was expressly totalizing: "it is understood that the workers who sign

There is something very abstract and concrete about the contract. In the colonial archive, it is only found either as an unused blank booklet from the administrative inventory, or as a ragged specimen confiscated from a deserter or forger. The *cartilla-contrato* or the "work-booklet" or "contract-passbook" was at the same time a pocket constitution, an identity card, a flexible surveillance registry, a passport, and the accounting book for wages and its underlying credit system. On the cover of this booklet was the name of the worker and the unique handwritten number of the contract. The number was sequential over the course of the year and started at "1" again at the beginning of the following year, corresponding to the *Curaduría*'s registry which ordered the contracts by this number in continuous annual volumes. The new labor office took over control of this centralized registry from the Governor's secretariat in 1901. The loose "copies" of the contract were emitted from this "master copy" in Santa Isabel at the *Curaduría* and any edits or modifications to the circulating copies could only be undertaken there under its supervisory stamp. When the *Curaduría* expanded its district branches in the 1930s, any partial pay outs or extensions were emitted and stamped as loose receipts or supplementary annotations by delegates and auxiliaries, but these had to be subsequently inscribed into the booklets during the obligatory stopover at the *Curaduría*'s headquarters, during final liquidation or intermittent renewal.

The single booklets did not seem to exist before 1901 – at least not in any uniform way. There had been individually confected agreements between recruiters and workers which listed names and salaries, but these would need to be inscribed in the *Curaduría* to be effective. During that step such agreements could be altered or transformed by the *Curador*. Only the names and affiliations, and starting and ending dates, listed in the columns of the *Curaduría's* tables "counted". Indeed, the *Curador* often doubled as a government statistician, collecting crucial aggregate data to foresee any bulk expiry of contracts which would require a push for renewals or the recruitment of new laborers. By 1906, both *braceros* and employers had "copies" of the contract, which was also theirs to keep after its expiry, though planters were known to hold onto the worker's copy during the duration of the contract itself.

The contract booklet starts with an eight page reprint of the valid labor legislation, but only its third section, the "obligations of employers and workers", articles 60 to 77 of the 1906 Labor Code which defined rations, housing condi-

---

or accept their contracts renounce their ability to exercise all civil rights which are not compatible with the fulfilment of their obligations they thereby incur." Cuba, *Reglamento para la introducción de los trabajadores chinos de la Isla de Cuba* (Havana: Imp. del Gobierno y Capitanía General, 1860), art. 34.

tions, the workday, and importantly the conditions for termination: death or "mutual agreement." The contract could also be revoked in exceptional cases where a worker was considered "useless" and "dangerous" or an employer had engaged in "cruel abuse." Then there is a passport-like identification sheet, consisting of wildly inconsistent toponymic and ethnonymic affiliations such as "tribe" (ranging from clan name to colony of origin), place of birth, place of residence before taking up the contract and "*señas particulares*," distinguishing features, which could include the idiosyncratic description of scars, skin-tone, the size of "eyes" or a distinct type of gait. This same sheet contained blank lines that could be filled out to further aid "identification," such as the name and place of work of a relative or their recruiter.

Only then comes the "contractual formula": "name" so and so, "obliges themselves, under the conditions determined by the current labor legislation to render their services" as a "*bracero*," to "D." as in *Don*, "employer" so and so, "for the duration" of "blank" years and "blank" months, with the starting and end date also left "blank," for the "monthly salary" of "blank" pesetas. There was no dedicated space for the "signature" of the *bracero* or employer, only the *Curador*'s stamp, though already in the 1920s, fingerprints as well as pictures could be superimposed at the bottom of this page as an added surveillance device. Only with the revised labor code 1953 was the requirement of a fingerprint as a substitute "signature" spelled out.[75] In a situation where "95 % of the workers do not of course know how to sign their own name," the ceremonial and communicative aspect of the signing was confounded by the fact that "at the *Curaduría* there [was] an interpreter who elaborates and explains the reach of the contract in a very limited way, in a mix Portuguese, English and Spanish and the dialect of the *Krumanes*" or Pidgin.[76]

Compensation and length of employment were rote numbers, as they depended on the labor legislation, with a duration of 24 months unless explicitly noted otherwise and a minimum monthly salary of around 15 pesetas in cash and 15 pesetas in rations from 1907 on; 25 pesetas from 1912 on, half paid out monthly and the other half only after the successful completion of the contract; 30 pesetas from 1936 on with the same 50 % retention and a part of that being paid in British pounds again; 35 pesetas or 45 pesetas if it was a second contract from 1945 on; 600 pesetas from 1958 on due the rapidly inflating peseta in post-

75 Peña, *Repertorio de legislación colonial*, 428, 484.

76 Peter Pan, "'Spanish' is a Synonym for Savages," *Sunday Times*, Lagos, March 4, 1962; DGMC (Jordana), 1928, AMAE, R887, E-52, "Trabajo en las Colonias españolas." For this faux translator to be present, the Spanish until the 1940s even charged a small fee that they deducted from the wages of the *bracero*.

war Spain, and so on. These labor costs were not meaningful, neither for workers nor employers, either because the provision of rations and facilities at the employers expense exceeded such monthly salaries or because of onerous deductions from the wage tally – for example ill-defined "absentee days", or the exorbitant "maintenance" costs between receiving the contract at the *Curaduría* and being interned in the plantation which could easily eat away, in one day, the first month's earnings. Most importantly, total labor costs were at least triple, sometimes tenfold, the official wage, because of the commissions and *dash* or "gift-advances."[77]

The final settlement and total costs were therefore far from rote or predictable, shifting with every turnover and the influx of new laborers by way of touts. To account for this complexity, the third and last section of the booklet contained an extensive classic double-entry bookkeeping table, with rows for 36 months, and two columns, "*debe*" and "*haber*". The left column, the "debit" side, listed the sums paid out to the worker during the duration of the contract, which after a 1912 reform consisted of an option of up to 50% of the monthly wage, though less or none at all was common, as the *Curaduría* was envisioned to function as a savings bank so that expired *braceros* would return home with sufficient money or goods and thus potentially promote new waves of eager immigrants. In the same left column, and scribbled over it, was the sum of the advance or *dash*, whose upper bounds were artificially capped at 300 pesetas in the 1930s. The employer was given loose individual receipts for each payment into the debit column, including the permitted advances and usually the unregulated *dash* as well. The right column, "*haber*," credit, or liabilities listed any outstanding monetary fines or deductions due to absences such as days spent absconded, in jail or sick. These sums were scribbled over the columns in the *Curaduría* according to the employers' accounts. At the end of this table was the empty equation: "*saldo*" or final balance, paid out to the liquidated *braceros* at the termination of their contract. Calculating the final balance sheet produced endless disputes over the sums of advances, gratuities, fines, and reasons for subtractions. This "clearing" of the final wage was complex, and money did not necessarily change hands at this interval either. The "accounting money" of the debit-wages and liabilities could cancel each other out in a constant flux between cumulative advances and arbitrary deductions. The positive or even negative *saldo* would also be often rolled over into a second contract if the employment relation continued, primarily because of the acceptance of a new *dash*.

---

77 Miranda, *Leyes coloniales*, 111, 206, 394, 1297, 1339; Peña, *Repertorio de legislación colonial*, 29, 289, 480.

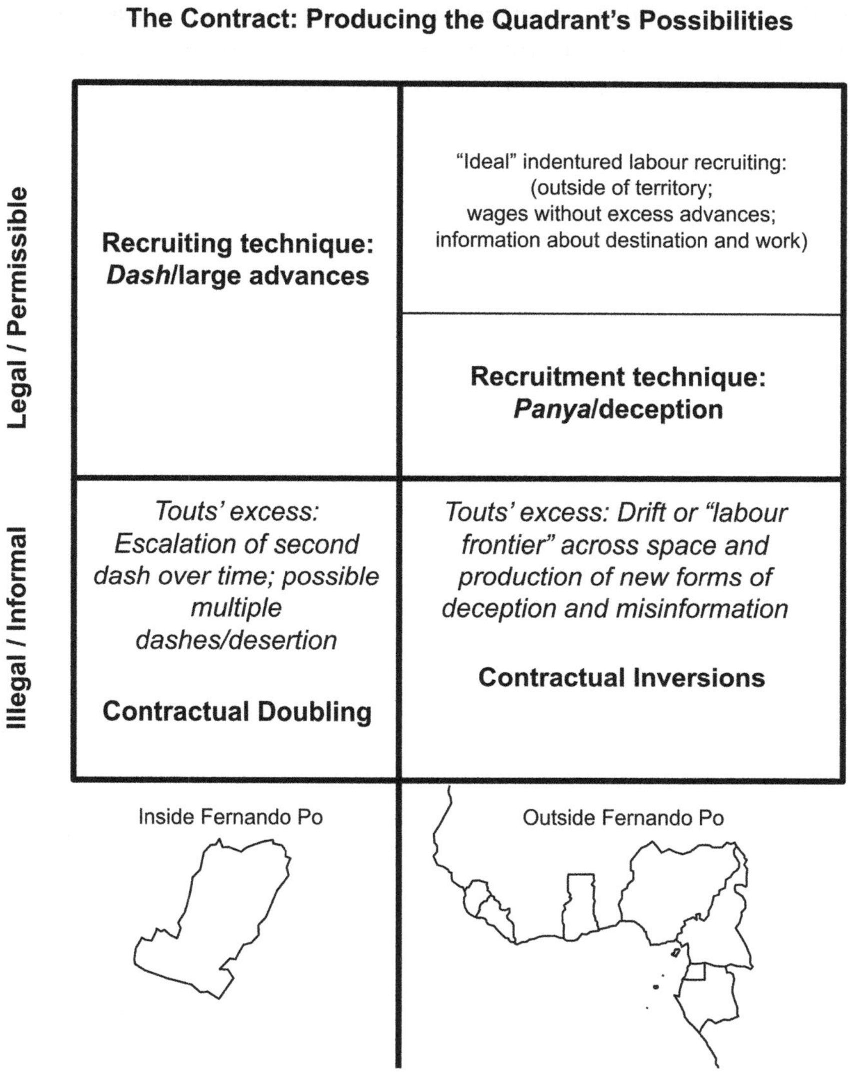

Figure 5: Quadrant of recruiting techniques produced by the contract. By author.

The *contrato* was not merely a dyadic document issued by the crown or state, with only its agents able to modify it, but the basis for producing the entire colonial economy and much of the dynamics of the new colonial society itself. It was only *within* its regulations that touts and various recruiting phenomena could elaborately appear. Recruiters were thus a main "outgrowth" of the contract form itself as provided by sovereign parameters. A focus on touts thus reveals the creative role that the imperial state had in instituting bondage and generating the colonial economy. The messy character of recruitment – recursive, embedded, inflected – is part of the history of the prefigurations and consequences of imperial formats.

2 Take or Give: Recruiting Techniques

> We have no intention whatever of doubting or despising the "revelation of history", for history is all and everything to us and we hold it more highly than any other previous philosophical trend, more highly than Hegel even, who after all used it only as a case against which to test his logical problem.
>
> – Friedrich Engels, *The Condition of the Working Class in England*

The compound terms for the two recruiting techniques I conceptually define in this chapter could also be "*panya panyarring*" and "*dash-peonaje,*" however for the sake of clarity, I refer to them as *panya* and *dash*, understood in the context of colonial labor recruitment. Both *panya* and *dash* are distinct Afro-European trading and exchange practices and are clearly traceable into early modern West Africa. Yet, I do not mean to imply that the precolonial practices of pawnship and kidnapping and the payment of obligatory gifts to unlock commercial gatekeepers, which had been integral to the slave trade and other trades on the West African coast, simply kept going in the colonial period. *Panyarring* and *dashing* underwent a reinvention, adapted to colonial conditions, specifically in relation to the Spanish imperial labor contract. After closely tracing the two concept-practices that Nigerian touts and workers creatively generated, this chapter takes them as a lens to read the comparable, widespread, and recurring recruiting techniques of quasi-kidnapping and quasi-debt-bondage across islands and enclaves of indenture more generally.

The historical transformations of *panya* and *dash* in the recruitment of contract labor oblige us to abandon the notions of "exchange" underpinning conventional political theories of wage labor and contracts. They stand for two parallel and asymmetrical modalities where axioms derived from the world of exchange do not add up, namely: theft and gifts. These practices of non-equivalence and escalating reciprocity were the very source of expansion and instability of colonial economics.

The implications for the formation of the labor market are simple: there was no cycle, no circular migration, no equilibrium. Labor recruitment and the growth of plantations ran on a sea of constant turnovers. *Panya* necessarily contained an intrinsic spatial spread of recruiters and the *dash* a similar dynamism that took the form of an in-situ competition for laborers between plantations. Both Claude Meillassoux and Chris Gregory made this original observation in different contexts, in relation to labor recruitment in colonial Ivory Coast and Papua New Guinea: recruiters were inherently "shifting," "recruiters would be forced to seek out new areas of supply, a new 'labor frontier,' and so it would

https://doi.org/10.1515/9783110755923-006

go on."[1] Here I add an examination of the preconditions and techniques that led to their expansive nature. Touts had to improvise and break new ground both extensively in new hinterlands, and internally, in the reshuffling of already contracted labor.

Panya: A Concept

Today, in Nigeria across various languages, *panya* (pájà) is the colloquial name for Bioko, formerly Fernando Po, from the pidgin rendering of *España*. Most commonly it is popularly conceived of as an imaginary and hellish plateau opposed to an ideal order in Nigeria itself; for example, when something extraordinarily terrible happens in Nigeria, one can hear the saying "I didn't think this could happen in Nigeria, only in *panya*." In West Africa, during the nineteenth century, the noun *Panyer* meant "a Spaniard" and was associated mostly with the Spanish Caribbean but also Fernando Po. In Igbo areas, Ugo Nwokeji says, "up to today, the word *panya* in Igbo folklore refers to forceful removal to the unknown."[2] Nwokeji notes that "to *panya*" can also be the Igbo verb form of *panyarring* and is strongly associated with the "child-stealing" practice of the Aro that continued well into the twentieth century. However, *panyarring* is quite different from *panya*, the former was widely defined in precolonial West Africa as an act of violent and unpredictable "seizure," while *panya* is more equivalent to being "taken" or "kept" by some "force" preventing one from coming back. *Panya* and *panyarring* have different etymologies but there was a mutual layering and transformation of both terms in twentieth-century eastern Nigeria. I argue that the term acquired specific new meanings through the experiences with the colonial economy of Fernando Po.

In southern Nigeria *panya* became a term to refer to various goings-on. On the Cross River delta in the mid-twentieth century *panya* was "a term usually used only by smugglers"; it was also a term used to refer to them, connoting "mischievous" "hustlers." In Igbo areas it was commonly compounded as *ahia panya* or "*panya* trade," meaning smuggling but also faulty and unsound commodity exchange.[3] At this point the toponym *panya*, in addition to being an ac-

1 Meillassoux, *Anthropologie économique des Gouro*, 41; Chris Gregory, *Gifts and Commodities* (London: Academic Press, 1982), 129.

2 Nwokeji, *The Slave Trade*, 127, 131; Nwokeji, personal communication, December 2014.

3 "Smuggling – Nigeria's curse," *Drum*, Lagos, January 1961; Donald C. Simmons, "Analysis of the Reflection of Culture in Efik Folktales" (PhD diss., Yale University, 1957), 26; Datguru, "Where Is PANYA In Nigeria?," *Nairaland Forum*, July 1, 2014, http://www.nairaland.com/1794650/where-

tual buying and selling hub for canoe-deploying smugglers, seems to have become the popular hellish plateau, because "no one receives news directly from anyone who goes to [work in] Fernando Po. Rumours of death, imprisonment and ill-treatment are current."[4] It was a figurative but "hard" place to where "misfits" and troublesome children and subordinates "feared" being sent off to, threats made by superiors usually in a facetious manner. Many people did in fact disappear to *panya*, and if they came back at all, they returned many years later, often "empty handed" with "nothing to show" in terms of "achievements" and gains: the meaning today of the expression "having come back from *panya*," regardless of where one disappeared to for a few years.[5]

Panyarring, as contrasted with *panya*, has its own pidgin etymology, most likely from the Portuguese word *penhorâr* to "pledge" or *apanhar* "to grab" or to "seize," but the term continued to have broad valency, as it referred to possession and theft in different contexts, such as spirit possession and "man-stealing" or kidnapping. According to various accounts by English traders, in precolonial Calabar *panyarring* meant the "seizing" of free people "by force or fraud" and was used by "both Whites and Blacks," who would resort to this seizure when there was a breakdown of promised debt repayments. Most commonly *panyarring*, across the West African coast, meant a type of seemingly arbitrary debt collection, under the permissible financial relationship of pawnship that could lead to enslavement.[6] Even if *panyarring* was a widely acknowledged legal institution for the enforcement of debt repayment, the process of seizing could be random, as potentially any kin or clan member of the debtor could be "rightfully" seized and in some cases even just any member of the same village or locality.[7] It is probably this coercive inclusion of uninvolved parties in commercial disputes that explains the common observation of enslavement through deception, found in even the earliest period of the transatlantic slave trade. As an early Dutch merchant on the Upper Guinea coast cited by Toby Green observed:

---

panya-nigeria; E. Nolue Emenanjo, "Slangs and Colloquialisms in Modern Igbo: A Preliminary Socio-Linguistic Study," *Ikenga: Journal of African Studies* 4, no. 2 (1980): 52.

4 Governor of Nigeria, Lagos to British Consul General, Douala, January 16, 1945, NAE, CALPROF 17/1/277.

5 Felix K. Ekechi, *Pioneer, Patriot, and Nigerian Nationalist: A Biography of the Reverend M.D. Opara, 1915–1965* (Durham: Carolina Academic Press, 2010), 60, 261.

6 Ranby, *Observations on the Evidence*, 83; See Paul E. Lovejoy and David Richardson, "Trust, Pawnship, and Atlantic History: The Institutional Foundations of the Old Calabar Slave Trade," *American Historical Review* 104, no. 2 (1999): 344.

7 Monrad, *Two Views from Christiansborg Castle*, 57, 220; Paul E. Lovejoy, "Pawnship, Debt, and 'Freedom' in Atlantic Africa During the Era of the Slave Trade: A Reassessment," *The Journal of African History* 55, no. 1 (2014): 78, 59. See also Brauner, *Kompanien, Könige und caboceers*, 523.

> [on] large canoes there are thieves called *Gampisas* in the [Biafada] language. They are like bandits [...] they are so canny that if somebody comes from the bush inland, they pretend that they want to welcome and host them, and welcome them into their homes; and, having had them there a few days, they put the idea in their heads that they have some friends by the sea, and that they'd like to take them there so that they can meet them and enjoy each other's company; and going to the ships they sell them; and in this way they trick many people.[8]

In the 1930s Major Orde-Browne, a prolific advisor on African labor matters to the British colonial secretary, says the principal feature of recruitment for Fernando Po's was characterized by "native touts who deceive" migrant workers "as to the nature and conditions of the work." Uncertain as to what these tangles of (mis)information would mean for the character of this movement, he concluded that the "decoying of labourers out of [Nigeria] may well be little short of slavery." Considering the numbers of Nigerians going to Fernando Po, Orde-Browne assumed that the "majority of people seeking work are probably doing so voluntarily," because practically no one who went to *panya* considered themselves a slave or enslaved at the point of recruitment. His hesitation on both fronts – "little short" and "probably" – is symptomatic of this internal inconsistency marking liberal conceptions of indentured labor.[9] A British intelligence officer noted in 1942 that the "traffic of labour to the Spanish Guinea falls little short of 'blackbirding'."[10] In the early 1950s a British Vice-Consul on the island says "for the last fifteen years and even before that" Fernando Po was seen "as a source of income by [those] who enriched themselves by shanghaiing unsuspecting Eastern Nigerians over here and selling them as labourers."[11]

"Blackbirding" and "shanghaiing" were terms for a modality of recruitment in the nineteenth-century colonial Atlantic and Pacific that meant kidnapping for work on the high seas or remote off-shore indentures in plantation islands and enclaves. Abolitionists and British officials in the wider imperial world considered it to be a "species of slavery or kidnapping." The wider literature on unfree labor sometimes places the "duplicitous inducements of indentured servitude" analytically uneasily alongside imperial naval impressment surges and

8 Toby Green, *A Fistful of Shells: West Africa from the Rise of the Slave Trade to the Age of Revolution* (London: Penguin Books, 2020), 37.

9 Orde-Browne, *Labour Conditions*, 47, 71.

10 Ministry of Economic Warfare, Special Operations Executive (Simpson), December 10, 1942, TNA, HS 3/77, "Final Report on Fernando Po and Spanish Guinea, 1942–1943."

11 British VC and LO (Bradley) to Commissioner of Labor, Lagos, April 2, 1952, TNA, 371/96714.

even the *panyarring* techniques of the West African slave trade.[12] I now turn to this practice in a comparative frame, to dispel the image that it was a largely independent and regressive technique employed only in what David Northrup called the "early phase" of indenture, within a progressive narrative of imperfect beginnings under chaotic and unsupervised initiatives.[13] I will show this through a reading of "Northrupian" scholars' own work. Such so-called "revisionist" works, which were motivated by a justified weariness of representations of indenture within the rhetoric of unfreedom and the pursuit of stories about victimization at the expense of all else, seem to either directly or indirectly vindicate the foundational insight of the "Tinkerian paradigm," as Tinker himself says in his *A New System of Slavery:* "fraudulent statements [and] false pretences" were constitutive of the world of recruiters who mastered the art of presenting a "picture of what was to come which was often distant from reality."[14]

Panya Comparisons

These related practices generated nebulous but oddly specific slang: shanghaiing, blackbirding, to be barbadosed, trepanned, phuslaoed or spirited by agents, enticers, sea-pimps, land-sharks, spirits or crimps in the British Empire, *arkatis,* literally "fish hooks," in Bengal, "snakes" in southern China, the blackbirder of the South Pacific,[15] runners and touts in South Africa; *enganchadores* in Latin America – literally "those who hook" or "press or trick others into performing a service";[16] an "erratic" labor market whose most widespread and consistent feature was "knavery," being "cajoled by plausible touts."[17] *Panya* occurs in similar junctions of a discontinuous global labor history, where the same pattern of recruitment is found, lasting also for one to several decades, and containing the

---

12 Niklas Frykman, "Impressment, Kidnapping, and Panyarring," 242; Laurence Brown, "'A Most Irregular Traffic': The Oceanic Passages of the Melanesian Labor Trade," in *Many Middle Passages: Forced Migration and the Making of the Modern World*, eds. Emma Christopher et al. (Berkeley: University of California Press, 2007), 185. See also Linebaugh and Rediker, *The Many-Headed Hydra*, 133.

13 Northrup, *Indentured Labor*, 6.

14 Tinker, *A New System of Slavery*, 116, 124; See also Kale, *Fragments of Empire*.

15 Hu-DeHart, "La Trata Amarilla," 169; Gerald Horne, *The White Pacific: U.S. Imperialism and Black Slavery in the South Seas after the Civil War* (Honolulu: University of Hawaii Press, 2007), 43.

16 Edward D. Melillo, "The First Green Revolution: Debt Peonage and the Making of the Nitrogen Fertilizer Trade, 1840–1930," *The American Historical Review* 117, no. 4 (2012): 1030.

17 Orde-Browne, *African Labourer*, 74.

same inherent spatial shift: between London and Barbados or Virginia in the 1640s, between Rhineland and Pennsylvania in the 1760s, during the Napoleonic Wars across Europe in the 1790s, across the early nineteenth-century American seaboard, first the eastern one then eventually on the west coast, and in the 1840s around many places, between the Caribbean, Peru, Panama or Queensland and the port towns in the Bay of Bengal, Xiamen and Macau, and Vanuatu, Solomon Islands or New Guinea.

Sprits or crimps were called upon or generated whenever military or commercial front lines in unpopular destinations needed replenishments in periods of acute scarcity. In the early modern British Empire, spirits' modus operandi was popularly imagined to consist of "diabolic cunning and assiduity"; "hordes" of "monsters" and "demons" "infest the metropolis," "deceiving" through "persuasion with 'allurements and deluding falsities'." "Men-stealers, termed otherwise Spirits or Kidnappers, whose whole employ is to collogue and seduce indigent, ignorant Souls [by] making Golden promises of things never likely to come to pass."[18] Their techniques and the imaginary used to describe such techniques are consistent over several centuries. Spirits, even if they are unmasked or arrested, reappear elsewhere in different guises, their presence and abilities arriving with new accents. Instead of trying to establish a timeline of abolitions and transitions or engaging in the matching or dispelling of orders of similitude, it is important to recall and realize the implication that labor touts were one of the afterlives of the original "spirits." The old and new literature on indenture has provided abundant examples of the creative and fiercely consistent ways in which those entering stretched labor markets would be "deliberately deceived about their real destination."[19] One should understand "destination" not only as geographic direction, but also as a place in the division of labor, because those who were promised acceptable jobs such as agricultural work in Nigeria, or desirable placements as trading assistants, clerks, and drivers, whether in Nigeria or Fernando Po, ended up in a type of plantation labor that was quite alien or even unknown at home.

In African history the *panya*-like techniques fully emerging in the colonial period proved to be particularly difficult to classify for colonial observers because the primary ideological coating of colonization was not only the goal of "suppressing the slave trade" but also "to prevent its revival under the guise

---

18 Carlyle, "Diderot," 197; John Stevenson, "The London 'Crimp' Riots of 1794," *International Review of Social History* 16, no. 1 (1971): 53; John Wareing, "'Violently Taken Away or Cheatingly Duckoyed': The Illicit Recruitment in London of Indentured Servants for the American Colonies, 1645–1718," *The London Journal* 26, no. 2 (2001): 6.

19 Allen, "European Slave Trading, Abolitionism," 2.

of contract labour."[20] Monica Schuler writes of "the slave trade" continuing "in the guise of indentured labour in areas where slavery had been abolished," being carried out by a class of "agents" who "emerged after the slave-trade" and "who brought colonial indentured labourers, into the same or new plantation zones." Schuler notes that while of course "Europeans recruited some voluntary indentured workers in Africa, most recruits were involuntary, and their acquisition involved deliberate violence, restraint, fraud and purchase." She says that such labor recruitment, for example in Sierra Leone in the 1840s for indentures in British and French Guiana, "combined the recruiting techniques of the African slave trade with the old European bond servant traffic."[21] Elsewhere in West Africa, the dual movements of rural displacement and the colonial regulating of mobilities made both contemporary observers and historians unable to disentangle the "blunted" "distinctions between slave, indentured servant, pawn and free labourer." For example Emmanuel Akyeampong notes that the recruiting techniques for the gold mines and cacao farms of the Gold Coast during the 1890s, such as "slaving, brigandage, panyarring and pawnship became fused in disconcerting ways."[22]

Why would the "slave trade" conceptually contaminate and merge with its then conceptual opposite – free contract labor – when it was revelated that typical and ongoing recruitment techniques involved only half-truths? Why did the existence of "deception" prove to be so confusing? The question of when deception or the consequences of deception became spotlighted or skipped over is revealing. By the 1980s, an intellectual frame for studying indentured labor started circumscribing the possibility that indenture was "founded on duplicity" and this vision took firm hold because it provided a misleading sense of the transparency and evenness of recruitment trajectories needed for a utilitarian analysis. They even speculated on the "inside" of the subjects of recruitment, who were grimly considered to be continuously weighing pros and cons and making "useful" decisions. They turned the fact that "most indentured migrants left their homes voluntarily" with "hopes of better conditions and opportunities" into a realization of volition and opportunity for "self-improvement."[23] Like the recruit-

---

20 Smith, "The Lagos Consulate," 415.

21 Monica Schuler, "The Recruitment of African Indentured Labourers for European Colonies in the Nineteenth Century," in *Colonialism and Migration: Indentured Labour Before and After Slavery*, ed. Peter Emmer (New York: Springer, 1986), 127.

22 McSheffrey, "Slavery, Indentured Servitude, Legitimate Trade," 360; Akyeampong, *Between the Sea and the Lagoon*, 70.

23 For a critical review of this strand, see Paul E. Baak, "About Enslaved Ex-Slaves, Uncaptured Contract Coolies and Unfreed Freedmen: Some notes about 'Free' and 'Unfree' Labour in the

ers who had unsystematically and clandestinely been organizing most "indenture" labor migration in the mid-nineteenth century, touts were considered a disturbance, an impediment to the smooth-flowing but highly regulated movement of people whose rational arrival at their destination was imaged to be the retroactive result of regulated and informed displacement, requiring both the state-surveyed infrastructures of registration and explanation and the ideological ideal of a self-sovereign subject.

This affirmation of transparency could be minimally maintained by pointing out a one-time stopover at a magistrate's office. For British India, as was the case for the Southern Nigerian Protectorate, Mckeown notes that during the "early attempts at indenture, private companies were given almost complete freedom to recruit in India, required only to take potential migrants before a local magistrate who would assure that they were departing voluntarily."[24] There was a confidence that affidavit-generating bodies in "home" countries could guarantee and make predictable the trajectories of movements, including destinations and types of work. Where such procedures failed, it could be attributed to naivete and manipulation that resulted in fraudulent and, in principle, invalid contracts. Where future workers were "seriously misled by unscrupulous recruiters" about their "duties and compensation," as Northrup implies, it was an imperfection that could be ironed out with further official explanations of the contract.[25]

Northrup, surveying the case of the recruitment of Chinese coolies for Cuba and Peru, expressed his incredulity at the fact that 80 % if not 90 % – anyhow, he says, an "improbably high" number – of the thousands of Chinese laborers in Cuba interviewed by a Qing dynasty commission of inquiry in 1874 reported that they had been "kidnapped or decoyed" by the "barbarians" in Macao who had sent out "vicious Chinese" recruiters.[26] Never mind that under related circumstances the regional academic literature has shown that "kidnapping was no mere sideline for the bandits that plagued South China during the nineteenth and early twentieth centuries, it was their primary modus operandi" or that even into the 1900s the Attorney-General for Hong-Kong "indicated that kidnapping

context of Plantation Development in Southwest India, early sixteenth century-mid 1990s," *Modern Asian Studies* 33, no. 1 (1999): 125. See of course Northrup, *Indentured Labor*, 7; Shepherd, "'The Other Middle Passage?'"

24 McKeown, *Melancholy Order*, 72.

25 Northrup, *Indentured Labor*, 6.

26 Northrup, *Indentured Labor*, 57; China, *The Cuba Commission Report: A Hidden History of the Chinese in Cuba: The Original English-Language Text of 1876* (Baltimore: Johns Hopkins University Press, 1993), 36.

was rife."[27] In Cuba, the petitioners explained carefully and clearly how in "recent decades, China is doing business with foreigners" who were "colluding [with] Chinese gangsters whose job is to abduct people. This practice originated in [the British treaty port of] Xiamen and prospers in Macao." Since the 1850s Chinese touts had "cast their nets in every harbor and their schemes block every road. No matter the wise or the fool, we are all trapped." A particularly lucid petitioner explained how

> some people used up thousands of gold pieces and were ashamed to go back to their hometowns. Some people were very poor and looked for a job alone. They met friends on their way. Some of these friends were heart-less. These wicked people pointed falsely at a gold mountain and promised to show the way. [They] grew a lotus under their tongues but hid a sharp blade in their stomachs. They deceived people into traps in order to make a profit. They lured people to a foreign land and didn't care about family loss and lineage. I didn't realize that I was tricked until the ship sailed to the middle of the river.[28]

Having perused these petitions, Northrup interjects that they "gave the answer they thought most likely to obtain their release" and approvingly cites the Qing Commission's own conclusions that laborers tended to be "'bad characters'" emigrating "to escape the results of gambling and crime" or otherwise were "'stupid fellows'" easily "ensnared by crimps." Northrup ends by saying that "the line between voluntary and involuntary is further blurred by the fact that the migrants' desperation and ignorance made them easy to cheat and deceive." This was the same line that colonial officers took in Macau, who talked of unscrupulous promoters of "false pretenses" who could find "easy prey" and "trick" people to "willingly accompany the[m] to Macao." For Northrup it is not decisive whether recruits were under the impression that they "would be working in Macao," while others, as Northrup speculates, after hearing "of the good fortune of clansmen or other villagers in California, undoubtedly offered themselves for employment, not knowing the difference between Peru and California." What happened downstream, on the ships onwards, was secondary to a fateful choice. If one looks closely to what the recruits reported the Northupian pillars collapse, for example as a coolie from Xiamen in 1852 says: "They were beguiled on board the barbarian ship as contract laborers by emigration agents and confined in the hold. After the ship sailed, the said barbarians gave each

---

27 James L. Watson, "Transactions in People: The Chinese Market in Slaves, Servants and Heirs," in *Asian and African Systems of Slavery*, ed. James L. Watson (Berkeley: University of California Press, 1980), 233. For the "Chinese touts" who recruited for South Africa, see Bright, *Chinese Labour in South Africa*, 89.

28 Yun, *Coolie Speaks*, 245, 96.

man in the hold a contract of servitude. If he did not accept, he was flogged." The basis of what recruited laborers called the "barbarian practice" was not about local middlemen and their "snake" qualities, but about sovereign imperial horizons stretched across the ocean, along treaty ports and its shipping and legal infrastructures.[29]

The persistent insistence to narrow down to an exception the incidence of deception in order to attach to contracts the aura of transparency speaks mainly to an ideology of self-will that either seeks to affirm its maxims or, alternatively, to propel a mode of fundamentally liberal critique, that searches for its absence only in specific moments in order to continuously condemn instances of its transgression. By bypassing its own contradictions, the only room left open for "critique" are then the pedantic affirmations that colonial contracts were incomplete, incorrectly applied or simply untrue. The concealed moral telos of this supposition is: if only there is continuing consent at ever shorter intervals registered by a paternalistic bureaucracy does the relation then become moral and legitimate. When discussing contracts in contractual terms one only peers into the ideology of its bearers, without learning anything about the contract's primary object or historical effect. Distorted communication was constitutive. Posing the problem in this way goes beyond the critique that even colonial officials could make, who reported that even though Chinese emigrants had signed an agreement written in Chinese and Spanish, the "truth of these statements is doubtful because it was unlikely that any of the emigrants could read and write, which meant they were at the mercy of whatever the coolie agents had told them."[30] As Jan Breman noted long ago, faced with systematic treachery and bungled ceremonies registering consent in the moment of signing, it is "nothing other than a colonial fantasy to maintain that a contract was entered into voluntarily."[31]

In the revisionist literature on indentured labor this systematic opacity was glossed as the "deception argument," as Marina Carter says in relation to *arkatis* or the touts in the Bay of Bengal who recruited indentured labor for Mauritius. While aware of the "persisting evidence of fraud in indentured recruitment," she, like many of the authors trained in the "Northrupian" paradigm coming primarily out of Oxbridge, manages to turn "specific" instances of deception usually "related to destination" into a minor and incidental detail. In the case of Sunil

29 Northrup, *Indentured Labor*, 57, 56, 58; Irick, *Ch'ing Policy toward the Coolie Trade*, 95, 205, 33.

30 Robert J. Plowman, "The Voyage of the 'Coolie' Ship Kate Hooper October 3, 1857 – March 26, 1858," *Prologue Magazine* 33, no. 2 (2001).

31 Breman, *Taming the Coolie Beast*, 132.

Amrith's account of indenture and post-indenture labor migrations across the Bay of Bengal, he argues that the idea that "agents practiced deception to lure the laborers with false promises" turns them into "passive victims," and because this notion was regularly entertained by "British officials" it actually speaks primarily to their "anxiety" and prejudice that "Indian migrants were incapable of agency"; "officials felt that the real 'agents' were the labor recruiters, known precisely by that term: as agents."[32] The brushing aside and away of "specific" instances which redraw the entire cartography of departure and destination and the fundamental experience of long-distance migration, seems to serve the attempts to equate recruitment within the empire with the "general" models of migration and labor that existed ideally in Europe and the Americas – even when they ventured into the "unknown". In this way the conceptual-political commitment, the equating of Europe and freedom, and the contract's role in enshrining and preserving it, could be upheld. The impetus behind this commitment was always to stem the polemical and chaotic tide of the metaphor of "slavery" – which were already proliferating as self-designations in Europe within the anti-capitalist labor movements themselves – being then applied to post-abolition imperial migrations by colonial reformers and critics. As Carter says – repeating what others had said before her and is still heard – the recruitment in the Bay of Bengal for Mauritius was thus "closer to white indentured servitude than to the system of slavery which had immediately preceded it."[33]

This conceptual rebalancing act however generated an overcorrected and pointlessly simplified classic liberal rhetoric of the recourse of choice or "freedom" in the labor market. The complicated ideology or better theodicy of liberal personhood and the transactional routes of self-improvement or even salvation, misses what can be called the *historical and hermeneutic dimensions* – in the sense of the interpretation of sources to approximate the meaning of the profound expressions of disappointment in them, as well as the theoretical underappreciation of the complexity of subterfuge and undecidability. Even the extensive regional literature on "white indentured servants" in the early modern

32 Amrith, *Crossing the Bay of Bengal*, 133.

33 Marina Carter, "Strategies of Labour Mobilisation in Colonial India: The Recruitment of Indentured Workers for Mauritius," *Journal of Peasant Studies* 19, no. 3/4 (1992): 230, 238, 243; Marina Carter, "The Transition from Slave to Indentured Labour in Mauritius," in *The Wages of Slavery: From Chattel Slavery to Wage Labour in Africa, the Caribbean, and England*, ed. Michael Twaddle (London: Frank Cass, 1993), 117. See also Crispin Bates, "Some Thoughts on the Representation and Misrepresentation of the Colonial South Asian Labour Diaspora," *South Asian Studies* 33, no. 1 (2017): 10. For an assessment of "deception" see Mohabir, "Servitude in the Shadow of Slavery?," 240.

British empire has consistently rejected an abolitionist free labor ideology and the literary trope of the so-called "free-willers" – the therapeutically "empowering" or mythological embracing of adversity dominating narratives of migration history – by simply showing how the "majority of indentured servants recruited in London were recruited illicitly," "mainly trepanned by the spirits rather than kidnapped by force."[34]

How did those recruited experience the procedure? The routes to Trinidad, Guyana, Mauritius, Fiji, Guyana, and Assam were largely paved by private Bengali recruiters, the *arkatis* who were said to work in "bazaar towns and pilgrimage centres" touting people semi-arbitrarily who may or may not even have been looking for work. In Assam, the colonial *Labour Enquiry Committee in the Recruiting and Labour Districts* simply concluded that "most of the people recruited under the present system have been phuslaoed by the recruiters."[35] *Arkatis* developed a particularly unsavory reputation. In the folkloric songs forged and recited by coolies in the Assam tea plantations in the late nineteenth century, the *arkatis* figures mythologically as trickster: *Shyam/Jaduram*. As Nitin Varma says of these narratives, it is the recruiters who carve the "path to the sites of 'oppression'," who through "deception (*Phanki*)" "lured them to contract (*Paka khata*) and facilitated their passage to Assam." The song goes: "Putting my name down in the (Contract) Oh nasty Shyam," "You deceived me to Assam," "Oh Jaduram You deceived us to Assam." "We saw the sky in Hooghly and thought we were going to Assam to pull *pankhas* but instead we were given spades by the *sahibs* to work." "Alas crafty Jaduram, you have deceived me and sent me to Assam by false promise."[36]

Arkatis from Calcutta were seen as purely commercial agents "who traded in labour for profit, thereby approximating 'traffic' in persons." They were the "dominant mode of labour mobilization in the 1860s" and when reforms attempted to formalize and regulate recruiting under corporate schemes and monopolies, the *arkatis* started venturing beyond West Bengal to Bihar and eastern Uttar Pradesh. Samita Sen notes that the distinction between the *arkati* "contractors" and the emerging *sardari* recruitment, where the *sardar* was "perceived to be an 'insider' recruiting within a proximate community and thus less likely to use force and deception in recruitment," was much emphasized in the colonial sources themselves precisely because officials wanted the latter to replace the

34 Wareing, "'Violently Taken Away,'" 4, 6.

35 India, *Proceedings of the Assam Labour Enquiry Committee in the Recruiting and Labour Districts, Vol. I* (Calcutta: Government Printer, 1906), 5; Bates, "Coerced and Migrant Labourers," 22; Balachandran, "Recruitment and Control."

36 Varma, *Coolies of Capitalism*, 116–120.

former. This discursive split around contrasting terms allowed colonial reformers to see, and imagine, the embedded moralities of the "new system," which however led to the same plantations and worksites.[37]

Ambitious colonial "Fordist" reformist promises of vertically integrating and supervising all aspects of indentured labor, including recruitment, were already fading away by the late nineteenth century and becoming replaced by pragmatic and fragmented recruitment. A focus on the dynamics during the massive growth of internal or intra-Asian labor movements by Ravi Raman, Sunil Amrith and more recently Ritesh Jaiswal, have been particularly insightful about the internal transformations of the new recruiting systems based around the so-called *sardari* or the *kangani* system, which moved away from an earlier system of recruiting. The *kangani*, the Tamil term for "headmen" or "overseer," was initially conceived as an embedded mediator who channeled labor to Ceylon, Burma, and Malaysia. However, as Jaiswal notes, from the 1880s on when the rapid growth of the *kangani* system commenced and came to replace formal indenture altogether, a change of *kangani* techniques and even of the *kangani* themselves had taken place, altering the "methods of recruitment, quality of recruits, nature of the labour regime, value of advances, [and the] indebtedness of labourers." Amrith notes the implications of this transformations of *kanganies* into touts – many of them former labourers "sent back to India by their employers to recruit more men on commission" paying out what was called the "coast advance" – yet still represents them as operating on a "small scale, recruiting largely among their fellow villagers," where "relations of caste and kinship could moderate the kanganies' power" and "make the bonds of debt more pervasive." During the recruiting for the tea plantations in Ceylon, Raman notes the *kangani*

> proceeded from one village to another, visiting fairs and other festive places where he would paint a rosy picture of the life on the hills: higher (money) wages, better housing and proper medical care. All forms of persuasion and coercion were employed to cajole the workers into migrating to the plantations. The poor workers often fell prey to these ploys, only to be cheated of the advance money promised to them, the kanganies often si-

37 Sen, "Commercial Recruiting," 7, 5. Compare Crispin Bates and Marina Carter, "Sirdars as Intermediaries in Nineteenth-Century Indian Ocean Indentured Labour Migration," *Modern Asian Studies* 51, no. 2 (2017): 472, 484, "The process of recruitment was thus far from being the ideal individualized market exchange," instead the "*sirdar* played a critical role as an intermediary in negotiations, securing the best possible terms for the engagement of himself and his body of workers"; "networks and social relationships are as important as innovation and production in a capitalist market economy and they remain so to this day," etc.

> phoning away this advance amount entrusted to them by the planters. In other instances, the workers received less than the amount claimed to have been decided on.[38]

The persistence of touts, as impersonal "strangers" who shifted their grounds of operations, rather than consistently connecting a specific employer or worksite with a specific village or group of villages, has been demonstrated for a period of over half a century in Southern Africa, at the junctions between Mozambique, Southern Rhodesia, and the Transvaal in different directions over time. There the generative process of "fraud and misrepresentation" by unlicensed "rapacious labour touts and criminal gangs" who made "promises which they did not intend to keep," were spoken of by local administrators and academics as having "degenerated into 'nothing more or less than a sort of slave trade'."[39] In what is the best article on recruiters in African history, "'Blackbirding' at 'Crooks' Corner': Illicit Labour Recruiting in the Northeastern Transvaal, 1910–1940," Martin J. Murray shows in great detail how these "unlicensed freelancers reaped huge profits," in part because they "used all sorts of tricks and ploys to ensnare unwary Africans and to smuggle this precious human cargo across the Limpopo." In a quasi-literary genre Murray even draws a picaresque portrait of an Afrikaans man, Cecil Barnard, and his recruiting "gang." He was a former soldier with the alias "Bvekenya" or "the drunk," "the one who swaggers as he walks," who became "Africa's leading illegal recruiter." Barnard and "his companions practically monopolised the labour recruitment of Shangaans" living in southern Zimbabwe. In "1917 alone, Barnard's best year, he single handedly recruited 3,250 Africans illegally and 'safely smuggled them past Portuguese and Transvaal police alike'." While his "gang" were "gun-toting" and quite predatory – Barnard "resorted to ambushing and hijacking labour from careless rivals" – an official South African WNLA (the monopoly recruitment branch of the Chamber of Mines that operated outside the Transvaal) recruiter in Southern Rhodesia made the important observation that "'no force is used and these Shangaans so far from objecting are very willing to go with Barnard' […] 'They go to the

38 Ravi Raman, *Global Capital and Peripheral Labour: The History and Political Economy of Plantation Workers in India* (London: Routledge, 2010), 100; Ritesh Kumar Jaiswal, "Mediated (Im)Mobility: Indian Labour Migration to Ceylon under the Kangany System (c. 1850–1940)," in *The Palgrave Handbook of Bondage and Human Rights in Africa and Asia*, eds. Gwyn Campbell and Alessandro Stanziani (New York: Palgrave Macmillan, 2020), 272. Amrith, *Crossing the Bay of Bengal*, 83.

39 Murray, "'Blackbirding,'" 382, 389, 380; citing letter by South African Police commander in the Zoutpansberg district from 1912; also cited in Jeeves, "Over-Reach," 407; MacDonald, "Forging the Frontiers," 157; Harries, *Work, Culture, and Identity*, 115.

Rand Mines with absolute regularity. Of course, this is illegal but the natives don't object'."[40]

The shift or drift of recruiters was gradual: "Officials knew that the fraud and misrepresentation which inevitably accompanied competitive recruiting frequently caused disturbances in the countryside, to the eventual detriment of the overall supply," so in their own South African districts the authorities tried to "eliminate some of the cruder forms of exploitation and fraud which had prevailed in the 1890s." However, "north of the Union's borders, no such controls operated at all." Between the 1890s and the 1920s and even into the 1940s "recruiting for the gold mines from beyond the Limpopo became an elaborate, highly organised business. For most of this period it belonged to unlicensed touts, and their black 'runners'." Although "economically weak" compared to the corporate mining monopolies, "these independents were able to dictate the terms on which labour was recruited for many years." Even when such networks were partially displaced though the 1928 bilateral arrangement with the colonial authorities of Mozambique, whereby the WNLA was allowed to recruit up to 100,000 workers per year for a "capitation fee" of £5 paid into Portuguese coffers, the miners in the Rand "routinely consorted with the unlicensed independents in their endless search for reliable supplies" of labor.[41]

Force or Fraud

The economy of deception in the recruitment of indentured labor is usually immediately attached to "force" by its analysts: blackbirding was "dishonest and violent," spiriting was "fraudulent and coercive," it meant being "violently taken away or cheatingly duckoyed," "either through deception or direct violence," "victims were kidnapped, tricked by offers of good jobs"; "all forms of persuasion and coercion were employed" by recruiters who painted "a rosy picture" and created "victims of empty promises"; all in all, a kind of "enticement/kidnapping."[42] The different segments of a recruitment trajectory are often col-

40 Murray, "'Blackbirding,'" 374, 380, 389, citing Cecil Barnard and Thomas Victor Bulpin, *The Ivory Trail* (Cape Town: Books of Africa, 1967), 164; see also Jeeves, *Migrant Labour*, 153–183.
41 Jeeves, "Over-Reach," 395, 401, 410. "The old ways died hard. In 1947, a syndicate of blackbirders was caught in the Waterberg, impersonating police and waiting in hideouts along the Crocodile River." MacDonald, "Colonial Trespassers," 271, 287.
42 Martin A. Klein, *Historical Dictionary of Slavery and Abolition* (Lanham: Scarecrow Press, 2002), 76; Wareing, "'Violently Taken Away,'" 1; Brown, "'A Most Irregular Traffic,'" 194; Miers and Roberts, *End of Slavery*, 21; Raman, *Global Capital*, 100.

lapsed in the category of crimping: the use of "persuasion, swindling, or coercion". The same range of conflationary vocabulary is used in more contemporary definitions of "trafficking in persons."[43] Indeed, already in 1925 the Anti-Slavery and Aboriginal Protection Society decided on a "broad principle" when deciding "what practices may be said to-day to amount to modern slavery," namely "any system in which force or fraud are exercised to secure control over the labourer for private ends."[44] This double bind of language and violence is connoted in *panya*, but they occur far apart, both logically, and in time and place.

The pattern of the technique is clear, first the trick then the force, first the farce then the tragedy. The first segment is referred to with endless synonyms for deception, that in comparison to "force" borders on the obscenely light-hearted, almost playful, infantilizing, and incredulous. The "trick" as vector of instrumental language for the commodification and obfuscation of desire is an axiomatic creative capitalist praxis, theorized in the psychoanalytic context of consumer society as "cruel optimism" by Lauren Berlant, and as the "gimmick" or the "cheap trick" by Sianne Ngai. The "gimmick," with an obvious relationship to labor and value, presents itself as something that can potentially save or augment time and money while at the same time those who tout it are "excessive," working "too hard" in their strained efforts to get attention.[45] *Panya* and the *dash* mobilized tremendous affective forces. Ill-fated managed fantasies saturated the grease that wheeled imperial labor recruitment. Touts were a symptom of the expansion of the internal limits of capitalism and its arenas of operation, every day commercial dealings with opaque others, containing hazards and seductions. They offered the crushing promises of the outside world and the need to connect with it through imaginaries and logistics.

Dash: A Concept

The word "*dash*" derives from the sixteenth-century Portuguese *doação*, meaning the process of gifting something to someone or that which "is given," from the Latin *dare* and *donum*.[46] In the introduction I cited Jane Guyer's precise

43 McKeown, *Melancholy Order*, 349–369.

44 Quirk, "Defining Slavery," 257.

45 Lauren Berlant, *Cruel Optimism* (Durham: Duke University Press, 2012); Sianne Ngai, *Theory of the Gimmick: Aesthetic Judgment and Capitalist Form* (Cambridge: Harvard University Press, 2020), 35, 72.

46 Paul Christophersen, "A Note on the Words Dash and Ju-Ju in West African English," in *Perspectives on Black English*, ed. Joey Lee Dillard (Berlin: Walter de Gruyter, 1975), 213.

and concise definition of the *dash:* "an ancillary to an exchange." It is a constitutive supplement, meaning it forms part of a transaction but is not formally defined by it even though the transaction itself could not be completed without it.[47] This ancillary moment contains at least two positions: those who need to give the *dash* within a certain range and interval, and those who expect or even require the *dash* and deem its quantity and quality – on top of the context of exchange or what the *dash* giver expects to receive and what the *dash* receiver can uniquely provide in turn. One *dash* produces this four-fold matrix, and each position must be distinguished to perceive the autonomous logic and power relations of the *dash,* including when it was attached as an indispensable part of colonial labor recruitment. This conceptual separation or positing is necessary to detect the source of instability and contradiction in exchange. A better term than "exchange" is conditional and asymmetric quasi-exchange, which is to say, the gift, because it is not inherently fungible and because there is no guarantee that it will elicit the desired return from the other.[48]

The *dash*-gift has little to do with the classical Maussian gift, where the idea is not about an exchange per se, but the power to carry and contain within it something of the giver's self, serving both as a reminder of outstanding debts and cementing bonds, turning into unconditional reciprocity or hierarchy at its most socially compelling – hospitality, generosity, and tribute. The decisive Maussian aspect for the study of debt bondage is the etymological-conceptual finding of the morally entangled "fatal gift" – as "gift" of course meant both "giving" and "poison" in Old High German, from *gaben,* as well as in Ancient Greek, *dosis,* the roots of the English words for "giving" and "dose."[49] The notion that

47 In colonial and post-colonial Nigeria the word *dash* can be accounted for, each with its own power-relation and social end, in any number of small- and large-scale transactions, from flashy sequences of marriage ceremonies to the quotidian life of underpaid staffers of bureaucracies. On this last manifestation Peter Enahoro put it satirically: "This barefaced robbery is delicately called 'service charge'. In fact it is bribery. Thus, while tipping is reward, the 'dash' is an incentive. I recommend the 'dash'. It reduces hostilities to the barest minimum." Peter Enahoro, *How to Be a Nigerian* (Ibadan: Daily Times of Nigeria, 1971), 35. Teju Cole, more recently, simply says: "For many Nigerians, the giving and receiving of bribes, tips, extortion money, or alms – the categories are fluid – is not thought of in moral terms. It is seen either as a mild irritant or as an opportunity. It is a way of getting things done, neither more nor less than what money is there for." Teju Cole, *Every Day Is for the Thief* (New York: Random House, 2014), 17.

48 Costas Lapavitsas, "Commodities and Gifts: Why Commodities Represent more than Market Relations," *Science & Society* 68, no. 1 (2004): 40; Alain Testart, "What Is a Gift?," *HAU: Journal of Ethnographic Theory* 3, no. 1 (2013).

49 Mauss, *Gift,* 81, 186; Marcel Mauss, "Gift, gift," in *Gift: Marcel Mauss' Kulturtheorie der Gabe,* eds. Stephan Moebius and Christian Papilloud (Wiesbaden: VS Verlag, 2006), 13.

wage advances are a sort of poison of entrapment lingers within scholarly and popular conceptual frames. This morally applied insight is, as we will see, incomplete at best, though certainly for the *dash*-giving employers the primary concern was a calculation of real returns in the "interest" paid through labor. A good translation would also thus keep the element of "dose" in the *dash*, a variable quantity given at a particular time during a transactional relation that could easily turn sour, but the concerns of the receiver were not limited to their liability or ability to cancel the "debt".

Much is hidden in the tensions of the four-fold matrix of the *dash* "exchange," with predictable and even mechanical elements accompanied by moments and strains of extreme uncertainty and opacity. Indeed, it is best to assume before an inquiry that the purpose and effects of the *dash* in different contexts are inscrutable, and that not all *dash* instances can be understood with the same underlying conceptual framework, supposing an economically rational or smooth quasi-equilibrated state that effectively guides commercial mutuality. As Guyer has repeatedly observed, innumerable aspects of socio-economic life in Nigeria combine the stable price inscribed in conventions and the *dash* as a demanded but negotiated part – an amount to be named, assessed, inspected, and deemed appropriate, usually without leaving a trace in the actual accounts of the calculations of the exchange.[50]

The first written recollection of the *dash* is found in a 1602 traveler's account penned by Pieter de Marees, at the cusp of the Dutch Golden Age which displaced the Portuguese from the Gulf of Guinea. In the Gothic typeface of the original, "*Dache*," along with *Negotie* and *Fetissero*, appear clearly in an arial-like font. The conjecture proposed by the translators of this text, whereby the "*dash*-system" or the "gifts" offered "before entering into an agreement or transaction probably existed prior to the arrival of Europeans on the coast" is undoubtedly true, but it is a somewhat misleading claim.[51] The *dash* fully shares

50 Guyer, *Marginal Gains*, 59; Jane Guyer, "Comparisons and Equivalencies in Africa and Melanesia," in *Money and Modernity: State and Local Currencies in Melanesia*, eds. David Akin and Joel Robbins (Pittsburgh: University of Pittsburgh Press, 1999), 237.

51 Filipa Ribeiro da Silva, *Dutch and Portuguese in Western Africa: Empires, Merchants and the Atlantic System, 1580–1674* (Leiden: Brill, 2011), 36, 194; Marees, *Beschrijvinghe*, 21–23; for an edited translation see Pieter de Marees, *Description and Historical Account of the Gold Kingdom of Guinea (1602)*, eds. Albert van Dantzig and Adam Jones (Oxford: Oxford University Press, 1987), 47n. In de Marees' short chapter titled "Why one must give them presents when they have bought something, and what 'Dache' means," the "them" were not the traders who came on board the ships but the "pilots" of the canoes who acted as interpreters and brokers. His story of the origin of the dash starts with the captain of one of three competing Dutch ships telling a canoe man: "Bring the Traders to me on my ship and I shall give you something." And

the hybridity of the three pidgin terms in de Marees' *Description and Historical Account of the Gold Kingdom of Guinea* and their obvious Portuguese etymologies – including *negócio*, business, and *feiticeiro*, fetish-maker. All three were located neither in an exclusively African or European tradition, but emerged in a stand-off and subsequent improvising of new associations on the commercial fringes of the coast.[52]

The *dash* is a well-known feature of precolonial coastal exchange practices, but in African economic and social history its internal dynamics have been undertheorized and underappreciated, sometimes barely mentioned at all and simply referred to as the "gifts" to "close out barter."[53] When European merchants on the West African coast lamented the "inconveniences" of barter, what they were often referring to was the "extra" component of the *dash*, not the fact of barter itself, because barter was a misnomer in a system of countertrade regularly fixed by conventional units of account bridging barter "ratios."[54] To give a schematic example: the "barter ratios" of imported goods were standardized and denominated in relatively stable prices given in imaginary units of account. Depending on the region and period these could involve local units such as the *brass* or *kroo* in the Oil Rivers of the Bight of Biafra which were "a purely fictitious standard of value" with a lagging peg to a European currency or staple trade good. In the nineteenth century, further west and south, the dollar or the five-franc coin was commonly used, again as an entirely imaginary unit since this physically absent "money" did not change hands. Each commodity,

---

indeed, these "Interpreters took the Traders to that man's Ship, for they are very greedy." Of course, now the second Dutch ship offered even higher *dashes* to attract trade via the touts, and slowly the "batmen," the pilots, says De Marees demanded "more better *Dache*," consisting of gold or linen, preferably gold, and "by that means" he concludes his origin story, the three Dutch ships "striving one with the other, they diminished one the other's gain." As Gutkind says, the touting, independent canoe men were "perceived by some as outcasts, as villainous, and always as lazy, but also cunning, ambitious, and determined to set themselves up as traders in their own right." The canoe-touts were made up from a mix of lineages – from pre-existing fisher communities on the coast, and from the cousins and fictive offspring of the Portuguese *lançados*, who had always lived outside of the European corporate fort compounds and who also were the commercial outcasts vis-à-vis Akan centers of political power. Peter C. W. Gutkind, "Trade and Labor in Early Precolonial African History: The Canoemen of Southern Ghana," in *The Workers of African Trade*, eds. Catherine Coquery-Vidrovitch and Paul E. Lovejoy (London: Sage, 1985), 40, 26.

52 G. I. Jones, *The Trading States of the Oil Rivers: A Study of Political Development in Eastern Nigeria* (London: James Currey, 1963), 20; William Pietz, "The Problem of the Fetish, II: The Origin of the Fetish," *RES: Anthropology and Aesthetics* 13 (1987): 36.

53 Brooks, *Eurafricans in Western Africa*, 124.

54 Du Chaillu, *Explorations & Adventures in Equatorial Africa*, 48, 222.

Figure 6: Canoes on the Gold Coast, 1602 (de Marees 1617, 49).

for example 20 yards of cloth or 20 rifles that could be traded for a slave or a barrel of palm oil, had a conventional peg to the unit of account, but the revising of this peg was a much longer process and was not quickly adjustable on the spot.[55] As the quality of each imported item could vary widely in the world of imperfectly uniform commodities and transport conditions, for example different types of rifles or gunpowder of varying quality, during each trade there would necessarily be a "scene" where items were assessed and inspected. The *dash* would then function as a supplement reflecting divergences from expectations: it could be a compensation when the trade goods in exchange were thought substandard without having to revise the exchange rate to the unit of account. An augmenting *dash* thus appeared in relation to non-equivalence and deviations from the convention.

55 Paul Einzig, *Primitive Money: In Its Ethnological, Historical and Economic Aspects* (Oxford: Pergamon Press, 1966), 140, 130; G.I. Jones, "Native and Trade Currencies in Southern Nigeria during the Eighteenth and Nineteenth Centuries," *Africa* 28, no. 1 (1958): 49; Marion Johnson, "The Ounce in Eighteenth-Century West African Trade," *The Journal of African History* 7, no. 2 (1966): 199.

It was a cliché to describe this component of exchange as "inconvenient" and "cumbersome" in the narrative accounts of both merchants and the late colonial African historiography. Most European slave traders and corporate diplomats considered the "trade-dash," the "shake-hands," the "bonus-gift" a "tedious and irritating" component.[56] The ideologically inflected and economically inadequate notional explanations of the *dash,* such as Jones' supposition, that the "modern" determination to have "fixed prices" brushed up against but nevertheless accommodated an African "indigenous culture" of "bargaining," become even clearer when closely read through economic logic, as exactly the reverse was the case: European merchants would have liked to haggle and threaten to go to non-existent sellers elsewhere, but they could not. The *dash* was an acknowledgment of this dependency on African suppliers. Indeed, those who received the *dash,* the coastal gatekeepers with the power to allocate, saw it in those terms, a non-negotiable sum that could be openly and unilaterally set and escalated.[57]

To take one example: "Trade is trade, but dash is dash" explained "Yellow Nako" to the British Rear-Admiral William Allen in 1841, the former a "veritable 'Lord of Isles'" in the Niger Delta, the latter on board the Wilberforce frigate dispatched to the delta to arrange the transition from the slave trade to "legitimate commerce." The former had brokered "all our bargains" says Rear-Admiral Allen, of the deal whereby the price of palm oil would be reduced, and the supply guaranteed and monopolized by Nako. The "dash," however, Allen notes, remembering his confusion, was not "reduced" or correspondingly devalued, not anchored as a percentage to the artificially lowered market rate. Nako's tautology, "dash is dash," distinguishes it first from "trade," and announces itself as a maneuver able to mark its own predicate, willing to accompany the attempts to dampen the volatility of supply and demand not only with its own more robust elasticity but with its own political trajectory.[58]

European sources are unambiguous about their misinterpretations: they constantly complain about the "greed" and "insatiable" "demands for gifts," and seeing that these *dashes* were in effect non-negotiable, wondered if these "gifts" were actually "tributes" or even a type of "wage" for the trade workers. In the literature, the trade-*dash* has often been conflated with the tribute *dash,* within a conceptual framework that gives both the same institutionalist-monetary "function": the reduction of risk and uncertainty between trading part-

---

56 Jones, *Oil Rivers*, 99; Austen and Derrick, *Middlemen of the Cameroons Rivers*, 38, 80.

57 Thornton, *Africa and Africans in the Making of the Atlantic World*, 43–53.

58 Allen, "Narrative of the Expedition," 235.

ners. The political-commercial *dash* is more prosaic than the ritualized-diplomatic *dash* which consisted in unique and high-value items for display given to recognized leaders to secure deals, concessions, monopolies, and the like. These "tribute-gifts" were called "custom", known locally as *kumi* or *comeys* depending on the region.[59] Paul Lovejoy and others have considered it mainly through the lens of a "tool" to gain an advantage. In this story European traders frequenting a certain part of the West African coast could motivate and incentivize an ongoing trade relationship with their counterparts through a generous *dash* and so shut out any competition, because the African merchants would reserve their export-slaves for them in the expectation of receiving a premium.[60] The *dash* as a sign of non-market relations of trust and reputability and fidelity.

A commonly disregarded but more important dynamic of the *dash* in precolonial West African trade practices, is the fact that it fluctuated depending on the volatility, inflationary pressures, and quality of trade goods. The *dash*, an obligatory but not regularly priced supplementary financial instrument, is not reducible to trade premiums, but indexes the qualitative dimensions of products and serves as a measure of reversible and localized power relations. The *dash* was not a stand-alone or self-constituting object: it was usually just composed of the very same currency or trade goods that made up the formal part of the transaction, such as brass basins, cloths, alcohol, and the like. It could be set in stable proportions for certain periods, but also increase or decrease with the value and volume of trade. At the same time it had its own inflationary and compensatory dynamics revolving around the specific qualities of the thing itself. In one direction, for the European traders or for example colonial employers, competing amongst themselves, experienced laborers on second contracts were prized and esteemed, and so a higher *dash* would secure it to their seeming advantage. Yet in the other direction, the lower the quality of the good, weather trade goods or for example the working conditions on certain plantations, the expected *dash* would be higher.

This doubly inflationary character of the *dash*, a premium for reliable quality from the perspective of the buyer, as well as a premium for substandard quality from the perspective of the seller, reappeared in the indispensable edge of the

---

59 Christina Brauner, "Connecting Things: Trading Companies and Diplomatic Gift-Giving on the Gold and Slave Coasts in the Seventeenth and Eighteenth Centuries," *Journal of Early Modern History* 20, no. 4 (2016): 416; Brauner, *Kompanien, Könige und caboceers*, 273–293; Silva, *Dutch and Portuguese in Western Africa*, 194.

60 Lovejoy and Richardson, "Trust, Pawnship," 342; Curtin, *Cross-Cultural Trade*, 56–60; John Middleton, "Merchants: An Essay in Historical Ethnography," *Journal of the Royal Anthropological Institute* 9, no. 3 (2003): 522.

dash employed in recruiting. The instability of this two-fold inflation compounded under highly competitive conditions. As I will detail in the *dash* chapter, the *dash* as wage advance had precisely these compensatory and inverse dynamics, where the conventional or rigged price was simply the inflexible official wage of the contract and planters with the worst reputation or most inhospitable locations had to offer the highest *dash*. Only in the mid-twentieth century did the *dash* generate a contradictory crescendo, but the same doubling of the *dash* was already present in nineteenth century Fernando Po, where labor conditions on the island produced not just widespread desertion, but also ever larger advances.

Initially in the 1860s, as Sundiata notes in relation to then prevailing Kru workers, with every passing steamer stopping over in Fernando Po a considerable number were lost "through desertion."[61] It seems every time a British ship was moored in the dormant and half-submerged volcanic crater of the port of Santa Isabel, a few dozen "Kruman would disappear"; "they make sure to flee from the island whenever opportunities arose." If "we don't find an energetic remedy" to the "flight of the *Kruman*," writes an early Spanish Governor, "it will be a stimulus to a series of successive desertions which will leave our Government and population without a single worker."[62] That a primary worry of the Spanish lay in desertion is clear from a 1862 labor treaty signed with the Kingdom of Bimbia on the shores of Mount Cameroon, located within a direct line of sight of the island. All five short articles are geared towards "King William I" of Bimbia "making his subjects fulfil the contracts with Spanish subjects" so as "to avoid the frequently arising problem" of desertion. Nevertheless this treaty did not produce any results; the British made sure to block any independent communication between these two authorities, and any other local authorities on the mainland, including with the "King of Calabar," "one of the most powerful in the region," who by invitation had visited Santa Isabel on his "small steamship" in 1861 to discuss opening up "commercial relations" with the Spanish.[63]

The Kru had no "kings," and the Spanish and other colonial states could not track them down with their own existing rudimentary methods. Notably, the Kru tended to always use quite eccentric pseudonyms on colonial paperwork, and only their "headmen" knew who the individual workers were – an example of

61 Sundiata, "Kru Power," 29; Brooks, *The Kru Mariner*, 25.

62 GG (Gándara) to DGMC, June 19, 1861, AGA, C-81/06941, cited in García Cantús, "Fernando Póo," 416.

63 Miranda, *Leyes coloniales*, 33; GG to DGMC, December 27, 1860, MAE, AH, TR 439 E-12, "Proyecto de convenio comercial con el Rey de Calabar."

the full names of 231 recruits sent from Maryland to Fernando Po, includes workers simply called Freeman (Headman), Deal, Willie No.3, Jaguar, George Labourors, Sea-Never-Dry, Teacup, Friday, Cheddar, Hunry, Boy, Sea Breeze, Friday No. 2, Tom No.3, Teacup no.2, Money Plava, Jon Try, Try-Best, Money Trouble, Coffee, Freetown, and so on.[64] These headmen were far from loyal collaborators or overeager contract enforcers.[65] The Spanish could do little about outward desertion, so they inverted it: in the 1870s it became official policy of the Spanish to offer a *dash* to those who deserted onto the island "from British vessels" stopping over at Santa Isabel.[66] This became one of the primary forms of recruitment as the Spanish were no longer able to send their own ships to the Kru coast. Here, at the harbor and on ships containing people already on the move, the localized touts could begin their arena of operation. The lowly labor touts waiting at the harbor to quickly board ships in transit made regular appearance over the next century. A British Vice-Consul noted that this new type of "native labour recruiters first made their appearance" in the 1890s, only following after "the period of headmen came to a close."[67] Much has been made of the distinction between headmen and recruiters, as with the opposition between *arkatis* and *sardars* in the Bay of Bengal, but in the case of *dash* dynamics they were almost indistinguishable.

Even for the earlier generations of mobile Kru work "gangs" of around twenty people, whose advances, labor conditions, payments, supervision, and repatriation were all mediated through their own "headmen," the headmen were precisely the figures who were able to first escalate the *dash* and organize the desertion for re-hiring elsewhere. The *dash* of the headmen was always clearly marked apart and significantly higher than the *dash* for plain or first-time workers. The "breakdown" of this pattern of "Kru migration to Fernando Po" as Sundiata notes, was not because headmen suddenly lost their ability to further develop these pioneering techniques in the late nineteenth century, but because of the rise of "external authority on the Kru Coast itself" or the "coercive machinery

64 Recruiting Agent (Allen Yancy), Maryland County, January 5, 1929, "List of Labourers shipped from Cape Palmes Maryland Country to the Spanish Protectorate of Fernando Po by the Cape Palmas Recruiting Company," AGA, C-81/7722, E-1.

65 Tonkin, "Creating Kroomen," 35; Frost, "*Work and Community*," 40; Mark-Thiesen, *Mediators, Contract Men*, 76–82.

66 GG (García Tudela), December 14, 1873, AGA, C-81/6939, cited in García Cantús, "Fernando Poo," 515.

67 British VC (Michie), February 28, 1941, TNA, FO 371/26908.

of the Liberian state" which came to monopolize the indenture-like emigration of its subjects in the early twentieth century.[68]

To better appreciate how the *dash* became attached onto the indentured labor contracts on Fernando Po while recovering its own historical logics, I will first draw out a brief comparative history of *dash* equivalents to show what makes it distinctive as a lens and what is revealed when similar arrangements elsewhere are explicitly read through it. This wider reading into the causes and effects of what is often inaccurately described as a "wage advance" allows a focused analysis of the escalations and doubly inflationary logics at work across a global history of labor mobilization and its expanding internal limits.

Dash Comparisons

In African history the discrete connections of pawnship and debt bondage, the passages of money before and after the bind, have been a central concern for studies of labor in the pre- and early colonial period, including in the common situations of "self-pawning" or people "selling themselves to get money" or "cowries."[69] The equivalents to the *dash* are considered to be the essential ingredient creating the conditions of what the Latin American literature refers to as "peonage" and the South Asian and most other literature calls "debt bondage." Historians and anthropologists continuously underline the ubiquity of debt in the creation of bonded labor. The entire premise and effectivity of the wage-veiled-as-credit, for example the "*girmit* (agreement) money" in the tea plantations of colonial Assam, was that it was so high that it become an unpayable debt, leaving workers unable to walk away.[70] Wage advances have also been thought to index a modicum of workers' "bargaining power" as well as various

68 Sundiata, "Kru Power," 30; Sundiata, *From Slaving to Neoslavery*, 129. For a similar argument see Mark-Thiesen, "The 'Bargain' of Collaboration."

69 Robin Law, "Finance and Credit in Pre-Colonial Dahomey," in *Credit, Currencies, and Culture: African Financial Institutions in Historical Perspective*, eds. Endre Stiansen and Jane Guyer (Uppsala: Nordic Africa Institute, 1999), 25; Law, "On Pawning," 55; Falola, "The End of Slavery among the Yoruba"; Mark-Thiesen, "The Dual Meaning of Debt."

70 Rana Behal, "Power Structure, Discipline, and Labour in Assam Tea Plantations under Colonial Rule," *International Review of Social History* 51, S14 (2006): 164; Geert De Neve, "Asking for and Giving Baki: Neo-Bondage, or the Interplay of Bondage and Resistance in the Tamilnadu Power-Loom Industry," *Contributions to Indian Sociology* 33, no. 1–2 (1999), 387; Prakash, *Bonded Histories*, 169, 142.

degrees of patronage and dependency – arguments made especially in the so-called "revisionist" Latin American literature on debt peonage.[71]

The principle behind categorizing peonage as a type of unfree "extra-exploitative" labor is the "advancing" of wages, which is said to secure "cheaper" labor, in comparison to a continuously hired free labor. Freely negotiated wages imply that laborers could capture wage spikes on a monthly or even daily basis. This bidding war would then accurately reflect the local scarcity of labor. Here, wages are simply a barometer for the competition amongst employers, and correspondingly the starting point and motivated interest for "advances" should also lie with employers. As Engels briefly noted, the potential "maximum of wages" is "determined by the competition of the bourgeoisie among themselves." If profitability is still expected, even though higher wages are deductions from corporate profit, then an employer will cumulatively pay "a trifle higher wages rather than let the whole profit escape him," so "one capitalist after another goes in chase of workers, and wages rise."[72] To halt this potential and "natural" steady rise, wages in unfree labor, instead of being drip-fed, are said to come in excessive lump-sums, to "immobilize" or "deproletarianize" workers and average down total labor costs.[73] In the words of Jairus Banaji, the depiction of "wages as loans" is a powerful transformation that serves to "control labour in conditions where the competition for labour is likely to drive up the bargaining power and wages of workers. It is a legal or pseudo-

71 Arnold J. Bauer, "Rural Workers in Spanish America: Problems of Peonage and Oppression," *The Hispanic American Historical Review* 59, no. 1 (1979); McCreery, "Debt Servitude," 744; for Mexico see the overview by Knight, "Mexican Peonage." The so-called "revisionism" begins quite early with Charles Gibson, *The Aztecs under Spanish Rule: A History of the Indians of the Valley of Mexico, 1519–1810* (Stanford: Stanford University Press, 1964), 248–256. Gibson argued peonage was not that common and that it was not even a form of servitude and that "the amount of the debt may be considered in some degree as a measure of the bargaining power of the worker." In the non-revisionist Latin American historiography debt peonage appears as the core of non-slave labour control which nevertheless appears as a type of wage labour, in the sense of contracts, recruitment, and modalities of payments. The canvas is discontinuous and concentrates in pockets until wherever revolutions tried to put a halt to it, from southern Mexico (especially Yucatán, Tabasco, and Chiapas) to the coastal plantations of Peru in the 1860s to the Western Amazon during the rubber boom of the 1890s. This critical history begins with Silvio Zavala, "Origenes coloniales del peonaje en Mexico," *El Trimestre Económico* 10, 40 (1944). See also Wolf and Mintz, "Haciendas and Plantations," 391; Banaji, "Modernizing the Historiography of Rural Labor," 90; Dore, *Myths of Modernity*, 28.

72 Engels, *Condition*, 111.

73 Moulier-Boutang, *De l'esclavage*, 5; Brass and Bernstein, "Proletarianisation," 17.

legal fiction used by employers to manoeuvre workers into a system of forced labour (which is still wage-labour) or contain their mobility."[74]

In peonage and debt bondage, the wage advance is considered then not an advance on wages but an excess that creates an ideological imaginary and material effect: a sum of money that is a "debt," where the currency of repayment is labor. In the words of Yann Moulier-Boutang, workers who "sign contracts of employment for the amount of time necessary to pay back the debt" find themselves "subjected to essentially a *corvée*, in the Medieval and not metaphorical sense of the term, since this obligation to work for the creditor is a substitute penalty for the debtor having defaulted on payment – the penal offense would entail imprisonment."[75] As the rate of interest may be ill-defined or more rapidly compounding than other earnings, the worker gets stuck in an interest repayment trap. This is the elementary operation of debt bondage.

This critical "calculation" however is partly tautological, as the putative mechanism can only be seen working out once the cycle is successfully completed. However, if this circuit is broken down into steps then the advance stands for an obvious excess well above market-clearing rates. The "cheap" "unfree" telos can only occur once all other forces institutionalize boundedness – commonly, the repayment of interest, the punishment for default, and, most importantly, the obstruction of escape. The poles to this set up need to be kept separate to see them colliding in the historical dynamics of recruitment and desertion. The paradox is that the initial ability to select employers in the context of a labor scarcity allows mobile workers to demand higher advances, which then subsequently leads them to become "attached" unfree laborers. However, at the other end, the "attachment" is under constant pressure and in impersonal contexts can readily fail. In a repetition of this set up the first condition – the rise of the demand and escalation of advances – surrounds the hirable worker again, in an intensified way. This is the elementary operation of what I call *dash*-peonage.

---

74 Banaji, "Fictions of Free Labor," 87. Another very concise definition is: "Advances lead to bondage when they capture a labourer into a debt trap, are accompanied by harsh labour conditions and exploitative wages, are buttressed by violence and coercion, and curtail a worker's bargaining power and ability to access alternative employment. Even if voluntarily entered, debt can lead to forms of bondage that remove workers' control over their own labour and tie them into bonds they can no longer escape." Carswell and De Neve, "From Field to Factory," 433. See also Brass, *Unfree Labour*, 14, 244–256.

75 Moulier-Boutang, "Forms of Unfree Labor: Primitive Accumulation, History or Prehistory of Capitalism?," *Viewpoint Magazine*, February 1, 2018, accessed February 1, 2018, https://viewpointmag.com/2018/02/01/forms-unfree-labor-primitive-accumulation-history-prehistory-capitalism/.

The *braceros* on Fernando Po, as elsewhere, were the "initiators of *habilitación*" – the cash advance – they "activated" it, and they were clearly "far from the passive victims of domineering *patrones* [employers] in need of cheap labour."[76] Rebecca Scott writes that the Cuban planters in late nineteenth-century Santa Clara complained that they "could not find workers" unless they "extended advances" to emancipated slaves or contract workers who had finished their indenture. She takes this to mean that "workers sometimes turned credit to their own advantage" because it "meant an effective increase in wages" – while being "risky business, since it could lead to [a] lasting debt" of peonage.[77] However, these "activations" were more explosive than they are usually given credit for and reveal the main colonial economic fault lines or the points at which the colonial economy could collapse when dispersed pressure mounted and concentrated on that point.

As Prabhu Mohapatra notes in relation to early nineteenth-century colonial Bengal, the "customary practice of receiving advances before commencing work" was not so much an imperial "imposition" scheming "to tie down labourers," but an "absolutely necessary compromise in face of workers' demands." The imperial wage advance in South Asia sprung from the indenture-like contracts made with sailors. As they were continuously amplifying their demands for them, the besieged British officials on site took it to be a principal "cause of their mutinous behaviour."[78] Coolies from the Bay of Bengal, along with *engagé* laborers from Mozambique and Madagascar, had started making very similar demands on the plantations in Reunion and Mauritius – but only during the second round of contracts from the 1840s on. Their "weapon: competition among employers," resulting in an uncoordinated rise of ever higher advances and rates of desertion. As in Fernando Po of the 1940s, there was no overarching entity "between estate owners" and workers would move "from one estate to another,"

76 Harry Walker, "Demonic Trade: Debt, Materiality, and Agency in Amazonia," *Journal of the Royal Anthropological Institute* 18, no. 1 (2012): 152.

77 Scott, *Slave Emancipation*, 235; see also Balboa, *Los brazos necesarios.*

78 Mohapatra, "Contract to Status?," 121; Nitin Sinha, "Contract, Work, and Resistance: Boatmen in Early Colonial Eastern India, 1760s–1850s," *International Review of Social History* 59, S22 (2014): 43; In "1800, British merchants accused lascars of wholesale arson: taking wage advances and then torching their ships so that they could abscond." Fischer, "Working Across the Seas," 34. The "Commander in Chief at Madras, seriously suggested that all British soldiers on foreign service be tattooed to prevent them taking the bounty [and] deserting." Singha, "Settle, Mobilize, Verify," 20. Only over the course of the nineteenth century were advances and capitalist bondage recast in the moral languages of hybrid debt ideologies of obligation. Prakash, *Bonded Histories*, 223–225.

becoming "fugitives" and "deserters."[79] In Mauritius, by the 1860s, "planters launched the first of several attempts to check the growing independence of time-expired Indians" by "reviving sweeping vagrancy legislation."[80] Planters took every chance they were given to denounce the "Indian propensity toward idleness, thievery, petty commerce, and financial irresponsibility," the last of which was projected in relation to their demands for advances. These "traits" were thought to lay behind the their "desertion and absenteeism."[81]

In Assam, British planters started complaining in the 1870s "that time-expired coolies" had "become 'complete masters of the situation' due to competition for their labour-power," and their seemingly automatic ability to venture "in search of the highest remuneration." A "bonus system had developed" where they were paid a six month advance "to reengage."[82] In relation to these new-found "'bargaining' capabilities" enabled through "garden sardars" operating "outside the legal-institutional framework," Nitin Varma cites a contemporary official in Sylhet who noticed "'the increase in desertion of [the] tea garden *coolie* [who] have learnt to sell their labour power in the most profitable market, and are not mere *adscripti glebae* of the garden for which they were imported."[83] But it was especially those "labourers sent up by professional recruiters," the *arkatis*, who "had no particular bond to a specific garden and would, if they could, abscond from their contracts if offered better conditions in another garden."[84] In Ceylon in the early twentieth century, tea planters complained not only about having "suffered shortness of labour, but they have also suffered to a very considerable extent by the large advances now demanded by *kanganies* and coolies." The escalations and desertions strung together by "unrecorded advances" were known in the Indian Ocean in this period by the term "crimping," which reversed the British meaning of the term, because in this case employers were seen as the crimp's victims. Their laborers were being "taken" from them through this mechanism guided by the new touts.[85] While the *dash* was not an oppositional movement, it could apply itself and at critical junctures redefine the

---

79 Stanziani, "Beyond Colonialism," 74.

80 Carter, "Strategies of Labour Mobilisation," 238, 230; North-Coombes, "From Slavery to Indenture," 109–113.

81 Allen, *Slaves, Freedmen and Indentured Laborers*, 59.

82 Behal and Mohapatra, "Tea and Money," 147; Singha, "Settle, Mobilize, Verify," 163.

83 Varma, "Coolie Acts," 53, 50.

84 Sen, "Commercial Recruiting," 9. "Sardari coolies were less prone to absconding, because of kin and community affiliation among new immigrants, the preponderance of married couples and a smaller number of solitary men and women, agreed inspecting officers in Assam."

85 Silva, *The Political Economy of Underdevelopment*, 206, 329.

flow of power. It could even overturn and invert colonial expectations and its received definitions.

When the *dash* appears in African labor history it is usually considered a credit-wage, even though it was not technically an advance but could rapidly become an excess that surpassed the official wages of a contract.[86] The efficacy and effects of the *dash* as an excess are usually accounted for in careful accounts. Outside of non-dialectical violence, the advance was the instrument that weaved through all aspects of colonial wage labor migrations: recruitment, stabilization,[87] and desertion.[88] In relation to the South Africa literature, the wage advance comes across quite clearly as the switch that accounts for much of the early trajectories of labor mobilization in imperial labor markets, setting them off, holding them together and undermining their very constitution. In much of West Africa, where contracts were not very long or labor scarcity not too intense, such as in the cities, in mining areas with a much longer history, or along well-worn migration routes, advances were really just that: advances amounting to the first few months of wages at most that would be deducted at some point in subsequent intervals during regular paydays.[89]

In the mining areas of South Africa around the 1910s advances had climbed to £30 or almost a full year's wages on contracts that were rarely signed on for more than six or nine months at a time – a *dash* outside but generated by the contract.[90] In the early twentieth-century gold mines of the Witwatersrand it seemed that "wage advances bound the voluntary workers" because they "had to accept employment on one of the mines," though it is clear that advances were so welcomed that many were accepting employment at two or more

86 As Orde-Brown, making a general and concise observation on the ground says: "The great majority of workers, when leaving home, wish to make various arrangements which entail small payments, and for this purpose they require an advance of wages. This then becomes an attraction in recruiting, and an agent who refuses to make any such concession will speedily find himself outdistanced by his more accommodating rival; further, a cut-throat competition may well set in when competing recruiters give increasing advances, until a point is reached where men are offered a large proportion of the whole of the pay due for the contract." Orde-Browne, *African Labourer*, 72.

87 Berman and Londsdale, "Crises of Accumulation," 76; Freund, "Labor and Labor History," 20–21; Cooper, *Decolonization*, 63, 155.

88 Van Onselen, *Chibaro*; 230–233; Harries; *Work, Culture and Identity*, 40–45; Atkins, *The Moon Is Dead!*; Cooper, *From Slaves to Squatters*.

89 Mark-Thiesen, *Mediators, Contract Men*, 65–77, 127; Rathbone, "West Africa, 1874–1948."

90 Kubicek, "Mining," 78. In Southern Africa advances were bulky partly because until the 1910s they often came in the form of indivisible and valuable cattle, see Beinart, "Joyini Inkomo," and Crush, "Swazi Migrant Workers," 33.

mines.[91] Mine touts "induced" potential wage workers to "enter into contracts [with] such large advances that the borrower 'remained in debt'." At the same time, mobile workers were "accepting advances from several agents" with evidently "no intention of honouring their debts to any of them."[92] Advances had become "so large that the incentive to desert before contract completion was considerable."[93] The literature has shown that all these internal logistics of the *dash* were largely arranged by touts.[94]

In the early twentieth century there were at least 175,000 people employed across South African mines and related activities. In 1905 over 100,000 new contracts per year were stamped. Before the unification of the British South African colonies in 1910, two thirds of the labor force in the Transvaal colony's mining industry were from Mozambique – largely brought in by touts. Though already in the late 1910s miners started depending on closer and more controlled channels, particularly from the Xhosa-speaking Transkei and Lesotho. A significant breakthrough was the 1928 "Mozambique convention" with its new indenture-like conveyance that implemented some of its classic features: it prolonged the contract to 12–18 months, capped the recontracting "bonus," and reduced total wages, half of which were paid out only on their return to thereby assure their subsequent and obligatory repatriation.[95] Other employers, particularly planters, sprung up besides the mines and its powerful recruitment lobby and exclusive license, and it was this second wave of employers who prolonged the flow of touts.

Wage advances, desertions, and forgery were the integral folds of van Onselen's "stop-go labor route" – a spiral which fully emerges in early twentieth-century Southern Rhodesia, looping ever further south across the emergent lunar scape forged by mining capital, a quest for just remuneration that led many Zimbabweans to the Witwatersrand, the "best labour market of all within the regional economic system." Ever more bulky advances for new or deserting recruits and "inducements" to "recontract" incited much of this movement, a dialectics of presence and absence, of stabilization and abandonment.[96] Van Onselen sketches the intricate itineraries of flights to portray a political-economic victory:

---

91 Jeeves, "Migrant Labour in the Industrial Transformation," 116.

92 Deborah James and Dinah Rajak, "Credit Apartheid, Migrants, Mines and Money," *African Studies* 73, no. 3 (2014): 462; citing Isaac Schapera, *Migrant Labour and Tribal Life. A Study of Conditions in the Bechuanaland Protectorate* (London: Oxford University Press, 1947), 109.

93 Stichter, *Migrant Laborers*, 114.

94 Murray, "'Blackbirding,'" 376; Jeeves, *Migrant Labour*, 3–34, 239–264.

95 Coquery-Vidrovitch, "Colonial Economy," 464; Jeeves, *Migrant Labour*, 10.

96 Van Onselen, *Chibaro*, 229; Worger, *City of Diamonds*, 288–289.

"a relative coup which improved their lot." Attempts to track down deserters were often hopeless and haphazard. Despite decades of imperial experiments in papered contraptions – obligatory contracts, registration regimes, pass-laws, and the like – most deserters, oscillating at around ten percent of the workforce, came out triumphant.

The "most radical way" to outmaneuver the pass system, as van Onselen says, was "simply to destroy them – a procedure widely resorted to by immigrant workers between 1904 and 1915." Destroying "what they knew to be a millstone around their neck," workers found their way, indubitably through the help of a knowledge economy saturated by touts, to some new "pass office on the northern borders" where "new certificates" could be bought.[97] The form of this "documentary regime" was considered by the mining lobbies to provide the "facilities" to "natives for desertion and re-engagement" – that is through "deserters leaving labour districts and re-entering them with fresh travelling passes, obtained from outside."[98] As van Onselen concludes: there "must have been some comfort in 'working the system' in such a way that it left the exploiters exploited!"[99] This carnivalesque element in labor history is well accounted for elsewhere, including in early modern Europe, where under similar situations during, for example, the development of rural labor markets in Prussia, Georg Friedrich Knapp says that suddenly "the master, who is dependent on free workers, becomes wholly dependent on them and the 'World is turned upside down'."[100]

As Keith Breckenridge has argued, the elements of an "archival government" – contract templates, normed administrative stamps and sundry cutting-edge identification techniques – were only deployed in colonial economies in the first place to try to regulate the mushrooming of both wage advances and the related desertions that accompanied "capital intensive forms of labour recruit-

---

97 Van Onselen, *Chibaro*, 230, 232. The 1910s saw the "state's drive for rigorous implementation of the Pass Laws" being churned out on a "significant scale." Breckenridge, "Flesh Made Words," 88; MacDonald, "Forging the Frontiers," 56. The "worker has almost complete control of the situation owing to the constant demand for his services. He is almost always able to find another employer anxious to engage him, so he can at any time leave his job and find another where conditions or type of work are more attractive." Orde-Browne cited in Cooper, *Decolonization*, 60.

98 Witwatersrand Native Labour Association and Transvaal Chamber of Mines, "Annual Report," April 1907, 576. Available through the catalogue of www.thevirtualminemuseum.org.za.

99 Van Onselen, *Chibaro*, 230, 232.

100 Georg Friedrich Knapp, *Die Bauernbefreiung und der Ursprung der Landarbeiter in den älteren Theilen Preussens*, vol. 2 (Leipzig: Duncker & Humblot, 1887), 140.

ment."[101] Commenting on the generalized system of "advancing wages," Orde-Browne recommended that "some written statement of any obligation of this nature should be drawn up at the time of incurring it" – keeping tallies obviously helped when trying to sanction defaulters.[102] The binding properties of "debt" did not emerge from the moral invocations of debt alone, but rather from the "organized violence" of those who measured and enforced repayment through labor.[103] In post-colonial Latin America, like in colonial Africa, the advances of *peonaje* "usually involved indebtedness and always involved the machinery of state to make the system work." Laws tried to set limits on such advances, officials kept tallies of receipts and police sanctioned defaulters.[104] This was the source of bondage in the labor relation, not the *dash*. The *dash* itself was simply a political-economic sign or signal, and the process of suppressing or reengineering it, cutting and driving it into place, required other monopoly forces.

This *dash* emerged from the contract form itself. Wherever the *dash* took shape outside of such contracts it had a different logic altogether. For example, the large plantations along the coast in Cameroon, which were mostly German owned until World War II, and under British-Nigerian authority since World War I, developed into a perfect inversion of ongoing developments on the adjacent island of Fernando Po. Conceptually distant, this quasi-plantation island on the slopes of Mount Cameroon had less hectares planted than Fernando Po but between 25,000 and 40,000 workers in the late 1930s.[105] As a British labor officer for the region observed in 1952, the workers in these plantations "were not contract labourers per se, if they don't show up to work, they don't get paid." The salaries were a little higher than the official ones in Fernando Po, but there were no *dash* advances. After the war, when the British took over production, their managers also handed out a "monthly bonus" of six shillings, about ten

---

101 Breckenridge, "Flesh Made Words," 88; Breckenridge, "Power Without Knowledge," 22. For the direct line of sail between archival South Africa and the paperwork surrounding indentured labor in Mauritius and Bengal see Carter, *Servants, Sirdars, and Settlers*, 193–200; Singha, "Settle, Mobilize, Verify," 163.

102 Orde-Browne, *African Labourer*, 72.

103 Taussig, *Shamanism*, 65; Prakash, *Bonded Histories*, 242; Graeber, "Debt, Violence, and Impersonal Markets," 107.

104 Dore, "Debt Peonage," 218; Washbrook, "'Una esclavitud simulada,'" 390.

105 Graf zu Trauttmansdorf, 1942, "Denkschriften über Arbeits und Sozialrecht, Arbeitseinsatz und Lohnfragen im Britischen und französischen Mandatsgebiet Kamerun und Vorschläge für die Neugestalltung," BArch, R2/4989. About 3,000 of them were Nigerian, mostly Igbo. They were brought by the same recruiters as Fernando Po. Within a decade Igbos made up most of the plantation workforce in Cameroon. See also Authaler, *Deutsche Plantagen in Britisch-Kamerun*.

percent of the wage, which was only paid out if workers "work over a minimum of 24 days a month." The turnover on these plantations was extremely high, around two-thirds annually.

The situation was similar in Nigeria where "the best employment a native of Nigerian can find as a *bracero* are in the banana, rubber and palm oil plantations, where the monthly salary can reach £3–10–4" or some 70 shillings, where at least five to ten shillings would need to be used for food costs. Contemporary studies note there was little to no desertion here; if workers were abused or changed their minds, they simply did not show up anymore, but this did not involve "breaking" contracts.[106] On the rubber and other plantations in Nigeria and the British Cameroons, prospective workers themselves had to *dash* recruiting agents and overseers to get a placement: "trying to get work on the plantations [involves] the exorbitant bribery which is nowadays practised to an almost unbelievable extent, [...] any labourers will be required to pay 30s or £2 to the foreman as a preliminary to being engaged." And without a continuous show of "occasional 'dashes'" to the foreman, he "will throw [the worker] out of the gang and engage another labourer on similar terms."[107] Here, following British managerial expectations, the world had been turned the right side up again, eliminating the dialectic of wage payments in contract labor.

Buying or Paying

The conceptual distinction between paying for or buying labor corresponds to the broad divide between slavery and wage labor and their respective relationships to credit. Slavery as ownership, mediated through purchase, implies slaves are assets, and under different circumstances could produce the basis of financial systems, including pawnship, amortization, collateralization, etc. In contrast, wage payments are defined as a liability for employers in the contract.

---

106 British VC, August 26, 1952, "Minutes of the talks about the revision of the Labor Treaty," AGA, C-81/12373, E-392. Ardener et al., *Plantation and Village*, 221. Though there were minor credit-arrangements for "stabilization," "wages are at daily rates but in order to discourage employees from leaving without adequate notice, it is customary to pay them monthly." It also became "general practice" to have workers paid provisionally "in the form of credit notes on the plantation's own store." Indeed, on some plantations "it is compulsory for employees to take part of their wages in credit notes," usually about "50 %, is paid in this form." Nigeria, 1938, "Report on the Administration of the Cameroons under British Cameroons for the year 1938," para. 187, TNA, CO 583/239/5.

107 Labor Officer, Buea (Nwokedi) to Commissioner of Labor, Lagos, April 5, 1948, BNA, Qd/a (1947)1; Konings, *Labour Resistance in Cameroon*, 61.

Wage payments and advances thus figured on the credit side of the employers' formal and informal accounting books. This sum had to match what the worker was owed if employers wanted them to renew or change contracts. Advances, at the point they reached the *braceros*, are therefore part of what accountants call a running expense or what Marx called variable capital. The economics of *braceros* on their second and third contracts are totally different than those initially passed onto the *Curaduría* for a "commission" by recruiters. The fact that contracts were owned by the state, and that the status of the *bracero* was created by the *Curaduría*, does not change the peculiar financial aspect of the layered and combined wage payments of typical *bracero* contracts. The customary informality of wage payments made them inherently more volatile and riskier, at the moment when workers were treating their labor as their own asset, leading to massive escalations and the increase of liabilities for employers. These sums could merely be fictitious "accounting money," growing though the contract's inherent temporal intervals and eliminated through deductions and prolongations. Here credit money expanded and contracted as a site of conflict.

This tidal motion underlies the superstructure of the colonial economy of labor and the plantation structure of Spanish Guinea. The longer history of labor market economics, as a section of political economy and a renewed neoclassical economic history, has never created useful starting points for the African history of labor markets because their "modelling" capabilities always came from the "final stage" of an enclosed and perpetual given, a pool of workers competing but each having a range of options to hire themselves to different employers to earn a necessary income. In classical and even mercantilist political economy wage payments were conceived as simply another outlay of capital to secure the inputs of production, derived from the mobilized savings of employers, or credits which they took out at their own risk and paid out in the expectation of recouping and profiting during the sale of the harvest. The labor market then simply becomes an extension and expansion of existing market mechanisms, including the frequent practice of advancing capital, to wage bills.

The advance as a key distinguishing feature of a type of wage labor with its own sites and volatile relations of conflict and negotiation remained undertheorized in classical political economy and social theory. Marx, in contrast, did lay great emphasis on the mystifications of the language of "advances" by early political economy because it concealed how it was the worker who effectively loans the employer the value of their labor, since the worker is only paid after a certain period while in the meantime the employer had already used up labor to make and eventually sell commodities. Being paid only after alienation and extraction is what enables the entire operation of surplus value extraction to go ahead relatively unnoticed: the free worker "everywhere gives credit to the capitalist," "weekly, monthly or quarterly, depending on when he is paid." It is this delay or what Marx calls the "interval of time" that makes possible exploitation through free labor markets, unlike in the direct trade and countertrade of commodities where "value" is simultaneously handed off and immediately objectified via the unit of account or general equivalent.

In one of his twists for his new political economy, Marx reverses the role of advances or *Vorschüsse*, to make his version of the labor theory of value work more precisely. Marx defined the essence of wage labor as a regular payout schedule only after the completion of defined tasks. In this way the logical conceptual circuit of valorization of "free" labor can be set up and function without any other relations of dependence or coercion than those which result from the "nature" of the market and its obfuscatory fetishism. These conditions of free labor are inseparable and presuppose each other, because a total dependency on smaller regular payment in money implies the mode of control whereby an entire class can be owned collectively by the owners of the means of production – instead of individually or by states. As Engels already noted in *The Condition of the Working Class in England:*

> The only difference as compared with the old, outspoken slavery is this, that the worker of today seems to be free because he is not sold once for all, but piecemeal by the day, the week, the year, and because no one owner sells him to another, but he is forced to sell himself in this way instead, being the slave of no particular person, but of the whole property-holding class.[108]

This conception of a complete dependency on the labor market to theorize the "proletarian" as a class owned collectively by capitalists, and to give the structural compulsion of money the role of medium substituting direct force is also how Weber conceives of labor relations: according to different structure of authority and immediate or more distant relations of command and obedience.

Marx insists that wage payments must, in "every country in which the capitalist mode of production reigns," come "customarily" within periods "fixed by the contract, as for example, the end of each week." Marx gives wildly diverging parameters of the proper "intervals" of free labor, calculated hourly, sometimes paid daily but usually weekly or monthly or quarterly. The interval needed to be "short," but also long enough so the liquidity provided by sold goods can return to the employer – in the range of weeks or months on average depending on the

108 Engels, *Condition*, 91. In *Capital*, this was reformulated as the interval of "alienation" which must only occur for a "definite period" of time, for if the worker would not just rent themselves bit by bit but sell themselves "once for all, he would be selling himself, converting himself from a free man into a slave, from an owner of a commodity into a commodity." Marx, *Capital*, 161.

(non-agricultural) industry. Any longer, and free labor, for which legislation necessarily "fixes a maximum for labour-contracts" and allows for equally short intervals that "regulate the mode of terminating this contract," becomes something else. In the worst case it regresses to a type of "slavery" usually "hidden under the form of peonage," as Marx continues in a footnote, taking examples from Mexico and the eastern Danube where he notes that laborers were recruited "by means of advances, repayable in labour, which are handed down from generation to generation," and where "not only the individual labourer, but his family, become, de facto, the property of other persons and their families." Marx ends the footnote with a brief mention of the revolutionary abolition of peonage in Mexico that was re-established by the Emperor Maximilian by decree, "which, in the House of Representatives at Washington, was aptly denounced as a decree for the re-introduction of slavery into Mexico."[109] Here, in a cursory historical footnote, the potential circuit of money-capital valorized in labor exploitation becomes engulfed by "peonage" – a type of feudal relation because money-capital metamorphosizes and hardens back into an impossible and directly oppressively inherited debt, a bottomless sink, instead of positively flowing out as a surplus for re-valorization through the market.

Only in *Capital* Volume II does Marx make the more fine-grained distinction between types of advance payments, around the terms "buying of" and "paying for." In paying for labor, after the "customary" period, the value extraction mechanism can continue concealed and undisturbed. If an employer actually "buys" labor power, purchases it, and then puts it to use, "then we can speak of advances."[110] The question of what status or category a "debt peon" descends to, after their labor is "bought" in this way, rather than paid for, is however less important than the effects of this modality of payment. A concern with the former leads to a range of static and fundamentally unresolvable research questions, posed by Alan Knight in his contribution to the volume *Slavery and Other Forms of Unfree Labour*, on "Debt Bondage in Latin America," where he asks whether the "debt peon" was a "surrogate slave or a surrogate proletarian":

---

109 Marx, *Capital*, 170 – 172. The footnote simply ends with a quote from Hegel's Philosophy of Right: "I may make over to another the use, for a limited time, of my particular bodily and mental aptitudes and capabilities; because in consequence of this restriction, they are impressed with a character of alienation with regard to me as a whole. But by the alienation of all my labour-time and the whole of my work, I should be converting the substance itself, in other words, my general activity and reality, my person, into the property of another."

110 Marx, "Das Kapital. Bd II," 217 – 230. "Kaufte der Kapitalist die Arbeitskraft, statt sie zu bezahlen, zahlte er also dem Arbeiter den Arbeitslohn per Tag, Woche, Monat oder drei Monate voraus, so könnte von einem Vorschuss für diese Termine gesprochen werden."

that is, was debt the "device to create a class of slaves long after formal slavery had been abolished?" or was "debt simply the result of cash advances, made in order to secure a basically proletarian labour force?"[111]

Historians and anthropologist have long engaged in creating new sub-classifications, derived from new sources, such as the late Roman "voluntary slavery" and the mediated partial pocketing of money for a usually temporary self-sale.[112] Like baffled Roman jurists, the social sciences have continued to generate "classificatory monstrosities" such as "*liber homo bona fide serviens*," "a free man but a bona fide slave."[113] Apart from buying and paying, to construct such hybrid or monstrous "anomalies" and "exceptions" requires continuous redefinitions and assessments along different "subjective" terms. As the comparative anthropologist Alain Testart observed, "only particularly hard contract conditions (being in pawn for many years, pittance wages, and so forth) make it true bondage," which raises the question of the intensity of such secondary criteria in a permanently "so forth" and qualitative state.[114] For Knight and the so-called revisionist Latin American labor historians the "voluntaristic" nature of receiving advances means that receivers were "really (temporary) wage labourers whose debts were advances to attract them to the plantations and who evolved into a rural proletariat," yet at the same time, when conditions were "bad" enough, they never fail to note that the "coercive debt peons forcibly brought into underpopulated territory in response to fresh and powerful (usually short-term) market demands" constitutes "slavery (in fact, the coerced peon's condition could be worse than that of the formal chattel slave)."[115]

Indentured contract labor, which only worked through recruiters and advances, cannot be plotted along these divides, because recruiters and the *dash* they handled produced unstable outcomes. Positing time (duration and the interval of renewal) and price (total wages) as the fundamental axis to define labor rela-

---

111 Knight, "Debt Bondage," 102; For a contemporary and theorized discussion of advances within classical political economy see Stephen Gudeman and Alberto Rivera, *Conversations in Colombia: The Domestic Economy in Life and Text* (Cambridge: Cambridge University Press, 1990), 90 – 97.

112 Morris Silver, "Contractual Slavery in the Roman Economy," *Ancient History Bulletin* 25 (2011): 76.

113 Finley, *Ancient Economy*, 69. Banaji cites a variety of sources, such as Dio of Prusa's discourse *On Slavery and Freedom* written in the first century AD, who noted that "'literally thousands of free-born persons sell themselves to work like slaves by contract, sometimes on the worst possible terms'." Banaji, *Theory as History*, 117; see also Kahn, *Wayward Contracts*, 63.

114 Alain Testart, "The extent and significance of Debt Slavery," *Revue française de sociologie* 43 (2002): 180.

115 Knight, "Debt Bondage," 102; Archer, "Introduction," 10.

tions cannot but lead to a statically computable quasi-statistical "continuum" of labor relations. Only by looking at the specific sequence and effects of wage payments can the economic and political contradictions of a colonial labor market appear. Its specific conditions – for example the need for long distance recruitment, and the desirability to retain already trained laborers after the end of a contract – meant that every time the contract was up for renewal a turnover or shift would take place. The power relations in which labor was priced at the beginning and the end of the contract were extremely volatile and they cannot be predicted with the conceptual baggage or backdrop assumption that stipulates permanent and smooth renewal.

In comparison to Marx, Weber spent more attention discussing and arranging forms of debt peonage and debt slavery within the "social history of all parts of the world," though he simply concludes there seems to be "an endless variety of forms" with "intermediate steps" and "gradual transitions" and thus making "sharp differentiation in concrete fact often impossible."[116] To recall Henri Poincaré's contemporaneous explanation for the conceptual creation of the continuum: between A and B "which are distinct, is intercalated another new term D, which we can distinguish neither from A nor from B". A contradiction emerges that can only be resolved or escaped by creating "the concept of a continuum formed of an indefinite number of terms" made up of a composite of two discreet parts "incessantly intercalating."[117]

The problem is that this proliferation of new hybrid or "blurred" half-terms along a continuum cannot account for the "transitions" of the emergence and collapse of free and unfree labor, and it is in these phases where we are confronted with recruiters. The conceptual notion of the spectrum nevertheless opens a metaphor for a different topology that can insist on the neither/nor. If we follow the recruiters from beginning to end, we must conclude that they are an inde-

---

116 Weber, *Economy and Society*, 214, 128. In the "free-unfree" labor historiography, this Weberian "spectrum" appears first in the work of the classicist Moses Finley over half a century ago. Finley was trying to pluralize the debate: "we are the heirs of the Roman law, filtered through the Middle Ages, and we are mesmerized by the notion that at the lower end of the social scale, in the work force, there are three and only three possible categories, slaves, serfs and free wage-earners." As a notable Weberian amongst the classicists, he shifted the attention of his colleagues from the "evils of slavery" arising from war and piracy to "the evils of short-term tenancy under the harsh Roman law of debt" as well as to "all sorts of other kinds of unfree labour" that existed in the first millennia of empire "to a far greater extent, I think, than most classical scholars and even ancient historians have realised." Finley called this range "involuntary" or "dependent" labor, which was "to a greater or lesser extent not free, a category for which our language provides no appropriate one-word label." Finley, *Ancient Economy*, 69, 65.
117 Henri Poincaré, *Science and Hypothesis* (London: Science Press, 1905), 24.

pendent third term, they neither are a "remainder" or relapse or revival of "slavery," nor a first step to free "wage labor," or something "in-between": they are a product of the contract, a "C," that turns the entire two-dimensional notion of the spectrum into an at least triangular or certainly into a more multi-dimensional constellation. In the elementary binary of zero and one, recruiters are not a fraction or a decimal, they do not appear "half-way." They emerge in pursuit of their own terms. They introduce new and original "code" that needs to be independently explored in its historical origins and effects.

3 *Panya:* Contractual Inversions

> For the contrast between truth and lie arises here for the first time. The liar is a person who uses the valid designations, the words, in order to make something which is unreal appear to be real. He says, for example, "I am rich," when the proper designation for his condition would be "poor." He misuses fixed conventions by means of arbitrary substitutions or even reversals of names. If he does this in a selfish and moreover harmful manner, society will cease to trust him and will thereby exclude him. What men avoid by excluding the liar is not so much being defrauded as it is being harmed by means of fraud. Thus, even at this stage, what they hate is basically not deception itself, but rather the unpleasant, hated consequences of certain sorts of deception.
>
> – Friedrich Nietzsche, *On Truth and Lie in an Extra-Moral Sense*

> During the abominable slave trade, hundreds, and probably thousands, were captured on the seas by the British, and liberated here [on Fernando Po], and some of them are now represented by the best African families in the capital [...] Others of these settlers have come to barter and trade, and may be seen in their wooden stores, with pens in their hair, bright intelligence in their eyes, and on their lips promises as safe as ready cash. It is a huge lie to represent all Africans as cheats, liars, and rogues. Authors and all other persons who call them such, are by far the bigger villeins. But, did Africans never cheat you? Of course they did, or how could I have thought them human? My friend, did Englishmen ever wrong you? Alas! far too frequently.
>
> – Henry Roe, *West African Scenes*

On a cloudless day from the Calabar coastline the silhouette of the volcanic peak of Fernando Po is discernible on the horizon. Writing in 1940, the British Vice-Consul on the island says that the "Spaniards have, during the last 40 years, recruited labour from most parts of the West Coast. Thanks to their methods they have been successively obliged to abandon Sierra Leone, Liberia, and the Cameroons [as] recruiting grounds." "Now," in 1940, "they have turned the attention of their recruiters to South Eastern Nigeria and this venture bids fair to be successful. The dozens of recruiters have ample funds at their disposal; the sea journey is short and the rewards are considerable." The "traffic is now well arranged, in Nigeria by the recruiters, and in Fernando Po by the Spanish Authorities and employers. The canoes generally sail in convoys."[1] With the archival material laid out in this chapter, we will meet the motley crew of touts, traders, merchants, and fishers who brought laborers to the island. The photograph selected for the cover of the book is them going about their business on a sandy part of Santa Isabel's port taken by the Vice-Consul in May 1944.[2]

---

1 British VC (Michie), February 28, 1941, TNA, FO 371/26908.

2 British VC (Robertson), May 1944, TNA, CO 554/139/5.

https://doi.org/10.1515/9783110755923-007

An account of the pattern and effectivity of their trajectories is important not only because this cross-border labor migration is one of the largest in colonial African history. If in 1938 the "influx of Nigerian boys into Fernando Po" was "undoubtedly on the increase," a year later recruiters operating out of eastern Nigeria had brought over an unprecedented and never again surpassed "12000 Nigerian labourers and all of them were smuggled in canoes across the sea."[3] Illegal migration peaked during the war-decade, spanning the Spanish Civil War and World War II, and during these years contemporaries spoke of workers being "virtually 'press-ganged' for Fernando Po."[4] As David Pratten has observed, "fears" of a "revival of the slave trade" developed "on a new axis during the 1930s with the dramatic increase in migration of Nigerian workers [to] Fernando Po off the coast of Calabar."[5] The idea of a "revival" is relayed not only allegorically and polemically in the only two existing empirical academic works on the subject. Both Henderson Tapela and Akinjide Osuntokun have spoken of a twentieth-century "Nigeria-Fernando Po 'middle passage'."[6] Early in 1939 Okon Archibong, a future anti-colonial political activist, let the chief provincial administrator at Calabar know of the "unrest that is existing in your Province" due to the revival of "a slavish act [that] had been absent from this Province for many years."[7]

There was no direct continuity with the recruitment techniques of the slave trade; the "likeness" suggested by Clarence-Smith is true but it needs to be inverted and specified: "even more akin to a slave trade was the clandestine importation of labour from south-eastern Nigeria [to Fernando Po] from about 1900, organized by African canoe owners."[8] Contemporary colonial reformers observed how laborers for the "large European-owned estates" were secured on the "mainland, often by methods reminiscent of old slave days."[9] Henderson Tapela says that illegal recruitment "began to take the character of the slave raiding of former days. Unwary travellers were kidnapped and canoe-paddled from

---

3 British VC (Twigge-Molecey) to Resident, Calabar Province, November 30, 1938, NAE, CALPROF 5/1/194; Supt. of Police, Calabar to Commissioner of Police, Lagos, December 30, 1938, NAE, CALPROF 5/1/194; "Fernando Po Labour Conditions," *The Nigerian Daily Times*, Lagos, July 13, 1939.

4 "Nigeria over the Water," *West Africa*, London, January 1, 1958.

5 David Pratten, *The Man-Leopard Murders: History and Society in Colonial Nigeria* (Edinburgh: Edinburgh University Press, 2007), 165.

6 Tapela, "Nigerian Labour," 51; Osuntokun, *Equatorial Guinea*, 40.

7 O. Archibong to Resident, Calabar Province, January 23, 1939, NAE, CALPROF 5/1/194.

8 Clarence-Smith, "Cocoa Plantations," 160.

9 Wieschhoff, *Colonial Policies*, 32.

Figure 7: Dug-out canoe on the Cross River. Lorenzo Dow Turner, 1951. Anacostia Community Museum, Smithsonian Institution.

the ports of Eket, Oron and Calabar."[10] There seemed to be a "reminiscence," but there was always a slight doubt, a "really" with a question mark: "What really looks like the indirect resuscitation of the old slave trade thought to have been completely stamped out, is being persistently and diligently pursued in this district [Calabar] in the form of organized labour recruiting to the Spanish island of Fernando Po by some individuals."[11]

Even though *panya* recruitment was a slaving genre of "kidnapping and smuggling" that continued in colonial Nigeria along the old supply routes of both the Atlantic and the internal slave trades, it was not the result of an inertia from the immediately precolonial period, subsisting only where "old elites" preserving an "old older" "survived."[12] Fernando Po's recruiters were initially drawn

---

10 Tapela, "The Cross River Basin," 210.

11 "The Nigerian Easter Mail Alleges Slavery in Oron," *The West African Pilot*, Lagos, January 21, 1939.

12 Lovejoy, *Transformations in Slavery*, 288; Afigbo, *Abolition*, 100; Patrick Manning, *Slavery and African Life: Occidental, Oriental, and African Slave Trades* (Cambridge: Cambridge University Press, 1990), 161. For the foundational thesis of the resilience of old elites, see Ralph A. Austen,

from groups who had previously had a hand in organizing (and abolishing) the slave trades in West Africa such as the Efik of Old Calabar, and the Aguda or Afro-Brazilians and Fernandinos and related Creole groups living on the island and along many emerging port towns on the Gulf of Guinea. Imperialism did not face vestiges or hindrances, instead it showcased its own immanent and dynamic unfolding.

When British district officers throughout eastern Nigeria started receiving many "complaints asking for information as to absent relatives in the island and alleging 'slave dealing'," it seemed obvious where to point fingers: the "recruiting of labour is largely carried out by the Efiks and people living in the area of the Cross River estuary."[13] The majority of recruiters were indeed Efik from Calabar and nearby settlements on the delta, or were from the so-called "Cross River Igbo" groups: Abam, Abriba and Aro, "mercenary" and "resident stranger" merchants with historical links to Calabar and many other river and creekside trading towns throughout the Eastern Provinces. In the 1950s "all Igbo migrants in Calabar" assured an American anthropologist that the "shrewdest and most successful Ibo traders are those from Abiriba." A reputation carried on into more recent times too: "The Abiriba man loves and follows the whiff of money to wherever it takes him, and no matter the risk involved," having "responded to changing economic opportunities" in the colonial period by "developing a strong trade in smuggled gin from Fernando Po."[14] However, decades after abolition and with imperial rule well cemented in Nigeria, a new generation of recruiters regrouped under the new structural templates provided by Spanish imperial rule and improvised with a radical discontinuity in their technique.

There were never more than 200 recruiters at any one time, even during the crescendo in the late 1930s, who their grandparents were or how the census grouped them had only a very loose bearing. For any specific individuals to become virtuosos of commercial life beyond the regulations of the state within the domain of the labor market, they required, as appreciated by the foremost colonial-era African labour studies specialist, the "exceptional and peculiar gifts of the able recruiter."[15] They belonged to quite distinct groups, but their actions were emergent properties arising from the entire configuration of the British

"The Abolition of the Overseas Slave Trade: A Distorted Theme in West African History," *Journal of the Historical Society of Nigeria* 5, no. 2 (1970).

13 DO Uyo, to Resident, Calabar Province, January 11, 1939, NAE, CALPROF 5/1/194.

14 Warren T. Morrill, "Two Urban Cultures of Calabar, Nigeria" (PhD diss., University of Chicago, 1961), 269; Ebere Ahanihu, "Abiriba and Ohafia: Two of A Kind," April 30, 2011, accessed July 2021, http://www.nairaland.com/657067/abiriba-ohafia-two-kind.

15 Orde-Browne, *African Labourer*, 52.

and Spanish colonial states and their colonial economic policies. Those involved in the recruiting boom were not a coherent group reproducing an existing status nor did they form an economic-functionally integrated ethnicity. The Fernando Po labor traffic was a spike of a defunct repertoire of the earlier Atlantic world, and of the post-abolition Indian and Pacific worlds, an admixture reaching back and forth across continents rather than unfolding along some anachronistic niche or trait perduring into the colonial period.

The argument can nevertheless be made that if the fifteenth-century island and river based trading network in the Gulf of Guinea initiated by the Portuguese witnessed the clear beginning of a commercialized system geared towards importing enslaved Africans onto colonial plantations,[16] it was on Fernando Po that this system met one of its unnoticed and confused ends in the middle of the twentieth century, in a vanishing Spanish empire that had wedged itself into an island in the Bight of Biafra. These final trajectories brought about duplicitous layers in bursts across space. It must be remembered that the initial and ultimate motive of the Spanish presence in the Gulf of Guinea was to welcome direct suppliers in the slave trade. In 1778, the navy commander of the failed Argelejo expedition that left Montevideo to claim Fernando Po noted with excitement that from the island "one goes to the coast with security and in a very short time; by means of which it would not be difficult to establish a continuous commerce there, and to oblige the inhabitants to come to Fernando Poo to sell their slaves in the large canoes or pirogues that they use."[17]

Fernandinos and Agudas, 1880s–1910s

Cacao plantations on Fernando Po were independently kick-started by individual Fernandino planters relying on British merchant creditors. The first export of a ton of cacao, requiring only a small number of *braceros*, was in 1884, and it went uphill from there.[18] The initial plantations were all situated along the is-

16 Miller, *Way of Death*, 115; Arlindo Manuel Caldeira, "Learning the Ropes in the Tropics: Slavery and the Plantation System on the Island of São Tomé," *African Economic History* 39 (2011).

17 García Cantús, "Fernando Poo," 50, 629. See also Crespi, "Enclave esclavista."

18 Already during the mid-nineteenth century a Fernandino, William Pratt, brought over cacao pods to the island after trips to São Tomé. Even in São Tomé only a few hundred tons of cocoa were being produced by large landowners in the 1870s, pioneered by Maria de Souza e Almeida, born in Principe of a Bahian father and an African mother, and who had made his "fortune in the Angolan slave trade" before buying up "abandoned estates" in the early 1850s. Clarence-Smith, *Cocoa*, 104, 158; Terán, *Síntesis geográfica*, 84; Sundiata, *Equatorial Guinea*, 24.

land's coast, an area of colonial encroachment the Bubi had stayed clear of since the height of the transatlantic slave trade in the Bight about a century previously. Fernandinos had acquired these parcels through a mix of government concessions, localized armed violence and as compensation from Bubi leaders to settle commercial debts arising from falling palm oil deliveries and prices and an increase of alcohol and other purchases. These first successful cacao plantations had been single-handedly set up by enterprising Fernandinos, such as the Barelycorns, Maximilano Jones, and the "fabulously wealthy" William Allen Vivour. They hailed from Freetown or the various Creole towns near Freetown. Their once enslaved parents or grandparents were from Nigeria, and very possibly Igbo.[19]

Vivour, a bricklayer by trade, had become a palm oil agent of the John Holt Company on the island in the 1870s and was used to travelling around the Gulf of Guinea, and even Europe. Vivour soon became the largest planter on the island. He had up to 100 laborers at any one point. He recruited with the help of "two Bassa-people stationed on the coast" – Bassa, a Kru coastal group whom a resident German scientist on Fernando Po in the 1880s paradoxically decided to describe as both "very lazy, and unsettled and restless, and who assimilate quickly into the ranks of the *Poto*" or Fernandinos.[20] To get *braceros*, these new generations of planters and recruiters traversed whatever port towns were connected by steamer, anywhere where "free immigrants" or "slaves escaping their servitude" had "flooded" the "coastal towns," including Accra and Loango, but especially Lagos and Freetown, both of which were becoming a type of "floating" "labour reserve for all of West Africa."[21]

By the 1890s several thousand *braceros* were working for hundreds of smaller Fernandino cash crop farmers as carriers and stevedores, and on the large plantations of several dozen notable Fernandino cacao planters, and increasingly on the *haciendas* or estates of a new generation of Basque and Catalan settlers and for large British and German firms led by dispatched managers. As Fernando Po's reputation headed off on a downwards spiral, new Kru laborers had stopped coming altogether. In 1900 there were 1,000 Liberians, mostly non-Kru, working on Fernando Po. That same year there were over 1,000 British West African la-

19 Sundiata, *From Slaving to Neoslavery*, 23. Sundiata notes that the British in Sierra Leone estimated in 1821, that 42% slaves leaving Old Calabar were Ibibio, and 56% Igbo.

20 Sundiata, *From Slaving to Neoslavery*, 130; Clarence-Smith, *Cocoa*, 80; On the "fabelhaf reich" Vivour and his recruiting see Oscar Baumann, *Eine afrikanische Tropeninsel Fernando Poo und die Bube* (Wien: Hölzel, 1888), 140, 138.

21 Phillips, *Enigma of Colonialism*, 34; Kristin Mann, *Slavery and the Birth of an African City: Lagos, 1760–1900* (Bloomington: Indiana University Press, 2007), 234.

borers on the island, many from Sierra Leone but also from Nigeria, categorized as "*de los lagos*" and "*Calabares*" or largely Yoruba and Ibibio.[22] Fernando Po could not hope to operate through attracting successive waves of immigrant labor within a "positive" and self-organized feedback system organized within kinship networks and communities. After the departure of *braceros* following their contract expiry, new sources of recruits had to be sought in separate locations. By the 1890s laborers had come from almost every port town of the Gulf of Guinea, but from early on most coastal groups were said to "detest Spaniards."[23] As a Spanish navy captain wrote in 1892, "rapidly unfavourable news spread about the treatment and suffering of immigrant Africans in our Spanish possessions" so that "in reality, at whichever point [in the Gulf of Guinea] we tried to recruit, as soon as they found out about the destination, they refrained from facilitating us *braceros*, with a palpable sense of repulsion."[24]

While there were Fernandinos who became landowners and successful agro-capitalists, many also became state functionaries and managers in the rapidly expanding European plantations during the 1890s and 1900s – when the Spanish colonial state had started dishing out 50 hectare land concessions to any Spanish settler who arrived. Most new Spanish settlers arrived from Cuba and Catalonia and were woefully unprepared to engage in the delicate and intricate task of informal recruitment on their own account. A Vice-Consul traced Fernando Po's "first" Nigerian labor tout onto a notorious figure named Bernadino Jose Reis from Brazil House in Lagos island. In the 1890s Reis began "importing Yoruba labour" from Lagos and Ijebu-Ode, a large Yoruba kingdom annexed to the colony of Southern Nigeria in 1892.[25] It would be onerous to place Reis at the origin as there were "other persons besides Mr. Reis who engaged labourers for Fernando Po." It is unclear who exactly he was except that he was related to a notable Aguda carpenter in Lagos and was known as the "Aguda man," and so a descendant of the freed Afro-Brazilian slaves who left Bahia and settled in Lagos in the first half of the nineteenth century, long before it was annexed by the British in 1861. Reis is nevertheless a great representation of the recruiter as tout, semi-anonymous in his commercial relation with both capital and labor and delinked from the colonial state, whose reign and movements into the first half of twentieth-century Nigeria I will try to follow in this chapter.

---

22 Sundiata, *From Slaving to Neoslavery*, 130, 129; Brooks, *Kru Mariner*, 25. It is unclear how many were Kru, as most "laborers leaving Liberia" seem to have been low caste Vai and Mandinka, and Kpelle.

23 "Escape of the Fernando Po Prisoners," *New York Times*, August 12, 1869.

24 Valero y Belenguer, "La Guinea Española," 218.

25 British VC (Michie), February 28, 1941, TNA, FO 371/26908.

Figure 8: Cacao trees with ripe pods (Baguena 1951, 50).

At the turn of the century over 500 *braceros* from Lagos and Accra, most of whom Reis recruited, went on strike to protest poor treatment and lower wages than agreed. In late January 1900 they had "marched to the Governors house in Santa Isabel with machetes in hand and refused to return to the plantations." The Governor realized he did not have a large enough armed force to suppress the "mutiny," so he negotiated with the strikers and offered to send them to work with the public works department and investigate their allegations of fraud in hiring. Within a few days, a British ship that was docked in Santa Isabel offered to repatriate them to Lagos, and more than 400 accepted the Governor's proposal to return to Lagos, under the condition that they would not receive any payment for the work already done. As the news spread, more *braceros* began to leave the plantations to be repatriated as well, but the authorities managed to convince them to "return" to the farms. Back in Lagos, over 200 *braceros* who said they were recruited by Reis lodged a complaint saying "they were cruelly treated," "their rations consisted of only one plantain for breakfast and a small cup of rice for dinner," and that "they had not been paid their wages, but some of them received advances either in money or in kind."[26] After what the Spanish called the "uprising of the Lagosians," the British embargoed labor migration to Spanish Guinea from Nigeria. They had already forbidden emigration from Sierra Leone in 1896, "as a large number of men are now being contracted to work in the Panama Canal and the Congo estuary, it has been necessary to suspend all shipments of labour from the colony [of Sierra Leone] not only to Fernando Poo but also elsewhere."[27] Soon, as a British agent of the John Holt company who also dabbled in illegal recruitment to the island said, the entire "labour markets in the French and British West African possessions" were "closed for supplying workers to the plantations on this dread island which shelters under the flag of Spain."[28]

The embargo was only partially enforced, and it became quickly "evident that a considerable unchecked traffic in illegally recruited native labourers of British nationality destined chiefly for the plantations of Fernando Po" continued to be carried out in various port towns in the Gulf of Guinea. Regular British and German steamers connected Fernando Po to its regional world and in the early decades of the twentieth century much of the palm oil and cocoa was still being exported to Liverpool and Hamburg, as well as increasingly and eventually almost completely to Barcelona. Indeed, a large receiver of this illicitly recruited labor were British cocoa exporting houses in Santa Isabel, such as the John Holt company, who "pay 5 pounds for each 'boy' landed" either for their various large cacao plantations on the island or more commonly in order to informally lend these *braceros* to various smaller African farmers on the island.[29] After the spree of Spanish decrees passed between 1904 and 1906 that regulated land, labor and colonial subjects, Bubi and smaller but more numerous Fernandino farmers could not officially hire labor at all. To contract *braceros*, exclusively done via the *Curaduría*, Africans needed a certified "elite" colonial subject status which granted the same economic and social rights accorded to all Europeans in the colony. Only a small number of mostly Fernandino elites with this certified status, confusingly also called *emancipados*, could employ

---

26 Henry Carr, Education Office, Lagos, February 20, 1900, "Report on the Condition and Treatment of Laborers just returned from Fernando Po," AGA, C-81/7789, E-2. On the strike see AGA, C-81/6488, E-2. Compare Hopkins, "The Lagos strike of 1897."

27 Francis Bertie to Minister of State, London, March 29, 1897, cited in García Cantús, "Fernando Poo," 576.

28 Harold R. Taylor, *Jungle Trader* (London: Jarrolds, 1939), 79.

29 British Consul General, Monrovia to FO, London, October 15, 1913, and June 30, 1913, TNA, FO 367/353; Sundiata, *From Slaving to Neoslavery*, 136.

contract workers.[30] The Holt company and other European merchants thus found a new niche to become a type of "sub-contractor of contract labor," leasing them for shorter terms and during punctual needs during the harvest or to open up new lands, to assure their smallholder cacao farmers could produce the output needed. The intermediary interest or premium was achieved through the underpaying of cacao producers at fixed and reduced rates.

Reis himself kept recruiting for decades. In the 1910s, someone accused Reis and a new associate, another "Lagos man" by the name of Thompson, of going "to Bonny and Warri" on the Niger Delta "to take little children to sell at Fernando Po. They have sold lots already." Reis and Thompson had a variety of liasons, as they would hire canoes to get to Rio del Rey in the German Cameroons "from whence there appears to be no difficulty in shipping them to [the] island of the Fernando Po group, where labour is very scare and in great demand."[31] A recurring recruiting experience in this period is that of a *bracero* called Ali, a "native of Lagos." "Ali complains that he was found by a man called Bruce in Accra, who told him that he was taking him to Calabar to work there. He was landed, he says, in Fernando Po and taken before the *Curador.*" Ali was then "told that if he did not sign a contract for three years he would be put in gaol. He therefore signed for three years." Comparable stories are repeated, almost endlessly. A recruiter by the name of "Mr. Davis" arrived on the island with "ten Elmina boys" from Ghana in 1912:

> Davis recruited them in Elmina, and promised to take them to Calabar at 1s per day. [When] the steamer left the coast and went in a direction they know to be not that of Calabar, they questioned Davis where they were going to. He said the steamer was first going to Fernando Po. When they arrived here, they were made to go ashore, and then taken before the Curador, who asked them to make a contract for five years. They said they had been engaged to work cargo, and were not to do plantation work. The Curador told [them] that if they did not

30 From 1938 on, *braceros* could only be contracted by those with a "canonical marriage" certificate. In the late 1950s, the so-called "cooperativas indígenas del campo de Fernando Poo" organized the Bubi farmers by villages and localities, and through these they could hire *braceros.* The 30 cooperatives only hired about 169 *braceros* in the late 1950s, see Patronato de Indígenas de los Territorios Españoles del Golfo de Guinea, "Datos para su historia y antecedentes y memoria del 1954," BNE, D/16263.

31 Joseph Asaba, Victoria, to Provincial Commissioner, Calabar, October 22, 1911, TNA, FO 367/254; German West African Trading Company, Rio del Rey, to Provincial Commissioner, Calabar, October 17, 1911, TNA, FO 367/254; Lieutenant Strong, to Admiralty, HMS Dward, Cape Lopez, November 10, 1911, TNA, FO 367/254.

> make a contract for five years he would send them to gaol [jail]. They then made a contract for three years.[32]

Even when African employers or inter-colonial British and German firms made their own recruiting arrangements on the coast, on their own negotiated terms, they had to cede to the Spanish state. A British firm found itself "under an obligation to see that the boys were sent back after" less than one year, to which the *Curador* replied: "that he was the *Curador* and that he would allow no one to interfere with him and he contracted the boys for three years." The "chief complaint" of British West African *braceros* in this period is "that they are brought here under false pretences. They are told that they are coming for a British firm and are then handed over to Spanish, Portuguese and [African] planters, from which they receive much worse treatment that what they are used to from a British masters."[33] The Spanish colonial authorities could feign a legal literalism, either sincerely or insincerely, and argued with the British that these migrations "cannot be described as 'forced'," as "laborers arriving from foreign territory into Fernando Po" had to make a "declaration" to "the effect that they are doing so out of their own free will."[34]

Other recruiters were operating simultaneously or followed in the footsteps of Reis and others, but always in different places. Calabar's first large scale recruiter in the early twentieth century was Ekpenyon John Boko, from the Cobham family in Duke Town, who was "suspected of inducing boys to leave Calabar for Fernando Po without either obtaining the consent of the head of their House, or entering into a proper contract of service."[35] He had been taking advantage of the rising number of deserters and the newly autonomous job-seekers generated by the abolition of slavery in Nigeria 1901 and the subsequent introduction of the House Rule Ordinance, under which former "slaves," now called servants, were obliged to render tributary service labour to their Efik "masters." The rate of flight was so high that even the "most important Chief[s]" in Calabar

---

32 British VC (Smallbones) to Curaduría, June 10, 1913, TNA, FO 367/353. Or take the case of Momo Bokory from Sierra Leone who arrived in similar circumstances. He was brought to Sekondi, also in Ghana, where he was promised by a Mr. Davis that he "would earn 3 l a month. When they arrived in Secondi, Davis said he was taking him to the Congo and work at that wage." He arrived in Fernando Po and "wanted one year" as had been promised by Davis, but he was forced to sign on "to four, under the same threat of gaol."

33 British VC (Smallbones) to CO, June 30, 1913, TNA, FO 367/353.

34 Ministerio de Estado (Prieto) to British Ambassador (de Bunsen), Madrid, February 9, 1912, NAE, CSE 9/1/6.

35 High Commissioner's Office, Calabar to GG, April 12, 1905, AGA, C-81/7789, E-2.

found it "difficult to secure enough labour for their trade canoes."[36] Dozens of letters reached the Governor in Santa Isabel from a demoted Efik aristocracy now classified as "chiefs," such as Abassi Ita of Duke House, asking about "the whereabouts of his runaway boys." The Spanish Governor happily ignored all of them and pointed the finger back "at the slavery being condoned by the English, who expect us to return these men who left their region freely."[37]

After the British promulgated the House Rule Ordinance they introduced the Roads and Rivers Proclamation of 1903 which gave "chiefs" the power "to recruit forced labour" for public works as well as resources to the "local police" to "secure the capture of the chiefs' runaway subjects." As Walter Ofonogaro says, "both the House Rule Ordinance and the government's forced labour policy created fugitives, many escaping to Lagos or Fernando Po, where they threw themselves on the mercy of the Spanish authorities of that plantation island."[38] Hundreds of "British subjects from Southern Nigeria" and particularly from Calabar were "found to be living in a Spanish island, in order to avoid the bondage of the House Rule Ordinance [and] fear[ed] to return home again lest they become 'enslaved' under it." In 1911 Jabez Linette was "anxious to return to his home in the Calabar district but dare not so because he would be arrested [and then] returned to his owner." The Methodists on Fernando Po had "purchased his liberty"; it is unclear whether they kept him on as a hired laborer. Vice versa, aristocratic Efiks had also started moving to Fernando Po pursuing various opportunities, and brought their old "servants" with them: "one woman from the island of Fernando Po visited Old Calabar, and was taking back with her a domestic servant. The woman was arrested and sentenced to a long term of imprisonment, which she is now serving in Old Calabar."[39]

---

36 Olatunji Ojo, "The Southern Nigeria Native House Rule Ordinance (1901)," *African Economic History* 40 (2012): 133.

37 Solicitor for Chief Marin Braid, Calabar to GG, October 18, 1905, AGA, C-81/7789, E-2; GG to DGMC, December 31, 1912, AGA, C-81/6945, E-20.

38 Walter I. Ofonagoro, "An Aspect of British Colonial Policy in Southern Nigeria: The Problems of Forced Labour and Slavery, 1895–1928," in *Studies in Southern Nigerian History*, ed. Boniface Obichere (London: Frank Cass, 1982), 237; Andrew C. Okolie, "The Transformation of Eastern Nigeria: From Self Sufficiency to Social Crisis," in *The Foundations of Nigeria: Essays in Honor of Toyin Falola*, ed. Toyin Falola (Trenton: Africa World Press, 2003), 455.

39 "The House Rule Ordinance," *The Lagos Weekly Record*, Lagos, May 8, 1911, 3, citing a letter from John H. Harris to the Secretary of the Anti-Slavery and Aborigines Protection Society. The House Rule Ordinance was abolished in 1912, see TNA, CO 520/107.

Touts in the Gulf Guinea, 1910s–1930s

It is worth turning briefly to Liberia and Río Muni, where we have important descriptions of the precise techniques of the recruiters, to underline the argument about their consistency and necessary drift through time and place. In addition, this serves to qualify the impression left by Sundiata and others that the labor treaty with Liberia, which between 1914 and the late 1920s had brought over a total of 7,268 indentured laborers, supplanted the type of recruitment undertaken by Fernandino recruiter-touts who had shuttled back and forth across the West African coast.[40] As Sundiata noted "by the late 1920s such an individual operation would have been almost unthinkable."[41] Reis and others did partially subside as they were being made less necessary by the upsurge of recruitment in both Liberia and Río Muni, organized more directly by state forces. However, there was still a flourishing of such "individual operations" throughout this period, which fully bloomed in the 1930s. An additional context of this period is that in 1916, 35,000 German and Cameroonian refugees arrived in Spanish Guinea: the entire German colonial administration of *Kamerun* and their loyalist soldiers and their families, when they finally fled from the last battles with the French and turned up in Río Muni en masse. With the end of the war, the Germans left to Madrid and much of the Cameroonian contingent returned home, but about 4,000 of them stayed on the island, which had a population of around 15,000 people, so this of course alleviated the labor question. The vast majority were "Ewondo" (Beti) from the area around Yaoundé, of the so-called Beti-Bulu-Fang group.[42]

While between 1914 and 1930 a large part of the about 10,000 "indigenous peoples impressed as contract labor" in Liberia for the Fernando Po plantations were taken under the command of a small group of senators who deployed their

---

40 Sundiata, *From Slaving to Neoslavery*, 117–123, 143; Sundiata, *Brothers and Strangers*, 81, 88–98, 249. For original treaty negotiations and drafts see AGA, C-81/6866. Liberia revoked the treaty in 1927 following an incident with its consul in Santa Isabel, who was recalled in protest because of racial discrimination when interacting with Spanish officials. Between 1928 and December 1929 a new "private recruiting deal" was made between various Liberian leaders – headed by the Postmaster-General Samuel Ross and the Vice-President Allen Yancy – and the Barcelona branch of the planter's lobby, the *Sindicato Agricola*. This final private recruitment deal brought over an additional 2,431 workers. The *Sindicato* paid Ross and Yancy $9 "a head" for "transportation and a bonus of £1,000 for each 1,500 laborers shipped," while Ross duly "paid $2.50 per head into the Liberian treasury" which was close to bankruptcy.

41 Sundiata, *From Slaving to Neoslavery*, 140.

42 Miquel Vilaró i Güell, *La internación de la Schutztruppe: la Guinea Española en la Gran Guerra* (Madrid: Letras de Autor, 2018).

frontier force to recruit laborers for "Fernando Po under the guise of contract labor," there were still touts operating in their distinct *laissez faire* mode.[43] The well-publicized League of Nations 1930 commission described the sequence of extortions and unpaid road-building programs aimed at extracting Liberian *braceros* for Fernando Po. This led to the ousting of certain political figures, including the Liberian president, Charles D.B. King, who were made responsible for the whole scandal. The League of Nations commission did not mention these other recruiters and their techniques as they focused on political targets.[44]

Just before the outbreak of World War I, the John Holt company called on Harold Taylor "to assist in the recruitment of labor." Taylor was a lowly British employee residing and working at a factory in Monrovia. Taylor says that "the best way to get results" was to venture into the "most remote of districts" in the "interior," where the term "Nanny Po" did not induce a "loathsome" reaction. Taylor proudly retells his linguistic feats. Exaggerating, he recalls how the "picture [he] painted [of Fernando Po] was so glowing with gorgeous colouring, that I eventually had all my work cut out to prevent the Chief himself from signing on and excluding all others from this golden promised land." Taylor notes that as soon as he crossed into districts where people had already come and gone to Fernando Po, touting became untenable.[45] Other private and informal recruiters who had been operating in Liberia were informing the planters on Fernando

43 Miers, "Slavery and the Slave Trade," 29.

44 League of Nations, August 1930, "Report of the International Commission of Enquiry into the Existence of Slavery and Forced Labour in the Republic of Liberia," 36. For a historically exceptional analysis of the "labour scandal" that focused also on the internal political machinations of other Liberian politicians, including Thomas Faulkner who lost the election in 1927 and then promptly denounced King as a slave trader to international organs and concluded that it was rather a case of "Colonial Powers arrogat[ing] to themselves an holier-than thou attitude" to "influence public opinion by propaganda that there was a recrudescence of classic slavery in Liberia" in order to control this Republic, see Ben N. Azikiwe, "In Defense of Liberia," *The Journal of Negro History* 17, no. 1 (1932): 31; Azikiwe, *Liberia in World Politics*, 186. Azikiwe also scathingly reviewed the ethnographic novel *Slaves Today: A Story of Liberia* written by the African American journalist George Schuyler, in the style of an ethnological inquiry and based on his own stay in Liberia to investigating this story. These early disputes of interpretation between these radically different figures, who would of course later become renowned and controversial in their own way, has been underexamined, however much would be learned from a detailed juxtaposition. Ben N. Azikiwe, "George Schuyler, Slaves Today, A Story of Liberia," *The Journal of Negro History* 17, no. 3 (1932), 382–83; George Schuyler, "Wide 'Slavery' Persisting in Liberia, Post Reveals," June 29, 1931, *New York Evening Post*, 1–2.

45 Taylor, *Jungle Trader*, 85.

Po that the "boys who had returned from Fernando Po gave it such a bad name that [they were] unable to induce more labourers to come here."[46]

Fernando Po's notoriety continuously spread, and so Taylor and his "native gangers" were forced to go into "ever more isolated parts of the interior" without laying "too much stress on the name Fernando Po [...] the very sound of it seemed to have a dampening effect on us." Taylor leaves his reader to imagine the conditions of the mobile encampments of recruits: "Within a month we had collected close on eight hundred labourers," but on the trek back down to the coast, over a third "just vanished into thin air" or "died en route from a variety of unexplained causes" or had been "left behind" because of "sickness." He dispatched the remaining recruits to Fernando Po on steamers even though the "British Captains were very averse" to "what they termed slave-running," so presumably he may have also had to rely on competing steamship companies that connected Monrovia to Santa Isabel, such as the German Woermann-Linie. Taylor also briefly expands on another principal – but less effective – recruiting method, which he says involved an "appeal to the cupidity of an impoverished Chief." Taylor offered a "payment of so much per head" to certain chiefs, who would then proceed to "round up all the young men" who had incurred real or imaginary debts with them – that is principally those young people a chief "suspected of having affairs with his many wives," whom he could thereby customarily fine. Those unable to pay these fines were "hand[ed] over, body and soul," and Taylor gave a "lavish commission" to those issuing the verdicts. This depended on the person and disposition of the local legal and political authorities. Just as often, Taylor says he would encounter someone like "Chief Nasty Chap" who refused to allow recruiters to get to work amongst "his people". "I have met only two with such a mean look in the whole of Africa, and this fellow was both of them." Taylor, "wishing to avoid all friction," left the area, the convoy meandering and leaking, as no one was bound or escorted.[47]

Despite the international and academic focus on the official recruitment for Fernando Po from Liberia, throughout the first third of the twentieth century most contract laborers arrived through informal individual operations that were in full swing in Río Muni, Cameroon, and Gabon.[48] Writing in 1931, a journalist on site noted that while "there are some 'monrovias' left, today the entirety of the human resources working on the island are being imported from the *continente* [Río Muni], the immense majority of the *braceros* on the island's planta-

46 British VC (Smallbones) to FO (Grey), June 30, 1913, TNA, FO 367/353.

47 Taylor, *Jungle Trader*, 85, 88.

48 For exhaustive details see my short book on these regions, Martino, *How to Create a Labour Market*, 38–46.

tions are 'pamues' [Fang]."[49] By the early 1930s they had almost all been brought by a "body of recruiters, technically clandestine but perfectly known, who replaced the rulers of Liberia, and turned Cameron and Gabon into their field of operations."[50]

Many of them were "misled" outright by for example being "promised work in the plantations of Cunha Lisboa," a large Fernandino planter from São Tomé who was "famed for the good treatment of his labourers." They of course always ended up elsewhere.[51] The first contract was always uncertain, recruits could never be sure they would end up where promised, and even then an apparent destination matching its initial description could be tenuous and reversible, as was the case with Ebosogo Esono, who was underage and therefore could only sign a contract for "housework duties," but instead he was "met by a master [Francisco Perez] who turned me from a domestic servant into a *bracero*."[52] In Río Muni, the usually Spanish or Portuguese *reclutadores* "laden with brandy, whisky, cloths and Virginia tobacco" always had "at least two or three *ganchos*, African subcontractors from the coast, who strategically camp out in the border villages."[53] *Ganchos* tended to settle and move around "along the border in the towns that have a direct communication to the French side, because it is much easier to recruit there." A Portuguese *gancho*, a true tout, Juan Ferreira, who spoke Fang, says he "only offered work in Bata to anybody he saw," "convincing them that [ALENA a forestry company on the coast] always treats its people well" – an outright deception, as they were almost all brought "to the island." "Those who sign up I give them some presents in goods and organize their meals until I deliver them." The Spanish investigator interrogated him "to get to the bottom of how these individuals proceed, with their illegal means, on the basis of deception and lies, which causes so much damage."[54]

While reading through the ILO's Forced Labour Convention of 1930, Juan Bravo Carbonell, a leading colonial ideologue, pondered why the concept of "voluntary" seemed to him to "be inadequate", "after all if we do not incline the *indígena* to work by deploying *dadivas o con alguna palabreria de una poca fantasia* [gifts or some verbiage with a dose of fantasy] he will never

49 Emilio Carles, *Misioneros, negreros y esclavos: Notas de un viaje a Fernando Poo* (Valencia: Cuadernos de Cultura, 1932), 33.

50 GG (Sánchez Guerra) to DGMC (Alvarez-Buylla), December 28, 1935, AGA, C-81/6867, E-5.

51 Curaduría (González Ordóñez) to Comisario de la Republica, August 26, 1931, AGA, C-81/6418.

52 Ebosogo Esono, in Curaduría (Guellin) to GG (Lluesma), May 18, 1934, AGA, C-81/8126, E-19.

53 Babiloni, January 1937, AGA, C-81/12427.

54 Juan Ferreria, August 20, 1932, "Declaración; Denuncia de Ernesto Ruiz Tejero contra Portuguese Juan Ferreira," AGA, C-81/8028, E-7.

offer us his *brazos*." Bravo even spelled out the stakes: "Without cunning and trickery they would have never come voluntarily to our zones of exploitation, and we wouldn't be able to harness the formidable sources of wealth that those fiercely fertile lands offer us."[55]

Law in Spanish Guinea

I now turn to the rupture of recruitment configurations during the Spanish Civil War, as it was precisely in 1936 when the planters on Fernando Po started to panic again, "feeling profoundly the *falta de brazos*" as "once the [Fang *braceros*] finish their contracts practically all of them return to their country, and no new recruits are taking their place."[56] Already in 1935 the majority of "any new *braceros* who arrive in our colony [were] all coming from Calabar."[57] Planters had started relying on an almost entirely new set of recruiters and labor hinterlands. As an undercover Nigerian police officer on the island observed in May 1936:

> Boys are very difficult to get over here for the [Fang] Spanish Subjects at Bata had completely refused to come over here at Santa Isabel [so] now the Spanish Farmers being in difficulty to get boys did all they could and so seduced the Nigerian traders especially the Calabarians to begin to recruit boys. For each boy recruited the Spanish Farmer pays the sum of three hundred pesetas.

He later adds, in an incidental sidenote, that many of these goods traders turned recruiters, were "Calabarian" or Efik women.[58] By 1939 the planters on Fernando Po had become "convinced that the only rapid and viable solution is an intense work of propaganda in Nigeria, which unlike us, has been spared an anxious lack of labor, and therefore we shall not fear that our efforts will be frustrated."[59] This was commonly referred to as the "external" or the "Nigerian solution."[60] Yet the initial influx of Nigerian migrants in the early 1930s consisted not of workers but of what the Spanish called "*los traders*," appearing on the island to engage in a range of licensed and unlicensed money-making activities in the towns and

---

55 Juan Bravo Carbonell, "De la Guinea española: El trabajo indígena," *El Sol*, Barcelona, June 3, 1930.

56 Cámara to GG (de Mendívil), April 1, 1937, C-81/8129, E-2.

57 GG (Sánchez Guerra) to DGMC, December 28, 1935, AGA, C-81/6867, E-5.

58 S. Muyiwa to Commissioner of Police, Calabar, May 24, 1936, NAE, CALPROF 5/1/194.

59 SubGG (Cabrera) to GG (Fontán), August 2, 1939, AGA, C-81/9017, E-18.

60 Bonelli Rubio, "Geografía económica," 200.

outside the plantation patios. Those who came more or less in accordance with their own intentions and designs were increasingly unwelcome. The "problem", as the Republican authorities (1931–1936) came to sharply define it, was how to bring over people and make them stay as *braceros*. Only recruiters, harnessing the power of the contract, could make this happen.

Santa Isabel was a key node strung along the West African steamship routes. The mostly Nigerian passengers on the steamships were itinerant self-employed traders or joining friends and family in the towns with an extendable visitors permit. They "arrive without any background checks, and with a simple municipal license fill a stall with fabrics and tinned food and start to work."[61] The economic shock and rural restructuring brought on by the global depression that plunged Nigerian palm oil prices, led to the first and wholly unexpected "mass immigration" alarm in Fernando Po. The Republican police chief of Santa Isabel worried that the "freedom to access our Colony could not be greater, whoever disembarks on our shores does not experience any discomfort except that of hopping off the steamer."[62] In the early 1930s the colonial office, slightly overestimating the dimensions, noted that there were now "some 2500 Yaundes, as well as an infinitely higher number of Hausas and Lagos, of English origin, and a quite considerable number from Calabar, Port-Harcourt, Victoria, Duala, Cribi, Tiko, Sierra-Leone, Monrovia, Accra y Opobo, which means that the number of resident foreigners on the island is far in excess of Spanish subjects." The new predominantly immigrant population on the island were seen as outsiders living within, and less as subjects to be molded. Spanish calls for "coercive" and "restrictive measures" found a new field of operation.[63]

The anti-vagrancy laws revamped in the 1930s became a structural pillar and precondition for the massive extension of recruiters into Nigeria. Only after 1936 was the law, where "anyone who declined to accept the contract placed before him" became "treated as a rogue and a vagabond," ironclad.[64] Specific anti-va-

---

61 "Hospitalidad Excesiva," *El Defensor de Guinea*, Santa Isabel, November 2, 1933, AGA, C-81/7720.

62 Jefe de Policía to GG (Manresa), March 15, 1934, AGA, C-81/8146, E-1.

63 DGMC (Alvarez-Buylla) to Presidencia del Consejo de Ministros (Montauer), July 20, 1933, AGA, C-81/6467, E-19.

64 British VC (Michie), February 28, 1941, TNA, FO 371/26908. The Francoists held this Republican code intact until the end of colonial rule in 1968. In Spain they similarly kept the new *Ley de Vagos y Maleantes* passed by the Republicans in 1933 until 1970; Salvador Cayuela Sánchez, "La biopolítica en la España franquista" (PhD diss., Universidad de Murcia, 2010), 172–178. While the colonial anti-vagrancy laws were quite like the metropolitan codes, one of the main modifications, the colonial adaptation, the mark of the extension to the plantation complex, was the clause, at the service of employers, specifying "desertion," the *fugados* "those, who

grancy ordinances supplementing the 1906 Labor Code were passed in 1908, explicitly "for the benefit of *la agricultura* of these lands, in light of the scarcity of *brazos*," and dictated that "anyone who arrives in this port, as soon as they disembark present themselves at the *Curaduría*." The ordinance reiterated the "requirement" that "*vagos* without employers" be put up "for contract in the *Curaduría*." However, its enforcement was not systematic, and neither were the other ordinances aiming to "reduce the possible number of *vagos y maleantes* [vagrants and miscreants] of colour who circulate through the towns, villages and pathways of these territories." Only the specific pass-laws targeting *braceros* were systematically upheld by the police, who were always on the lookout for deserters or *fugados*. If found outside plantations *braceros* would be "asked" for their "pass, plaque, or card," inscribed with the "name of the carrier, place of work, date of contract and signature of the master."[65]

Already in the late 1920s, with the tripling of the number of *braceros* since 1909 and the still growing smaller Bubi and Fernandino farmers, a lucrative "underclass" was taking shape in a parallel economy alongside the plantations to service small farmers and the Cameroonian, Liberian, and Fang *braceros* of large estates. The new informal, lumpen economy was primarily populated by liquor-vendors, medicine-sellers, paper-forgers, and cacao smugglers – "ambulant buyers of cacao," "especially Lagos people, who are eminently of the commercial type."[66] The motley groups were often crystallized in the image of the "unassimilable" "Hausa mafias," Muslims from northern Nigeria who had originally arrived with the exiled German Schutztruppe in 1916 as their horse dealers and keepers. Their leadership were known to "rule" the "slums," the so-called Campo Yaounde and Campo Hausa created on the grounds of the German en-

---

are under contract and escape without a justified cause [and who] show an aversion to work." The planters' influence is evidenced by the comparatively reduced "correctives" or being "interned in an establishment with a work regime, for no less than a month, nor more than a year" – in Spain "petty" vagrants were interned for two to four years. The penal sanction for runaways in the first labor code of 1906 specified that "once recaptured the *fugado* will suffer a correction that shall not exceed ten days in jail," after which they were immediately "reintegrated" back into the workplace. Miranda, *Leyes coloniales*, 1468.

65 Miranda, *Leyes coloniales*, 401, 876, 627. The importance of the pass-laws was reiterated in 1926: "In order not to cause damage to employers and *braceros* with the gathering of vagrants ordered by this Government, and until the identity bracelets are received and acquired by them for their servants, the latter will be provided with a paper, plate or card on which the owner, manager or master will state their name class of work and contract number."

66 Jose Pinto Guimaraes to Inspector de los Servicios del Golfo de Guinea (Ferrer Barbero), August 15, 1931, AGA, C-81/8095, E-17.

campments and temporary barracks in the outskirts of Santa Isabel during their refuge from Cameroon.

Hausa-led or monopolized activities included cattle-importing and slaughtering, "landlordism" in the migrant "slums," currency conversions, and the selling of animal hides and handicrafts to settlers. They were also believed to be "poisoners" and "quack-doctors" – "the Hausa, who dedicate themselves to fetish-making and medicine."[67] Hausa healers were held in high esteem by *braceros* from all over the Gulf the Guinea. They were "reputed healers and diviners of causes of ill-health and prescribe remedies against evil by selling a simple ram's horn for 500 pesetas [or] a little piece of paper written in Arabic wrapped in a black cloth for 25 pesetas." When accosted by the authorities they could "defend themselves with the *papel de libertad*" needed to work in the autonomous and self-employed professions, as tailors or carpenters for example, and "they leave with an air of triumph to secretly return to their penchant for selling medicine."[68]

When the Republicans were preparing their "delicate study of the material" on new vagrancy laws, they came across the "indispensable colonial regulations that have been implemented since distant times, the French since 1853 have had decrees related to immigrants workers in their colonies, similar norms have been taken up by England, Portugal, Italy and Belgium," norms that would "avoid that the colonies become places of refuge for *vagos y maleantes* and undesirable people of a political order."[69] The *Gobernador*, Estanislao Lluesma, quickly passed a decree in December 1933: "All those overstaying a thirty-day visitation period [and] those immigrants who are known, or suspected to be in a condition of *vago*, shall be interned in the *barracones* [jails] of the *Curaduría*." Those who "lack licit means of living, will be kept in jail until they contract" or until they are "repatriated and deported."[70] Lluesma left office within a few months and it seems the decree was not immediately enforced; in any case the type of paperwork required to avoid arrest could still be acquired, and a widely applied vagrancy law only hit the ground in August 1936, their last month in office.[71] A whole new range of registration regimes were being prepared by the Republicans at considerable expense – reordering cabinets, importing the latest identification templates, the streamlining of taxation with stamps, etc. – but their implemen-

67 Pélissier, *Territorios españoles*, 48; García, *Fernando el africano*, 35; Baguena, *Manuales del África Española*, 52; Cámara to GG (Fontán), April 13, 1938, AGA, C-81/8126, E-1.

68 B.P., "Brujerias de Extranjeros," *La Guinea Española*, Santa Isabel, September 17, 1939.

69 DGMC (Duque) to GG (Lluesma), December 8, 1933, AGA, C-81/8156, E-3.

70 Miranda, *Leyes coloniales*, 876; see also AGA, C-81/8126, E-1.

71 Miranda, *Leyes coloniales*, 1468; Cordero Torres, *Derecho colonial*, 160 – 162.

tation was interrupted by the outbreak of the civil war in Spain. The new vagrancy law was one of the few Republican colonial reforms the Francoist kept without interruption.

"*Los traders*" necessarily dispersed with the advent of harsh anti-vagrancy laws but it was these that allowed them also to partially regroup, and splinter off to become Fernando Po's most effective recruiters yet. The shift between miscellaneous petty traders to lumpen-brokers was quite sudden in the mid 1930s, as a undercover Nigerian police officer in Fernando Po, Sargeant Muyiwa, writes: "the inducement that the Spanish Farmers offered these recruiters" had caused a few "Ibo and Calabarian traders" to "totally abandon their good trade of local food-stuffs and cling to shipping of human cargos into Fernando Poo" – "these dealers in slavery now believe or take this traffic to be the means of living."[72] Many of the new Nigerian *braceros* were themselves hoping to assist in or undertake common petty trading activities and so willingly travelled on the steamers to Fernando Po. A trader from Lagos reported that he came across some recruiters who disembarked with a group of unwitting recruits whom they had brought "under the pretext" of being trading assistants, hired to carry trade goods in and out of the island: "boys whom they have impressed with the notion of FERNANDO PO being an El Dorado for the unemployed and depression in Nigeria and upon their arrival are made over to some farmers for some inducive amounts of money."[73]

In 1938, Alfredo Jones, one of the earliest and "principal" buyers of new Nigerian *braceros* for his plantations in San Carlos, said: "The Nigerian government might not sympathize with the agents of Fernando Poo who facilitate the voyage to the island [...] insinuating that this has an element of 'SLAVE TRADE'," but, he insisted, the "poor" of Nigeria were "subject to a miserable life without the possibility of liberation." Jones admired the "migrants" who were "defying the danger of capsizing canoes and being eaten by sharks that abound in these waters, to redeem themselves from the hardship suffered in their own country." These "*braceros*," he could conclude, were "received" in Fernando Po "with alacrity and glee, and they find work from the second they arrive. Their employers start by serving them plentiful and healthy food rations." Alfredo Jones was one of the sons of Maximiliano Jones, the fabled "richest" man in Spanish Guinea who turned the slopes above San Carlos Bay into the most productive cacao producing area of the island. The plantations in San Carlos employed Nigerian

72 S. Muyiwa to Commissioner of Police, Calabar, May 24, 1936, NAE, CALPROF 5/1/194.

73 Olatunji Sapara, n.d. [January 1934?] contained in Commissioner of Police, Buea, Cameroons, to Resident, Calabar, January 31, 1934, NAE, CALPROF 5/1/192.

laborers earlier than other parts of the island; indeed, the links between Fernando Po and Nigeria were commonly thought to have started as links between San Carlos and Calabar, because of the direct canoe traffic between them.

Alfredo Jones had studied in Spain for four years at the military academy of Zaragoza and by 1939 had embarked on an illustrious and tenured colonial career, starting out at the all-important and powerful Agronomy Department that decided who received which lands. He was one of the few Africans occupying a "European post in the government," and by the early 1950s headed the Anglo-Spanish Employment Agency set up Calabar after the labor treaty, and in the 1960s he was appointed the Spanish consul at Calabar.[74] He became a highly respected figure during the Francoist period, and his imprint on the island's labor question was profound, probably without equal. It was the vision expressed in his 1938 report prepared for the new governor, Juan Fontán y Lobé (1937–1942), that won over the initially confused new Francoist authorities when they took over the island and were deciding what to do with the Nigerian touts. Indeed, Fontán had initially cracked down on the lumpen-brokers and their irregular steamship itineraries, as he favored a new state-led push into Río Muni to gain new *braceros.* By 1939 Fontán came to share Jones' attitude, and brough it with him to the colonial office in Madrid when he was appointed Director General in 1942.[75]

The Francoist invariably added layers to the anti-vagrancy ordinances, such as one from 1940 where customs officers at Santa Isabel were given the mandate to "let no one board ships, except those duly authorized," barring those who had "outstanding obligations in these territories," or who were "considered *vago* and who cannot show the required documents."[76] Those widely classified as *vagos* could not leave the island except through deportation or a "freedom paper" issued after the expiry of a contract. The juridical status of the *vago* thus became strictly a sub-set of the contract: "if *indígena*s from a neighbouring colony should not find work within 15 to 30 days, they enter into the category of *vago.*"[77] On Fernando Po it was not only that there were types of *Master & Servants* penal sanctions for the breaking of contract but that prison or a forced contract was the default: "Unemployment is not known here. In fact, there are regulations

---

74 Alfredo Jones, December 1938, "Memoria sobre el problema de la mano de obra en la isla Fernando Poo," AGA, C-81/08128, E-1. See also Alfredo Jones Niger, *Memoria del homenaje a D. Alfredo Jones Niger* (Barcelona: Casa de la Guinea Española, 1963), BNE, Afr C/7010/1.

75 For a piece dedicated to understanding the Francoist mindset and response to the "Nigerian labor solution", see Martino, "Corrupción y contrabando."

76 Secretario General to GG (Fontán), July 9, 1940, AGA, C-81/8806, E-1.

77 SubGG to GG (Bonelli), June 8, 1944, AGA, C-81/8182, E-6.

for compulsory employment – any person who failed to produce satisfactory evidence of being in employment is arrested and detained," says a puzzled British official in 1960.[78]

Nevertheless, most British colonial officials did not hesitate to consider the contract a type of free labor, opposed to slavery and new systems of slavery, because even if contracts were effectively obligatory, one could still enter them willingly with the appropriate procedures, so its free character remained uninterrupted.[79] The "sole mission" of the *Curaduría*, writes the *Curador*, David Carrillo in 1936, was "to exercise a tutelary function for the *indígenas*, both nationals and foreigners, and to prevent that these be enslaved in any form." Carrillo continues down this logical path: "while our ordinances contain only the most just and humane orders," it is only when these are "transgressed" that "*peonaje* follows, and in some sense, this is similar to classic slavery."[80] While Carrillo had the involuntary and obligatory bondage of penal labor in mind, or *peonaje* as a debt to society paid by the criminal, the "transgression" of non-work is already there as the default setting in the first article of the labor code, valid as soon as one stepped into the territory itself.

The principal ideological-historical effect of liberal conceptions of the contract was that it allowed the Spanish to successfully weather accusations of "illegitimate" exploitation or "modern slavery." This shared sense reigned amongst colonial authorities and their international fora too. Contracts were considered as a stand-alone entity of private or civil law conducted between persons and opposed to a state, or a social condition of tort or violation. The Spanish could and would insist that they were rigorously applying their own laws and were simply unaware of the exact conditions of recruiting undertaken by agents that were never "directly" authorized. The invocation of the "contract" could ideologically function this way precisely because it was categorically excluded and considered apart from slavery and new forms of rampant state-administered forced labor. In most African colonies, the ILO conventions regarding slavery (1926), forced labor (1930), and the recruitment of "indigenous workers" (1936) were followed by new or reformed colonial labor departments and legislation, with important backdoor clauses for "exceptions" creating the permissible conditions of forced labor which could be flexibly redefined, such as convict labor and anti-vagrancy measures with penal sanctions, bracketed into criminal law. The Spanish delegate at the ILO meetings for the different conventions in this period, which Spain almost

78 British VC (Harriman), April 22, 1960, TNA, FO 371/146562.
79 Gerald A. Cohen, "Capitalism, Freedom and the Proletariat," in *The Idea of Freedom: Essays in Honour of Isaiah Berlin*, ed. Alan Ryan (Oxford: Oxford University Press, 1979), 11.
80 Curador (Carrillo) to GG (Sanchez Guerra), July 4, 1936, AGA, C-81/8028, E-6.

immediately signed on and ratified, observed with relief that nothing was said about contracts as this "would have complicated our position," because any modification – such as making contracts revocable – would have immediately caused the cacao plantations and its recruiting mechanisms to break down.[81] Plantations would have immediately been run to the ground if anything like negotiated wages as well as the ability to withdraw from a contract would have played out in the "scarcity." As Ibrahim Sundiata has reasonably surmised: already in the 1890s "voluntary labor migration became increasingly difficult to maintain; given a free play of forces, plantation agriculture on the island would have probably collapsed."[82]

Money in Nigeria

Recruitment outside of Spanish Guinea could not operate through direct relations of political domination but only through the intense commercialization of both intermediation and social life. The notable absence of direct or even "structural" compulsion in recruitment was a feature repeatedly emphasized in diplomatic communications, as a Spanish representative at the ILO asked rhetorically: how could the "agents" of Fernando Po's planter be "slave-traders," "as it is unthinkable that nations like France and England, from whose colonies our labor power arrives, would have allowed us to employ procedures that require violence and coercion." He even ventured to claim that the *braceros* were "freer" than workers in the metropole because they did not technically need money-wages to purchase food or "subsist" in their own societies.[83]

A depictable moment of uprooting violence on land was absent. Significant migrations to the towns in eastern Nigeria, in particular, Enugu, Aba, Port Harcourt, Onitsha, and Calabar, were propelled in the late 1920s when the British introduced a poll tax. The background to rural flight and revolts that emerged in response to the poll tax was closely linked to the diffuse depreciation versus the pound of precolonial currencies such as manillas which were still in daily

81 El Consejero Tecnico a la XIX Conferencia Internacional de Trabajo (Cavestany Anduaga), May 22, 1935, AGA, C-81/12422. See also Cooper, *Decolonization*, 25–107; Brass, *Labour Regime Change*, 230.

82 Sundiata, "Kru Power," 38.

83 El Consejero Tecnico a la XIX Conferencia Internacional de Trabajo (Cavestany Anduaga), May 22, 1935, AGA, C-81/12422.

use in local markets.[84] The established idea that the introduction of colonial taxation forced an external monetary dependency and drove proletarianization overlooked crucial semi-autonomous financial aspects of early colonial economic life.[85] The poll tax burden was low – in the 1930s it did not exceed 15 shillings, about the cost of two nights with a prostitute in Calabar. In comparison Igbo bridewealth would normally be around £25 in the 1930s, and up to £100 in the 1940s.[86] Nevertheless the effect of the tax was magnified in conjunction with local modalities of exploitation. The rural inhabitants of eastern Nigeria moved away to "escape" the new "tax," "definitely to escape tax" says a British district officer in 1930 who had been stationed near Aba during the tax revolt known as the Women's War. The sudden tax obligation of seven shillings was often paid out in bulk to district commissioners by appointed village chiefs. For those who suddenly found themselves debtors to chiefs, interests quickly accumulated to up to £3, and they would be "summoned for this amount and they place[d] themselves in bondage" to creditors and chiefs who "take all our money," says a resident in Aba in 1930. "On account of the tax and various other matters people have pawned themselves," says another.[87]

In eastern Nigeria most peasants could expect an annual income of around £12, higher of course in certain boom periods and plummeting in the case of the palm oil areas after the great depression. In the densely farmed palm oil growing districts of Owerri, Aba, and Bende where most *braceros* were from in the 1940s, the selling and pledging of land became unusually common. In this period, putting up land as "collateral" quickly replaced the credit institution of pawning people. In the "hope of gathering the first instalment to pay for a bicycle or a [palm oil] press," land pledges were being accepted as a "security for a debt." Land could be seized by creditors for failing to pay back loans with extremely high interests rates, something which had "driven many away from farming to seek their fortunes abroad."[88] Recruiters operating out of these areas populate

84 Ben Naanen, "Economy within an Economy: The Manilla Currency, Exchange Rate Instability and Social Conditions in South-Eastern Nigeria, 1900 – 48," *The Journal of African History* 34, no. 3 (1993): 426; Walter I. Ofonagoro, "From Traditional to British Currency in Southern Nigeria: Analysis of a Currency Revolution, 1880 – 1948," *The Journal of Economic History* 39, no. 3 (1979); Igwe and Obiakor, "The Effects of Permanent Migration," 182.

85 Cooper, *Decolonization*, 27; Manchuelle, *Willing Migrants*, 161.

86 John Iliffe, *Honour in African History* (Cambridge: Cambridge University Press, 2005), 269.

87 Nigeria and Aba Commission of Inquiry, *Notes of Evidence Taken by the Commission of Inquiry Appointed to Inquire into the Disturbance in the Calabar and Owerri Provinces, December, 1929* (Lagos: Government Printer, 1930), para. 18675, 18570.

88 A.F.B. Bridges, June 1938, RHL, Mss. Afr. S. 697 (1), "Report of Oil Palm Survey, Ibo, Ibibio and Cross River Areas," para. 3; see also Martin, *Palm Oil and Protest*, 119 – 125; Korieh, *The*

the archival record; for example Michael Ikeocha, from Oloko, in Bende division, was living in the compound of Chief Udo Edem in Calabar, and made "his journeys" to Fernando Po from Creek Town, and was regularly "away," canoeing up the Cross River directly to Bende, almost certainly finding potential new recruits.[89]

As Nigerian historians of this period have noted, the "greater number of Cross River people who migrated to seek employment" abroad ended up in "Spanish Guinea." Yet at the same time "an Igbo saying has it that 'no one who was comfortable at home ever opted for Fernando Po'."[90] Indeed, the pattern of recruitment seems to have been distinctively opposed to a typical "migration model" where a series of focal village-groups produce networks of emigrants, creating a collective dependency on emigration as a communal and rural economic strategy. Rather, most of those who ended up in Fernando Po seemed to have been picked in a fragmented way and belonged to disaffiliated and marginalized groups of people from innumerable villages across a wide region. According to the local Methodist chaplain in Santa Isabel:

> It is no exaggeration to say that Lagos, Port Harcourt and Calabar are swarming with 'unemployed and down and outs'. Our Nigerian missionaries have informed me that they are constantly paying the railway fares of destitute 'boys' who have become stranded while searching for work in Port Harcourt. Fernando Po on the other hand, has large plantations of cocoa and coffee and yet she is so scantily populated that without imported labour, the plantations cannot be properly worked, and are in constant danger of going 'back to bush.'[91]

Low-level British officials in the region, who drew on local informants for their regular reports, noted that in this period the wages and conditions in Fernando Po made the island attractive only to the most "miserly situated labor" in Nigeria, and that migrants to the island tended to arrive "completely destitute and penniless," and many "had never worked before" in the imperial sense. They were drawn from the ranks of those who for assorted reasons could not find work in Nigeria, including absent social and kin relations that facilitated money making opportunities and the sums of money needed to pay the initial *dash* that would secure placements, training, and apprenticeships in Nigeria it-

Land has Changed, 259–262; Okolie, "Transformation of Eastern Nigeria," and Robins, *Oil Palm*, 139–141.

89 British VC (Michie), February 28, 1941, "Appendix C: List of Recruiters and Canoemen," TNA, FO 371/26908.

90 Tapela, "Cross River Basin," 210, 212; Ejituwu, "Anglo-Spanish Employment Agency," 50.

91 Ewart Shepherd, "Nigerian Labourers in Fernando Po," *West Africa*, London, May 13, 1939.

self. Some also had their own reason for "a hasty exit from Nigeria, e.g. debts, taxes unpaid, family disputes," for example one Ekepenyon Essien Ekepenyon, formerly a clerk of the Native Court at Awa who was wanted by the police for absconding from his post with over £100 and who escaped a seven-year prison sentence by going to the island.[92] The "evil" reputation of Fernando Po advanced at the same pace as the spread of the "illegal recruiters in the widely scattered areas of recruitment."[93] Touts quickly "gained a very unsavoury reputation" in almost the entire colony of Nigeria after "cases of kidnapping were brought to light," but colonial officials assumed they achieved "some success," "because the very dense population in Onitsha and Owerri Provinces had created a class of landless peasants, who were compelled to turn to wage earning for a livelihood."[94] But on closer inspection it was clear to those doing the investigative groundwork, such as the British district officer of Itu, that only "through such agencies as may exist in Calabar," that is "through the instrumentality of a 'recruiting agent'," would anyone "find" their way into the island's plantation contracts.[95]

Unauthorized emigration and unlicensed recruiting were banned in Nigeria as part of the Labour Ordinance No. 1 of 1929 which was formulated and directed at Spanish Guinea specifically. The code targeted laborers themselves who were presumed to only leave Nigeria to escape family and government obligations. British subjects were not permitted to accept foreign contracts "without the sanction of an administrative officer, under a penalty of £25 and/or three months imprisonment." The officer had to "satisfy himself that the native is fit to work, is over the age of 16, is not abandoning any dependent relatives, and is not absconding to avoid liability under native law."[96] While British district officers were generally pleased to see the "acceleration of the drift," as they called the emergence of a "pool of surplus labour" or the "tendency of young men to drift to centers of semi industrial employment," they worried about the "drain of labour to foreign possessions," but not only for mercantilist reasons. This "drain" was imagined to arise from both the "avarice" of recruiters and the pro-

92 British LO (Evans) to British Consul General, Douala, August 31, 1945, NAE, CALPROF 17/1/278; British VC and LO (Bradley), July 4, 1956, TNA, CO 554/1346; Chief Secretary Office, Lagos to GG (Manresa), July 7, 1930, AGA, C-81/8146, E-1.

93 British LO (Lewis), Calabar to Commissioner of Labor, Lagos, December 6, 1943, NAE, CALPROF 5/1/193.

94 Nigerian Secretariat, Lagos, August 1953, RHL, 600.18 s. 21/XI (10).

95 DO Itu to Resident, Calabar Province, January 11, 1939, NAE, CALPROF 5/1/194; Commissioner of Police, Calabar to Resident, Calabar Province, August 1, 1935, NAE, CALPROF 5/1/192.

96 Aworawo, "Decisive Thaw," 93: Orde Browne, *African Labourer*, 154.

miscuous expectations of "the uneducated young man, in search of easy money."[97]

Fernando Po's recruiters were not integral members of the colonial or corporate bureaucracy, nor did they tend to be the accommodated sons and daughters of the former aristocratic families of Calabar. In relation to the smuggling of laborers to Fernando Po, the political activist from Uyo, Okon Archibong, rhetorically asked as to the cause of the revival of "this slavish act" and unambiguously answered: the "United Africa Company are to blame, because they compete our traders and women," rendering "the country [Nigeria] economically helpless. People therefore resolve to undertake inhuman industry."[98] Nigerian journalists and writers endlessly discussed British monopoly capital: "When we come to think of the activities of some [British] mercantile houses among us, our souls simply rebel [for] these representations of big buisness [...] skin the people to the very bones in the matters of purchasing their produce." Others asked a series of soul-searching questions, posed in a strange rupture of the British empire, along a breaking point of colonialism and anti-colonialism, balancing at the seams of a resuscitated Atlantic practice:

> why waste time talking of exploitation by [British] interest, of pools and combines and other inequities, if we can contemplate with equanimity the sale and purchase of our youths and young men into foreign servitude? Is it nothing to you that shameless Nigerians are waxing fat on the sale of the sons of this country? If this does not make your blood boil, then the New Africa is a mirage and a worthless dream.[99]

Economies of Deception

A Spanish petty functionary on the island writing in December 1936 explains the modus operandi: "deceitful methods operate in la *recluta* and this is well known by all, well if it wasn't for the manipulation of appearances, the *indigenas* would not come to work for us."[100] Another colonial official noted that while it was "not always necessary to employ cunning and trickery and other despicable proce-

97 DO Opobo to Resident, Calabar Province, June 20, 1947, NAE, CALPROF 3/1/1447; Resettlement Office, Uyo to Resident, Calabar Province, July 1, 1947, NAE CALPROF 3/1/1447.

98 O. Archibong to Resident, Calabar Province, January 23, 1939, NAE, CALPROF 5/1/194.

99 J. Abala Egbe, "Mr. Sosoo," *Eastern Nigeria Guardian*, Port Harcourt, February 22, 1945; "Spanish Slavery, *The Nigerian Eastern Mail*, Calabar, March 11, 1939.

100 Babiloni, January 1937, AGA, C-81/12427.

dures, but at least half" were "set up" this way.[101] It was a good estimate, as various surveys confirm that at least half the Nigerian recruits in this period "claimed ignorance of knowing that they were being taken to work in the Spanish Cocoa plantations."[102] Timothy Farley Smith, a one-man British commission of inquiry and negotiation delegation sent to the island during the whole summer of 1939, rounded down his own similar estimate that around "50 %" of those "taken" to Fernando Po were not "willing to go there," to "possibly 15 %." These "15 %," he says, were apparently "for the most part, credulous youths lured there under false pretenses."[103]

Farley Smith had rounded down this figure because like other British colonial officials who had investigated this "traffic," he considered himself able to "detect carefully prepared lies" and discern "carefully crafted stories" from sight and sound alone – imputing a calculating shrewdness to the recruits that was simultaneously denied to them.[104] He "arrived at this figure" after "listening to complaints and making inquiries on the Island" and excluding those "for whom it is natural that having gone willingly and finding they do not like the conditions make as good a story as possible in their efforts to return to Nigeria before completing their contracts."[105] "On arriving at the farms they find the work hard and the hours long" and "no doubt," says the resident British Vice-Consul, "their contract and forced stay of two years appear to be insufferable, hence their pitiable appeals for assistance."[106] An undercover Nigerian policeman reports that "they are all now in the Spanish Plantations serving their term regretfully [...] really suffering a lot and many of them had died – death occasioned by brutal and hard treatment unaccustomed to from the time of their Birth."[107]

A better barometer attesting to the fact that most *braceros* did not want to be there, even if they agreeingly followed misleading expectations, is a revealing incident in the summer of 1940, echoing the exceptional strike of the 500 Yoruba

101 Guillermo Cabanellas, *La selva siempre triunfa: novela del África española* (Buenos Aires: Editorial Ayacucho, 1944), 35.

102 Ejituwu, "Anglo-Spanish Employment Agency," 47.

103 Nigeria and Timothy Farley Smith, *Report on Employment of Nigerian Labour in Fernando Poo* (Lagos: Government Printer, 1931), para. 6.

104 British VC (Smallbones) to FO (Grey), October 13, 1913, TNA, FO 367/353; British LO (Evans) to British Consul General, Douala, January 31, 1945, TNA, FO 371/49598.

105 Nigeria and Farley Smith, *Report*, para. 6; Governor's Deputy, Lagos to Sec. of State for the Colonies (MacDonald), London, August 23, 1939, TNA, FO 371/23171.

106 British VC (May) to Resident, Calabar Province, September 13, 1934, TNA, FO 458/126; also in NAE, CALPROF 5/1/192.

107 S. Muyiwa to Commissioner of Police, Calabar, May 24, 1936, NAE, CALPROF 5/1/194.

braceros from 1900. Spain was neutral during World War II, but the British considered them potential enemies and the island was initially a safe harbor for Germans and Italian subjects and ships until the British navy was able to embargo all enemy commercial interests in the region by squeezing them out of shipping routes through so-called "navy-certs." There must have been much tension in the air as a "rumor had spread" among "the Nigerians residing on the island" that a British navy ship was waiting at the harbor in Santa Isabel to "repatriate all British subjects." *Braceros* started "abandoning their place of work en masse"; descending from the "plantations on the hills," they "started to fill the *Plaza de España*," the central square of the capital by the harbor. They were "gathering on the docks too, and all were carrying their heavy luggage with them." Planters were of course "very alarmed, they thought they would lose all their *braceros*, as you know, the *indígenas* of Nigeria make up over ninety percent of all the *braceros* of this island."[108] The militarized police, the *Guardia Colonial*, returned everyone to the plantations, because of the planter's perennial concern: "imagine the damage to our agriculture and our colony, if the only source of labor that is available to us now would meet with any sudden interruption."[109]

The recruiters used "lies, deceit, and stealth to get labour from Nigeria," says a journalist in the Nigerian Eastern Mail during an outpouring of the reading and writing public in the Nigerian and international press in 1939.[110] Scholars who have seen a range of sources say that "recruiters resorted to deception to entice young men to leave their homes." Recruiters "were in the habit of making exaggerated promises [and] of hiding the fact that the labourers were going to Fernando Po." The "sweet-tongued recruiter convinced his victims that Fernando Po was a haven of wealth easily extracted from apprenticeships, shop-assistantships and domestic stewardships."[111] As Farley Smith says, the recruit was "stuffed with sufficient falsehoods to induce him to accompany the recruiter to Fernando Poo or sufficiently far on the journey as to make it impossible for him to turn back when he finds out the truth."[112] David Aworawo notes that those "drawn to a new land by the better-than-factual stories," went side by side on the same canoes "smuggled across the waters in the Bight of Biafra," with those that may have experienced the movement as conforming to predictable

108 Secretario General to GG (Fontán), July 9, 1940, AGA, C-81/8806, E-1.
109 Cámara (Carbonell) to GG (Bonelli), June 17, 1947, AGA, C-81/8179, E-5.
110 "The Fernando Po Slave Traffic," *The Nigerian Eastern Mail*, Calabar, February 25, 1939.
111 Pratten, *The Man-Leopard Murders*, 166; Osuntokun, *Equatorial Guinea*, 27; Tapela, "Nigerian Labour," 48.
112 Nigeria and Farley Smith, *Report*, para. 6.

or transparent expectations.[113] Touts were not a service bureau and operated at a significant "distance," creating a space of manipulation and indifference. They wielded no weapons, they could not even be too intrusive, they simply latched on to people who were already on the move, redirecting the desire of migrant laborers and leading them to thwarted hopes and an unwilling fate on Fernando Po.

Dandeson Green, a Krio from Calabar, a friend of Alfredo Jones, and a "veteran Calabar reporter" with pro-colonial credentials, writes that while "many Nigerian labourers went to Fernando Po of their own accord, [a] very considerable number are taken, either by force or with the promise of 'Utopia', by ruthless smugglers and illegal native recruiters."[114] Ruthless peddlers of "utopia": the "chief trouble is caused by the army of recruiters who entice young people away, their story of Fernando Po being a land 'flowing with milk and honey' is, however, true," says another journalist with experience on the island.[115] Spanish and Fernandino colonists had always been trying to spread this paradoxical message, which is why they were often confounded by and in denial about the constant transformation of a positive and promotional self-image to a negative reputation: "The island of Fernando Poo has achieved a good reputation along the entirety of the coast, it is known as a place of abundance, an easy life, of richness for the black worker, who on his days off has plenty of money to spend, and where all *braceros* can acquire a wife or wives."[116]

The chief Methodist in the region based in Nigeria, Frederick Dodds, visited the island several times in this period and reported publicly how he was impressed by the facade of a fascist colony that in one stroke imprisoned or hired "vagrants" en masse. During "the whole" of his month-long trip in the spring of 1939, he "did not see a single ill-nourished" or "ill-clad" person. The Igbo- and Ibibio-speaking Dodds talked to hundreds of Nigerian *braceros* in the congregations who apparently only complained about the absence of "women" and the "lack of Bibles." Dodds obviously also "condemn[ed]" how

---

113 Aworawo, "Decisive Thaw," 92.

114 Dandeson Green, "Recruitment of Labour to Fernando Po is done under Treaty with Spanish Govt," *Eastern Nigeria Guardian*, Port Harcourt, April 17, 1947; Dandeson Green was in 1952 appointed "Labour Delegate to the Agency" for licensed recruitment to "provide propaganda which will encourage recruitment and to combat any adverse criticism by the popular press in the Eastern Region, Nigeria." British VC and LO (Bradley), September 31, 1952, TNA, FO 371/96714.

115 "Fernando Po Labour Conditions," *The Nigerian Daily Times*, Lagos, July 13, 1939.

116 Juan Bravo Carbonell, "Politica de España en África. Los braceros liberianos para Fernando Poo," *Luz*, Barcelona, December 22, 1932.

"much of the labour for the island is now being recruited. There is a constant stream of canoes filled with Nigerians, many of whom have been lured into taking the passage under promise of being taken elsewhere."[117]

The resident Methodist reverend, Ewart Shepherd, also went out of his way to publicly praise the wealth produced on the island and the access to food rations and healthcare for plantation workers. Shepherd did this as he watched the "wholesale system of smuggling across in canoes" become "in vogue." "Dozens of these canoes land their human cargoes in a little haven close to Santa Isabel. They come out of the creeks between Calabar and Victoria and the Nigerian Government is powerless to prevent them."[118] Farley Smith was "very surprised at the wholeheartedness of the praise of labour conditions" loudly voiced by the British Methodists in the British press. He presumed they feared being expelled by the new Catholic fundamentalist administration, and so Shepherd and Dodds had gone out of their way to hold up the virtues of the territory. Dozens of members of Shepherd's "flock" submitted "complaints" to Farley Smith during his tour, and he did "not believe" that the complaints "were all brought because they knew I was visiting the island and though that a good moan, however unfounded, would do them no harm and might be instrumental in improving their position."[119]

The beneficiaries of the massive smuggling operations and the seemingly fabulous wealth produced by the colonial economy of Fernando Po were always highlighted by the Nigerian press. Recruiters were said to "import foreign men to suck dry its honey."[120] For the mix of official and underhand payouts from the Spanish labor officer and individual planters, the recruiters were "prepared to shangai, trick or, by any method open to them to persuade their countrymen to come over here, provided that they themselves make a handsome profit out of the deal."[121] The "recruiters at certain seasons asks and gets as much as £15 per head [with] no questions asked," a sum higher than the wages for a

117 Dodds, July 1939, "Notes on Visit to West African District, February to June 1939," SOAS, MMS, MMS/Special Series/Notes and Transcripts/FBN 1 (fiche 15 – 17); Rev. F.W. Dodds, "Nigerian Labourers in Fernando Po," *West Africa,* London, June 24, 1939.

118 Ewart Shepherd, "Nigerian Labourers in Fernando Po. Dr. Haden Guest Misinformed? Allegations of Slavery Cannot be Substantiated," *West Africa*, London, May 13, 1939; Leslie Haden Guest, London to Sec. of State for the Colonies (MacDonald), February 20, 1939, TNA, CO 554/119/5.

119 Farley Smith, Lagos to Nigerian Secretariat, Lagos, August 2, 1939, TNA, FO 371/23171.

120 "Writer vehemently condemns idea of Labour Recruiting to Fascist Territory," *Eastern Nigeria Guardian*, Port Harcourt, March 1, 1945.

121 British VC and LO (Bradley) to Commissioner of Labor, Lagos, April 14, 1953, TNA, FO 371/102612.

two year contract and about the same as the average annual income in the Nigerian Eastern Provinces.[122] Indeed it was the "lucrative commissions" which Fernando Po's recruiters could command that gave their activities, in the eyes of scandalized colonial contemporaries, "the character of a slave trade."[123] These commissions were seen by British colonial officials across the empire as "a reward for extra cunning in inducing coolies [or even as a] compensation for the risk run in unlawfully inducing or compelling them to go." It "was risk-money, an incentive to 'iniquity' or outright crime."[124]

As noted by an earlier Spanish governor, for new recruits "planters would not only pay for their transport costs, but for taxes, passports, the wage advances that aren't usually deduced from the wages, etc. This etcetera is actually the lions share, and includes expenses which it would be prudent of us not to declare" – the "lion's share" was always the recruiter's commission.[125] The commission went well beyond the costs surrounding their labor of logistics which covered the ensemble of paddlers, bribes, and arrangements upstream and downstream. Because of this, "judged solely on the question of motive" – the "thought of nothing else but the prospect of earning the promised commission on the transaction" – recruiters were considered by one newspaper columnist after another "to stand on practically the same footing as the local slave dealers of the early days."[126] Such a high share was always formally illegal, but the recruiters escalated it by playing off competing employers against each other, and so for obvious reasons, even amongst the regular planter clients, "the feeling [was] very strong against these middlemen recruiters."[127]

Where did this commission come from? Recruited *braceros* effectively wound up paying for their own displacement. The credit circuit of delayed and recouped costs can be seen more clearly in the early 1930s when Nigerian recruiters operated through the steamship companies. A ticket to Santa Isabel, even from nearby Nigeria, was expensive, half a pound or several months' wages of a *bracero*. The recruiters paid for tickets, bribes, the necessary counterfeit paperwork, and

122 Minister of Economic Warfare, Special Operations Executive (Simpson) to Commissioner of Labor, Lagos, December 20, 1942, TNA, HS 3/77; British LO (Nery), June 17, 1943, TNA, CO 554/127/15.

123 Carles, *Misioneros, negreros y esclavos*, 34.

124 Sen, "Commercial Recruiting," 15, citing Deputy Commissioner of Ranchi (Streatfeild) to Commissioner of the Chota Nagpur Division, Ranchi, April 13, 1899.

125 GG (Manresa) to DGMC (Canovas), May 16, 1931, AGA, C-81/8095, L-2, E-20.

126 "Matters of Moment," *The Nigerian Daily Times*, Lagos, July 15, 1939; "Spanish Slavery," *The Nigerian Eastern Mail*, Calabar, March 11, 1939.

127 Commissioner of Police, Calabar to Inspector General of Police, Lagos, May 22, 1936, NAE, CALPROF 5/1/194.

other travel expenses, but those recruited were "made to sign an I.O.U. acknowledging that should they fail to take up contract on the island they would owe three pounds to the recruiter."[128] By the mid-1930s hundreds of new Nigerian recruits were arriving every month on steamers, "their passages" had been paid "by a recruiter against an IOU," but only "if they do not contract to work in Fernando Po will the IOU be enforced," meaning once a "labourer is here he is more or less forced to contract although he may not like the conditions on closer acquaintance."[129] This type of debt ticket system did not always operate on the canoe traffic, as touts tended to offer a "free ride," without tickets, only arrangements and their errant potentials. This made the barrier or "cost" of emigration effectively non-existent.

On arrival in Santa Isabel "the police department takes charge of them and see that they all get employment."[130] Immediately after disembarking "the workers are usually lodged in the Barracon a species of lodging-house under the control of the Curador" who "supervis[ed] everything to do with the contracted workers." Future *braceros* were then

> taken before the Curador Colonial or one of his staff and told that they are going to contract to Señor [so and so] for two years at five dollars a month; before this statement has sunk in they are outside the office and their contract books are being filled in. They have been contracted and it is too late for them to 'change their minds' as some of those who have persisted stating that they did not wish to contract are accused of doing.[131]

British labor officers in Fernando Po and elsewhere worried endlessly on the precise explicative moments of this contract signing, because more often than not "the contracts were so ill-explained that the effect upon the illiterate" hired worker "was the same as if they had been deliberately cheated."[132] The Vice-Consul noted that "boys are ignorant of the condition of plantation labour here, and agree to everything that is put to them in accordance with the suggestions of the recruiters."[133] "The recruiters assist in this procedure as much as they can (and they can do a great deal) in order that there shall be no argument over the fee

128 British Consul General (Yapp), Monrovia, September 17, 1936, "Report on Employment of British Coloured Labor in Fernando Po, as the Result of a Visit made August 29th-September 1st, 1936," TNA, CO 554/105/3.

129 British VC (May) to Chief Secretary to the Government, Lagos, July 6, 1936, TNA, FO 458/126.

130 Kicks-Dadzie, "Confidential Report," NAE, CALPROF 5/1/195.

131 Nigeria and Farley Smith, *Report*, para. 14, 20.

132 Mhone, *The Political Economy of a Dual Labor Market in Africa*, 78.

133 British VC (May) to Resident, Calabar Province, September 13, 1934, TNA, FO 458/126; also NAE, CALPROF 5/1/192.

that they have already agreed to accept from the prospective employer." It goes without saying that recruiters would invariably "fail to mention that employment conditions were unlike Nigeria in that the workers would be bound for two years, with very little chance of changing employer and no chance to visit home."[134]

The recruiters "name the farms or masters with whom they will work. These claimants sign for them and the [*braceros*] are taken to the Curaduria" to receive a copy of their contract. According to J.W. Kicks-Dadzie, an investigative journalist from the *Nigerian Daily Times*, it was this commission "which most of the labourers resent when they happen to hear of it." This commission was received by "unlawful recruiters mostly" or otherwise "old hands who return with boys to his Master," former employees who returned with new *braceros.*[135] For "new arrivals" the extent and amount of commissions handed over to recruiters was often "completed over their heads," they were "not aware that the tout had made capital out of the recruitment and that the employer has had to pay far more than may appear."[136] Canoe passengers "found themselves to their dismay, being disembarked at Santa Isabel (Malabo) and auctioned to waiting plantation owners."[137] The substantial wage advances that were sometimes promised to them usually just became added to the recruiter's commission. Touts may or may not have divided it again and paid out a part of it to laborers, but this possibility is rarely mentioned in the archive, so it seems that almost no one ever saw the *dash* the first time around. Instead, they were met with an irrevocable contract lasting a minimum of two years, with formal monthly wages equivalent of the local sale price of three large yams a month.

Ekpe Eyo, a Christian convert from Uyo, managed to get a letter through to his father via the Methodist mission in Fernando Po, written in Ibibio, and naming his recruiter, a trader who frequented his home town: "greet Etim Asibong warmly for me for he brought me here to stay here, and went back in peace and earned his money and ate things and live and let me die and suffer."[138] An anonymous letter from a laborer in Fernando Po does not explain how he has was recruited, and irrespective of whether he was deceived as to the destination, he says that "an eket man has brought me here to sell for 7£, if god keeps me alive until it reaches the years for which he sold me, i shall come

134 Nigeria and Farley Smith, *Report*, para. 20.

135 Kicks-Dadzie, "Confidential Report," NAE, CALPROF 5/1/195.

136 British VC (Lewis) to Commissioner of Labor, Lagos, June 11, 1946, NAE, CALPROF 17/1/278.

137 Tapela, "Nigerian Labour," 48.

138 Ekpe Eyo, Santa Isabel to Eyo Ubon, Afaha Atai, Uyo, Calabar Province, September 2, 1938, NAE, CALPROF 5/1/194 [original in Ibibio in NAE, CALPROF 5/1/195].

home."[139] An Ibibio petitioner on the island representing a group of imprisoned workers denounced the "traders bringing the people to this country in awfully way" because they were "saying that we were going to Tico or Victoria," on an offer to work in the large British and German plantations in British Cameroons. Many of these plantations on the mainland were only accessible by water and the laborers there were increasingly from Nigeria who were "for the most part recruited by Efik contractors belonging to Calabar" and were brought "by canoe from Oron." The petition ends with a thesis which is difficult to interpret but suggests the element of being cheated out of the advances: "I am telling you fact and clearly that [the] canoe-men [are] total selling person to those people [planters] by a great lot of money. That's why slave is better than us in thousand upon thousand way."[140]

Only the disappointment arising from deception could amplify the experience of enslavement. For those who were able to report about what happened to them, the delayed realization of *panya*, the meaning of the commission and the awareness that the entire process of advanced valorization came at their expense and immediate future is why they unambiguously considered themselves enslaved. They were bound only on site and working off non-existent debts they had not even successfully contracted. It is not a coincidence that the recruitment fee, the "good sum of money" paid "to these so called labour 'organizers' whose secret rendevouz is reported to have been around Oron," was exactly the same sum, if not slightly higher, than the price of a slave two generations earlier. Before the outlawing of the largest and most frequented slave market of the Cross River at Itu in 1901, upriver from Oron, and largely run by Efik, Aro, Abam, and Abriba slave merchants, "the price of a slave was approximately five pounds sterling."[141]

In 1939, the journalist Kicks-Dadzie interviewed the new Spanish police chief, Miguel Llompart Aulet, and implored him to "chase the wicked canoe traffickers out of the Island," to which Llompart flatly replied that he could "not possibly put a stop to it" as otherwise "they will not get labourers at all." Yet, even Kicks-Dadzie went on to publicly praise the "highly scientific farming" of

139 "Letter to Etim" [n.d., received by the Resident at Calabar from the Hope Weddell Institute in July 1934], NAE, CALPROF 5/1/192.

140 Petition signed "Your Prodigal Sons" to Resident, Calabar Province, March 24, 1936, NAE, CALPROF 5/1/194; Orde-Browne, *Labour Conditions*, 74.

141 Uchendu, "Slaves and Slavery in Iboland," 126. These £5 would be equivalent to about £8 in 1939 and £15 in 1945, and similarly to the £2 to £3 pounds a European slave trader would have paid an Efik merchant in 1840 for a slave. Lovejoy and Richardson, "The Initial 'Crisis of Adaptation,'" 45.

Fernando Po's large settler plantations as well as its "full" employment policy, as this allowed "no room for idlers, vagabonds and thieves."[142] The entire situation was heavy with paradoxes: rejections of regressive revivals of the "slave trade" combined with a simultaneous embracing of the "most advanced" agricultural economic form, the imagining of a peaceful and prosperous economic order and the undertaking of awry and absolutely deviated journeys to get there, profound tragedies mixed with attempts to allocate, weigh, and divide culpability. A famous columnist in Calabar, in 1947, signing off with the name *Candidus*, writes without adding punctuation as the two points are related: "We are told that these recruits are officially designated as *lazy Nigerians* and it is slur on ibibo and ibo tribes to allow them to be sold onto slavery in foreign lands."[143]

Henderson Tapela makes the strong distinction between outright abduction and misinformation-based kidnapping. The former forms part of the topos of the slave trade and is usually referred to as such in the sources. Such instances seemed to be subdivided into two: the kidnapping of children on the one hand, and on the other of literate and educated adults, often professionals. There "was evidence that children were being stolen and sold to the island of Fernando Po in a manner similar to the kidnappings of the precolonial period," and some of the evidence suggest that such children accompanied some of the better placed migrants to the island, to work in their households.[144] On the other hand, it was quite common that the victims who were "shanghaied from Calabar" and "taken to Fernando Po against their will and arrangement" were actually ordinary passengers, "teachers, traders etc. going on business boarding canoes" which departed daily from "Oron or Calabar by night," once the colonial ferry services stopped running.[145]

Rumors of kidnapping saturated semi-anonymous intersections, but people still needed to be on the move, obligatory transit points became infused with in-

---

142 Kicks-Dadzie, "Confidential Report," NAE, CALPROF 5/1/195; Special Correspondent [Kicks-Dadzie], "Fernando Po Labour Conditions," *The Nigerian Daily Times*, Lagos, July 13, 1939.

143 Candidus, "Recruitment of Labour to Fernando Po," *The Nigerian Eastern Mail*, Port Harcourt, April 5, 1947. On aliases in Nigerian political and print cultures see Stephanie Newell, *The Power to Name: A History of Anonymity in Colonial West Africa* (Athens: Ohio University Press, 2013).

144 Aderinto and Osifodunrin, "'500 Children Missing in Lagos,'" 102; Secretary's Office, Eastern Provinces, Enugu to Commissioner of Labor, Lagos, July 14, 1949, NAE, CALPROF 7/1/458; "I was sold as a slave [to someone African in Fernando Po] at the age of two," *Daily Times*, Lagos, June 11, 1958; Robin P. Chapdelaine, *The Persistence of Slavery: An Economic History of Child Trafficking in Nigeria* (Boston: University of Massachusetts Press, 2021), 64.

145 British LO (Nery), June 17, 1943, TNA, CO 554/127/15; O. Archibong to Resident, Calabar Province, January 23, 1939, NAE, CALPROF 5/1/194.

security and alarm. Calabar sits on the eastern shore of the unbridgeable Cross River delta and the only way to reach this provincial capital was by canoe or ferry from the port town of Oron, where the "trunk" road that connected all the provinces of Eastern Nigeria started or ended. The only links to Port Harcourt and Lagos and elsewhere were likewise through ferries and boats in Calabar and Oron where at least a thousand or more people passed through every day. As Misty Bastian shows, in her classic study on women's vulnerability in the motor-parks of Onitsha, such junctures are always the "location of chicanery" where the figure of the *wayo* can fully emerge, finding victims by persuading them to board their taxis, only to either rob or sexually assault them or force them to sell their soul. Elements of the stories combine the fear of circulation and loss of autonomy, and the social dangers of an exodus of rural young people, with a moral panic – a shared, uncontrollable, and delusional medium in which the increasingly unlikely and surreal could propagate more easily. This must have been the case as well in colonial Oron and the mood of its vast hinterland. Underlying the generalized social panic, and a direct instantiation of it, was also a clear moral cosmology of the "market-place," where the treatment of people as "objects for commodification and sale" splits from the customary "positive sense" of trade or *ahia* – in contrast to *ahia panya* or faulty and unsound commerce.[146]

Even in areas far from Oron or Calabar where vulnerability was less obvious people could be cast out in deep waters, such as Peter Udo who reported that while he was "on his way home from a Cameroons plantation" he was told by the canoe-man "to change canoes" only to be "transported to Fernando Po" with five others.[147] The same canoes carried both the "misled" who were looking and expecting to work somewhere, and the outright kidnapped who disappeared from their ordinary itinerary; for example in July 1944 one canoe carried a "schoolboy from Calabar" who boarded it having been promised a job as a trading assistant on the island, "deceived by the canoeman whom he knew," as well as "a soldier who had been up country to visit his relations" making the "trip from Oron to Calabar." Both woke up the "next morning on the Island, and [were] sold and contracted."[148]

146 Misty L. Bastian, "Fires, Tricksters and Poisoned Medicines: Popular Cultures of Rumor in Onitsha, Nigeria and its Markets," *Etnofoor* 11, 2 (1998): 118; Julien Bonhomme, "The Dangers of Anonymity: Witchcraft, Rumor, and Modernity in Africa," *HAU: Journal of Ethnographic Theory* 2, no. 2 (2012): 226.

147 DO Eket to Resident, Calabar Province, January 16, 1939, NAE, CALPROF 5/1/194.

148 British VC (Lewis) to British Consul General, Monrovia, July 12, 1944, TNA, FO 371/39661.

Victims were accused of being heedless and unmindful by the colonial authorities and others. Key British officials managed to turn the way to *panya* into the failing of "simple minded natives" who "have been induced to join the canoes in the expectation of being given a lift downstream, only to find themselves landed in Santa Isabel."[149] In the late 1930s – the Governor in Lagos, Bourdillon, and the British Consul, Twigge Molecey for example – foregrounded not only a vocabulary designed to demonize mediators but also one that accused the victims themselves of backtracking or "changing their minds": on hearing the stories of those "falling into the hands of the slave-dealers," they would say that "the 'slave dealers' have little or no difficulty in obtaining persons who are willing to go with them to Fernando Po, but the latter after 6 months try to abscond as they naturally miss their freedom and are unaccustomed to hard work."[150] Some kidnapped workers also blamed themselves, but for different reasons, as Ekpe Eyo, the Ibibio who wrote to his father, said: "it was I who looked for money hence let this happen to me."[151]

District officers throughout the Eastern Provinces pithily summarized the spate of inquiries submitted by "relatives worrying over the whereabouts" of their family members who had been "taken away by strangers to work at Calabar." But not having "been traced," their "relatives fear that they have been shipped to Fernando Po." Recruiters were shifting further north and west, and everywhere they had been seen "prevailing on youths by specious promises and glowing accounts of conditions obtaining in the plantations near Calabar and in the Cameroons, to accompany them" only to end up being "taken to Santa Isabel."[152] Colonial authorities fixated on the narrative that the broker could get away with subterfuge because of the "gullible" and "ignorant peasants from the Ibo and Ibibio areas" who were being brought over to the island by "unscrupulous native 'black-birders' who earned a lucrative livelihood by kidnapping them."[153] It is as if they were displacing blame onto the absence of an internal-

---

149 British VC (Twigge-Molecey) to British Consul General, Monrovia, February 18, 1939, TNA, CO 554/119/5.

150 Commissioner of Police, Buea, Cameroons to Resident, Calabar Province, January 31, 1934, NAE, CALPROF 5/1/192; British VC (Twigge-Molecey) to Resident, Calabar Province, November 30, 1938, NAE, CALPROF, 5/1/194; Governor of Nigeria (Bourdillon), Lagos to Sec. of State for the Colonies (MacDonald), London, February 15, 1939, TNA, CO 554/119/5.

151 Ekpe Eyo, Santa Isabel to Eyo Ubon, Afaha Atai, Uyo Division, Calabar Province, September 2, 1938, NAE CALPROF 5/1/194.

152 DO Uyo to Resident, Calabar Province, January 11, 1939, NAE, CALPROF 5/1/194; DO Abak to Resident, Calabar Province, May 10, 1939, NAE, CALPROF 5/1/195; DO Opobo to Native Court Clerks, Ibibio and Annang, January 1939, NAE, CALPROF 5/1/194.

153 Nigeria, *Annual Report 1943*, 11.

ized concept of "due diligence" prior to a transaction, while still able to express a cold pity towards beings they considered not yet appropriately twisted within a political economy – paranoiac, pre-emptive, never at ease, shrewd from the outset, gliding across space only through sovereign movements.

The fine-grained archival material – hundreds of depositions, letters home, voices from police and press reports, etc. – reveal that each recruitment case or scenario had its own iteration of creative opacity and varying degrees of misinformation. Experiences varied, for example: Affiat and a group of his friends were recruited by "one lady in Henshaw-Square at Calabar named Ne Edak" who was "making a great craftiness before she" brought them to a plantation belonging to a Spanish lawyer, Estrada, "the worst farm in the Fernando Poo"[154]; Denis Ama from Owerri, in contrast was completely unfazed by recruiters and did not raise any issues regarding working conditions. He says he went "to Calabar to search for work" and had been a laborer at a British colonial "palm factory," then at an Efik-owned plantation at Adiabo and then at Fernando Po, where his "duty is general clearance and cocoa seed plantation – we dig holes and lots of grass clearing"[155]; Akpan Okono accompanied his brother on his journey to Fernando Po because he had heard "there was much money and that it would be easy to save up"; Okpay Awa, from a village in Bende, had "followed his friend Kalu Ukay who told him he was going to work in Victoria" but Kalu "brought him to Oron and handed him over to the canoe-man Sambo Ekpa"[156]; Bronwson Edem Ekong of Eket had started to trade foodstuffs but "lost his money and became stranded" on the island and so he hired himself to a plantation where "tobacco, snuff and free medical treatment" was provided, and subsequently embarked on a short career as a tout until he was arrested in 1938[157]; Anele Nwosu and Elijah Chiolu of Owerri were

> at Nwaniba, Uyo, as part-time labourers to U.A.C. [United Africa Company] and at other time as petty traders [when] one Abriba man advised us to accompany him to Victoria

154 Petition signed "Your Prodigal Sons" to Resident, Calabar Province, March 24, 1936, NAE, CALPROF 5/1/194.

155 Denis Ama, Calabar, October 10, 1933, "Deposition," NAE, CALPROF 5/1/192.

156 Inspector de Trabajo (Blesa Boloix), Santa Isabel, June 20, 1948, "Informe: Finca de Don Antonio Fernandez y Cia," AGA, C-81/8214, E-1.

157 DO Calabar to Resident, Calabar Province, December 3, 1932, NAE, CALPROF 5/1/192; The names of the other five arrested recruiters were George Oke, Stephen Onwutibe, Bassey Umo, Bassey Okon, and Peter Esien, "two of whom are Ibos, three Efiks and one Ibibio." Supt. of Police, Calabar to Commissioner of Police, Lagos, December 30, 1938, NAE, CALPROF 5/1/194; British LO (Lewis), Calabar to Commissioner of Labor, Lagos, December 6, 1943, NAE, CALPROF 5/1/193.

> as traders. The two of us conjointly bought 100 yams (£5), two bags crayfish (£1.16/-) and two tins of palm oil (18/-). We all embarked on a canoe at Nwaniba. To our surprise the Abriba man (Eni) clandestinely brought us to Fernando Poo and contracted us to work for Aselope at Bispa;

Wilson Bassey, a "probationary Teacher" who in 1944 "resigned due to my aim of joining the army," but on his way to Calabar the "junior clerk in John Holt Office called Utche deceived me not to join the army" by promising him a clerical job "in the shop" of a merchant in Fernando Po. In a moment of indecision that he came to regret and remembering his anxiety during his job search, he confides to the British Consul whom he petitioned: "as you know an applicant's heart is always in a circulation and not steady." Wilson had been in *panya*, he had been taken: "a matter of no help as I am under contract, I am serving as a labourer in the plantation of Finca el Pino. It is a great pity to me as I am such great suffering."[158]

The final pages of this section are dedicated to a quite typical case of *panya* recruitment, described with as much detail as the archive makes possible. Late in 1938, the District Officer (DO) of Eket went on tour of his division and at Okopedi, the last town on the road to Oron from Aba, his translator, out on a late evening stroll, "Mr. J.I. Peter, met a party of 19 Ibo men" marching "on foot to Oron." This party was unusually quiet, they "had removed [their] boots for the night march," but "he overheard [them] grumbling to each other that they could not see why they should be made to travel at night." They had "started out from Aba in a lorry" that morning and at Okopedi they stopped to meet the paddling crew, to plan a rendezvous in "one of the little creeks near Okopedi where canoes will be waiting." Startled and after some commotion, the party was led to the nearby rest house where the DO was staying the night. The DO tried to arrest the only non-Igbo among them, while remembering being quietly impressed with "George Matthew Offiong, alias Asuquo Bassey" whom he described as a "literate, rather smooth-tongued person."

Under interrogation "Offiong insisted that he had been sent by Mr.H.G. Brown Manager of the Adiabo Plantation", a U.A.C. rubber plantation east of the Cross River near Calabar, "to recruit labour, but he had no document to prove this." Offiong had "represented to the men" the same story, and by "his own statement" recounts how he had "secured introductions" to "a chief (whose name, the men say, is Abang Chibwu) and by means of those persons re-

158 "Statement of Anele Nwosu of Ameke Owerri and Elijah Chiolu of Umuochita Diobu, Ohoada Division," in British VC (Lewis) to DO Uyo, February 17, 1949, NAE, CALPROF 7/1/464; Wilson Bassey to British LO, June 9, 1946, NAE, CALPROF 17/1/279.

cruited 19 men." Before they left Aba, "the men demanded that the conditions of service be given to them in writing"; insisting that they "would not have gone unless they had the conditions in writing." Offiong did produce a document, it was indispensable and incriminating, its strength and weakness was that it could be deployed with brazen confidence and meticulously inspected. It was a sheet of paper with the header – typo and all – "Robber (sic) Plantation Adiabo." This was a felicitous spelling mistake, both because it caught the DO's eye and confirmed his suspicion, and because Offiong, while not exactly a "robber" or bandit, was almost an expert at total dissimulation. His hermeneutic literacy came from being able to show people what they were looking for, and lay pictures over traps, in a tout's pose, with arms and hands tucked behind one's back.

While the DO was "convinced, he was trying to carry [them] away to Fernando Po" he "had no charge against Offiong." There had been no "offence in the nature of deprivation of liberty" as there was "nothing in the Criminal Code to prevent a person inducing another to accompany him under false verbal promises." The DO called it a night and "advised" the recruits to "keep an eye on" Offiong, and this "they did, and when Offiong tried to go away during the night, they stopped him." The "next morning" Offiong changed his story and tried to persuade the DO that "in fact he was recruiting labour, not for the United Africa Company, but for 'his father's plantation at Akpabuyo near Calabar'."[159] Michael Offiong was sent to Eket prison – not for beguiling or controlling representations in the minds of others but for "forgery and uttering false documents." It is not clear how long he was in prison – not long for sure – the DO was unaware that he had stumbled on one of the main recruiters based out of Calabar, operating since the mid-1930s with a handful of large Spanish planters as regular clients and a small fleet of five canoes at his disposal, with at least 60 rowers.[160] Within a few years of the incident at Okopedi, Michael Offiong alias Asuquo Bassey was back in Santa Isabel, and with a trail of forgeries and bribed officials in his wake, in a single day in December 1942 he passed on 100 future *braceros* to the police and labor office combine at Santa Isabel.[161]

The larger recruiting operations continued to operate and expand, or if some figures in the chain were arrested and removed their absence was temporary as

---

159 DO Eket to Supt. of Police, Aba, November 24, 1938, NAE, CALPROF 5/1/194; DO Eket to Resident, Calabar Province, January 16, 1939, NAE, CALPROF 5/1/194.

160 Michael Offiong was a prominent name on an early list of "persons suspected of recruiting" when the traffic was conducted on the backs of forged permits and colonial steamships. Commissioner of Police, Calabar to Agent, Elder Lines, Calabar, June 4, 1936, NAE, CALPROF 5/1/194.

161 AT Santa Isabel, December 8, 1942, "Relacion de los reclutadores que salen para Calabar," AGA, C-81/15865, E-12; British VC (Michie), February 28, 1941, TNA, FO 371/26908.

others took their place. A well-known recruiter, Louisa Souza, known as the "Dahomey woman," who the Vice-Consul in 1936 was told by "various Calabar natives here, [was] a notorious recruiter," was more active than ever a decade later, and over time she relied on different recruiters down-stream. Interrogated on the island by the Vice-Consul she simply responded that she was "a counsellor and friend to the boys in their journey to Fernando Poo."[162] She was related to a large Fernandino planter, Amado M. Souza, who decades earlier had come from Benin and belonged to a notable Aguda family. In 1945, the "Dahomey woman" was still "regularly going to Nigeria by canoe" and she continuously reappears in the archive as one of a large handful of shanghaiing culprits. Friday Akpan was one of her victims and he reported her accomplice, the canoe owner Godwin of Abak from Eket, who "took me here and handed me to Serra," or Vaz Serra, a big Portuguese planter in San Carlos who regularly received labor from Louisa Souza: "I have not been paid for three months. I went to a farm and reported my trouble to my relative. I was caught there and sent to prison. I am still in the prison. My employer said that she paid a fat sum to Godwin and that I am her slave."[163] Apart from the other insights this letter communicates, the relationship between Souza and the "canoeman" Godwin was not fully coordinated or integrated but rather ad hoc and transactional, one of supply and delivery, as was her relationship with Vaz Serra. Among recruiters themselves there were also many strictly commercial conflicts. For example, a recruiter, Mary Bassey Duke, from Duke Town in Calabar but who intermittently lived in an apartment in Santa Isabel rented from the Fernandino Collins, actually initiated proceedings against Luisa Souza in the civil court of Santa Isabel in 1940 for having "the 11 *braceros* she sold to the Casa Perez e Hijo taken away" from her by the "Dahomey woman."[164]

162 British VC (May) to Resident, Calabar Province, January 15, 1936, NAE, CALPROF 5/1/194 or TNA, CO 554/105/3.

163 British VC (Lewis) to British Consul General, Douala, November 30, 1944, TNA, FO 371/49598 or NAE, CALPROF 17/1/227; British VC (Nery), June 17, 1943, TNA, CO 554/127/15.

164 Contador de la Sección Económica de Hacienda, October 6, 1942, "Relacion nominal de los patronos que han sido sancionados," AGA, C-81/08128, E-13; AT Santa Isabel, June 2, 1940, "Palabra Civil: Interesados Marry Bassey Luisa Sousa relativo a la reclamacion de 11 braceros," AGA, C-81/8527, E-40.

Control or Blame

The British Labour Ordinance of 1929 regulating emigration hoped to "ensure that illiterate or inexperienced men were safeguarded against rapacious employers, traders and others," but this concern about undue influences or duress coming from stranger-brokers was not one the colonial state could enact or pursue.[165] The British administrative impulse was to "de-victimize" emigration by removing randomness and innocence, though this by itself did not lead to reducing exploitation nor the commission – the entire "engine" of recruitment. Even when the British overhauled their surveillance – the first base of the colonial Nigerian navy was eventually created in Calabar for precisely this reason – the border state unfolding beyond the customs wharf and check-points was being consistently outmaneuvered. Fernando Po's touts concealed many things but not themselves, and so they could tout undisturbed at riverside markets and junctions simply without mentioning the destination, riding on one of the many thousands of canoes that regularly travelled the waterways up and down the Cross River and its tributaries and delta.

Many British officials considered the tout a "modern successor of the slaver," capable of "any sort of roguery or deceit to cajole his victims."[166] The transference of this label left them in a quandary, because they could not directly interrupt the "flow." To beguile is to steal time through language; there is no place to physically "cut" it. The "lie" in British colonial law, as in many other juridical traditions, had a "natural" legal impunity, and the actual prosecution of fraud in civil and criminal courts notoriously required substantial evidence. Touts treaded on fine lines and legal grey areas; they only became liable to significant punishment and penalties when they crossed a border out of Nigeria. In Nigeria the prescribed punishments in the Labour Ordinance, amended in 1932 (No. 17), in the sections "Unlawful recruiting of Labour" as well as "Assisting a native to leave Nigeria," could be up to £100 or two years imprisonment, but made room for higher fines of up to £500 or five years imprisonment in cases where "labourers who are illegally recruited for service abroad may find themselves in a state of servitude from which they have no means of escape." Yet in the courts, fines were rarely higher than £50, usually around half that, around the same amount as the commission for depositing two new *braceros* at the *Curaduría*.

While British officials said they were keeping a "strict watch" and "all illegal recruiters against whom evidence exists are prosecuted," they papered over their

165 Nigerian Secretariat, Lagos, August 1953, RHL, 600.18 s. 21/XI (10).
166 Orde-Browne, *African Labourer*, 50, 54.

own inaction by claiming that touts were "skilled in the art of evasion and arrests are rare."[167] Up until 1938 the British "had a motor launch which was used to pursue" these "smugglers of human souls," but due to budget cuts this "service was stopped" for over half a decade, and so, as David Aworawo says, "the illegal traffickers had a field day."[168] During this key spike in the canoe traffic, the "water police" forces were themselves only being "equipped with canoes." In 1939 there were at least a hundred canoes going to Fernando Po on a regular basis. These canoes "generally sailed in convoys," "large convoys of canoes up to 20 in number" that gathered off-shore in this formation so that they could disperse in all directions if pursued by the "water police" who "proved too slow to intercept some large sea-going canoes which were said to have shown a clean set of flashing-paddles to the launch as they escaped."[169] By the end of World War II the British tossed a small sea launch into the Cross River delta, but should it "call upon the canoes to stop" practically all "escaped." British officials could only conceive of continuous armed surveillance as an effective solution: "until a regular twenty-four hour patrol can be maintained it is likely that the flourishing illegal canoe traffic will persist."[170]

British district officers watched on as some of the "great canoes of the Niger and Cross River deltas" that could be up to "seventy feet long" and carry up to 100 people including "pull-a-boys, or paddlers," "put out to open sea and make the coasts of Fernando Po, at its nearest ninety miles away."[171] The effects of World War II in Nigeria compounded recruiting to Fernando Po, as there were suddenly new dimensions that forced young men to look for alternatives to the ramping up of forced labor in the mineral industries and the even more persistent military recruiters for the war front in Burma who were sweeping the nation. In addition, demobilized soldiers were said to avoid returning home after undertaking such long travels and difficulties without first pursuing further and potentially higher renumerated work, including Fernando Po.[172]

167 Nigeria, *Annual Report 1943*, 11.

168 "The Fernando Po Slave Traffic," *The Nigerian Eastern Mail*, Calabar, February 25, 1939; Aworawo, "Foreign Policy and the Travails of Nigerian Migrants," 26.

169 Supt. of Police, Calabar to Commissioner of Police, Lagos, December 30, 1938, NAE, CALPROF 5/1/194.

170 British LO (Evans), Calabar to Commissioner of Labor, Lagos, September 23 and 18, 1943, NAE, CALPROF 5/1/193.

171 Jeffreys, "Review of Water Transport," 106.

172 British VC (Michie), February 28, 1941, TNA, FO 371/26908; Osuntokun, *Equatorial Guinea*, 36–40; Chima Korieh, *Nigeria and World War II: Colonialism, Empire, and Global Conflict* (Cambridge: Cambridge University Press, 2020), 120–124.

Colonial authorities struggled to follow and understand the organization of people smuggling. Unless they caught a canoe near Fernando Po their criminalization policy met with little success. British justice found that "illegal recruitment" was "extremely difficult to prove."[173] Leads sent in by family members who received letters from relatives did not result in convictions until the entire instrumentarium and theaters of proof could be mobilized in the local courts. In a case of 50 laborers from Ogoni and Eket working in Fernando Po in 1935, not a single person could come back to court and the magistrate did "not accept SWORN STATEMENT" as there would have been no opportunity "for cross-examination."[174] Nevertheless the six prosecutions for illegal recruitment to Fernando Po in the district courts of Calabar, Aba, Owerri, Ikot Ekpene, and Opobo in 1938 rose to over 100 in 1941, and even more in 1943.[175] This sum, in a single year, was more than double the total number of convicted cases of "child kidnapping" in Nigeria during the entire decade of the 1930s.[176]

Kicks-Dadzie, the first Nigerian journalist to enter the island after it fell to the Francoists, standing over the canoe-landing cove in Santa Isabel, observed that "the canoe traffic goes on in great number, and if any one sees the number of canoes at Fernando Poo Bly-Beach, it will appear as if our Police Department are not doing anything to stop it." It "seemed that the arrests and heavy fines are of no avail to the canoe people."[177] Kingsley Mbadiwe, a former court official and later member of the inner circle of Azikiwe's political party, the NCNC, remembered: "In the early forties one of the commonest crimes in the Eastern Region was illegal recruiting: the Region was infested with people who by specious promises, induced other people to seek employment in Fernando Po." Nevertheless, the various laws that "deal with slave dealers" proved to be "ineffective as a deterrent" as there were "always others ready to take their place because the traffic was very profitable"[178]; "the canoe men undoubtedly are seeing that they can get £20 for each labourers they can contract."[179] Touts could be arrested or

173 British LO (Lewis), Calabar to Commissioner of Labor, Lagos, December 6, 1943, NAE, CALPROF 5/1/193.

174 Commissioner of Police, Calabar to Resident, Calabar Province, August 8, 1935, NAE, CALPROF 5/1/192.

175 Supt. of Police, Calabar to Commissioner of Police, Lagos, December 30, 1938, NAE, CALPROF 5/1/194; British LO (Lewis), Calabar to Commissioner of Labor, Lagos, December 6, 1943, NAE, CALPROF 5/1/193.

176 Nwokeji, "The Slave Emancipation Problematic," 337, 342; Afigbo, *Abolition*, 106, 90.

177 Kicks-Dadzie, "Confidential Report," NAE, CALPROF 5/1/195.

178 Mbadiwe, "Nigerian Workers in Po will be protected: Government promises," *West African Pilot*, Lagos, August 26, 1954; see Lynch, *K. O. Mbadiwe.*

179 British VC (Lewis) to Supt. of Police, Calabar, January 22, 1945, NAE, CALPROF 17/1/277.

change profession; but they were an open category, constantly supplanted by various members of outlier elements of a highly commercial society, by fisherman from the Cross River delta, by traders from Dahomey who only in certain years made up "most of the offenders" arrested for "illegal recruiting," and of course former contract workers themselves.[180]

The patterns of how the ventures were financed unfortunately does not come across clearly in the archive, but it is important to note that it was not simply "canoe owners" who could undertake the traffic. Canoes could be purchased or hired, and new ones could be easily commissioned – combinations of teams and leaders shifted, and upstarts seem to have regularly appeared. Their organization recalls the distinct "unit" of the "canoe house" peculiar to "the Eastern Niger Delta," described by Nimi Warikobo as a "highly commercial, aggressively competitive" entity in "which nothing could afford to be static," and which could only continue "to function as long as it was dynamic, flourishing, and profitable."[181] In any case, it is likely that financing was the result of reinvested recruitment windfalls from the 1930s, or otherwise based on the anticipation of guaranteed commissions in Santa Isabel with profit-sharing used to organize canoe owners and the rowers, who even in the era of the slave trade traditionally received compensation partly on the outcome and success of specific ventures.

The distinctive feature of the "large sailing canoes" that could reach Fernando Po was their cloth sails that were hoisted when riding on wide stretches of water. Their use was "confined to the Calabar River estuary," especially around James Town, south of Oron and close to the ocean. The re-mobilization of the canoes was capital-intensive. The "great dug-out canoes which one sees round James-town are the most valuable possessions of their owners" costing "up to a hundred pounds or more." The price depended "not only on size and workman-ship, but also upon the character of the indwelling spirit." The landscape of the Cross River delta consists principally of mangrove, and construction of canoes was undertaken by the Ijaw people who sourced the timber "from the forested region of the upper Benin river," the "canoe forest."[182]

180 Governor of Nigeria (Bourdillon), Lagos to Sec. of State for the Colonies (MacDonald), London, February 15, 1939, TNA, CO 554/119/5.

181 Nimi Wariboko, "A Theory of the Canoe House Corporation," *African Economic History* 26 (1998): 143.

182 Simmons, "Efik," 118; Percy Talbot, *Life in Southern Nigeria: The Magic, Beliefs, and Customs of the Ibibio Tribe* (London: Macmillan, 1923), 206; Robert Smith, "The Canoe in West African History," *The Journal of African History* 11, no. 4 (1970): 521.

Figure 9: Dug-out canoe with sail on the Cross River Delta. Lorenzo Dow Turner, 1951. Anacostia Community Museum, Smithsonian Institution.

Canoes and canoe rowers could be hired from the most preponderant owners of these, the large aristocratic "houses" of the several Efik clans based in Calabar. The Efik gentry, "the lineage heads and the wealthier professional and business members of the lineage liv[ed] in Duke Town or in Creek Town" in or near the urban nucleus of Calabar. They maintained their wealth by still having a stake in the canoe trade, this time a clandestine one: they "owned most of the canoes that plied the river and sold most of the spirits that were found in the market."[183] For example, Michael Offiong, the forger of the "Robber plantation" caught almost red-handed by the District Officer at Itu cited above, belonged to the Ntiero (Eyamba) House in Calabar, the most prominent slave trading "house" of Old Calabar in the nineteenth century. However, there was no direct continuity. Why groups of canoemen, merchants, fishermen and others turned into lumpen-brokers can only be understood by constant reference to the material consequences of the solidification of British colonial rule.

---

183 Anthony I. Nwabughuogu, "From Wealthy Entrepreneurs to Petty Traders: The Decline of African Middlemen in Eastern Nigeria, 1900–1950," *The Journal of African History* 23, no. 3 (1982): 369.

By World War I "the entire waterways of Eastern Nigeria were under the control of European merchant firms." By 1928, the head administrator of Calabar Province, the so-called Resident, boasted that the concerted effort to eliminate the "older style of African middlemen" had more or less been completed.[184] Only Eket, Itu, and Ikang, "the last stronghold of the middlemen," still needed to be "attacked" by colonial export monopolies who were trying to determine their own prices. The "attack" came in the form of ever larger fees, and by requiring trading canoes to have a corresponding license number "painted on [their] prow."[185] Many canoe-based commercial ventures who had up to then dedicated themselves to the palm oil trade were forced to turn to fishing, especially of shrimp or "cray-fish," which was profitable up to a point. The economy of Calabar had sunk from its economic heights in the early nineteenth century, and in the next century "the Efik talked nostalgically of the good old days with the offshore British merchants."[186]

In the 1930s there were around 20,000 Efiks out of the 54,000 inhabitants of the Calabar district, a small number compared to the mostly Ibibio farmers of Calabar Province and even smaller in relation to the very densely settled Igbo areas of the Nigerian Eastern Provinces with several million inhabitants. By the early 1930s the "majority of Efik trading middlemen had withdrawn from the trade" in palm oil. Many Efik emigrated as "clerks and technicians" to other parts of Nigeria, while others turned to various forms of self-employment and "landlordism" if they could – "the occupation most favored by the Efik." With "few exceptions the EFIK is not successful as a clerk," notes a British colonial officer: "[they] have acute intellects which they seem best able to apply when they have complete independence. As soon as they come under control lethargy overcomes them."[187]

Complicating matters was the fact that agents of the Nigerian administration were partaking in or benefiting from the traffic. The extent of the involvement of the Nigerian police and other officials is not clear. Sergeant Muyiwa, the police officer with a heart of steel who went undercover to Fernando Po in 1936, shone a light on some of his colleagues, who he says had "decided that BRIBERY is the

---

184 Kannan K. Nair, *Politics and Society in South Eastern Nigeria, 1841–1906: A Study of Power, Diplomacy and Commerce in Old Calabar* (London: Routledge, 1972), 205, 210.

185 N. Mylius, 1931, "Report on Calabar Division with Special Reference to the Efik Clan," NAE, CALPROF 53/1/553.

186 David L. Imbua, *Intercourse and Crosscurrents in the Atlantic World: Calabar-British Experience, 17th-20th Centuries* (Durham: Carolina Academic Press, 2011), 130.

187 Mylius, "Report," NAE, CALPROF 53/1/553; see also Forde and Jones, *Ibo and Ibibio-Speaking Peoples*, 90.

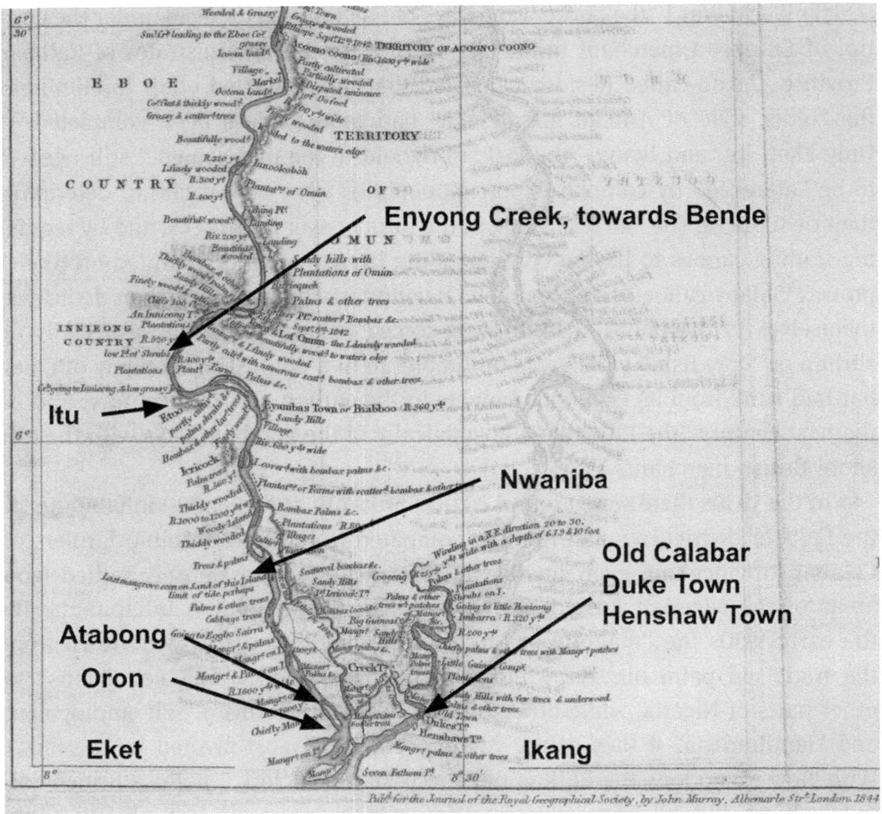

Figure 10: Cross River in 1844 with old and new relevant place labels superimposed (Beecroft and King 1844, 284).

best means of living today at a laudable manner." The "inducement made the irresponsible recruiters to corrupt many a faithful servant of the Nigerian Government for many [had] been so degenerated that some of them serve as instruments to the Recruiters."[188] Slices of these £15–25 per head found their way into various pockets. A British Colonel in 1944 found "it difficult to believe that the Calabar police really can do nothing in the matter," having heard "reports that both African policemen and Customs Officials are themselves seriously involved."[189] The Oron "native authority council" wrote to their district officer in

188 S. Muyiwa to Commissioner of Police, Calabar, May 24, 1936, NAE, CALPROF 5/1/194.
189 Security Liaison Officer for West Africa (Colonel P.E. Russell), May 17, 1944, "Illicit Traffic between Nigeria and Fernando Po," TNA, FO 371/39661.

1938 saying that the reign of a now fully insinuated colonial police force had actually promoted

> the daily increase of the number of Rogues and Criminals of all classes in Oron Clan, making the Oron Town their headquarters for evil practices. It is beyond doubt that he [the police corporal in Oron] encourages crimes and sides with these Criminals, this making the Oron Town more dangerous to stay in than in the past when there was no Police Detachment.[190]

The recruiters' central nodal point was the colonial boom town of Oron, which had a large transient population of "Ibo, Hausa and Yoruba communities," though the principal "stranger community" was "composed of Efiks from the Henshaw house" of Calabar who occupied "land owned by them."[191] Oron had been an Efik fishing settlement that by the early twentieth century was totally transformed when direct links to the "cargo boats from Liverpool" were, literally, cemented, through the mass requisitioning of forced labor to prepare the gravel for a port and to drain the creeks, after which "the merchants of Oron stated that trade grew by leaps and bounds till" it rose "to about three times that of Calabar."[192] In addition, the touts operated from the "strongholds" of Ikang and James Town close to the Atlantic coast, and the completely inaccessible delta island of Atabong, that served as "the port of embarkation and return of canoes that do the smuggling" with Fernando Po, not only of labor, but a variety of other goods. It is important to note that the delta island of Atabong and the surrounding marshlands did not belong to a particular group but was a "kind of Alsatia for surrounding tribes," "owing to the ease with which supervision can be avoided," as described by the early ethnographer of this region, Percy Talbot, who had been a district officer based in Calabar.[193]

Traffic or Treaty

The *Gobernador*, Faustino Ruiz (1949–1962), christened his long reign as the "great flourishing" of Spanish Guinea. Even the metropolitan Spanish authorities were "pleasantly surprised that cacao production has doubled since 1943

---

190 Chief Ntak Ikam Eba on behalf of Oron Native Authority Council to DO Eket, February 22, 1938, NAE, CALPROF 3/1/1953.

191 DO Eket to Resident, Calabar Province, February 29, 1936, NAE, EKETDIST 1/2/146.

192 Talbot, *Life in Southern Nigeria*, 256; Ofonagoro, "British Colonial Policy," 237.

193 British VC (Lewis) to Supt. of Police, Calabar, November 25, 1944, NAE, CALPROF, 17/1/277; Talbot, *Life in Southern Nigeria*, 317.

[and] timber exports have quadrupled," generating growth rates of between three and ten percent in the post-war decades, on the heels of a recovering Spanish metropolitan economy.[194] The conditions of this "great flourishing" were obviously linked to the growing presence of Nigerian *braceros*, but it is important to show that the "growth" itself was always negotiated with the "threat" to carry on or restart the canoe traffic even after this source had been supplanted by regulated "treaty laborers". The more or less official Spanish approach was to always leave the option open to reconnect with the illegal touts in Nigeria itself: "It is of course regrettable, but even if the Spanish Authorities want to put a halt to it, the *bracero* scarcity will always lead planters to take any necessary private steps to solve their stifling *problema*."[195] To show their upper hand and establish the tenor for negotiations, in 1945, the *Cámara Agricola, the* cacao planter lobby, petitioned the Vice-Consul for an increase of the quota of contract laborers set to go through the treaty channels, from 400 to 1,200 new workers a month for the island, in addition to a further 3,400 monthly contracts needed for the unrealized but projected growth of logging works and coffee plantations in Río Muni – signing off with the brazen bottom line of 55,000 *braceros* per year.[196]

The threat to release touts into the interior of southern Nigeria was effective because coercion existed in the ends not the means, subsisting in the structure of imperial contract law. Future *braceros* were at no point accosted or assaulted up until they refused to sign a contract at the *Curaduría*. After describing the distressing day-long passage on the ocean-going canoe, Ekpe Eyo relates how on firm ground in Santa Isabel's *Curaduría* he "argued that I will not stay, but they said that I would be sent to prison until after two years then we go."[197] Anyone "lured to the Island [had] little chance of avoiding entering into a contract once they are there,"[198] though the drift of violence could certainly start on the canoe when communication stopped. An imaginary of necessary violence retroactive infused the entirely trajectory leading up to a workplace that could be cruel and deadly. As Kingsley Mbadiwe recalls from his days collecting depositions and court files, the "recruiters did not always stop at promises of work" as "all too often a man who had to make a journey along the coast" would find

194 MAE, March 10, 1962, "Desarollo," AGA, C-81/13039, E-392.

195 Camára (Arriaga) to Anglo-Spanish Employment Agency (Serna), Calabar, October 21, 1948, AGA, C-81/8214, E-1.

196 British VC (Rylands) to Cámara (Arriaga), October 20, 1948, AGA, C-81/8124, E-1; British Consul General, Yaounde to Governor of Nigeria, Lagos, February 12, 1945, TNA, FO 371/49598.

197 Ekpe Eyo, Santa Isabel to Eyo Ubon, Afaha Atai, September 2, 1938, NAE CALPROF 5/1/194.

198 Governor's Deputy, Lagos to Sec. of State for the Colonies (MacDonald), London, August 23, 1939, TNA, FO 371/23171.

"that the canoe was putting to sea: if he asked where it was going, he would be told that it was bound for Fernando Po, and that if he didn't want to go there he could jump overboard."

Unless a canoe was already beyond the Cross River delta in Atlantic waters there would be barely sufficient reason for an accusation of false imprisonment; though definitely of reckless endangerment, as the canoes, several a year, "from being overcrowded often upset, with the loss of everybody in them."[199] Kicks-Dadzie met and even photographed "a batch of kidnapped labourers who were conveyed by canoe just a few weeks before" who told him: "Do all you can to stop the canoe traffic for [the] majority of us had perished in the Sea." They also "told [him] that on their way coming, whenever the Sea became rough, the canoe traffickers will suddenly seize one or two or more persons and case [cast] them into the Sea as sacrifice for the angry Sea god. When a canoe capsizes, not one kidnapped labourer will be saved."[200]

What happened on the open ocean is unclear. This is the only first-hand source on the matter, though there were many reports of missing canoes presumed capsized due to strong waves or tornados. Approaching this source briefly and hypothetically, it is important to note that human sacrifice had been common in Old Calabar and was conducted collectively and openly with much ceremonial pomp until the British prohibited it in the mid-nineteenth century. It was partly a targeted terrorizing submission, as only those from the new class of agricultural slaves in Akpabuyo, the growing export-orientated plantation areas opened up and owned by the Efik during the transition to "legitimate" trade, were picked as offerings. If such sacrifices did happen a century later, it would likely have occurred, as was customary, only at the beginning and end of seasonal weather patterns. In any case, the delta was also given this reputation by outsiders to the region. In the early twentieth century, a Yoruba police officer from Lagos who was accompanying Talbot on a canoe trip near Oron is supposed to have "burst into loud weeping," after water started pouring "in through the cracks on every side" of the canoe, and said: "the paddlers were bad men who would 'Drown us all for water'."[201]

---

199 Mbadiwe, "Nigerian Workers in Po," *West African Pilot*, Lagos, August 26, 1954.

200 Kicks-Dadzie, "Confidential Report," NAE, CALPROF 5/1/195. His series of unique photographs from his report are available at http://www.opensourceguinea.org/2014/11/the-kidnapped-labourers-referred-to-in.html.

201 Talbot, *Life in Southern Nigeria*, 43–44, 318. The Efik Ndem was the "tutelary deity at Old Calabar," a serpent like "male Juju, who lived on Parrot Island in the Cross River," the site of mooring British slave ships, from where it was the deity's duty "to send children, keep canoes from sinking, and help in trading ventures" by keeping the entrance from the ocean "open" with

Figure 11: Kidnapped *braceros* at a Libanio Vaz Serra plantation, San Carlos, 1939 (NAE, CALPROF 5/1/195).

Ekpenyong Etim, a trader from Calabar on the island saw how "boys came out in quantum" and "was sad when seeing them, because [they] come and die," having been brought by "those tradders [who] make tradding of boys, [not] only the tradding of goods" who "signed the boys with bad amount of 10/- [wage] in bad farm they died away hopeless." Echoing the chickens or "fowls" as a common

wealth. The sacrifice was likely to a hybrid regional variant of Mami Wata, known in Efik as *udominyan*, who was depicted in shrines as part-snake or "a fish body with a woman's head and upper torso" and epitomizing "beauty" and caprice. She "inhabits rivers, at the bottom of which she has a fine house and also fantastic wealth since she obtains everything that falls into the river from capsized canoes," and in turn she bestows those riches on the world above the surface of the water. If a pact or exchange was entered into with her, neglecting it would lead to her wrath and your ruin. Mami Wata wore jewels and gold medallions identified with trade goods, specifically artefacts of Portuguese traders, who had arrived on these same shores in the late fifteenth century, including Fernão do Pó, the voyager, himself. Talbot, *Life in Southern Nigeria*, 37; Simmons, "Efik," 347; Nkparom C. Ejituwu, "Old Calabar Rediscovered," and Martha Anderson, "From Adumu to Mami Wata: Central Ijo Water Spirit Imagery," in *The Multi-Disciplinary Approach to African History: Essays in Honour of Ebiegberi Joe Alagoa*, eds. Ebiegberi Joe Alagoa and Nkparom C. Ejituwu (Port Harcourt: University of Port Harcourt Press, 1998), 135, 260. See Robin Law, "Human Sacrifice in Pre-Colonial West Africa," *African Affairs* 84, no. 334 (1985).

sacrificial object in eastern Nigeria, Etim continues saying that "Nigeria's boys simple die like fowls, some are in the hospital with cuts because of bad treatment, and some died away with poisonous injection being given."[202] *Braceros* regularly reported human sacrifice on the island – an "accidental" by-product of production and usually related to delayed causes of sudden or mysterious deaths arising from workplace injuries, such as hernias and internal bleedings. They spoke in terms of "deliberate killings and burning of labourers by Spanish and Portuguese planters allegedly for fertility rites. Ashes from the burnt up for corpses were allegedly spread in the plantations as fertilizers."[203] A petition from a group of *braceros* who saw their friends taken away to a site of "care," the hospital, only to disappear, claimed "they are purposefully killing them in the hospital, by injecting them with a long needle mixed with potash."[204]

Potash, a common fertilizer, was imaginatively incorporating the dead, an association brought on by the shock Nigerians experienced when learning of the traditional Spanish medical tradition of cremation, producing ashes instead of an appropriately processed and buried body. As Jonathan Parry has observed in similar accounts of crushing and pulverizing human sacrifice in industry, the deteriorating relationships "between men and masters" led to a transformation of the "classical variants of sacrifice" where the "victim must represent something of value to the sacrifier," and have been "his possession or purchase," into a more aleatory and anonymous selection of victims for "modern industrial sacrifices" where "he is kidnapped or tricked" into becoming the sacrifice. The corpse or its ashes were then characteristically incorporated back into components that uphold and grow production, such as under a cement foundation or pillar, or into the growing fruits of cash crops themselves via fertilizers.[205]

---

202 Ekpenyong Etim to [n.n., probably Resident, Calabar Province], June 2, 1936, NAE, CALPROF, 5/1/194. One of Simon Ottenberg's informants in mid-twentieth century Igboland, while sacrificing a hen, called upon a deity to keep "Ibe's brother, who was working at Fernando Po [to] remain well." Simon Ottenberg, *Igbo Religion, Social Life, and Other Essays* (Trenton: Africa World Press, 2006), 113.

203 Ejituwu, "Anglo-Spanish Employment Agency," 45.

204 Anonymous, July 19, 1938, "An agonish report from Nigerian boys to the above Captain of English man of war," TNA, FO 371/22669. The Vice-Consul on the island who received copies of this letter says: "Most troubles other than those which can be surgically treated, are dealt with by injections, and it is inevitable that in cases which are incurable and the patient dies, the reason for this may be put down by the untutored native to being the result of the injections." British VC (Twigge-Molecey) to Consul General, Monrovia, July 22, 1938, TNA, CO 554/114/10.

205 Jonathan Parry, "The Sacrifices of Modernity in a Soviet-Built Steel Town in Central India," in *Religion on the Margins*, eds. Frances Pine and João de Pina-Cabral (Oxford: Berghahn Books), 240.

In negotiations with the British, the Spanish tried to pass themselves off as "absolute enemies of this system of *reclutadores.*" They tried to convince the British to legalize recruitment as the principal effect of the "presence of the prohibition" was to "foment these *reclutadores*, who with inhuman methods propagate what could alternatively be to the great benefit of the *braceros.*" Their ultimatum in these diplomatic negotiations would be based on a "reality that no one can fail to accept," the unquestionable demands of the planters that beckoned the confluence of touts and canoes. The *Gobernador*, Juan Fontán, did not consider he was asking for much, "only that they should not lay down any obstacles to our recruiting work, which in our good judgment will be to the benefit of both our colonies."[206] The British had until then repeatedly rejected various requests by the Spanish for a formalized indentured labor treaty. In response to such a request in 1930, a top diplomat in the British Colonial Office, Cecile Bottomley, recommended to his Spanish counterpart to "encourage [the] natives to work on their account, that is to say outside a regime of contract or servitude."[207]

Finally in May 1939 the British sent Farley Smith to draft up an agreement, meticulously cross-checked with various relevant League of Nations and ILO conventions. Nevertheless, when World War II broke out in September 1939 the British stopped pursuing the negotiations, it seems because the British Ministry of Warfare had planned for a possible invasion and annexation of the island. Destroying the "sovereignty" of Spanish Guinea would have only put an end to the matter if they dissolved the *Curaduría* itself.[208] Indeed one of the factors keeping Spain "neutral" during the war was the otherwise likely immediate loss of their last colonies in Africa, including prized possessions in North Africa. At the same time, the Spanish also froze the negotiations between 1939 and 1942, because they were convinced that an Axis victory could signal the expansion of their colonial territories. Franco's notorious list of "excessive" requests made in his meeting with an irritated and dismissive Hitler in 1940 at Hendaya included

---

206 GG (Fontán), January 12, 1939, "Instrucciones para el viaje a Nigeria," AGA, C-81/8131, E-3.
207 Spanish Ambassador (Barcenas), London to DGMC, June 25, 1930, AMAE, R887, E-52. Key republican reformers agreed with the characteristic British line of fearing an African proletariat: "We should guarantee the future with the existence of an indigenous capitalism, which apart from being more productive, staves off the dangers of full immersion in our civilization, which is to convert the totality of the *indígenas* into salaried workers." Eugenio Arizcun Carrera and José María Martínez y de Pons, "Memoria sobre los territorios españoles del Golfo de Guinea" (n.p, 1935), 126, BNE, AFR/13541.
208 Ministry of Economic Warfare, Special Operations Executive (Simpson) to Commissioner of Labor, Lagos, December 20, 1942, TNA, HS 3/77.

possession of French North and Central Africa as well as the parts of Nigeria and Cameroon surrounding Fernando Po in the Bight of Biafra.[209]

Only in December 1942, with effect in May 1943, was the treaty finalized on the insistence and initiative of Bourdillon, the Governor at Lagos, for whom it seemed like the best solution to "the plantation owners difficulty at present in obtaining indentured labour" and the "clandestine recruitment" of kidnapped laborers.[210] The arrangement allowed the Spanish planters' lobby to forge legal recruiting paths in Nigeria through their licensed recruiting agency, the Anglo-Spanish Employment Agency. It also provided for a British labour officer to make "attestations" of the voluntariness of the contracting before embarking on a Spanish steamship in Calabar. This paper trail for the declarations of consent was a way to have labor movements conform to the laws of exchange. It was a bureaucratic mechanism that would disenchant the labor market through a congruent arrangement of expectations and realities, make its brutal realities and disappointments finally appear legitimate, and dispel the mysticism of amoral archetypes.

The British strategy was to only allow enough laborers to start flowing out through the channels of the treaty in order to gain sufficient leverage to enforce a complete halt to illegal recruiting – to make a potential "threat to abrogate the treaty" effective. However, as the British Labour Officer who was renegotiating the terms of the agreement in 1945 says, "the Spaniards can easily call our bluff," as to "abrogate the Treaty would probably restart the human smuggling trade unless the Government is, at long last, able to provide a sufficiently strong preventative service."[211] In the early 1950s the so-called "treaty" laborers were still not "forthcoming" in sufficient numbers and the Vice-Consul feared that the Spanish would introduce new "instructions to get labour by any methods and we shall have illegal recruitment again, with all its inherent evil."[212] A series of modifications to the treaty in December 1950 and a thorough revision of its scope in October 1954, to the benefit of the Spanish, permitted the association of Spanish planters to increase the number of licensed recruiters in Nigeria to over two dozen, who were now allowed to operate across the whole of the densely populated Eastern Provinces.

---

209 José César Banciella y Bárzana, *Rutas de imperio: Fernando Póo y Guinea* (Madrid: Librería General de Victoriano Suárez, 1940), 88; see also Nerín and Bosch, *El imperio que nunca existió.*
210 Governor of Nigeria (Bourdillon), Lagos to Sec. of State for the Colonies (MacDonald), London, March 8, 1939, TNA, CO 554/119/5.
211 British LO, Calabar to Commissioner of Labor, Lagos, April 6, 1945, NAE, CALPROF 7/1/457.
212 British VC and LO (Bradley) to British Consul General, Barcelona, January 4, 1952, TNA, FO 371/96714.

Figure 12: Spanish recruiting steamship in Calabar Harbour. Lorenzo Dow Turner, 1951. Anacostia Community Museum, Smithsonian Institution.

By 1951 the Spanish had still "not been able to sensibly increase the number of Nigerian *braceros* [through the treaty], and moreover as those who were brought here are now leaving, in larger numbers than new arrivals, the *problema* is being aggravated day by day."[213] Until the very late 1950s they were not even close to filling the new permitted quota of 10,000 – and eventually 15,000 *braceros* a year recruited by less than a 100 official touts, under the revised "agreement" between Spain and Nigeria of May 1963, "for the recruitment of Nigerian adult male workers" with "the object of working in the Spanish Ecuatorial Provinces of Fernando Póo and Rio Muni." The late British colonial and early Nigerian policy was to continue to expand the "official channels" of recruiting: "the Spanish territories need Nigerian labour [and] in the absence of an Agreement the chaotic conditions that existed prior" and alongside the Treaty "would return with all their ensuing misery and suffering."[214]

---

213 Anonymous, Santa Isabel, August 17, 1951, "El problema de braceros en Guinea Española," AGA, C-81/12373, E-392.

214 Nigerian Parliament, *Report of the Parliamentary Delegation to Fernando Poo & Rio Muni 1957* (Lagos: Federation of Nigeria, 1958), 11.

Illegal recruitment only came to a meandering end in the 1950s, and never to a final resting point. By the 1950s, outright *panya* occurred only "on a very reduced scale." In any case such illegal recruits were no longer being brought into Santa Isabel directly, but were "landed in the more out of the way places" and were said to be "sold to Portuguese" planters. The Spanish police had certainly started to crack down, by handing out hefty fines and arresting touts, and so "illegal recruiters" were suddenly "finding it difficult to dispose of their wares and have taken to hawking them round the bars in the town and even then finding no buyers."[215] The Spanish authorities had even made minor concessions by promising "to allow only persons holding satisfactory travel documents to land or remain on the island." As a British colonial secretary said optimistically in 1953: "This meant that illegal recruiting – the virtual kidnapping of men against their will – came to a stop and all migration was through controlled channels which provide that the journey is made freely and without duress."[216] However, when the *Gobernador*, Faustino Ruiz, paid a visit to his counterpart in Lagos in 1953 aimed at quadrupling the annual quotas for recruitment to 10,000 a year, he "told" his counterpart in Lagos: "sure your mission is to protect Nigeria and to make sure it stays part of the British Empire, but mine is to safeguard the wealth and the economy of Spanish Guinea, and while, yes, true, the [treaty-arranged] *recluta nigeriana* is to our benefit, if push comes to shove we will get *braceros* through whatever means available to us" – in a not so veiled threat to kick-start the canoe traffic again.[217]

Panya recruiting dynamics were accentuated because of the island's consistent and renewed notoriety, so that after *braceros* returned to their home regions a new generation of workers did not follow in their footsteps but had to be sought out from elsewhere, where touts would improvise the same techniques and add onto them ever more elaborate fabrications and false guarantors. Only because of this constant drift of touts internally in Nigeria and previously across the entire coast of the Gulf of Guinea could *panya* keep working. Around 1950 there seemed to be only a large handful of "illegal recruiters still operating in the northern half" of the Eastern Provinces "where the people are more ignorant and where they can get victims by promising them work in Port Harcourt or

215 British VC and LO (Spencer-Cooke) to Commissioner of Labor, Lagos, June 26, 1950, TNA, CO 554/169/1.

216 Nigerian Secretariat, Lagos, August 1953, RHL, 600.18 s. 21/XI (10).

217 GG (Ruíz) to DGMC (Díaz de Villegas), March 25, 1953, "Impresiones de mi viaje por Nigeria," AGA, C-81/12373, E-392.

Calabar."[218] The smuggling of new labor never ended. In 1961 Gowdin Amadi of Owerri explained that he had turned up at the treaty recruiting agency in Calabar, penniless, but was turned back by the medical officer, possibly due to being under the age of 16. He was given "nine shillings and two pence to return to his village whence he accidentally met MARCK OTURU," a Nigerian tout from Bende, who "promised him help for 20£ to be returned once he's earned wages on Fernando Po, which he gladly accepted."[219] The promised relaying of the advance or *dash*, even though it ate into their commission, continued to be a key tout technique. The next chapter turns to this *dash* dynamic.

Touts did not and could not operate within a fixed hinterland: they unleashed themselves in waves and operated necessarily on a patchwork of ever-new fringes, constantly pursuing new victims to disappoint, or impressing well-versed hopefuls with the promise of ever-larger advances. *Braceros* tended to leave after two years, after their first contract, or they stayed on for a further two or four years, after which they returned home or turned to small scale cash crop farming or sought out other more desirable ways of earning an income at other emerging colonial towns along the coast. On a biennial cycle, new workers had to fill the ranks, either from an expanding labor frontier or internally, as we will now see.

218 British VC and LO (Spencer-Cooke) to Commissioner of Labor, Lagos, June 26, 1950, TNA, CO 554/169/1.

219 Jefe de Policía to GG (Ruíz), June 22, 1961, AGA, C-81/8215, E-5.

4 *Dash:* Contractual Doubling

> The essence of trading is the giving of one object in exchange for another. The one hand tenaciously holds on to the object with which it seeks to tempt the stranger. The other hand is stretched out in demand towards the second object, which it seeks to have in exchange for its own. As soon as it touches this, the first hand lets go of its object; but not before, or it may lose both. The crudest form of cheating, when something is taken from someone without any return being made, corresponds, translated into the context of climbing, to falling from the tree. To prevent this the trader remains on his guard during the whole transaction and scrutinizes every movement of his opposite number. The profound and universal pleasure men take in trading is thus partly explained by the fact that trade is a translation into nonphysical terms of one of the oldest movement patterns.
>
> – Elias Canetti, *Crowds and Power*

> If the gift and the counter-gift are unequal, then there's a winner and a loser, and possibly exploitation and trickery. If, on the other hand, they are the same, then there's apparently no difference between the gift and a rational, self-interested mercantile exchange. In short, either the gift results from uncharitable motives and is therefore illegitimate or it is non-existent, illusory.
>
> – Jacques Godbout and Alain Caillé, *The World of the Gift*

Why did tens of thousands of labor migrants re-indenture themselves to the planters in Fernando Po in the decades after the Spanish Civil War? H. Rylands, a district officer previously stationed in Owerri, where the mostly Igbo *braceros* were from, says he had "heard all about the 'evil' conditions of Nigerian labourers in Fernando Poo from those who [had] previously been" there. In 1947 he was dispatched to the island as Vice-Consul and concluded that the "illiterate candidate for the Fernando Poo labour market knows more or less what to expect."[1] The "candidates" could expect openly practiced police torture and overseers committing manslaughter with impunity: so why did the majority stay on for a second and sometimes a third contract, but almost never a fourth? And why were the informal modes of payment of these subsequent contracts a remarkable instance of a vast countermovement that brought the order of planter power to its knees? The answer to all three questions is: the *dash*.

From the Spanish archive there appears a distinct and internal recruiting technique, made up of *reenganchos* – "re-hooked" laborers signing onto a further contract – containing the heightened *dash* component. The *reenganchos* were drawn from the ranks of clandestinely recruited first-time laborers, deserters, and new illegal immigrants, and must be analyzed as a collective and polit-

1 British VC and LO (Rylands) to Commissioner of Labor, Lagos, January 8, 1947, NAE, CALPROF 17/1/278.

https://doi.org/10.1515/9783110755923-008

ical phenomenon, not only because the tracing of individual routes in the existing archive is quickly frustrated by so many aliases and hidden *dash* renegotiations; discontinuous, dispersed, and overgrowing. Only the *dash* jammed a plantation island that was depending on conned and kidnapped Nigerians bound by long contracts during World War II and warded off what would become a small cousin of Apartheid's labor recruiting system in the late 1950s. After World War II, the canoe-going clandestine recruiters started encountering a revamped Nigerian navy and the number of smuggled labor dropped sharply. It was Nigerian *reenganchos* who were signing most contracts. They were the first generation to radically escalate the *dash*. They renegotiated its 20-fold increase (not adjusted for inflation) in a little over ten years – doubling the nominal wages of *braceros* every time they were released from an expired or sabotaged contract. Thrown and kept in the bottom rung of the colonial economy because of an initial ruse, a dire need, or dreams of excess, they figured out a way to stay on the plantations only as long as necessary. This they did in collaboration with touts.

Dash-Peonage in Post-war Fernando Po

The "peculiarity of the process of contracting labor," writes a Spanish planter in the 1940s, "is the age-old custom of giving advances to the *braceros* the moment a contract is made."[2] The Spanish called this advance *regalo* or *prima* – a present or bonus at the outset – while the Nigerian migrants on Fernando Po, most of whom learned to speak Pidgin on the island, called it *dash*, a legacy of the Kru workers who brought the language, term, and even technique to the island. In a first instance, the *dash* of *dash*-peonage was simply the advance made possible by long-term bondage contracts. In principle, and as a matter of policy, indentured labor contracts tended to enshrine "bondage in exchange for advance payment."[3] The *braceros* who demanded and invariably received this "very substantial inducement to recontract" found themselves between contracts already on the island.[4] The *dash* was not reducible to something else – to an extension of credit used to uproot or to cover initial transport costs.

The *dash*, an axiom of West African commercial life, had its own autonomous trajectory and political meaning. As the *dash* became inextricably part of the contracts on Fernando Po it produced its own sociality and space of rene-

2 Cámara (Sola Galvez) to Curaduría (Llompart Aulet), October 17, 1949, AGA, C-81/8130, E-3.
3 Stanziani, "Beyond Colonialism," 71.
4 British VC (Lewis) to British Embassy, Barcelona, July 5, 1946, NAE, CALPROF 17/1/278.

gotiation that riddled the plantations with a contradiction and came to destroy their viability. Recruitment techniques involving debt generated a two-way movement, a mobile form of submission and subversion, a friction that both enabled and undermined imperial plantation economics. Without credit-wages, the ancillary dispensing of lump sums, the plantations on Fernando Po would have fallen apart; none of the Nigerian *braceros* would have stayed on the island. At the same time, plantations repeatedly almost fell apart because of these same *braceros* continuing to sign contracts under informally renegotiated advances.

Contracted *braceros* had their official wages withheld until the very last day of a contract to ward off desertions and make the accounting of deductions easier. But for those signing onto a second contract there was also a supplementary unregistered payment at the outset – immediately preceding a further uninterrupted and irrevocable two-year bind. This bind could be doubled and extended, "because the system of wage advances over and above the salary means that the workers are frequently indebted." This gave the planters in the "always present conditions of labor scarcity and reticence a way to oblige *braceros* to work off their debts" by signing on to a "further contract," in the words of Juan Velarde Fuentes, a prominent Spanish economist, published in the prestigious academic journal of the Spanish Ministry of Labor after coming back from an intense period of colonial research in the early 1960s.[5] However, the "casually authoritative way" this economist refers to the device of debt in Fernando Po's hiring arrangements should cause a pause, not only because it skims over the many moments of actual violence within the "deceptively transparent" relation of peonage, but because it papers over the history of resistance generated by those who demanded the advance.[6] The analytical and explanatory endowment given to "debt" systematically overlooks its pliability and the intricacies of brokerage.

Braceros were not there to make a career or seek "stability," "security" or any long-term "guaranteed employment" as imagined by Alfredo Jones, the assiduous cultivator of the labor connection to Nigeria.[7] The principal aim of the *braceros*, as noted by a resident colonial social scientist, was to "exit the colonial contract" world completely "as soon as the internal circumstances that forced

5 Velarde Fuentes, "Problemas de Empleo," 174.

6 Taussig, *Shamanism*, 62. Certainly, outstanding debts were explicit reasons for limiting mobility even for the non-*braceros* on Fernando Po who could not leave the island if they were indebted to the treasury for taxes and unpaid fines.

7 Alfredo Jones Niger, December 1938, "Memoria sobre el problema de la mano de obra en la isla Fernando Poo," AGA, C-81/8128, E-1. Less than 1% stayed on, on the plantation hierarchy. By the late 1950s many *capatazes* were Nigerians who would also "inflicted corporal punishment when need be." "Fernando Poo," *Eastern Nigeria Guardian*, Port Harcourt, August 14, 1957.

him to contract cease."[8] However, without a nullified contract "the labourer is unable to leave the island by orthodox means and the military control of the island is such that it is virtually impossible for him to leave by canoe."[9] A prominent trader from Lagos, Lola Martins, while visiting Fernando Po, wondered why no one "absconded. Not under the Spanish Government. There is no way of escape in Fernando Po except to run into the sharks surrounding the island."[10] Breaking or cutting short a contract was close to impossible, except through desertion. As Peter Enahoro said with a dose of earnestness: "It is easier to divorce a catholic than to break a contract on Fernando Poo."[11] While the archive reveals scattered traces of very risky exploits, such as a group of Nigerian *braceros* stealing "a canoe" and trying to "row themselves back," desertion took the shape not of a permanent subtraction, an outwards escape or a flight onto the mountain tops, but as a cleft, spiraling inwards.[12]

In Fernando Po the *dash* engendered but also contradicted the arrangement of debt bondage. The *dash* was demanded outright by reengaging workers and relayed by a set of unruly resident touts. The place of the *dash* outside the contract, the timing of its payments and its outright negotiation, carried its own distinctive "gifty" code that generated both new forms of exploitation and resistance. It was the conditions of this very bondage, the attempts at "attachment" by competitive employers vying for scarce labor, that allowed a distinctive and radical form of workers' resistance to unfold. It is precisely in the struggle around the sum and negotiation of the *dash* where the relative strength and unstable relations between workers and employers and the colonial state can be detected. The balance of this struggle directly affected the boom and crises cycles of the colonial economy and forced a constant push to keep widen-

---

8 Rafael Romero Moliner, "Apuntes sobre la estructura social de Fernando Poo," *Cuadernos de Estudios Africanos* 7 (1949): 46.

9 British LO (Nery), June 17, 1943, "Nigerian Labour in Fernando Poo," TNA, CO 554/127/15.

10 Lola Martins, "African Tradition Abused in Fernando Poo," *Express*, Lagos, February 22, 1962.

11 Peter Pan, "'Spanish' is a Synonym for Savages," *Sunday Times*, Lagos, March 4, 1962.

12 Policía, "Registro de Incidencias 1953," 464 [entry of November 10, 1953], BNM [no call number]. Already in the 1890s the Consul reported that "British West African subjects had escaped by canoe from Fernando Po after being duped that they were going to work in Nigeria." Sundiata, *From Slaving to Neoslavery,* 132. This was rare unlike for example in São Tomé, Clarence-Smith, "Hidden Costs," 164. It does however resemble slave marronage in eighteenth-century Mauritius, as Megan Vaughan says, "many maroons were urban runaways," working as hired subjects under negotiated terms of payment and with a variety of forged permits and identity papers in hand; "a much more threatening prospect," she suggests. Vaughan, *Creating the Creole Island*, 172.

ing the circle of potential recruits. The fluctuation has little to do with "scarcity" as such, as the number of contract workers in this period was quite constant, but with the changing composition of the workforce and the exploration of gaps at material points in the order that tied *braceros* to the Spanish colony, such as the documentary and inspection regime.

Rather than being a predictable fold in the interplay of domination and subordination, the *dash* was a slippery and unwavering trigger, heralding promises of "plenitude" and producing a plethora of tactics for "unsanctioned" wealth.[13] As I will go on to detail, with every contract came a higher *dash*, whether *braceros* acquired it after deserting or not. This double excess – the inherently inflationary, the incitement to escalation – is the principal social dynamic in Marcel Mauss' *The Gift*. This fundamental instability and potential for reversibility is an underestimated counterforce in studies of debt bondage. The double excess created by the *dash* – prolonged indebtedness and incited desertion – produced both the bind and the flight. On Fernando Po, the *dash*, the cash that employers intended to advance as a debt-trap, left colonial capital in retreat, trying to fend off the escalations on the front line populated by *reenganchos*. The *reenganchos* were accompanied by relatively small but disproportionately effective groups of *ganchos* and *fugados* – "hook-people" and "fugitives" or recruiter-touts and deserters. For the rest of the chapter, I follow the intersecting movements of these three figures along the archival sources they made an appearance in.

Island Touts, 1940s–1950s

The "*regalo*," the *dash*, "through times past has served as an index of the variable scarcity – but always scarcity – of labor power on this island."[14] In the three decades of colonial Francoist rule thousands of new settlers and a heavy presence of large corporate plantations rushed onto the island. The axiomatic "labor scarcity" was obviously intensified: in 1948 barely half of the island's self-declared "labor needs were being met."[15] A resident social scientist notes around the year that the *dash* as well as the "labor scarcity" was reaching "a distressing and agonizing limit of which everyone is sadly very well aware": "demand has been so intense that the *primas*" the *dash* "given to the *braceros* the moment they sign the contract are swelling day by day. On the shoulders of

13 Guyer, *Marginal Gains*, 16; Roitman, *Fiscal Disobedience*, 83. For advances in relation to consumption see James and Rajak, "Credit Apartheid," 462.

14 Cámara (Sola Galvez) to Curaduría (Llompart Aulet), October 17, 1949, AGA, C-81/8130, E-3.

15 DGMC, January 15, 1948, "Informe sobre braceros," AGA, C-81/12373, E-392.

this desperate necessity, the *braceros* have organized a *picaresca laboral,*" a picaresque labor movement that "has been very much to the benefit of the unscrupulous *bracero* and pretty damn onerous for our agriculture."[16]

The Vice-Consul, to his own surprise, was forced to speak of "the labour force [that] is, in many instances, exploiting the employers."[17] By the early 1950s wages for a two-year contract had been revised upwards with the inflation of the peseta, though overall the wage sum was still stable vis-à-vis the pound. The wage was revised to a constant 700 to 1,000 pesetas, while the *dash* briefly reached 7,000 pesetas (or £60), at which point the *reenganchos* were pocketing the entire surplus value being produced on the plantations – in particular cases twice as much. The "uncontainable rise" of the *dash* made "*las fugas,*" desertion, "become habitual. The *braceros* had been changing their names, and hired themselves to multiple employers, creating a malign indiscipline and an invitation to continuous fraud."[18]

The authorities did not publish figures for desertion consistently, though judging by discontinuous data for individual years and statements of the *Curador* recorded at various meetings, it tended to be over 3% and less than 10% of the workforce at any one point. In the early 1960s the "principal problem" was still "related to, above all, the breach of contract" statistically aggregated under "absenteeism," which according to the calculations of one prominent economist constituted an average of "five days a month per worker" or "15%" of total labor time. The economist, Velarde Fuentes, was the president of a vast 1963 colonial economic development commission sent to the territories, referred to as overseas "provinces" since 1958, to provide a glowing report about conditions in Spanish Guinea, with the aim to discourage the calls for decolonization with "development" statistics. In his report he collapses and makes invisible the category of desertion by folding it into an aggregate "absenteeism" – divided only into "medical causes, 5,6%" and "other causes 8,7%". In a separate article on the "problems of employment" in Spanish Guinea, Velarde Fuentes also distributes the reality of desertion within the other "problems" related to contract labor: "punctuality, theft, and the non-return of debts," in the context of workers trying to cut short their contracts after receiving advances.[19]

---

16 Rafael Romero Moliner, "Crónica de los territorios de Guinea," *Cuadernos de Estudios Africanos* 17 (1952): 91.

17 British VC (Lewis) to British Embassy, Barcelona, July 5, 1946, TNA, FO 371/60392 or NAE, 17/1/278.

18 Peña, *Repertorio*, 350. *Orden* from May 12, 1952, "Ordenanza prohibiendo las primas o regalos en la contratación."

19 Velarde Fuentes, "Problemas de empleo," 174; Comisión, *Plan de desarrollo*, 37.

The original 1942 labor treaty allowed an association of Spanish planters to pay licensed recruiters small commissions, to construct a large depot in a converted military barracks in Calabar and to send a dedicated steamship to make bi-monthly pick-ups. British colonial top-down schemes offered single channels of supervised declarations of consent and reduced advances to keep total wages low and avoid the charge of debt bondage. In the early 1950s, revisions to the labor quota of the 1942 labor treaty with Nigeria were hiked to "meet the demand," up to 10,000 *braceros* per year, however during the first decade of operation it never managed to sign up more that "about one third of this figure," and sometimes as little as a thousand per year.[20] Under the "treaty" prospective *braceros* signed their contracts in Calabar and received a small *dash* officially capped at five shillings, ostensibly so that laborers would not become "heavily indebted."[21] These "treaty-laborers" were attached to planters proportionately according to a list prepared by the *Cámara*, which only included the labor needs of its members. After a minimum two-year contract with an option for a further 18-month renewal they were repatriated and paid out on their return. Nevertheless, until around 1959 *dash*-touts proved to be more effective than any diplomatically negotiated labor-importing agreements. Indeed, to subsist during the Francoist period many planters had to rely on touts as they were being excluded from the flow of "treaty-laborers" by the more powerful Spanish planters. The dynamics of this illegal and informal recruitment shifted in the late 1950s when the *braceros* were overwhelmingly new recruits arriving through this regulated treaty channel, later kept by the Nigerian state. As the Vice-Consul noted, still pondering how to try to help end the "illegal system of inducements": the *dash* system "would disappear entirely if the numbers" of new recruits under the treaty could be "increased."[22]

The labor treaty provided for altogether modified entry points for touts, as licensed recruiters were stripped of the ability to mediate advances and were reduced mainly to handing out flyers with many images on them about earning money in Fernando Po. However, as recruits reported, they now had to *dash* the staff of the Anglo-Spanish Employment Agency (ASEA) in Calabar themselves if they wanted non-*bracero* jobs – paying up to 15 shillings to a "junior officer clerk" to be placed as "shop boys" or "office boys" or "house boys,"

---

20 British VC (Lewis) to GG (Bonelli), June 8, 1946, AGA, C-81/8130, E-1; Llompart, "Nigerianos," 66.

21 Resident, Calabar Province to Editor, Nigerian Eastern Mail, Calabar, August 5, 1945, NAE, CALPROF 17/1/278.

22 British VC (Lewis) to Commissioner of Labor, Lagos, June 11, 1946, NAE, CALPROF 17/1/278; British VC (Lewis) to Cámara (Carbonell), May 6, 1946, AGA, C-81/8130, E-1.

but nevertheless ending up "working as laborers in the Finca El Pino." Licensed recruiters in Nigeria and staff at the ASEA inserted themselves into the informal field of allocation, through and beyond the official recruitment procedures and fanned out through a series of sub-touts in Fernando Po, "the tout's stooge[s]," as the Vice-Consul called them.

These "stooge-touts" on the island promised planters that they could get staff at the ASEA to make laborers sign on for certain farms, and "for the privilege" the "stooge commands and receives 50 pesetas." Employers would then pay the "real tout a further 100 pesetas, if the tout can persuade the employer that it is through his efforts that the labourer has come to Fernando Poo," to their specific farm. Planters it seems sincerely did "not know that such recruitment is illegal because all the boys eventually pass through the recruiting Agency." Downstream, the official recruiters in Nigeria of course handed out a "substantial dash" to these laborers in Nigeria who were "recruited at the Agency for the particular farm." This bustling activity of touts upstream and downstream even for "treaty labour" helps explain why there was such a high rate of desertion, at times up to 30% of new treaty laborers after they willingly arrived on the island on steamers, instead of canoes.[23]

Touts prescribed, brokered, or sold any supporting documentation to deserting or newly smuggled laborers, and had obvious access to rubber stamps and urban photography studios to create or supplant portrait photographs on documents issued by all sorts of administrative offices, such as the freedom paper of the *Curaduría*, customs and travel permits, medical certificates and the like. This was usually arranged beforehand, because the "detaining of immigrants without the appropriate papers" was almost instant. Dozens of detachments and roadblocks of the *Guardia Colonial*, were placed around the only road that by the 1940s had encircled the island – a road built and maintained by imprisoned Nigerian *braceros.*[24] As Isaac Pepple, a Nigerian journalist arrested on the island in 1956, found out from "a group of five thieves [in the] prison cell": "strangely enough," the Nigerians who had "smuggled themselves" onto the island or bypassed the treaty, did so "because as free men, they can bargain for high wages" – in the form of a *dash.*[25]

British colonial authorities in Nigeria thought "for reasons quite unknown illegal immigration offers certain attractions to the immigrant," but surmised that the "principal reason, not the least among them," was of "an economic na-

23 British VC (Lewis) to Commissioner of Labor, Lagos, June 11, 1946, NAE, CALPROF 17/1/278.
24 GG, September 25, 1963, "Circulares Indocumentados," AGA, C-81/8781, E-3.
25 Isaac Pepple, "Free Ticket to Hell," *Drum*, Lagos, April 1957.

ture."[26] Spencer-Cooke, the Vice-Consul, thought it "strange that so many workers are persuaded to come here [but] the fascination of being promised such a large sum of money as £15 to £30 is a temptation hard to resist [for someone] who has probably rarely handled a greater amount than 1/-" – that is one shilling, 20 shillings to a pound. The "hopes" of these new smuggled recruits were "never realised of course," a first time *bracero* was "lucky to get £3" at the end of their contract, while "the remainder" invariably went "into the pockets of the illegal recruiters."[27] Okon Archibong, a political activist in Calabar sums up the mood amongst these *braceros*, once they realized what type of exchange had just taken place: "Every thinking man can prove beyond doubt how these victims felt when they were landed at Fernando Po," their "wages" meaning their potential *dash* "having been paid to the middle-men."[28] "They always sell man two years called sign," as a letter from a group of *braceros* explains.[29] Another petition by a group of *braceros* tells how after a week into their first contract "we saw one man who shows us road back to the town" where they complained to the *Curador*, who "reply us that the parties who brought us here have claimed £6–0–0 per each head [and] so we must go and work for the farm for good 2 years." When they "strictly refused" to be interned in the plantation the *Curador* "held us in prison until we are agreed to go back to the farm, as up to date we are in prison with heavy punishment."[30] The *Curador*, an agent of neo-slavery, pulled the carpet from under the feet of new *braceros*; but this only happened once.

This Atlantic crease was upended by *reenganchos* who transformed the *dash* from being a part of a recruiter's capitation fee into a moving medium for assessing and asserting their own bargaining power. The "odd thing," says a slightly surprised British Consul General in 1953, "is that although men who are sent to Fernando Po by illegal means, such as trickery or kidnapping, tend to be resentful at first, many of them give in and agree to the conditions." The Consul General's subdued way of phrasing these realities concealed preposterous overstatements – "agree" – as well as understatements: "it is also odd that although

26 Secretary, Eastern Provinces, Enugu to the Resident, Calabar Province, June 9, 1951, NAE, RIVPROF 2/1/53.

27 British VC (Spencer-Cooke) to Commissioner of Labor, Lagos, January 8, 1950, TNA, CO 554/169/2.

28 O. Archibong to Resident, Calabar Province, January 23, 1939, NAE, CALPROF 5/1/194.

29 Petition signed "Your Prodigal Sons" to Resident, Calabar Province, March 24, 1936, NAE, CALPROF 5/1/194.

30 Petition signed by A. Afiatai, addressed to "District Officer, Nigeria," October 28, 1932, NAE CALPROF 5/1/192.

in some ways the Spaniards are strict, if not harsh, in their relations with their African workers, many Nigerians stay on there for years."[31]

The Nigerian press-storm that regularly formed over Fernando Po in these decades, sometimes daily for months, had vivid and haunting titles of incarceration and damnation that drew on a Euro-African imaginary of satanic mills and cruel dungeons: a "Biblical Hell," a "Hell on Earth," an "Island of No Return," the "Brutal Island," with "Wickid Laws and Wickid Rulers," where a warp or short-circuit had spawned "paid slavery."[32] Journalistic exposés contained interviews with returning laborers who told "newsmen in Calabar that they had suffered 'the most inhuman, hellish and brutal treatment' they ever had heard of in their lives" – principally at the hands of the colonial police. For the prominent writer Peter Enahoro, the prickly question was that of an apparently irrational consent to voluntary "servitude": "In Fernando Po, I was ashamed. I WAS ASHAMED that in spite of the treatment they got, they still came in numbers."[33] In the hundreds of press articles covering or commenting on the scandals coming out of "Hell's Island," the *dash* was rarely named directly, though if it had been, it might have been described as a deal with the devil.

In the early 1940s, David Evans, the British Labour Officer on site gathered from some of the migrant workers who served as his paid informants that those who were "completing their contract" were not going back home just yet with nothing to show from many years of arduous work abroad but had instead started to "put a high premium on their future services." The "recruit soon learns that without his services the employer will be ruined and at the expiration of his first contract he may himself employ a tout to offer his services for re-engagement to the highest bidder." Evans describes the *reenganchos* as being "fully alive to the possibilities," and "out to make capital of the situation." During this reshuffling for the second round of contracts he also witnessed how "intermediaries who have scented the elements of a racket are springing up wholesale. These 'agents' – themselves Nigerians – haunt Santa Isabel and the neighbouring farms in

31 British Consul General, Brazzaville, June 12, 1953, "Tour," TNA, FO 371/102621.

32 Candidus, "Recruitment of Labour to Fernando Po," *The Nigerian Eastern Mail*, Port Harcourt, April 5, 1947; V.S, "Hell on Earth," *New Times*, Lagos, May 1962; Isaac Pepple, "Free Ticket to Hell," *Drum*, Lagos, April 1957; Peter Pan, "Wickid Laws and Wickid Rulers," *Sunday Times*, Lagos, February 25, 1962.

33 "We were Tortured, Starved," *Nigerian Outlook*, Enugu, January 28, 1961; Peter Pan, "The Brutal Island," *Sunday Times*, Lagos, February 18, 1962. Enahoro wrote under the moniker "Peter Pan." Enahoro's vicarious sense of disgrace was also projected onto colonialists: "I WAS ASHAMED for the Spaniards -good Catholics all of them- who treated their fellow men like beasts of burden."

search of likely recruits and, of course, take their cut out of the bonus offered."[34] This was a novel shift. A German scientist stuck in Fernando Po at the outbreak of World War II observed that "usually the Nigerian *Gastarbeiter* returned home" after a first contract "with three to five pounds in savings."[35] In 1937 it could still be said that "the labour question" was "likely to become serious" since those "who finish their contracts show little desire to sign a new one."[36] The labor question took a serious turn not because of the refusal to sign second contracts and the absence of new arrivals but because those already there redeployed themselves.

Gancho-touts were a discontinuous and unrelated group, who often started off very modestly and, again, armed themselves only with the capacity to handle and inflate language and money. They were drawn from the ranks of lowly and landless Spanish and Portuguese *pichinglis*-speaking settlers, from the community of urban Creoles or Fernandinos and West African self-employed immigrants, from the existing entourage of Calabar-based recruiter kingpins, or they were former *braceros* themselves with a few contracts under their belt. Everyone was "well aware of the existence of 'ganchos' whose mission it [was] to capture those *braceros* who presently find themselves in Santa Isabel because they just completed a contract" – and no one could stop them. In 1946 the planter's lobby had even tried to propose a tax on the *reenganchos* who hired themselves elsewhere, about "half the going rate of a *regalo* to be paid to the *Cámara*," to disarticulate the relation between a "new employer and his 'gancho'." With almost theatrical pathos, planters started complaining that the *ganchos* were "twisting the will" of the *braceros* who were abandoning them after their first contract.[37]

The Spanish settler Fernando García Gimeno worked as a labor contractor for a group of Portuguese planters and fondly recalls in his memoirs how he enrolled a small but peaceful army of Nigerian *ganchos*. García's parents arrived on the island after the Spanish Civil War and started working at his aunt's restaurant in Santa Isabel where he was also a waiter. He says his "*ganchos*" would "bring potential recruits to the best farms we had" – often not the ones "they were actually going to be destined to." Complaints about being misled about

34 British LO (Evans) to British Consul General, May 26, 1944, TNA, FO 371/39661; British LO (Evans), June 30, 1945, "Native Labour, Monthly Report, No. 16," TNA, FO 371/49598; British VC (Lewis) to Commissioner of Labor, Lagos, June 11, 1946, NAE, CALPROF 17/1/278.

35 Wolff, "Wirtschaft von Fernando Poo," 98.

36 Governor of Nigeria (Bourdillon), Lagos to Sec. of State for the Colonies (Crimsby-Gore), London, October 29, 1937, TNA, FO 371/22669.

37 Cámara Bata to GG (Bonelli), August 3, 1946, AGA, C-81/8129, E-1.

the eventual place of work were bracketed under the "daily conflicts of a minor sort," such as "being destined to plantations other than those promised." This "confusion," he says, could arise because the "majority of firms had different 'patios', one in Basakato, the other in Fistown. The workers were promised work in the farm closest to the city, but in the end he was sent to the one further away." To "win new recruits over" García would "invite them to lunch and things. We even paid for a session with a woman of the night." This Dionysian pampering, an inversion of the plantation's unchanging and imported food rations of rice and stockfish that came with the contract, served to "screw the competition" out of laborers, as García says.[38]

This liminal phase corresponded to the validity of a 14-day *papel de libertad* or "freedom paper" handed over to *braceros* when finishing a contract so they could buy a ticket and wait for the bimonthly steamer to take them to Nigeria, or so they "may look for work without risk of being taken by the police."[39] A contract was always laid out at the end of this strangely self-imploding grid of reallocation and inducements, because of the enforced vagrancy ordinances on the island. The *dash* could only appear in a reign of long contracts, but its flourishing was the outcome of touts and workers combining. *Gancho*-touts of course pocketed commissions, proposed unnecessary fees, and often conducted scams. However, the dispersed sets of touts were the ones channeling and bidding up the informal advances, relaying but also cracking open the edifice of imperial bondage on the final African shores of the Spanish Empire. Out of it came a realization and a practice that effected a radical coup against an arrangement that officially only promised poverty wages and a high risk of being killed – there were one to two deaths per day – by what can euphemistically be called the guardians of public order and work-related injuries.[40]

Up until the early 1930s there was an officially registered *regalo* of exactly 300 pesetas "for re-engagement [which] changes hands in front of the Spanish labor officer" – a small sum, about the price of 15 bottles of olive oil or ten dozen eggs or 25 meters of cloth in the markets of the Santa Isabel, that almost

38 Garcia, *Fernando el Africano*, 45–48.

39 British VC (Robertson) to British Consul General, December 30, 1944, TNA, FO 371/49598 or NAE, CALPROF 17/1/277.

40 "During this quartile for example 26 Treaty workers and 41 non-Treaty workers [...] have died." Counting only the treaty workers the Vice-Consul says: "Up to March 1952, 508 deaths had been reported which represents 3.6 % of a labour force of 14,174, 13,666 of whom were repatriated during the period May 1943 to March 1952." This death rate was "11 times greater than in [the rubber plantations of] Calabar." British VC and LO (Bradley), October 1, 1952, TNA, FO 371/96714.

exceeded one year of official *bracero* wages. In the 1940s, however "outside the door of the Labour Office" around the negotiations of decentralized tout-emissaries "an unofficial and much more substantial dash" was being exchanged.[41] This "unofficial *regalo*," laments a planter, "has been consecrated by the reality of the bargaining power of labor."[42] In 1949 the *Curador* refused to inscribe the real amounts of this "free playing system of *primas*" in his registry or onto contracts. The "300 peseta limit," he says, one imagines in a voice growing louder, was the "only way to put a brake on the *regalos* of the underground market of labor which have been elevated to absurd levels." For the *Curador*, Sebastian Llompart – who was annually being rewarded some 45,000 pesetas for performing his duties – the "regime of *regalos*, free playing as to its quantity is a danger," not only because it "defrauds the fiscal regime," since it was tax free, but because he saw it as driven by the "venality of the uneducated native and the maliciousness of men in general, when they are moved by economic reasons alone."

His immediate reasons lay in a more prosaic and typical anxiety: the workload of paper-shufflers. "Today," he says, "the handing over of the 300 peseta *regalo* is always the same, it is done automatically, and everyone knows the quantity given and received." He then engages in rhetorical arithmetic: "it would take at least 4 minutes to hand over 1500–2000 pesetas," counting the labor of the "cashier, then the necessary European supervisor has to count the bills, and the *bracero* who is contracting would have to count the bills as well." The "average number of contracts presided over" by the *Curaduría* per day were "approximately fifty," and so the process of counting and inscribing a variable "*regalo*" in the books "would take over three and half hours more per day". His "office", he says, was already "knee-deep in work" and unable and unwilling to extend into elaborate "cashier" duties.[43] During the post-war decade it was *reenganchos,* "as many as 25,000 non-Treaty labourers" in 1952, who were making most contracts.[44]

Until the early 1950s the "system in force" for "re-engaging workers on second contracts was quite irregular," to say the least, as "the personal copies of workers contracts" were kept by employers for "safe-keeping." Spencer-Cooke, the Vice-Consul, goes on to explain that it was "sufficient for an employer," *without* the *bracero*, to appear "in the Spanish Labour Office and state that the par-

41 British VC (Lewis) to Commissioner of Labor, Lagos, June 11 and 20, 1946, NAE, CALPROF 17/1/278 and CALPROF 17/1/279.

42 Cámara (Sola) to Curaduría (Llompart), October 17, 1949, AGA, C- 81/8130, E-3.

43 Curaduría (Llompart) to GG (Bonelli), November 8, 1949, AGA, C- 81/8130, E-3.

44 Nigerian Secretariat, Lagos, August 1953, RHL, 600.18 s. 21/XI (10).

ticular [*bracero*] wished to enter into another with the same employer." The *Curador*, Sebastian Llompart Aulet – a post he held between 1943 and 1962 – seems to have happily stamped these unsigned *reengancho* contracts that were being justified on the grounds of the outstanding debts generated through the "undesirable" and "illegal system of inducements." As "all employers keep the personal copies of workers contracts this practice was all too easy."[45] Llompart Aulet would eventually authorize the release of people after they had completed a few contracts; in this sense *peonaje* on Fernando Po was akin to Igbo precolonial "debt-slavery," in that it promised an in-built but sometimes ill-defined expiry date. Ekechi even makes the observation that "the status of a pawn [in] some Igbo communities" seems to be "analogous to that of an indentured servant or laborer" because "a limit of several years was imposed" after which a pawn was "to be released 'whatever the amount of the debt'."[46] Precolonial forms of peonage have, particularly in West African history, been artificially divorced from the worlds of imperial labor.

An amendment to the labor code from 1913 closely defined the conditions allowing contracts to be lengthened or declared expired. This is also the only moment where the term "freedom" appears in the labor legislation, used in the narrow context of the freedom to choose another contract with the same or another employer after the expiration of a first contract. This "freedom" came only after the completion of a first contract, measured not in calendar months, but in working days. Article 5 of the 1913 amendment ordered "that once his contract is terminated, a *bracero* will have to continue serving his employer for as many days as he has been detained, for which purpose the corrections will be noted in the contract books so that the time calculation can be made later and the *braceros* will be warned so that they are aware of them."[47] It is unclear to what extent this amendment allowed employers to try to extend the contract along the same reasoning of outstanding debts, as such conditionalities of "debt relief" seemingly also depended on the disposition of the individual *Curador*.

The *Curador* always regularly added to the agreed period the "absentee" days, with one example from 1936 reading: "I have examined the annotations on punishments" that appeared in a particular worker's contract book, and "if we sum up the 138 days of detention and 59 days of absconding, that is a

45 British VC (Spencer-Cooke) to Commissioner of Labor, Lagos, January 8, 1950, TNA, CO 554/169/2; British VC (Lewis) to Cámara (Carbonell), May 6, 1946, AGA, C-81/8130, E-1.

46 Uchendu, "Slaves and Slavery in Iboland," 128; Ekechi, "Pawnship in Igbo Society," 169, citing Talbot, *Life in Southern Nigeria*, 698.

47 Miranda, *Leyes coloniales*, 396.

total of 197 days that he stopped rendering his services and therefore, not having fulfilled his contract, as a consequence of the law, he must continue rendering his services until he completes 18 months of effective work."[48] It is suggestive that in 1950, the highest number of complaints by *braceros* related precisely to the issue of prolonged contracts, and related techniques to the same effect, such as the fact that payment was "delayed in the Spanish Labour Office," which would often leave *braceros* bound "to recontract with same employer" as they awaited or were refused the 50% of the official wages paid out only at the end of a contract's final liquidation.[49]

Restructuring Plantations

For the "prospect of returning to Nigeria with £24 in their pockets" – that is with the *dash* of a *reengancho* – the *bracero* was "prepared to risk work in Fernando Po [even] if he is unlucky to find a bad master."[50] Contracts on the island were irrevocable and fixed in length. The *dash* marked the entry into them, a threshold with a very ambivalent sign: "it [was] generally recognized by the labourer that the higher the 'dash' the worse the conditions are on the farm, but quite often their cupidity gets the better of them". Once on the island however, the *reenganchos* were "very discerning when signing second contracts: they naturally seek the best pay and amenities," and this was the only "stimulus" for "employers to make their farms more attractive."[51] *Reenganchos* tended to stay clear of planters "who had a reputation of ill-treating the labourers." Planters with a reputation "sufficient to frighten [*reengancho*] labourers away" were forced to replace the ranks of abusive Portuguese, Spanish, Fernandino and British West African overseers if they wanted anyone to "recontract." When they did, as a local administrator notes, planters were "able to find labourers from other farms, who are prepared to serve their second contract with" them.[52] For those planters

48 Curador to GG, November 24, 1936, AGA, C-81/8153, E-1.

49 British VC and LO (Spencer-Cooke) to Commissioner of Labor, Lagos, September 30, 1950, TNA, FO 371/89597.

50 British LO, Calabar to Government, Lagos, March 23, 1945, AGA, C-81/8130, E-1; British LO, Calabar to Government, Lagos, November 15, 1945, AGA, C-81/8130, E-1.

51 British VC and LO (Bradley) to Commissioner of Labor, Lagos, March 31, 1950, TNA CO 554/169/1; British VC and LO (Bradley) to Commissioner of Labor, Lagos, March 20, 1956, TNA, CO 554/1346.

52 British VC and LO (Bradley) to Commissioner of Labor, Lagos, January 2, 1952, TNA, FO 371/96714.

who did have a large contingent of "the *reenganchos*" this served as a kind of "badge of honor and reputation for the planters, and benefits the *bracero* too because it represents an increase in salary and a guarantee of good working conditions."[53]

The achievement of the cumulative and iterative effects of the *dash* become clear when we consider what type of "working conditions" were being eliminated through these decentralized methods. Just by way of example: Domingo Alvarez Cruz was a Portuguese plantation manager who survives in a small vignette left in a labor inspector's report from 1941. The inspector had been on the job for years, yet the report was his very first on his tour of only a handful of plantations on the east side of the island, only reachable by surfboat. This inspector was struck by the figure and presence of Domingo Alvarez. With an emphatic distance the inspector depicted him as "a tall and slender man, sinewy, with a cold and penetrating stare, of a forceful and uncompromising character," with an "opinion" he repeatedly expressed: "the *bracero* is indolent and one needs to make them work to extract from them the maximum yield." Unsurprising then that at this plantation there were "several *fugados* and almost no *recontratados*, no one prolongs their contracts for normal motives."[54]

The "unbreakability" of the contract was a given. The Vice-Consul noted in 1952 that the Spanish "medical authorities continue to be reluctant to certify workers who become physically incapable of completing their contract and this is certainly a contributory factor to the high death rate amidst Nigerian workers."[55] In 1941, a Nigerian *bracero*, Eyo Udo, requested the help of the Vice-Consul to get the authorization necessary to travel to the hospital, it "being dangerous to just wait and die as happened with the other *braceros*." Explaining his situation, he remembers his recently deceased brother "Isaiah" who "had a wound on his foot," and instead of "receiving treatment at the Hospital" as he had requested, he was taken "to the warehouse" of one of the plantations of Antonio Perez Lopez, a planter well connected to the *Cámara*, and whipped several "times with a rubber tubing" and "locked inside during the night." His foot injury festered, and he still refused to work; the Spanish overseer sent Isaiah to the hospital four days later as a corpse. The pick-up truck that brought him there carried away "the cadaver of another *bracero*, who had also died due to mistreatment at work in the same farm." Udo explained to the Vice-Consul that the Spanish authorities "take it as joking we don't know that it fact they say." And indeed,

53 Carles, *Misioneros, negreros y esclavos*, 38.

54 AT Santa Isabel to GG (Fontán), December 17, 1941, AGA, C-81/8128, E-13.

55 British VC and LO (Bradley), October 1, 1952, TNA, FO 371/96714.

the *Gobernador*, Juan Fontán, replied to the Vice-Consul regarding this case, insisting "that the veracity of such declarations are untested." Fontán then sent him a copy of the coroner's report which conveniently declared: "natural death caused by organ failure." Throughout this period coroner's reports and official statistics about "causes of death" were instruments to cover up manslaughter.[56]

The *dash* for *reenganchos* exceeded the commissions commanded by clandestine recruiters because planters were paying out extra for experienced hands – the skilled wielding of long-armed sickles making exact incisions on the millions of dangling cocao pods without which any later blossoming was irreversibly lost; the keeping constant of furnace temperatures in the over 100 tin-roofed chimney-sprouting cacao drying houses peppering the island, etc. The value of experienced labor is difficult to quantify, but indirectly readily evident. In the 1940s the numbers of "treaty" *braceros* did not increase significantly, in fact, writes the British Vice-Consul in 1950, "since 1946 the labour force has fallen steadily in numbers but production figures have not," compensated by the experienced "workmen" who were still often "kept under pressure all day from 6.30am to 5.30pm without any established rest period," at least during the harvest season.[57] As the renowned Spanish economist noted, the "high productivity of these most diligent *reenganchos* quickly generated a group of agent entrepreneurs, the *ganchos*" or recruiter-touts.[58] The "tout, called 'gancho' which means 'hook' in Spanish receives 400 pesetas for every recruit whom he claims to the employer."[59] But like some recruiters from Calabar before them who "took commissions" on "the same *braceros* from at least three employers," the "result being a very profitable business," the worker-tout assemblage that took over the island in the late 1940s could recombine all the same elements and coil up the system to the extreme.[60] The *dash* was fanned by refractory mediators who never operated with the full blessing of the planters and the administration.

In the mid-twentieth century a colonial accountant found himself somewhat anxious by the fact that the "custom of the *pequeño regalo*" had become the "single largest expenditure" for running a plantation: the *dash* was having an antag-

---

56 Eyo Udo, September 8, 1941, AGA, C-81/8128, E-12; GG (Fontán) to British VC (Michie), November 27, 1941, AGA, C-81/8128, E-12.

57 British VC and LO (Spencer-Cooke) to British Consul General, Barcelona, November 8, 1950, TNA, FO 371/89597.

58 Velarde Fuentes, "Problemas de empleo," 165.

59 British VC (Lewis) to Commissioner of Labor, Lagos, June 11, 1946, NAE, CALPROF 17/1/278.

60 Curaduría (Guixeres) to GG (Guerra), June 29, 1936, AGA, C-81/8153, E-1.

Figure 13: Plantation infrastructure, 1920s–1950s (Terán 1962, 50; Rodríguez 1924, 50; Spain 1955, 130–134).

onistic seizure with obvious "repercussion on the costs of production."[61] When in 1952 the *dash* had "risen to amounts oscillating between 6000 and 7000 pesetas the benefits of the harvest [were] squarely falling into the hands of the *braceros* themselves or to the intermediaries who intervene on their behalf." The convulsion and acceleration of the *dash* was paid for by large Spanish and capital-rich corporate plantations who were the ones "needing a large amount of *braceros* and constantly renewing the contracts of their recruits." Until the early 1950s these hegemonic planters were busy fueling the *dash* in order to drown out the undercapitalized small farms owned by Spaniards, Portuguese, and Fernandinos, who had not been "able to stand the pace" of the *dash* and had "no alternative but to sell out to the larger concerns." Only during what could be called the "peak-*dash*" of June 1952 did the *Câmara* call upon the Governor to "resolutely intervene in order to immediately cut rising labor costs."[62]

Within three weeks the Spanish colonial authorities had "put in motion a study to wipe out the escalating *regalo*," but they found that they could not get rid of it. They partially rearranged it into a registered bonus, into a reduced "lump sum paid out only at the end of a contract, [because] the total suppression of the *prima* would have completely paralyzed the agriculture of the island."[63] The Vice-Consul gathered that *braceros* "did not take to this new method at all."[64] Those "who completed their contracts had no interest in staying" on the island because their "calculations or estimation of the *regalo* were no longer being taken into account," as Llompart Aulet himself noted. The Spanish attributed the decline in new arrivals and a falling *reengancho* rate after 1952 to "Nigerian electoral politics" and the scandal hungry elites, even though there was certainly almost no correlation.[65] The number of recruited treaty *braceros* peaked shortly after independence in 1961 during the most intense media scandal involv-

---

61 Delegacion de Hacienda, Santa Isabel to GG, n.d. [1950 – 1951], "Oficio Num. 150," AGA, C-81/12373, E-392.

62 Vicepresidente del Comite Sindical del Cacao, Barcelona to DGMC, May 5, 1952, AGA, C-81/12373, E-392; British VC and LO (Bradley) to Commissioner of Labor, Lagos, April 10, 1951, TNA, CO 554/169/2.

63 GG (Ruíz) to DGMC (Díaz de Villegas), June 17, 1952, AGA, C-81/12373, E-392.

64 British VC and LO (Bradley) to Consul General, Barcelona, July 4, 1952, TNA, FO 371/96714. For treaty-workers the bonus was paid out in Calabar at the end of a double contract, 42 months in all, for a total of around £20. "Deferred wages are paid into an account in Calabar controlled by the Department of Labor. The current balance awaiting disbursement on the return of the labourers concerned is £117,000."

65 Llompart, "Nigerianos," 68; Comisión, *Plan de desarrollo*, 233.

ing a roaring back and forth between notable journalists and various Nigerian ministers for almost a year.

New *dash* prohibitions notwithstanding, over a third of the planters continued to pay upfront and off-the-books to subsist; otherwise they were simply unable to harvest their crop. Many of these smaller planters had to rely on touts as they were being excluded from "treaty-labor" by the more powerful Spanish planters. This group of tout-dependent planters was made up of small Spanish planters, and small and large Portuguese, Fernandino, and German planters who made up over a third of employers. As was mentioned earlier, the 1943 treaty gave the Spanish-only executive committee of the *Cámara* a monopoly to "fairly distribute and allocate" any new *braceros* arriving from Nigeria, but the growing number of cheaper "treaty-labor" was "blatantly" directed to the *Cámara*'s own members. No new *braceros* were "allocated to foreigners," and "very few to Spanish emancipated natives," so the large Portuguese and German plantations and the Fernandino and Bubi farmers had to "rely on retaining their pre-treaty labour or obtaining illegal labour [or deserters] in order to carry on."[66] If medium-sized Fernandino planters of very diverse backgrounds dominated agriculture in the early twentieth century, then by the first decade of Francoist rule, bar a handful of exceptions,[67] they were wiped out.[68] The planter class was always in motion, joining, consolidating or disappearing, and partly because of

---

66 British VC and LO (Spencer-Cooke) to Commissioner of Labor, Lagos, September 30, 1950, TNA, FO 371/89597; British VC and LO (Spencer-Cooke) to Consul General, Barcelona, November 8, 1950, TNA, FO 371/89597.

67 San Carlos was known for its Fernandino agriculture, but even this was the situation in the 1940s: the biggest planters were Libanio Vaz Serra with 1300 h; Veiga y Avendano with 1,200 h; Antonio Perez with 850 h, Casa Drumen with 582 h, Mera y Compañia with 500 h; Comapañia Colonial de Africa with 500 h, and the Herederos de Maximiliano Jones with 280 h. Only the last were Fernandinos. The 40 European plantations in San Carlos employed over 8,000 *braceros*, each between 20 to 700 *braceros*, while only four plantations of Fernandino *emancipados* (excluding Jones) hired about 60 Nigerian treaty labourers on some 200 h. AT San Carlos [tabular data between 1944 and 1949], AGA, C-81/8129, E-4, "Movimiento de braceros: estadística Delegación de trabajo."

68 Clarence-Smith, "African and European Cocoa," 199. They were also decimated through systematic fines. The most common fine for employers was not "depositing 50% of the income of *braceros* in the prescribed intervals," a deposit system where half of the wages were banked by the *Curaduría* and only paid out at the end of the contract. This obligatory arrangement was officially to guarantee final payment but also to disincentivize desertions. Many of the smaller Bubi and Fernandino farmers were thus penalized for running their plantations on credit and having liquidity only after the sale of a crop to one of the commercial houses. Delegado de Haciendo to GG (Alonso), November 30, 1942, "Sanciones por incumplimiento de la Orden de 4 de Agosto de 1942," AGA, C-81/8128, E-13.

the *dash* the island underwent a full polarization where the "employers" were all "Spaniards and workers [were] all Nigerian."[69]

Bracero Finance

The "point of view of the *bracero*" was to "never want to remain a *bracero* but for as short a period of their life as possible, or at least that is their intention."[70] The Nigerian *reengancho* found himself in "Fernando Po with the sole object of making his fortune in his small way" – figuring out an overriding purpose: to "make money as quickly as possible."[71] A 1949 survey of 500 new recruits were asked at the labor department in Calabar as to their "purpose for seeking to earn money under contract." The answers were: to earn enough money to then "engage in petty trading," 36%; or "to pay dowry for a wife," 23%; or "to purchase a bicycle," 10%; or "to assist parents or other relations," 9%. The questionnaire is a nonsensical format since all four reasons contain and presuppose each other, and much else besides.[72] A former *bracero*, who in the 1950s turned himself into a prosperous smuggler of canes and batons, remembers the Fernando Po of the booming late colonial heyday as "a place of many profits," "money everywhere, if something was a luxury in Nigeria, [in Spanish Guinea] it was in abundance."[73]

Thousands of Spanish settlers – when not bossing and attacking people on the plantations or manning most administrative positions – were largely busy running the "many, many, many *factorias* that plague Santa Isabel. The Europe-

69 "Nigeria over the Water," *West Africa*, London, January 1, 1958.

70 Romero Moliner, "Estructura social," 42.

71 LO Calabar to Government, Lagos, 23 March 1945, AGA, C-81/8130, E-1; Osuntokun, "Relations between Nigeria and Fernando Po," 10. Similar to Nigerian labor migrants in Cameroon: "on the whole do not intend to stay longer than is necessary to obtain capital with which to return to Nigeria." Ardener and Ardener, *Kingdom on Mount Cameroon*, 198.

72 Nigeria, *Annual Report 1949/50*, 24. "[O]ther purposes named by small numbers of workers were to improve knowledge, to get experience by travel, to buy farm land, to build a house, and to pay school fees. The desire to possess a bicycle is in the Eastern Provinces from which the recruits come, inspired by more than the mere pleasure of riding one. Bicycle carriers are a special feature of both Ibo and Ibibio country and serve the needs of the population in place of carts and taxis. A bicycle owner thus possesses a means of livelihood." All 400 "were asked to state their previous occupation, with the following results": Occupation-Number, Farmer-132, Petty trader-60, Artisan-44, Labourer-32, Fisherman-28, Domestic servant-24, Carrier cyclist-24, Palm tree cutter-24, Student-20, Clerk-8, Teacher-4.

73 Interview with [anonymized], July 2013, Malabo, Equatorial Guinea.

an emigrant is quite a fan of commerce. Santa Isabel is full of their factories, selling all sorts of goods, and almost all are in their hands."[74] These merchant shops openly catered almost exclusively to a clientele of wholesale brandy and tobacco smugglers from the Cross River delta and the Wouri estuary of Douala who sailed to the island on large ocean-going canoe convoys. By the 1950s they had orchestrated the largest contraband smuggling network in coastal West Africa.[75] While on a fundraising tour in Santa Isabel the secretary of the Ibo State Union whose members on the island were being continuously arrested, beaten, and deported remarked that "it is truly a 'market country', throughout the island one can scarcely distinguish the shop fronts from the government offices. In its entirety it is filled with gigantic mansions and warehouses with innumerable merchandise for sale."[76]

After completing a contract, it was possible under certain circumstances to obtain "a trading license," which allowed *braceros* to stay on the island for a further month without being picked up by police.[77] In the words of a former British district officer: in "reality, the Ibo went for two reasons: to make money and to take advantage of the opportunities the island presented for smuggling." The "return trip" of the "great sea canoes filled with Africans being taken to Fernando Po for illicit engagement" were "laden to the gunnels with brandy, guns and trade good for sale in Nigeria. Labourers also at the end of their contract shipped contraband."[78] The *dash* was also being poured into expensive "bicycles and gramophones" or Spanish-made "sewing machines, before returning home."[79] Laborers made it "clear" to anyone who asked them that the "principal attraction of [a] term of employment in Fernando Poo [was] the acquisition of a lump sum" – "the inability of the individual to save when employed in Nigeria on even well paid work is well known."[80] One "Mr. Chinedu Echu, from Okigwi" after returning from a four year contract on a coffee plantation told a journalist in Port Har-

---

74 Pozanco, *Guinea mártir*, 25. In the 1960s there were about 1,500 Europeans employed in "commerce" in Río Muni and 1,000 in Fernando Po. Pélissier, *Los territorios españoles*, 46, 75.

75 "Smuggling – Nigeria's curse," *Drum*, January 1961.

76 Ibo State Union, Delegation to Fernando Poo, 1954, AGA, C-81/8223 E-1. See van den Bersselaar, "Creating 'Union Ibo.'"

77 British Consul, Yaounde, May 4, 1961, TNA, CO 554/2502.

78 Ian Brook, *The One-Eyed Man Is King* (London: Cassell, 1966), 196, an autobiography.

79 British VC and LO (Bradley) to Commissioner of Labor, Lagos, April 14, 1953, TNA, FO 371/102612; Gabriel B. Hart, "Public Opinion: Recruitment for Fernando Po," *Nigerian Daily Standard*, Lagos, July 30, 1957; Adro Xavier, *España en Africa: ayer y hoy* (Barcelona: Ferma, 1960), 16.

80 Minister of Labour, Lagos, January 18, 1956, "Report of the Federal Minister of Labour and Welfare on visit to Fernando Poo, 4th-8th January 1956," TNA, CO 554/1346.

court that "the conditions" on the plantation where he worked "were fine," and he was even considering "heading off again to said place." Echu had managed to earn "some 35£," because, he said, "there was also a bonus given by employers" and indeed "every labourer receives this bonus."[81]

One of the Vice-Consul's informants gave him the impression that "the majority of labourers, on receiving the lump sum bonus on contracting, paid a large part of it over to a woman and this gave them the right to spend the night with her, whenever they came to Santa Isabel."[82] This was only partially true; these figures were more than sexual liaisons. Several thousand Nigerian and Cameroonian women ran and staffed the market stalls, and brothels and bars that populated *Nu Billi* (New Village) or *Campo Yaounde*, the migrant slum of Santa Isabel.[83] These women acted as the so-called "money-keepers" accounted for elsewhere in West Africa, because informal *dash* money was obviously unbankable.[84] The peseta lost fourfold its value vis-à-vis the West Africa pound between 1936 and 1952, so it made sense to quickly convert the *dash* into fixed assets such as liquor bottles that could eventually be smuggled back and easily sold in Nigeria – a delayed conversion with various steps usually arranged by these women.

Braceros never actually held on to the *dash* money for long. Keeping unattended valuables in the housing barracks of the plantations was not a good idea – theft was common. Though theft of each other's possessions was clearly marked off from the appropriation of planters' property: "It seems that the saying that there is honour amongst thieves is very apt in this case, for whereas all labourers seem to consider robbing their employers as all in a day's work, they do not rob each other with the same monotonous regularity."[85] Also, as there were no official receipts for the *regalos* higher than the regulated amount of 300 pesetas, *braceros* would need to avoid carrying around large sums of cash for fear of being accused of theft and immediately thrown into jail – or rather the road-gangs of the public works department. Many *braceros*, at the end of

---

81 "Fernando Poo," *Eastern Nigeria Guardian*, Port Harcourt, August 14, 1957.

82 British VC and LO (Bradley) to Commissioner of Labor, Lagos, April 14, 1953, TNA, FO 371/102612.

83 Policía, "Registro de Incidencias 1953," 278 [entry of September 28, 1953], BNM [no call number]; Paul Iregbulam, Jefe de los Ibos Owerri, Santa Isabel to AT Santa Isabel, December 14, 1955, AGA, C-81/8601, E-5. See also Chapdelaine, "Marriage Certificates and Walker Cards."

84 Berry, "Stable Prices," 309; Guyer, "Gains and Losses," 148; Gustav Peebles, "Rehabilitating the Hoard: The Social Dynamics of Unbanking in Africa and Beyond," *Africa* 84, no. 4 (2014).

85 British VC and LO (Bradley) to Commissioner of Labor, Lagos, March 31, 1950, TNA CO 554/169/1.

the working day, derived extra income from participating in the informal economies of the island; "producing charcoal,"[86] "stealing firewood [to bring] to the town for sale," catching crabs from the innumerable rivers streaming down the volcanic slopes and selling them to passing cars on the road, or gathering fruits from the shadow trees of the plantation, and selling them.[87] These activities were often followed by the accusation of "alleged robbery." The "stealing of coffee beans from the plantations" was a systematic affair, as these could be sold on to a highly organized underground circuit of Hausa intermediaries.[88] It should be emphasized that in colonial work sites, as elsewhere, this type of wisely opportunistic pilfering was "certainly not considered [to be] criminal behaviour"; those involved in it "talked openly about forging exchange and selling networks."[89]

A British missionary, responsible for a mostly Nigerian congregation in an isolated plantation area, noted in 1934 that "lots have been terribly disillusioned and suffer terribly from home-sickness. Behind them they have left their families, parents, tribal chiefs, laws and restraints [and here] except to their employers and the country laws, have no other allegiances. Soon they acquire new sins and vices."[90] Already since the 1920s, on Sundays, *braceros* were "given ample liberty to visit the many bars and vagabond women of the Island, the principal import from Spain is a cheap wine chiefly for indigenous consumption." British visitors on the island observed this as a "state of freedom. There are plenty of cafes and idle women on the island, and the chief import from Spain is a crude wine for native consumption only."[91] The Methodist Reverend on the island lamented that his churches were being "neglected" because the *bracero* went on Sunday shopping trips to "spend his money in shops [with] fine displays offering a bewildering variety of cheap Spanish drinks" for export and consump-

---

86 British LO (Evans) to British Consul General (Lawrence), Douala, July 31, 1945, NAE, CALPROF 17/1/278.

87 British LO (Evans) to British Consul General (Lawrence), Douala, August 31, 1945, NAE, CALPROF 17/1/278.

88 British LO (Evans), April 30, 1945, TNA, FO 371/49598.

89 Ralph Callebert, "Cleaning the Wharves: Pilferage, Bribery, and Social Connections on the Durban Docks in the 1950s," *Canadian Journal of African Studies* 46, no. 1 (2012): 26; Harries, *Work, Culture, and Identity*, 114.

90 W. H. Collins, "Fernando Poo Today: A weekend visit to San Carlos by Rev. W.H. Collins," *Kingdom Overseas* 2 (1934): 222.

91 Curaduría (Romain Ordoño) to GG (Manresa), July 16, 1931, AGA, C-81/8125, E-2; Murray, *The School in the Bush*, 25.

tion.[92] Given the commercial intensity of the island it was unsurprising that *braceros* were "tempted to fritter away" the "ill-gotten gains" of the *dash* on "wine, women and tobacco," while "the more prudent of them," says the Vice-Consul in 1950, "invest the money in goods with which to trade on their return to Nigeria."[93] In a rare archival find, the confiscated diary of a *bracero* from 1961, a politically conscious and torn convert, a young unmarried man called Monde, reads: "Shameful, I had over doze shots of illicit gin and palm oil wine and adultered and woke up to 12 noon at the premises in the Afonta local Bar. My action when I was very high was rewarded as madmans way of life."[94] Those with the nerve to stay on the island for several contracts, says Israel, a former treaty-*bracero*, were given the appellative "*griho*": "this simply means that those people were carried away by the high life in Fernando Po that existed in the form of women and alcohol."[95] *Griho* seems to have been a common sobriquet derived from the Spanish word for cricket, *grillo* – awake and noisy at night.

Bracero Politics

The 1952 decree that tried to ban the *dash* was also explicitly geared "to stop workers deserting and recontracting under false names, with false documents in order to obtain the engagement bonus."[96] Deserters "appeared to consider that the risk of breaking the law is well worth the 'dash', which they would receive for contracting, if they were not caught."[97] The labor market into which the *fugados* inserted themselves into was characterized by an excess of paperwork. It was a costly routine, but a routine nevertheless, to acquire certain stamped forms in the different labor, medical, and police departments and fill the pockets of one of the "at least 400 functionaries who easily succumb to the temptation to falsify a paper or document as soon as the opportunity presents itself." A Francoist official in the late 1930s already made the prejudicial ob-

92 David Lawrence, (unpublished memoirs, 1999), "Faith Hope Love: A Legacy," 42, SOAS, MMS, MMSL MSS/028.

93 British VC and LO (Bradley) to Commissioner of Labor, Lagos, March 31, 1950, TNA CO 554/169/1.

94 Monde Obongue, October 15, 1961, "Annals 1961" [Diary booklet], AGA, C-81/8803, E-622.

95 Oham, "Labor Migration," 62.

96 Peña, *Repertorio*, 350; British VC and LO (Bradley) to Commissioner of Labor, Lagos, April 14, 1953, TNA, FO 371/102612.

97 British VC and LO (Bradley) to British Consul General, Barcelona, January 5, 1952, TNA, FO 371/96714.

servation that the Fernandinos, the "landowner" and "elite caste" of English-speaking Protestants, "feel hate for Spain" but "nevertheless for inexplicable reasons they also make up the greater part of African staff in our colonial bureaucracy."[98] Marck Oturu, a Nigerian tout from Bende who was "inscribed as a peddler residing in this city," was arrested and held in the police headquarters of Santa Isabel and assured the new Spanish Chief of Police in 1961 that any "necessary paperwork could all be arranged for here," by which he meant either Santa Isabel or the police station. Oturu's case related to the acquisition of paperwork necessary to hire newly smuggled labor under usurped identities of departing laborers, for which there was a considerable market.[99]

Deserting *reenganchos* again enlisted the collaboration of Campo Yaounde's bar owners, who "protect[ed] *fugados* in their homes" when they needed to await a supply of new paperwork. In the 1950s the colonial authorities started delegating the task of finding *fugados* to the handful of prominent Nigerian and Cameroonian "chiefs," one for each main "ethnic" immigrant group on the island, well-represented in Campo Hausa and Yaounde. A local *Jefe de los Lagos* or Yoruba "chief" had already existed since 1887 and a *Jausa* or Hausa paramount chief since World War I, but the positions were not formalized until 1947 – when they needed to be instrumentalized with the rise of urgent surveillance needs related to the *dash.* During the early Francoist period there were numerous requests to recognize new "chiefdoms," including the "Chiefdom of the Calabars" led by Juan E. Boco, a "professional photographer" of the powerful Efik Cobham family of Calabar. In the early 1950s, the chiefdom of the Igbo "Oweri" followed. The chiefs were voted on internally by "ethnic" associations and were sites of mutual aid and dispute resolution, organizing charitable works for "needy countrymen and burial of the dead." By the late 1940s these Nigerian "chiefs" became key municipal agents, spreading and translating new decrees and supervising the markets of Campo Yaounde. They were also enlisted in the search for escaped *braceros* and the denunciation of "vagrancy," with the incentive of keeping a third of the corresponding fine extracted thereby.[100] By the late 1950s a dozen Nigerian chiefs had been appointed, "to fulfil the laws of Public Order, especially

---

98 Romero Moliner, "Estructura social," 43; Babiloni, 1937, AGA, C-81/12427.

99 Jefe de Policía (Jaime) to GG (Ruíz), June 22, 1961, AGA, C-81/8215, E-5.

100 Policía, "Registro de Incidencias 1953," 174, [entry of August 9, 1953], BNM [no call number]. The Campo Yaounde chiefs, at the behest of the local administration, organized the sending of "Ibos and Calabares" to do "cleaning jobs and *chapeo*" in the slum, "without pay" and "against their will." AT Santa Isabel to GG (Bonelli), May 15, 1946, "Campo Yaounde," AGA, C-81/8601, E-1.

amongst the Nigerian population." They "were authorized to arrest any delinquent, bringing them to the Police or to the courts."[101]

The carceral landscape of Francoist Fernando Po was unusually intense. In the Francoist decades around five and up to ten percent of the island's population passed through a jail in any one-year period, principally Nigerian *braceros* and traders. Just the series of jails run by the *Guardia Colonial* on the island housed between 600 and 1,000 prisoners a day.[102] In the island district of San Carlos, the "number of prisoners driven" per day in 1955 ranged between 300 to 500. San Carlos had a population of about 8,500 contracts workers. Nevertheless, prisoners were known to be able to escape often, as they were always "outside" doing extra-mural penal labor: "at the end of the work day at 7pm when we take the prisoners to rinse themselves off by the water they always manage to *fugarse*."[103] Their escape was most likely aided by touts again.

In the late 1930s the *Curaduría* had 17 staff – desk clerks, guards, a driver, a cashier, and its own team of detectives dedicated to the full-time pursuit of "*braceros fugados*." The *Curaduría* has its own police force with wide-ranging powers to raid homes and plantation patios without notice: to "keep in continuous fear *the braceros fugados o maleantes* [miscreants]." In addition, eight guards supervised the forced labor of those *braceros*, usually 80–150 on any given day in the Francoist period, arrested on minor work-related "anti-vagrancy" charges such as malingering or being caught out at night outside the housing units of the plantations. The *Curaduría* held them in their own *barracones*, which were separate from the prison and other sites of arrest, organized by the *Guardia Colonial* and the municipal police.[104] Most *braceros* were held by the *Guardia Colonial* who had outposts and jails distributed throughout the island and closer to remote plantation. If "a labourer's employer has any sort of grounds of complaint he can send the labourer along to the Police and have him soundly flogged."[105] As Mateo Ríos, a Spanish sailor passing through the colony, notes in the early 1950s, there was "no need for brute force on the plantations" as it was "suf-

101 "Nine Nigerian 'Chiefs' appointed in Fernando Poo," *Daily Times*, Lagos, August 22, 1958.
102 Guardia Colonial, 1950, "Memoria," AGA, C-81/8183. See especially Celeste Muñoz Martínez, "La ley contra la costumbre. Segregación, asimilación jurídica y castigo en la Guinea Española bajo el franquismo (1936–1959)" (PhD diss., Universitat de Barcelona, 2020), 297–369.
103 Guardia Colonial, 1955, "Memoria," AGA, C-81/15865, E-9. In San Carlos, 7,500 *braceros* were Nigerian, 800 "Spanish" and 430 "French."
104 Curaduría, 1936, "Inventario," AGA, C-81/8126, E-28; Curaduría, September 1934, "Reglamento de la Policía de Curaduría," AGA, C-81/7722 E-1.
105 British VC and LO (Rylands) to Commissioner of Labor, Lagos, January 8, 1947, NAE, CALPROF 17/1/278.

ficient to threaten the worker with dropping him off at the police station, and out of fear he returns to work. The *barracón de la Policía* is a '*tabú*', there he will be beaten with a rubber truncheon wrapped in leather for as long as the Guards wish, while he serves out a sentence of forced labour."[106]

Spanish officials systematically took all signs of labor abuse and complaints as a feigned, distorted, and staged instigation. Workers were constantly being fined and punished for "producing false denunciations of abuse, as the complainants pretended to collapse when assaulted" by an overseer. It was a well-known fact by all parties that an "excessive" or "illegitimate" abuse as vaguely defined by the 1906 labor code could merit an all-important early release of a *bracero* from their contract. The *Curadores* expended much perceptive energy and paranoid incredulity to claim a divide between "disciplinary slaps" and "cruel beatings by masters," to channel all violence into the permissible category of supervisory discipline.[107] As the Vice-Consul noted in 1952, "when labourers complaints are proved to be false, they are detained for a week or a fortnight for making false accusations against their employers," which, he added, "is, alas, a very necessary step as otherwise both this office and the Spanish Labour Office are inundated with unfounded complaints." In many cases it was impossible to reconstruct the incidents as all that circulated were "witness" testimonies of the same incident that claimed different "minor" but vital details that could be the ground for terminating a contract. The longest serving British Vice-Consul, Bradley, sympathized with

> an African employer, [who] quite rightly, considered that his eight labourers were idling their time away. He took them round to the local post of the Guardia Colonial and persuaded a soldier to beat them. The men concerned stated that they each received 50 strokes but the employer and the solider stated they had each received 5 strokes. As there were no marks on the bodies of the men concerned, I believe the employer's and soldier's version.[108]

Another Vice-Consul, Spencer-Cooke, opined in 1950 that the "award of arbitrary sentences [on] workmen [who] are insubordinate or act in any malicious manner on a farm is possibly deserved." Off "the victim goes to prison where I under-

106 Ríos, *La España ignorada*, 55.
107 Curaduría to GG, August 8, 1930, "Malos Tratos a Braceros," AGA, C-81/07720.
108 British VC and LO (Bradley) to British Consul General, Barcelona, January 4, 1952, TNA, FO 371/96714.

stand he is greeted with a flogging as a preliminary to serving his sentence."[109] One of the first active labor inspectors in the Francoist period – almost half a decade after they taken power – observed in 1941 that in the plantations of the *Compañia Colonial de Africa* a twelve-hour working day was the norm, but "the work day has been reduced to ten hours." There were "corporal punishments, especially the whipping of the *braceros* who are unwilling to work" – this was permissible if it did not cause irreversible bodily disfiguration. The inspector also observed that while *braceros* "were generally well-behaved in order to avoid corporal punishments in the *fincas*" he proposed that "there is the pressing necessity of creating within all army outposts the *brigadas de castigos* [punishment brigades] employing the prisoners with heavy pickaxe and shovel work, which is what most upsets the *indígena*."[110]

Under the Francoist the so-called *brigadas disciplinarias* expanded considerably. These disciplinary brigades spread through policing institutions, supplied a "special regime of regeneration" where "indigenous delinquents are obliged to work," and were "dedicated to the maintenance of roads and tracks, or other works of analogous hardness."[111] A group of *braceros* told George Dove-Edwin, a Nigerian Krio lawyer visiting his brother-in-law on the island, that "a note from anyone of their employers was sufficient not only to confine them in prison but for them to be treated as convicts" – the sign of the "convict" in Nigeria as elsewhere in colonial Africa was primarily extra-mural penal labor.[112] The road-

---

109 British VC (Spencer-Cooke) to Consul General, Barcelona, November 8, 1950, TNA, FO 371/89597; "[C]orporal punishment invariably administered on entry into the prison," British VC and LO (Spencer-Cooke) to Commissioner of Labor, Lagos, September 30, 1950, TNA, FO 371/89597.

110 AT Santa Isabel to GG (Fontán), December 17, 1941, AGA, C-81/8128, E-13.

111 Miranda, *Leyes coloniales*, 1487. The prison became not only a place of systematic torture but infinite toil. In the early 1960s when a governmental circular reached the *Guardia Territorial*, instructing them to withhold severe corporal punishment, the Governor quickly reissued a clarification: "An incorrect interpretation of the instruction of 9 of February [1961] it seems, has led to the festering among some prisoners of an apathy towards work, possibly caused by their false idea that they cannot in any case be subject to corporal punishment; such apathy results in a decreased work performance rendered by the inmates, which I am in no way willing to tolerate." He adds that those in charge of the "prison regime are my most effective collaborators; they are undertaking an aspect of such transcendental importance for the policies that my Authority is developing in these Territories [...] and out of respect to my own position I cannot consent to any deviation or passive resistance." GG (Ruíz), March 28, 1961, "Instruccion sobre trato a los reclusos," AGA, C-81/8221, E-4.

112 George Frederick Dove-Edwin to British VC (Robertson), January 31, 1944, NAE, CALPROF 17/1/277; British VC (Spencer-Cooke) to Consul General, Barcelona, November 8, 1950, TNA, FO 371/89597. See Bernault and Roitman, *Prison and Confinement*.

gangs of the public works department were a place of dread. As an "agonish report from Nigerian boys" explains in 1938:

> When we finish contract from each of his master's farm where there is hell, that's a bad master, and refused to go back there, they will put the boy or boys to jail. Some are numerable in that road they call caratera [road] which is the worst of all punishments in Sta Isabel beating us to death by their policers with big rubber and to carry a heavy pan of stones, plenty boys have sick and died away.[113]

The terrain of value between capital and labor on Fernando Po was often jarring, verging from absolute injustice to spectacular coups. Planters clawed back their profits by extending contracts and adding arbitrarily imposed jail time. As Nnamdi Azikiwe, the media mogul and first president of Nigeria, observed early on in relation to Liberian *braceros* on the island, the prison system was primarily a device to extend the duration of *bracero* labor on the island and doubly exploit it: "instead of 'punctual repatriation' Spain devised a subterfuge to prefer a criminal charge against laborers whose contracts are nearing termination, and by imprisoning them, it derives an unjust benefit from free convict labor."[114]

There was much spontaneous and insurgent pushback against *capatazes* or overseers, making deserting a wise decision. The planter Jose Ramirez from San Carlos lodged a revealing complaint: on a Sunday in January 1954 when it was "customary to have some festivities in the patios," he ordered "his *braceros* to go to sleep and rest for the next day, whose order they all obeyed without exception." But when Ramirez approached a rowdy room in one of the barracks, "at this moment an unknown *indígena*, without prior warning and without an exchange of words, punched him in the face, bruising his left eye and nose." The protagonist of the surprise attack was a young Cameroonian form Mamfe, a *bracero* from a nearby plantation. When arrested he "pretended to be drunk" while being held by the guards, and then "pretended that he needed to urinate"; it turned out he was actually "quite sober" and he "used the opportunity to flee." Caught again later that night, his defense was alcohol: he had "stumbled upon a fellow countrywoman" and "with a guitar" they sat "together and drank a little, with seven others. We drank four bottles of wine and one cognac." He also confessed to "try to get away because he knew that if he disappeared the *massa* whom he punched in the face would not be able to recognize or locate

---

113 Anonymous, July 19, 1938, "An agonish report from Nigerian boys to the above Captain of English man of war," TNA, FO 371/22669.

114 Azikiwe, "In Defense of Liberia," 40.

him."[115] Only the *massa* could arrange for his pursuit – he was confident that none of his drinking companions would inform on him. Nevertheless, he got caught and was sent to the *brigada disciplinaria* for one year followed by deportation, all of which he was forced to pay himself. It seems he either returned destitute to Cameroon or otherwise he may have deserted from jail and hired himself under a different name and in a different plantation zone or possibly in Río Muni.

Such incidences were common, though many came out the other end unscathed. For example, Jose Ocoyo from Calabar, a "*bracero* working for Casa Lampert," a German contractor, and the "alleged author" of a "head-wound" inflicted "with a shovel" on "Mr. Garcia," the overseer or *capataz*. Ocoyo wisely "fled apparently to Santa Isabel," untracked, the Spanish police gave the vague markers: "approximately 35 years of age, heavy built and very dark."[116] However, hitting the planters where it really hurts was someone who went by the female alias Okpara Anita.[117] In 1962 Anita fled back to Nigeria with a forged "freedom paper" and then proceeded to send a personal letter taunting his former employer "Mr. Pedro." While working a seemingly prime job at the recently inaugurated Pepsi-Cola bottling plant, he was temporarily entrusted to deliver an envelope, that allegedly contained 46.600 pesetas.[118] From the safety of his own country, to which he had "flyed away by avion" – or airplane, as he says in a mix of Spanish and English – and insisting on the more or less ethical conduct of his operation, he says: "the money was given [to] me by Master Pinga, not by night or hidden thing it is in day time." Like the *dash*, money changed hands in broad daylight, the cosmological opposite of stealth or night-time banditry.[119] Unlike

---

115 AT San Carlos (Matres Calvo), January 25, 1954, "Atestado" and "Manifestacion de Edet Elachea," AGA, C-81/8215, E-5.

116 Guardia Colonial, Comandante de Puesto, Concepcion to AT San Carlos, April 7, 1941, AGA, C-81/15865, E-11.

117 In Fernando Pó and elsewhere in colonial Africa, the "very casual use of names" amongst "African labourers" was a pre-emptive defense grounded in wit and well-founded paranoia: "he fears that some unknown and probably oppressive use may be made of any information about himself which he may supply, and he therefore frequently purposely gives false particulars; he may even adopt a vulgar or indecent pseudonym as an excellent joke in the vernacular for the amusement of his fellows who alone understand it," Orde-Browne, *African Labourer*, 77. On aliases as a strategy against pass-laws in South Africa and the flailing dialectics of fingerprints and photography, which were only implemented on Fernando Pó in the mid-1940s and even then in easily forgeable templates, see MacDonald, "The Identity Thieves," 254; MacDonald, "Forging the Frontiers," 168.

118 Jefe de Policía (Ramirez Togores) to Alfredo Jones Niger, Calabar, January 24, 1962, AGA, C-81/8803, E-s/n 622. For information on bottling plant, see AGA, C-81/11850.

119 Bastian, "Bloodhounds," 154.

the *dash*, linked directly to the contract, this was a case of outright theft, but much is revealed in his letter about the moral and political strategy of a bold lumpen action.

The letter is at times incomprehensible or open to wide interpretation, but Anita seems to suggest that his theft-desertion was the sublimation of the resentment of subordination realized by outwitting his employer: "end your higher knowledge." His act of flight would be vindicated by the added respect that would accrue to other workers because of the employers' unease: "Through two years ill treatment in we black men end your higher knowledge have brought you to this point of heard I known which is always brother to master hate. This is simple when you see any black man working under you respect him through: to his colour." This last sentence is also cryptic, but another laborer, who was immediately deported after several months of hard labor for what he said, puts the gist of Anita's letter more clearly, as paraphrased by the Spanish Police Chief: "it's very easy to say yes to the orders that the Europeans give us, well because the only words of Spanish we have been taught are 'si señor', which one has to say even if you are thinking the opposite. In Nigeria this is not how it works, everyone responds man to man."[120] In any case it was poetic that the bottling plant where Anita worked and fled with the money from, was called *El Cayuco*, or the canoe.

While the range of strategies of informal and criminal counter-practices on the island's workplaces do not all correspond to the specific anti-structural dynamics I identified in the escalation of the *dash*, the world of wage negotiations borrowed and resided freely within the lumpen economy on the island. Not least in the fact that the sabotage of *dash-peonaje* worked only if performed with theatrics and props – with aliases, assumed identities, forgeries, and a stash of documents – in the plain light of day rather than through the stealth of the predatory lone burglar. If deemed just or worth the risk, a laborer could "contract himself to five different employers in the course of a month, each time receiving a handsome 'dash'." "One man [who] had 13 current contracts" might have broken a record with all except one of his hopeful employers denouncing the *bracero* as a *fugado*. A "great many Treaty labourers" were also defecting to the spiraling *dash* by simply "adopting a new name." They "realise that if they run away and obtain false papers, which can be bought [they] receive a 'dash' of

120 Akpara Anita to Pedro de la Cia. Pepsi-Cola, November 24, 1961; Policía to Secretario General, May 4, 1962, AGA, C-81/8803, E-s/n 622.

some £30."[121] Ato Santos, an "Ijaw from Opobo," signed a treaty contract in Calabar but soon fled back "to Nigeria on a canoe" and two months later he came back, "paid FIFTY PESETAS to a nurse of the Sanitary Services who gave him a medical certificate with a changed name," with which he could then hire himself under the false name of "Patric Chinaka Alaga" to "another employer."[122] He was unlucky to be caught.

Escalation

The deserter-tout nexus reassembled by deploying techniques of financial capitalism – generating speculative debts based on their labor – within a state of generalized corruption. Touts could not generate their own kingdom, only the knowledge of whom to approach and where to go. Touts were driven by their share of the *dash*, but they were also personally solicited as they enabled a radicalization of workers' strategies and expectations. Together they produced an extraordinarily creative praxis, a co-operative but risky logistics, that tuned the colonial order through a savoir-faire and rejected its preformatted rules of contract labor exchange. Recruiters could surprise the imperial economics of labor demands; they could lean into and jam the force of an entire agro-capitalist plantation island and make it collapse onto itself.

The outcomes and success of desertion were necessarily serendipitous and mediated through opportunism. Because of this, "desertion" has often been considered a "conservative," "inhibiting" and fragmentary form of resistance or even as not a form of resistance at all.[123] The labelling of something as "resistance" at the point of a contradiction simply implies the identification of a pressure point where the economy could be paralyzed, and power relations renegotiated. In relation to the tin mines in Nigeria, writing in a period when strategies of industrial labor relations were still a considerable concern, including in Nigerian sociology departments, Bill Freund even conceived of mediators as a primary obstacle, with the "struggle" needing to be "directed against the network of contractors and other parasitic intermediaries who stand between labour and capital" be-

121 British VC and LO (Bradley) to Commissioner of Labor, Lagos, April 10, 1951, TNA, CO 554/169/2; British VC and LO (Bradley) to British Consul General, Barcelona, July 4, 1952, TNA, FO 371/96714; British VC and LO (Rylands) to Commissioner of Labor, Lagos, January 8, 1947, NAE, CALPROF 17/1/278.

122 Jefe de Policía (Jaime) to AT San Carlos, July 22, 1960, AGA, C-81/09006, E-1.

123 Harries, *Work, Culture and Identity*, 42; Isaie Dougnon, "Migration for 'White Man's Work': An Empirical Rebuttal to Marxist Theory," *African Identities* 7, no. 3 (2009).

cause it is "their strength, rather than the migrant nature of labour" that explains the "weakness of class struggle by mineworkers."[124] Even when faced with a similar constellation of facts, where workers "fled so early in the term of recruitment that they had not yet worked off the advances," and indeed gave "false names to the recruitment agency in order to more easily cover their tracks once they fled into the wage labor market," this historical action was misread as resistance, says Eric Allina, mocking the image of workers who had been represented not "merely" as "actors" but as "nimbly planning ones who schemed to exploit their would-be exploiters."[125] Clearly the tout-workers were not modelling themselves on the naïvely affirmative connotations of the term "agency" of critical social theory; if "agency" is to mean anything it is the capacity for actors to surprise and create original techniques for making history, under conditions not of their own choosing and with their own past weighing upon them immeasurably.[126] In practice, the crossing, staying, appropriating, experimenting, and redeploying of whatever was circulating in the confines of the colonial economy of Fernando Po easily amounted to an outright anti-colonial action of the most fundamental kind.

The dual spiral of the *dash* – escalating advances and multiple desertions – did not of course involve any syndicalist organization. On Fernando Po collective "politics is a forbidden fruit"; "in that island of terrorism and brutality strikes are illegal and agitation is criminal."[127] "In this part of the world" says the resident British Consul, "labour relations," meaning the industrial sociology of deliberated negotiations, "are unknown." Any "attempt to discuss or argue an issue with the employer would be regarded as an affront and the labourer may find himself in serious trouble."[128] In the literature, the surreptitious movement to and from contracts has often been downgraded to a technical search "for slight better wages,"[129] sustained by a "spontaneous and ephemeral" "communications network" strung along by touts in "a continuous, although unofficial, level of organization." While delineating the ways in which "migrant workers" and touts informally "combined" in South Africa and Mozambique without reaching levels of "radical" self-organization, Patrick Harries says that for the "transient and shad-

124 Freund, "Labour Migration," 83.

125 Eric Allina, "Resistance and the Social History of Africa," *Journal of Social History* 37, no. 1 (2003): 192; also Allina, *Slavery by Any Other Name*, chap. 4 and 7.

126 Walter Johnson, "On Agency," *Journal of Social History* 37, no. 1 (2003).

127 Lola Martins, "Laborers Go Singing: Life with the Nigerians in Fernando Poo," *Express*, Lagos, February 22, 1962; Peter Pan, "The Brutal Island," *Daily Times*, Lagos, January 27, 1965.

128 British VC (Harriman), April 22, 1960, TNA, FO 371/146562.

129 Cooper, *Decolonization*, 45; Bolt and Green, "Was the Wage Burden too heavy?"

owy tramping system," equivalent to the *dash*-system, "it was the very obscurity, ephemerality, and flexibility of this form of organization that was their greatest weapon."[130] The *dash*-system sustained and enacted a mortal critique of the colonial contract system itself.

The *dash*, with and without deserters, was well on its way to finish off the plantations for good – until "reforms" and new sources of external *braceros* were brought in. The *dash* – and the touts who made the connections between the respective *dash* parties – appeared from the new voids of registration surrounding the *Curaduría*, from the thwarted ability of dirigiste political power to make *reenganchos* stand in an orderly queue behind unilaterally stipulated terms of payment. Such state coordinated contract monopsonies had been set up across imperial islands and enclaves of indenture to drive down and cap wages and worker bargaining power.[131]

It was only outside or between contracts that *reenganchos* opened the space for a form of contestation that first managed to get rid of the most abusive overseers and planters and then gutted the plantations at their very core – their declining rate of profit. The escalating *dash* was supported by the self-organized working relationships between *braceros*, touts, forgers, corrupt functionaries, prostitutes, money keepers, smugglers, illegal immigrants, thieves, convicts, drunks, etc., relationships I will try theorizing in the next and final chapter. Though as is already clear, the lumpen groups did not only reside in a parallel "second economy" but navigated and configured the breakthroughs and contradictory interdependencies between "wage-earning and self-employment."[132] Drawing on the repertoire of *dash* negotiation techniques – self-evident demands, up-to-date scripts, masks made with forged papers – the *reenganchos* outwitted the imperial capitalist stamp that tried to engineer low-wages, and this, with an indispensable dose of confidence and dexterity; a remarkable maneuver.

Even though bound by the "grotesque nuisance"[133] of a chain of imperial contracts, passes and "freedom papers," the *reenganchos* escalated the *dash* through an uncompromising commodity economics based on the price of their labor. The autonomous escalations of the *dash* took place entirely besides imperial self-definitions of "free" contract labor, and indeed outside liberal notions of

---

130 Harries, *Work, Culture and Identity*, 40, 45.

131 Arrighi, "Labour Supplies," 200; Van Onselen, *Chibaro*, 21, 231.

132 Janet MacGaffey, ed., *The Real Economy of Zaire: The Contribution of Smuggling & Other Unofficial Activities to National Wealth* (Philadelphia: University of Pennsylvania Press, 1991), 12; Bolt, "Waged Entrepreneurs," 116.

133 Breckenridge, "Flesh Made Words," 88.

the self-regulating market. Across the boundaries of imperial states as well as those of the cellular plantation patios, an alliance of *braceros* and touts opened borders and doors where these had been closed. Even though the coup of the *dash* was a provisional and rare feat, the self-propelled trajectory of the *reenganchos* on Fernando Po was sustained by a "just" praxis – a moral economy of radicalized economics – in one of the most structurally violent colonies of its day.[134]

For *braceros* the *dash* was a relevelling moment pulled out from inside a colonial state-imposed device for calculating bondage, a rare point of leverage around "fixed" colonial law. The devices that capital and bureaucracy deployed to infiltrate and gain strength – the forced distribution of paperwork to enforce and detect as well as the social control enabled by debt – could be rendered inoperative by ever more audacious incursions. Employers attempted to deploy the *dash* as a bind to keep experienced labor power, but the ploy of the *dash* got out of hand. The gifty code of the *dash* came back to haunt the planters by providing the *braceros* with the tool to peacefully arm themselves on the island. The cumulative play of flight was one of withdrawal and tactical re-entry, a guerrilla without bloodshed.

134 See also Valenciano-Mané, "Morals and Politics of Price in Equatorial Guinea."

5 Lumpen-brokers

> If exchange is the criterion of generality, theft and gift are those of repetition. There is, therefore, an economic difference between the two. [...] Marx's theory of historical repetition, as it appears notably in The Eighteenth Brumaire of Louis Bonaparte, turns on the following principle which does not seem to have been sufficiently understood by historians: historical repetition is neither a matter of analogy nor a concept produced by the reflection of historians, but above all a condition of historical action itself.
>
> – Gilles Deleuze, *Difference and Repetition*

Only a concept as loaded and stretchable as the assembly of workers and touts can suit them. Only a concept that can explain why and how they matched, and how they could consistently shift and escalate their extreme and effective techniques, can capture this oscillating movement. A worthy concept needs to show the power of combination of the same elements. The same contracts, often the same recruiters, and the same workers, altered their own assemblages, leading to vastly different outcomes. In one constellation recruiters allowed the island's cacao plantations to flourish on the backs of an unprecedented influx of quasi-kidnapped laborers in the 1930s and 1940s, and in the next step and decades, many of these same recruits combined with touts to unleash themselves on the colonial economy of the island.

The idea to rigorously develop the concept of "lumpen-brokers" to provide conclusions about their contradictory historical effects in labor markets needs to be prefaced with a precautionary note: the lumpenproletariat was very much a concept of its time and language. Marx and Engels were the only authors to consistently use the term in their lifetime, and most mentions are found in miscellaneous note-essays and semi-published manuscripts used to label different groups in different historical periods – sometimes it was applied to Irish immigrants in Manchester for their insalubrious dwellings and weekends spent hawking and peddling, or for their role as the "surplus" population keeping wages low; other times it was a distinctive invective against the pan-European *lazzaroni*, originally a Neapolitan underclass of the Bourbon era, characterized by their "unplanned" lives and being easily susceptible to bribery and thus easily engaged in reactionary alliances; sometimes it was applied to what Marx initially called *Tagelöhnerpöbel*, the unorganized daylaborers without property in the early modern towns; and initially it was used to designate the Roman class demographically called "proletarians" or "plebeians, midway between freemen and slaves, [who] never succeeded in becoming more than a *lumpenpro-*

https://doi.org/10.1515/9783110755923-009

letariat," because they were not creating value in the Roman slave-based productive economy that depended on the "constant" importation of "new slaves."[1]

The inconsistent definitions of the term and its awry application in different historical settings could lead to the pre-emptive conclusion that the concept was never meant to be central for the analysis of social structure or the labor market or part of an outline of a genuine theory. The concept has usually been treated in the same way as the groups it supposedly designated, as an extraneous and superfluous idea, an "unproductive" "flotsam." Instead, I offer what I think is a more precise interpretation of it as an economic category well beyond the object of criminology and social work, "the milieu of beggars and thieves," found and sent, as Marx says, "to the work-houses and lunatic asylums, to the bar of justice, to the dungeon and to the scaffold."[2] This chapter proposes a strict economic logic of the lumpen, with their own "financial science" as Marx called it. This particular reading moves away from the received understanding of the lumpenproletariat as a primarily moral-political category that designates unreliable and corruptible factions of a radical political movement seeking allies and improved organization, or alternatively, as simply an old-fashioned catch-all term equivalent to the unregulated, criminal, outcast, precarious or informal sectors of the economy.[3]

Brokers and Merchant Capitalism

Brokerage or the figure "the broker" is a well-studied and theorized one, especially in financial markets and as political and cultural intermediaries. In other dimensions only loosely related to the labor market, they were usually seen as assimilated or assimilating agents, helping propagate and translate

1 Marx and Engels, "The German Ideology," 84. Written in early 1846, and first published in full in 1932. The best overview of the contradictory and inconstant usage of the term is Peter Stallybrass, "Marx and Heterogeneity: Thinking the Lumpenproletariat," *Representations* 31 (1990).
2 Raymond Huard, "Marx et Engels devant la marginalité: La découverte du Lumpenproletariat," *Romantisme* 59 (1988): 7; Marx, "Class Struggles in France," 50–51.
3 See the dismissal of the term on these grounds by Marcel van der Linden and Karl Heinz Roth, "'Marxism' or Marx's Method? A Brief Response to Tom Brass," *Science & Society* 82, no. 1 (2018); and the original and unconvincing critique, which botches the concept of the lumpen, by Tom Brass, "Who these days is not a subaltern? The populist drift of Global Labor History," *Science & Society* 81, no. 1 (2017). See also Franco Barchiesi, "Precarious Liberation: A Rejoinder," *South African Review of Sociology* 43, no. 1 (2012): 104; Clara Han, "Precarity, Precariousness, and Vulnerability," *Annual Review of Anthropology* 47 (2018): 332–334.

new colonial political, legal, and economic orders.[4] In a wonderfully recuperative review article, Johan Lindquist has excavated a conceptual genealogy of the broker trope in the history of the post-war social sciences. He notes how the figure ballooned in the era of decolonization for its obvious interest as a missing link in between the various stages of "modernization." Early studies by Eric Wolf and Clifford Geertz, pioneers of a new "political anthropology," dedicated themselves to these figures as the almost exclusive mediators between communities and imperial or post-colonial bureaucracies. Wolf, in his study of Mexican politics and economy from the early 1950s, linked the nineteenth century rise of "brokers" to the milieu of the "lumpenproletariat," where "loosely-structured settlements of casual farmers and workers, middlemen and 'lumpenproletarians' who had no legal place in the colonial order" developed in-between the haciendas, mines, or mills. He adds that "colonial records tended to ignore them except when they came into overt conflict with the law."

The form and abundance of documentation of recruiters in the archives I consulted speaks well to this point: they were not demarcated or serialized objects of administration but appear in dispersed chains of incidence reports at points of constant conflict. Wolf goes on to focus on the more political brokers drawn from the ranks of landowners of the haciendas as well as the post-revolutionary *ejido* leaders, who were themselves independent from the government, and who were often the only representatives or point of contact for marginalized people who approached them for a variety of principally economic concerns. Wolf's recuperation of the "broker" for social analysis led to his research into what he called the "integration into larger systems" of the communities which until then anthropologists had been studying in an isolated way, by way of these "crucial junctures or synapses" that were "Janus-like, they face in two directions at once." Long before the "articulation" of Marxist theoretical jargon became en vogue in the 1970s, and still not able to use the word "contradiction" in the American academy, he says the "study of its dysfunctions" would be most revealing, as these concentrate much of the "tensions" and hold a "grip" on the contradiction, "lest conflict get out of hand and better mediators take their place."[5]

Brokers also captured the attention of the then main conceptual alternative in the rapidly developing post-war social sciences, namely the Goffman-inspired

---

4 In African history see especially the excellent collection Benjamin Nicholas Lawrance, Emily Lynn Osborn, and Richard L. Roberts, eds., *Intermediaries, Interpreters, and Clerks: African Employees in the Making of Colonial Africa* (Madison: University of Wisconsin Press, 2006).

5 Lindquist, "Brokers and Brokerage," 871; Eric Wolf, "Aspects of Group Relations in a Complex Society: Mexico," *American Anthropologist* 58, no. 6 (1956): 1072.

characteristic thematizing of powerful characters that the transactionalists from the 1960s onwards set their sights on. Brokers were highly magnified points of action and authors of decisive acts. Deborah James, in her own recent review of the genealogy of the broker in social theory and anthropology, writes of them as not merely a bridge between the poles of either the "state" or "market" and the "people," but as uniquely having a "bricoleurs" toolkit with which they generate social positions and identities. They are "producers," not products of the social. She even notes their paradoxical embodiment of "the people," of collective deliberations and communal desire, as they seem to blend "re-emerging traditional authority" with a consensus-based egalitarian ethos.[6] The more skeptical and sobering and market-defined conception of them as "a professional manipulator of people and information who brings about communication for a profit" has of course always remained.[7] It is wise not to lose sight of this opportunistic and short-term dimension of motivated actors when painting them in a completely different light, but even if they are reduced to their economic dimension, a much more ambivalent and encompassing picture appears.

Brokers were a well-defined figure in Roman and Medieval European law, clearly distinguished in jurisprudence as a dedicated but supporting element of trade. In other mostly literary sources, they were looked down upon and associated with failed or aspiring merchants, particularly in the realm of sordid businesses. While sometimes the broker was synonymous with small dealers and commercial agents or factors they are clearly distinguished from commissioning or proxy agents who were empowered representatives, as brokers would operate independently seeking out buyers or sellers on behalf of each, a messenger who brings two parties into a commercial relation with each other, quickly and secretly if need be.[8] Theoretically, they are supposed to facilitate and ease transactions with their knowledge of both supply and demand to bring buyers to willing sellers and vice versa. They were rarely professionalized and licensed: in the labor market there was always at least some agents who would be, but these formal agents never formed the beginning nor the end of the recruiting operations.

---

6 Deborah James, "The Return of the Broker: Consensus, Hierarchy, and Choice in South African Land Reform," *Journal of the Royal Anthropological Institute* 17, no. 2 (2011): 319.

7 Joan Vincent, "Political Anthropology: Manipulative Strategies," *Annual Review of Anthropology* 7 (1978): 176.

8 Morris Silver, "The Role of Slave Markets in Migration from the Near East to Rome," *Klio* 98, no. 1 (2016); Wilhelm Endemann, *Handbuch des deutschen Handels-, See-und Wechselrechts*. Vol. 3 (Berlin: Fues's Verlag, 1885), 132.

In his early and short book on the stock exchange, written with a first-hand account of the newly elaborated steps involved in this advancing form of European financial capitalism, Max Weber offers a particularly nuanced reading of a continuum between agents and brokers, and between brokers, merchants, and speculators, which are useful to transpose to this financially mediating element of the labor market. Weber distinguishes brokerage (*Makelei*) from merchant trade (*Handel*), because the broker is initially only a hired sub-agent charged with seeking out willing sellers. The commission of the broker is thus a kind of finder's fee for the work of seeking out a counterparty "willing to accept the conditions set by the person placing the order," especially in opaque and illiquid markets where it is difficult to find a willing seller at the offered price. The broker enters a mediating role not merely as a transmitter of this offer, but in two individual relationships established with the buyer and the seller respectively. In financial markets this is called the "spread" of a price, and the higher this straddled uncertainty about the closing price of an exchange the higher the broker's profits in exchange.

In terms of the labor but also other markets, the effective broker must make digestible the employer's fixed offer by making the "uncertain" seem certain, including with embellishments and misrepresentation. Brokers, like recruiters, could operate with speed and secrecy and conduct both commercial propaganda and hands-on improvisation. Their second role, and the basis for the *dash* recruiting technique, is their flexible relationship to the buyer or employer. This involves the setting and negotiating of the final price itself, since if the offer the buyer initially puts out is perceived as too low or unrewarding no exchange will take place and the buyer will have to agree on a higher price to purchase what they need from a broker-mediated labor market. The broker appears as an intrinsic parameter in the price mechanism itself, in independent and specific power relations with buyers and sellers or "supply and demand." Weber notes how the initially dependent or subordinate broker can become a "self-employed broker" or "*Propermakler*" by transitioning from fulfilling orders or completing assignments into becoming themselves those who acquire goods to sell on the other side, seeking "their business in the difference between the two." In this new position, the broker's power to determine the price increases and they can effectively corner the market with either a monopoly or an effective monopoly when they are the only available source for the commodity that buyers by necessity require for their production and thus are willing to pay almost anything for.

Only in the final and idealized stage, with the robust and free-flowing competition of liquid markets and without "shortages" of either buyers or sellers, does the broker becomes superfluous and blend into the operations of quasi-mechanical and decentralized "arbitrage" or the harmonizing of a price differential. It is this last fully formed domain that is considered the essential formula of merchant capitalism, flourishing at full capacity rather than in erratic and irregular semi-commercial bursts. The source of profit is the repetition of this same operation, taking advantage of price differentials in different locations, save the costs of custody, storage, and transport. Weber saw in this increasingly liquid, predictable and harmonized "price" the culmination of an economically rational, "*ökonomisch berechnet,*" space based on ever smaller, distributed, and recurrent monetary calculations. Only in this "gradual and imperceptible" way does capitalist business emerge in a "pure" form. At this stage, the broker or "market maker" becomes a synonym for price and a practical embodiment of cost, but at the level of transactions they suddenly lose their parameter-setting character and their ability to act beyond the laws of exchange.

Yet even in Weber's schema, once rationalized, the brokers reappear and burst at the "top" in the uncontrollable, chaotic, and irrational, because unpredictable, force of speculation. For Weber, speculation appears automatically in an accelerated market, because it is just a predicted extension of the moment of exchange into the future. Calculating and expecting alterations of supply and demand would just present another opportunity for "arbitrage" between the present and the future, an abstract profit which substitutes both commissions and commissioning agents. Delinked from the organizational or political growth of a specific enterprise, the goal then becomes imagining and augmenting any final exchange value. Speculation in this sense means marking up prices in a scarcity through this very mechanism, and so Weber notes that "speculators in the most genuine sense of that word" are also just a type of broker, and in turn, no one can prevent a "self-employed broker" from "speculating."[9] As the planters in Spanish Guinea never failed to remind officials, touts were "neither planters nor merchants, nor are they even actual proxies or company agents.[10]" A planter pleaded: "make the intermediaries disappear, for, as a rule, they are *persona extraña*" – external, but also strangers, strange, startling – "to *real* colonial interests, their only aim is the acquisition of maximum wealth with minimum effort, and for sure they do not create the permanent wealth" that agro-capitalist planters, like himself, liked to think of themselves as generating.[11]

---

9 Max Weber, "Commerce on the Stock and Commodity Exchanges [Der Börsenverkehr]," *Theory and Society* 29, no. 3 (2000): 359.

10 Joaquin Jose de Sousa to GG (Manresa), September 17, 1931; Curaduría to GG (Manresa), September 26, 1931; Primitivo Alvarez to Chris Nordenholz, March 14, 1931, AGA, C-81/8126, L-1, E-34.

11 Cámara (Estrada), May 15, 1930, "Nota sobre el problema de brazos en Fernando Poo," AGA, C-81/06415, E-13.

Weber's doctoral dissertation, *The History of Commercial Partnerships in the Middle Ages*, was precisely on the type of budding and germane trade associations called the *commendas* of the Italian city-states. His concern was the creation of the legal balance of profits and liabilities for failed or faulty ventures, in the formal and informal agreements between an investing partner, someone who fronted the money expecting a return, and the traveling partner, who organized the commercial enterprise and expedition, usually overseas. Braudel noted how this boom in capital or capitalization turned "the entire Venetian population" into "so-called capitalists," because the entire townsfolk, even those of "very modest means," were "advancing money to the merchant venturers, thus perpetually creating and renewing a sort of commercial society." The constant and "spontaneously offered supply of credit" created a new landscape of commercial temporary associations whose profits often depended on other brokers downstream, usually in territories colonized by the Venetians, who together would divide or expand the totality of profits from a successful venture or suffer complete losses if the arrangements failed.[12]

This commercial churning successfully instituted and streamlined a range of payment instruments, such as bills of exchange and accounting-money, but also innovations in labor recruiting and wage payment such as dynamic premiums linked to the success of the venture, making the laborer in effect also part of the brokerage enterprise. Before each voyage active "taskmasters" involved in the venture "signed on" sailors, carriers, guards and the like who were "paid" in advance the sum of the "entire voyage, which could last up to one year" while being provided with "daily rations (comprising biscuits, cheese, salt pork and wine)." Workers who received "wages beforehand and then failed to report at the ship's departure, hiding or pretending to be ill," paid off their "debt" by being "forcibly recruited" – an increasingly preponderant mode of recruitment when Venetian traders faced "acute" labor shortages. Sudden labor scarcities led to the extension of credit-led and force-backed recruitment, particularly of foreigners beyond the Venetian colonies.[13]

Jarius Banaji recently published a fragmented book, full of insights and loose ends about the chain-like "trading machines" of merchant capitalism, titled *A Brief History of Commercial Capitalism*, where he partly addresses the or-

12 Fernand Braudel, *Civilization and Capitalism, 15th-18th century, Vol. III: The perspective of the world* (Berkeley: University of California Press, 1992), 548.

13 Milios, *Origins of Capitalism*, 120, 159 – 160, 169. The usual protagonists were of course the commercial brokers Natalie Rothman called "trans-imperial subjects," with their ability to straddle and mediate more than one world and make money off that difference. Rothman, *Brokering Empire.*

thodox conceptions of the history of capitalism that had brushed off merchant and even financial capitalism as non-productive. Merchant capital was traditionally conceived as being mediating or circulatory and peripheral to the identification of capitalist dynamics and contradictions, which missed the obvious importance of the magnitude of accumulation coming from the expansion of new markets as such. Critics of Banaji, who would label him the most sophisticated of the so-called "neo-Smithians" or better post-Gunder-Frankians, cannot explain the extraordinary booms and windfalls of imperialism and colonization that far outpaced growth rates in the metropole, even while having to cling to the only unanimous definition of capital as the successful and compounded accumulation at a global scale.

In a chapter on the "Relative Autonomy of Brokers," Banaji characterizes the new imperial dynamic in the "produce trade" starting in the late nineteenth century as one of increasing competition and concentration, with large volumes of "variable capital," or fluctuating wage-like components "circulated as advances." Even though the largest and most consolidated corporate firms in the colonial world tried to exercise "tight control over the prices paid to producers" in the end, entire economies seemed to only operate by way of advances "circulated via brokers and middlemen." Analyzing Fieldhouse's regional study on the United Africa Company in Nigeria and his figure of up to 3,000 middlemen and contractors operating in different produce sectors in 1930s Nigeria, he notes that the "advances" were constantly discussed as a system open to "abuses," such as concealing the quality of the palm oil or simply selling palm oil to other firms for higher prices. They became an impossible to reform element as broker groups were either dispersed or coalesced into formidable units, into an "oligarchy of brokers." They underpinned almost the entire volume of the wholesale trade. There was what Banaji calls a "'structural' impossibility of doing away with brokers."[14] The same is true of the labor brokers of the Bight of Biafra, and those elsewhere. To further refine the unique positions and operations of labor brokers, I now turn to justifying how the "broker" can be appended to the more political category of the "lumpenproletariat".

---

14 Banaji, *Commercial Capitalism*, 117–118, citing Fieldhouse, *Merchant Capital*, 443. To keep this footnote brief, for reference to the Banajian tendency and the alternative English-centric currents in the "origin of capitalism" debates, see Milios, *Origins of Capitalism*.

Lumpen: A Category of Political Economy

A historicist impulse would locate the concept in the intra-philosophical disputes of the Hegelian left during the *Vormärz*, as Marx picked up the term from Max Stirner in a critical and ironic way in the 1840s; or as part of the polemical dividing line between communist and anarchist political factions in the First International in the 1870s, as Bakunin explicitly tried to rescue and revive the concept against Marx; or in its consistent popularity as an insult in the later Kautskian period of German working class union and party organizing. There is no shortage of extreme contextualizing, including its literary motifs, such as those popularized by Marx's favorite authors, Balzac and Victor Hugo, where characters from the underclass and hidden overclass regularly figure as a brazen and immoral counter-society, operating like an "inverted monarchy" that worked cosmologically against efforts to recreate political power in the surface world.[15] In the 1970s, and particularly in the past decade the concept has been subject to rigorous assessments and genealogical explorations, with entire doctoral dissertations and book length manuscripts dealing with it, with the explicit and semi-explicit aim to sharpen contemporary political analysis and help explain late-capitalist breakdowns and the decomposition of classes and parties in formerly industrialized countries.[16]

To define the worthy and dynamic object – the proletariat – its opposite had to appear in an endlessly negative way: not productive or parasitic in the social structure, politically unreliable, characteristically dishonest, and dishonorable, etc. The category worked through this negative ideal that captured the impediments and imperfections of a revolutionary movement. The concept of lumpen itself thus appears not as an analysis of social differentiation or its representation but as a political and strategic opposition in the heart of a messy and overlapping division of labor. It is easiest to find passages in Marx and Engels where these "heterogenous" groups are bunched and maligned in an absurdly lyrical way. However, it is important to note that the impetus behind the coinage of the term was to rectify their absence from political and economic analysis,

---

15 Dominique Kalifa, *Vice, Crime, and Poverty: How the Western Imagination Invented the Underworld* (New York: Columbia University Press, 2019), 30, 60 – 81.

16 Hal Draper, *The Concept of the "Lumpenproletariat" in Marx and Engels* (Paris: Institut de Science économique appliquée, 1972); Peter Bescherer, *Vom Lumpenproletariat Zur Unterschicht: Produktivistische Theorie Und Politische Praxis* (Frankfurt am Main: Campus Verlag, 2013); Clyde Barrow, *The Dangerous Class: The Concept of the Lumpenproletariat* (Ann Arbor: University of Michigan Press, 2020); Bennett Dempsey Carpenter, "Lumpen: Vagrancies of a Concept from Marx to Fanon (and On)" (PhD diss., Duke University, 2019).

and to show their essential role in periods of political instability and in the creation of new social forms emerging in convulsive peripheral markets.

Figure 14: "Before the Sunrise" by Mikhail Dzhanashvili (Karl Marx and Friedrich Engels walking in London at night). Reproduced with permission of akg-images / SNA.

While the term has been etymologized to bits, it is worth briefly delving into an underexplored philological dimension. Lumpenproletariat, the untranslatable portmanteau coined by Marx and Engels in their long unpublished *The German Ideology* (1846), is mostly glossed as the "rabble" or "ragged" proletariat, as it was famously defined in the *Manifesto* as the "rotting mass thrown off by the lowest layers of the old society." There has been an acknowledged problem of mistranslation, as depending on the decade of popular English translations of key works it was rendered not only as rabble but as "slum proletariat," "ragamuffins," "dangerous classes," and even "scum."[17] If one could create a more neutral translation truer to the original, then it would be something like rumple-proletarian, with its textile, unsmooth and disheveled imagery; or with its political significance, the "pro-rogue-letarian."

The stand-alone noun *Lumpen* is translatable as fabric waste or rags, and while it has maintained this formal definition, its popular use is different and more varied. In the regional dialects of Bavaria, *der Lump* was a term not only

17 Barrow, *Dangerous Class*, 28.

for vagrants and beggars, its earliest early modern definition, but also specifically referred to dishonest and sordid knavery: a "crook," a "scoundrel," a "rascal," a "good for nothing." *Lumperei* was specifically the use of "miserable tricks." Lump was a prefix for dozens of portmanteaus in southern spoken dialects, from the technical *lumpen-sammler*, or rag-picker, to the *lumpen-ding*, trifling things, to *lumpen-geld*, debased money or something cheap and worthless, and finally, and most commonly, in the expression *sich nicht lumpen lassen*, literally "not to be taken for a lump," a synonym for showing honorable and generous behavior – which is the expression Marx gives quasi-theoretical form too in defining the proletarian in opposition to the *Lumpen.*[18]

The *Lumpen* as a social category was introduced by the Bavarian Max Stirner into the German socialist and literary scenes of the *Vormärz* period and designated the pauperism at the outer edges of a new advancing society, including of the working class. Marx criticized Stirner precisely because of this equation of proletarian with grime and misery, in the 300-page section of *The German Ideology* dedicated to Stirner, written in 1846. Practically all studies of the concept locate the "birth" of it in Marx's critique of Stirner, but it is seldom remarked that it was used entirely ironically by both authors in critiques of each other. Stirner used the term interchangeably with the propertyless "proletarian" *Habenichts*, have-nots, and posited it as the support base and end-result of political socialism. Stirner's only book, *The Ego and his Own*, published in 1844, uses the figure of the *Lumpen* as an ironic critique of the moralizing "social liberalism" of Moses Hess, who was the young Marx's leading mentor in Left Hegelian circles – and evidently also a key formative source of Marx's lingering idealist view of money as an alienating corrosive Mammon.[19] Stirner polemically linked socialism to a secularized Christianity and mocked its vision of the "state" and "society" as a tool of redistribution through seizure of property that would end up in equal impoverishment or a "Communistic society where we could call ourselves

18 Kuettner, *New and Complete Dictionary*, 496.

19 Michael Heinrich, *Karl Marx and the Birth of Modern Society: The Life of Marx and the Development of His Work* (New York: NYU Press, 2019), 33. Hess is said to have even helped Marx draft his reply to Stirner, as his handwriting is on the original manuscript. "Money make us vampire. […] What God is to the theoretical life, money is to the practical life in this inverted world: the externalised (entäussert) capacity of men, their sold-off life-activity. Money is human value expressed in figures; it is the mark of our slavery, the indelible brand of our servitude. Money is the congealed blood sweat of the miserable wretches who bring to market their inalienable property, their most personal capacity, their life-activity itself, to barter it for a caput mortuum, a so-called capital and to consume cannibalistically their own fat." Moses Hess, "The Essence of Money," *Rheinische Jahrbücher Zur Gesellschaflichen Reform*, 1845, available at https://www.marxists.org/archive/hess/1845/essence-money.htm.

a 'ragamuffin crew' [*Lumpengesindel*]"; "Let property be impersonal, let it belong to – society. Before the supreme proprietor we all become equal – ragamuffins."

In his original critique Stirner also mocks the social figures created by varieties of socialism, which were populated only by exemplary "powerful persons (and) so-called 'moral persons,' ghosts," vanguards and designated model followers, a card-carrying titled membership group separated from an undifferentiated mass. Stirner has been misconstrued through the lens of Marx's reading of him as wanting to introduce the *Lumpen* as a revolutionary subject: as models of a utopia of "egoists" behaving like "care-free ragamuffins."[20] Stirner's undeservedly small reputation and original thought consisted in being a kind proto-Nietzschean rejector of "morality," which, as he says, in the economic sphere is: "a solid business, an honourable trade, to lead a moral life," and to anything opposed, "the swindler, the whore, the thief, robber, and murderer, the gambler, the penniless man without a position, the frivolous man," the "doughty commoner designates the feeling against these 'immoral' people as his 'deepest indignation'." That critique still hangs like a long shadow on the use of the concept by vulgar political Marxism.[21]

---

20 Max Stirner, *The Ego and Its Own: The Case of the Individual against Authority* (Cambridge University Press, 1995), 120 – 122. In a new translation from 2017 by Wolfi Landstreicher, published online at www.theanarchistlibrary.org, under the title *The Unique and Its Property*, the word lump appears as "pauper" instead of as the "ragamuffin" of the original and most widespread 1907 translation. The position attributed to Stirner by later Marxists was precisely Bakhunin's position in 1872, when he was expelled by the Marx-led First International, because of his rejection of the idea that state power should be taken over by despotic "socialist savants." Bakhunin insisted that "the flower of the proletariat is not, as it is to the Marxists, the upper layer, the aristocracy of labor," but "precisely the great rabble of the people (underdogs, 'dregs of society') ordinarily designated by Marx and Engels in the picturesque and contemptuous phrase Lumpenproletariat. I have in mind the 'riffraff,' that 'rabble' almost unpolluted by bourgeois civilization, which carries in its inner being and in its aspirations, in all the necessities and miseries of its collective life, all the seeds of the socialism of the future." Bakunin, "The International and Karl Marx," 294.

21 Stirner, *The Ego and Its Own*, 101. The orthodox interpretation can be traced back to the revival of the term by Karl Kautsky in the Erfurt Programme of 1892, where it was translated as the "slum proletariat": "The capitalist system of production has greatly increased the slum proletariat. It constantly sends to it new recruits." Kautsky was the foremost proponent of a negative definition of the lumpen, "compelled either to perish or to throw overboard all sense of shame, honor and self-respect," living "parasitically" as scroungers or "*schmarotzer*" of the wages and value produced by the productive classes. He normalized the imaginary of a "great gulf between the working-class proletariat and the slum proletariat." He also gave it a universal character: "The slum proletariat has always been the same, whether in modern London or ancient Rome," Karl Kautsky, *The Class Struggle (Erfurt Program)* (New York: Charles H. Kerr & Co., 1910), 170.

The German Ideology contains the first known and arguably the most accurate usage of the term: "the entire proletariat consisting of ruined bourgeois and ruined proletarians, a collection of *Lumpen*, who have existed in every epoch and whose existence on a mass scale after the decline of the Middle Ages preceded the mass formation of the ordinary proletariat."[22] The category was born split from the creation or preservation of national wealth and mushroomed into a pan-European class of roguery and *déclassés*, resulting from the socially aimless and commercially corrupted fragmentation of both the bourgeoisie and proletariat. An unacknowledged piece of early writing on the lumpen is Engels' 1850 book on the sixteenth century *Peasant War in Germany*, where he already gives it a quasi-universal character: "This low-grade proletariat" consisting of "ruined members of the middle-class and that mass of the city population which possessed no citizenship rights: the journeymen, the day labourers, and the numerous beginnings of the lumpenproletariat" was a phenomenon which "in a more or less developed form can be found in all the phases of society hitherto observed." It was a matter of not having a "definite occupation and a stable domicile," but retaining parts of, what he calls, a "peasant nature," without the extreme "degree of venality and degradation which characterise the modern civilised low-grade proletariat."[23] The latter, Engels characterized elsewhere as being fermented in the "hell of modern England," and needing secularized Christian impulses to combat "the lack of principle, the inner emptiness, the spiritual deadness, the untruthfulness of the age."[24]

In 1847, Engels includes the term for the first time in a published pamphlet about the history of the German class structure, where he notes that the *Zersplitterung und Zerstreung* or fragmentation and dispersal of the working classes into "farm labourers, day labourers, handicraft journeymen, factory workers and lumpen proletariat" renders them unable to mobilize together and to become easily instrumentalized with "payment," making them all individually "an aux-

---

22 Marx and Engels, "The German Ideology," 202. Marx's main critique in this text is that Stirner represents communism as the equal distribution of wages.

23 Engels, "The Peasant War in Germany," 407. In the 1870 preface to the book Engels changed the emphasis, in light of the political experiences of revolutions in urban Europe, where he dismisses them as potential "allies" of the "class of the population which entirely and permanently depends on wages," the proletarians, who still being "a minority of the German people" were "compelled to seek allies" among the "petty bourgeoisie, the low grade proletariat of the cities, the small peasants, and the wage-workers of the land", but definitely not the "lumpenproletariat, this scum of the decaying elements of all classes, which establishes headquarters in all the big cities" as they are "absolutely venal, and absolutely brazen." Engels, "Preface to the 2nd Edition," 98.

24 Engels, "The Condition of England," 445.

iliary army for the class employing them." With the "*Lump*" he says, there is always a ready mercenary force, willing to "fight out with his fists the squabbles between bourgeoisie, nobility and police" for "a few thaler," whether on the political or economic terrain.[25]

In some of the longest and most notable list-like definition of these heterogenous elements in Marx's 1850 analysis of a tumultuous period of French politics, he defined them not so much sociologically, as a "mass sharply differentiated from the industrial proletariat," but rather ethically as the "recruiting ground for thieves and criminals of all kinds" and after a long and colorful exposition, which varies "according to the degree of civilization of the nation to which they belong," he says irrespective of what "nation" they belonged to, they never "renounce their *lazzaroni* character."[26] This novel pan-European *lazzaroni* "character" is defined by a relationship to money. As Engels says in a short article on Swiss immigrant workers, they are "still largely what one describes as lumpenproletariat, prepared to sell themselves to anyone who will make extravagant promises."[27]

The concept of the lumpenproletariat can be recuperated as a tool of social and historical analysis, if we subject it to the same procedure that was used to create it: incorporating Stirner's critique to transform this hot potato of a concept to reveal the productive logics and political protagonisms emergent in an unstructured *Lump*. As Marx says in his 1857 *Outlines of the Critique of Political Economy*, the "mass of such rabble" includes everyone "from whore to pope," and even the "honest and 'working' lumpenproletariat belongs here as well; e.g. the great mob of porters etc. who render service in seaport cities etc," – or the "'suitcasers' who have until now have dedicated themselves in Calabar to trying to carry the suitcases of passing passengers in order to live off the tips," as a Nigerian journalist says of the model target recruits, quoted in the introduction.[28] Working through the economic modes of organization and techniques of the lumpen-brokers and their recruits overcomes the original nebulousness and ambivalence of the concept, which were simply features of its function as a "limit" category. Its distinguishing limit was of course the "unproductive" element of mere circulation without value creation through labor. The serious pursuit of this dialectical and global concept implies giving an autonomous movement to the creation of the differentiation machine, the division of labor, and its dynamic filiations through money. The dialectical transformation that

25 Engels, "The Constitutional Question in Germany," 83.
26 Marx, "Class Struggles in France," 62.
27 Engels, "The Model Republic," 43.
28 Marx, "Outlines of the Critique of Political Economy," 203.

Marx undertook with the concept when he wrestled it from Stirner needs to be kept in mind when considering its renewal for social and colonial history, in particular the way the "bottom" can appear at the top, with a force and role in political analysis and political economy.

"Rogues and Vagabonds" in Labor History

The final ossified and misperceived limit is its supposed "European" nature – a static cross-section of the underclass of an advanced industrial city – which Fanon dissolved long ago. This type of analytic pastiche serves to ply apart an old reflex which was inextricably strengthened through the intellectually common nineteenth century association between the European urban underclass and remote and yet to be colonized worlds. The mutual transferring of motifs between the colonized "barbarians" and the internal "dangerous classes" was already generalized in Paris and London of the 1840s, where "tribes of rag-pickers" were endlessly discussed and said to lead a life that is "totally nomadic and almost savage," culminating in a swamping of the Victorian mind with all things "dark." In Henry Mayhew's four volume *London Labour and the London Poor* published in the 1850s the protagonists of "uncivilized" life in the metropole were those figures inherited from early modern anti-vagrancy laws: "those that will not work," which he labelled the "wandering tribes," including "vagabonds, idlers, petty jobbers, gamblers and speculators."[29] These shared templates are also clearly visible in Engels' encounter with the Irish in Manchester in 1841, where in his chapter of *The Condition* dedicated to their immigration, up to 50,000 a year "packed like cattle" on steamships, he begins by citing Thomas Carlyle's account of the "uncivilised Irishman" and "his squalor and unreason," "degradation and disorder," and adding that except for Carlyle's "exaggerated and one-sided condemnation of the Irish national character, Carlyle is perfectly right." It is in this chapter that Engels scents the concept of the Lumpen during his tour of Manchester's slums, where the "filth and comfortlessness that prevail in the houses themselves" are "impossible to describe," "a heap of straw, a few rags," *Lumpen*, "utterly beyond use as clothing, suffice for his nightly couch."[30]

Vice-versa, descriptions of Africans drew in turn on the imaginary of Europe's outcasts, for example the "unassimilable" Nigerian Hausa traders and dis-

29 Kalifa, *Vice, Crime*, 158–163, 106. This shared lens is of course well established, but not in terms of the "labor question," see McClintock, *Imperial Leather*.
30 Engels, *Condition*, 103.

putatious *braceros*, as I described in the *panya* chapter, were easily incorporated into the long-standing polarized schema of the Castilian cosmography of "Jews and gypsies." This transference was often explicit, but was never meant to be more than analogical: for example, the Fang were described by an early official as being "very similar to our Gypsies," as "they have a fierce character, tend to be loquacious, argumentative, shameless and somewhat fond of stealing. In business dealings they are used to haggling to the point of being tiresome."[31] This transposition was doubly strengthened by the inordinate expansion of the anti-vagrancy apparatus already fully elaborated and deployed in the *ancien régime* legislation, abolished or limited in moments of political reforms in the nineteenth century, but brought back in full force into the colonies, and further elaborated as colonization progressed.[32]

The interwar period in Africa saw the development of a new colonial situation where "criminality" was no longer considered a niche occupation or marginal site, but where at times well over half of the population could be classified and targeted in one way or another with these revived codes – not only with anti-vagrancy and anti-smuggling laws but a whole range of specific ordinances related to, for example, liquor production or currency counterfeiting which aimed to combat, not unemployment, but alternative means of income generation.[33] If in Europe the juridico-discursive impetus was to differentiate and specify delinquency, at least in Foucault's *Discipline and Punish* schema, then there was a great divergence in the colonies, where an old range of vague labels, from "undesirables" to "idleness" to "vice" were concretely reapplied to swathes of the rural and urban population, what the Spanish in legislative discussions called both *mal vivir*, crooked modes of livelihood, and *buen vivir*, extravagant

---

31 Almonte, *Los naturales de la Guinea Española*, 12.

32 Polanyi, *Great Transformation*, 81–136; Robert Castel, *From Manual Workers to Wage Laborers: Transformation of the Social Question*, trans. Richard Boyd (London: Transaction Publishers, 2002), 191–280; In African history see especially Ocobock and Burton, "The 'Travelling Native'"; Keese, "Slow"; and Stacey Hynd, "'... a Weapon of Immense Value'? Convict Labour in British Colonial Africa, c. 1850–1950s," in *Global Convict Labor*, eds. Christian De Vito and Alexander Lichtenstein (Leiden: Brill, 2015).

33 Bernault, "The Shadow of Rule"; Laurent Fourchard, "Urban Poverty, Urban Crime, and Crime Control: The Lagos and Ibadan Case, 1929–1945," in *African Urban Spaces in Historical Perspective*, ed. Toyin Falola (Rochester, NY: University Rochester Press, 2009); Laurent Fourchard, "Crime and Illegal Work"; Ayodeji Olukoju, "Social Prestige, Agency, and Criminality: Economic Depression and Currency Counterfeiting in inter-war British West Africa," *International Journal of African Historical Studies* 54, no. 2 (2021). Laurent Fourchard's new range of comparative in-depth studies have traced precisely how such a category of "undesirables" came about in Nigeria and South Africa, particularly as discursively and administrative constructed.

and carefree. The change in the structure of the colonial economy – the growth of towns, warehouses and plantations with the added intra-imperial goal of monopoly and core-periphery autarky – generated a tremendous accentuation of colonial "discourse." As elsewhere in early colonial urban Africa, in Spanish Guinea the early contours of a racist colonial ideology of "disease and inactivity" quickly shifted by the 1930s to the superimposed label of "criminality" and uncontrolled circulation.[34]

In post-war social and economic history, the concept of lumpen along with many other uniquely Marxist ones were partly revived through new editions and translations of unpublished works from the Marx and Engels oeuvre. However, the immediate tendency was to dial back the dialectical potential of the category and keep it either as a synonym for pauperism and criminality or split it even further, to extract further politically notable and noble figures from the "mass," such as Hobsbawm's "social bandits," which he vigorously distinguished from ordinary criminal "rogues."[35] In the political context of the 1960s, the rediscovery and explicit revalorization of the concept in Fanon's *Wretched of the Earth* led to its spread into various New Left formations as well as to fringe Maoists groupings who recalled Mao's fondness for what he called the "bandits, robbers and prostitutes," because as existing outlaws they were obviously more likely to risk joining illegal revolutionary parties.[36] These global political currents revived the concept outside of the African context of the struggles of decolonization and its specific contradictions and possibilities which Fanon put his finger on. The fate of the "academicization" of Fanon as a psychological theorist of racist encounters to be responded to with a "poetics" of counter-violence, distorted his legacy as the acute first-rate class analyst of colonial and decolonizing society that he was.[37]

---

34 Odile Goerg, "De la ségrégation coloniale à la tentation sécessioniste: 'l'urbanisme sécuritaire'," in *Security, Crime and Segregation in West African Cities Since the 19th Century,* eds. Laurent Fourchard and Isaac Olawale Albert (Paris: Karthala, 2003), 256; Eckert, "Urbanization," 214; Glasman, "Unruly Agents," 91.

35 Eric Hobsbawm, *Bandits* (New York: Pantheon Books, 1981), 102–108. See also Ralph A. Austen, "Social Bandits and other Heroic Criminals: Western Models of Resistance and their relevance for Africa," in *Banditry, Rebellion and Social Protest in Africa*, ed. Donald Crummey (London: James Currey, 1986), 89–108.

36 Mao Zedong, *Selected Works of Mao Tse-Tung* (London: Lawrence & Wishart, 1954), 80, 115.

37 Bashir Abu-Manneh, "Who Owns Frantz Fanon's Legacy?," *Jacobin*, October 12, 2021, accessed October 12, 2021, https://jacobinmag.com/2021/12/postcolonialism-socialism-wretched-earth-class-violence.

By the 1980s a consensus in various academic currents pushed the same conclusion: while the concept offered "striking metaphors" it could not offer sociohistorical, descriptive nor "analytical power."[38] The suspended state of the concept is most visible in Peter Linebaugh and Markus Rediker's classic *The Many-Headed Hydra*. Their study of the potent, spontaneous, and ruthlessly suppressed outlier assemblies, does not broach it except in passing. Instead, they employ rich and contemporary metaphors of unbreakable heterogeneity used by early modern English intellectuals of "order," who imagined though Greek myth and biblical imagery. They nevertheless decide to give their key concept of "motley crew" a conceptual meaning related to *Lumpen* but one which, they say, highlights its "inter-racial" character, as "motley" was the multi-colored garment of the jester who would bring carnivalesque disorder and subversion by telling the truth, and by extension it could refer to any "colorful assemblage." The lumpen proper, "the lumpenproletariat, *lazzaroni*, or underclass," they write, was only a "*dramatis personae*" of a sub-group of bandits and thieves "who rejected wage labor."[39]

In labor history, Marcel van der Linden notably slotted the concept into one of five "subaltern classes or semi-classes in capitalism," along with free wage laborers, the petty bourgeoisie, the self-employed, and slaves, and defines it as those "who fall outside the legalized labor market altogether." By his own account, this schema follows quite closely the outline provided in the 1972 article, "The Meaning of the Working Class in Africa," written by a communist trade unionist sent by the ILO to Nigeria in the 1960s. Its author, Vic Allen, gives it an even more prominent place, because, he was overwhelmed by the observation of the "large number" of "*lumpenproletarians*" in Lagos. More recently van der Linden has dismissed the category for its moralizing and non-analytical character, and reduced it to a intellectual history, in particular Wallerstein's Fanon-inspired reading of the term, as merely the reflection of a political urge during the late colonial and early post-colonial "search for those who truly had nothing to lose but their chains" – "what is variously called the subproletariat, the lumpenproletariat, the unskilled (often immigrant) workers, the marginal, the chronically unemployed."[40]

38 Bussard, "'Dangerous Class'," 688; Cohen Robin and Michael David, "The Revolutionary Potential of the African Lumpenproletariat: A Sceptical View," *Institute of Development Studies Bulletin* 5, no. 2 (1973).

39 Linebaugh and Rediker, *Many-Headed Hydra*, 28, 63.

40 Van der Linden, *Workers*, 21–22, 298; Vic L. Allen, "The Meaning of the Working Class in Africa," *The Journal of Modern African Studies* 10, no. 2 (1972). For a more sociological and rural angle, see Henry Bernstein, *Class Dynamics of Agrarian Change* (Halifax: Kumarian Press,

Dedicated studies of the lumpen in African history were inspired by trends in European social and urban history such as Stedman Jones' 1971 *Outcast London.* Foremost and unsurpassed is Charles van Onselen's *New Babylon, New Nineveh: Everyday Life on the Witwatersrand 1886–1914* as well as Andrew Burton's *African Underclass: Urbanisation, Crime and Colonial Order in Dar es Salaam.* Burton studied the *wahuni*, translatable as those who wander without a purpose, "vagabonds," but also specifically unmarried and lawless "wastrels," as well as the urban milieu of unlicensed traders, brewers, rickshawpullers, prostitutes and the like. Van Onselen expanded his earlier pieces on crime, gangs, and banditry in Johannesburg and through dedicated deep and chance archival finds turned that unique African industrial metropolis into a canvas of the fragmented new world of liquor sellers, prostitutes, cab drivers, washermen, domestic servants, transport riders, and brickmakers, etc.[41] He uses the term lumpen mostly in passing, and as either synonymous with crime or with the "informal economy." The southern African social history increasingly distanced itself from the category for good, opting to flesh out the less politicized or technical vocabulary of an "underclass" or a "subordinated class" in the African "hidden" histories of primarily urban contexts of survival and "control."[42]

This academic cordon sanitaire around the concept is closely related to intra-academic schisms as well as a sense of political contamination after the coming to power of Marxist-Leninist regimes, such as the Derg in Ethiopia in 1974, who explicitly used the category of the lumpenproletariat to designate

2010), 54. In Bukharin's famous manual in the section "The Classes and the Class," he includes a little table schematizing the difference between peasants, workers, and the lumpen, only the latter are "unproductive" and "unexploited," but like the peasants, the lumpen only work as "individuals" and like the other categories, may also be poor and oppressed, but not necessarily in the same way. Following Lenin, Bukharin emphasized their "shiftlessness, lack of discipline," and "impotence to construct or organize anything new"; this nonworking class moved only through "foolish caprice" and leaned politically to a "vacillating and hysterical anarchism." Nikolai Bukharin, *Historical Materialism: A System of Sociology* (Cosmonaut Press, 2021), 332.

41 Charles van Onselen, *New Babylon, New Nineveh: Everyday Life on the Witwatersrand 1886–1914* (Johannesburg: Jonathan Ball, 1982), 148, 387; Andrew Burton, *African Underclass: Urbanisation, Crime & Colonial Order in Dar es Salaam* (Oxford: Currey, 2005), 5, 10.

42 Charles van Onselen, "South Africa's Lumpenproletarian Army Umkosi Wa Ntaba – The Regiment of the Hills, 1890–1920," *Collected Seminar Papers. Institute of Commonwealth Studies* 21 (1977): 80, 90; Martin J. Murray, "The Triumph of Marxist Approaches in South African Social and Labour History," *Journal of Asian and African Studies* 23, no. 1 (1988). For incidental rhetorical uses see Jean Comaroff and John Comaroff, *The Truth about Crime: Sovereignty, Knowledge, Social Order* (Chicago: University of Chicago Press, 2016), 61–68, 137; and for its general disappearance see, Ralph Callebert, "Rethinking the Underclass: Future Directions in Southern African Labor History," *International Labor and Working-Class History* 82 (2012).

"dangerous vagrants" and "criminals, beggars and coolies" that could be "employed" or pressed for "agricultural development projects."[43] There was of course a distinct aversion to applying the term "proletariat" to African history, and needless to say for the lumpenproletariat category this new feeling was compounded. The micro- and narrative-prioritizing E.P.-Thompsonian side of African social and labor history that came to predominate by the 1980s had always vigorously opposed what they perceived as a structuralist tendency excessively concerned with precise class composition and neo-Marxist jargon reified by the offspring of Althusser in Africanist circles.[44]

An argument to overcome this distinctly stagnant Anglo-French schismogenesis, needs to draw on the unresolved and encompassing terms of the discussion as they were emerging in the 1960s, or even the 1840s. As Peter Worsley, in his remarkable 1972 essay on "Fanon and the Lumpenproletariat," forecast, the concept seemed to be destined for a clear analytical revival by forcing us to abandon "looking at the twentieth century through nineteenth-century eyes," and by implication, what he called the "Third World" through European eyes. Worsley's sociological turn to this new shadow added to by Fanon was already then unorthodox, and failed to manifest. Excoriating the excoriators, or those who used or heard the term in a disparaging and overly moralizing way, he notes the obvious importance of it in the world-historical context of the "explosive growth of urban populations composed of immigrants from the countryside," where "thousands

---

43 Marco Di Nunzio, *The Act of Living: Street Life, Marginality, and Development in Urban Ethiopia* (Ithaca: Cornell University Press, 2019), 114, citing "Lumpen Proletariat Here Begin New Life," *Ethiopian Herald*, December 18, 1977.

44 Abdullah, "Rethinking African Labour," 82; Mike Morris, "Social History and the Transition to Capitalism in the South African Countryside," *Review of African Political Economy*, no. 41 (1988); Frederick Cooper, "Work, Class and Empire: An African Historian's Retrospective on E. P. Thompson," *Social History* 20, no. 2 (1995); Bellucci and Freund, "Work across Africa." I can already pre-emptively point to the best critique of a "mad" Platonism by Althusser's harshest critic and former student, Rancière, in his "Althusser, Don Quixote, and the Stage of the Text," originally published in 1990: "But also this anguish of speech that does not get through, of the story that doesn't manage to be written, of men whom neither speech nor time link as subject of a story, is an old anguish, an inaugural anguish that Marxism localized and exorcized in the concept of the lumpenproletariat. Despite the praiseworthy efforts made to give it an economic-social materialist genealogy, the lumpenproletariat is first of all a phantasmagoric name, a stage name, the theatrical embodiment of all the disasters of scholarly speech, the generic name of nonmeaning, of disconnection, of non-relation. This stage name fixes non-relation in place and denies it by giving it form in the system of social relationships." Jacques Rancière, *The Flesh of Words: The Politics of Writing* (Stanford: Stanford University Press, 2004), 139. I will readily drop any future mention of the *lumpen*, if another idea can explain *touts* and *braceros* in one go.

of new recruits flock to the favelas, barriadas, bidonvilles, and shanty-towns." The sociological profile he gives of the new lumpenproletariat is an almost perfect characterization of both the recruiters and the recruited, broadly "petty entrepreneurial" aspirations and "unstable family" situations:

> In the early days of colonialism, they had to be forced out to work on plantations and in factories. Now they go readily, [...] they have no steady jobs; they live from hand to mouth, sell a few stolen goods here and there, [...] sometimes they get a brief job as a coolie; a vast mass of them live off their relatives. Many of them come as 'target' workers, hoping to make money which they can invest (usually in land or in a shop) back in the village later. These people have no intention of becoming permanent city-dwellers. They are not even necessarily men who have lost their land.

Worsley opts for the term "sub-proletariat" following the French *sous-proletariat* and the cue of Amilcar Cabral who in an analysis of the social composition of Guinea chose to isolate the "easily identifiable" groups of "beggars, layabouts, prostitutes, etc." as the "lumpen-proletariat, if we had anything in Guinea we could properly call a proletariat," from the second type of sub-proletarians or quasi-*déclassés*, the "large number of young folk," usually "without any training" who "come from the countryside, and retain links with it" and who do not yet form part of the "wage-earners." To use the Cold War development economics jargon of the period, they were "unmodernized" "target workers," that is those that wished to gain, as quickly as possible, a certain "target" sum through wage work, even if it meant heightened periods of extreme exploitation, in order to return "home" once their target had been met. On the way to and even at the "industrial" or other formal worksites, they still had to dwell in and navigate through local stratification systems such as caste and the harsh seniorities of social kinship networks, as well as what would later be called the translocal "informal economy" led by itinerant traders.[45]

Worsley's, and even Cabral's application of the concept to African social analysis and theory, contrasts with the tactical and inspired writings of Fanon. Fanon's positive revalorization of the "classless idlers" as a political force was extremely original: in an often cited passage he describes how the "workless less-than-men," the "pimps, the hooligans, the unemployed, and the petty criminals," and even the "prostitutes too, and the maids who are paid two pounds a

45 Worsley, "Frantz Fanon and the 'Lumpenproletariat'," 200, 209; see also Ibrahim Abdullah, "Culture, Consciousness and Armed Conflict: Cabral's Déclassé/(Lumpenproletariat?) in the Era of Globalization," *African Identities* 4, no. 1 (2006). On "target" workers, see Elliot J. Berg, "Backward-Sloping Labor Supply Functions in Dual Economies – the Africa Case," *The Quarterly Journal of Economics* 75, no. 3 (1961).

month, all who turn in circles between suicide and madness," will "throw themselves into the struggle like stout working men." Fanon himself warns, like Engels had, that "colonialism" can readily use the lumpen to "manoeuvre" its domination by simply being "ready to pay a high price for the services of this mass" as quasi-mercenaries. Nevertheless, he leans his high hopes on this rising force of the "uprooted" urban lumpenproletarian, giving examples of the anti-vagrancy laws that intensified yet again in Kenya and Congo during the 1950s, precisely because neither "the brimming activity of the missionaries nor the decrees of the central government can check its growth." He says plainly, echoing Stirner, without a sense of decay or decadence: "They won't become reformed characters to please colonial society, fitting in with the morality of its rulers."[46]

The "Financial Science of the Lumpenproletariat"

What is usually missing in the lumpen-thematizing history and lumpen-adjacent social theory is the original dialectical encompassment of the "top," which already clearly forms part of the category from the beginning, or at least starting in 1852, with the publication of Marx's *The Eighteenth Brumaire of Louis Bonaparte*. In this political analysis of the 1851 coup through which the initially elected Bonaparte would eventually crown himself the new emperor, Marx unambiguously names the strategy of his success: by becoming the "Chief of the Lumpenproletariat." The "Chief" gained the confidence or votes of – in a wild enumerative definition of personae, legal classifiers, occupations, and souls – the

> vagabonds, discharged soldiers, discharged jailbirds, escaped galley slaves, swindlers, mountebanks, *lazzaroni*, pick-pockets, tricksters, gamblers, pimps, brothel keepers, porters, literati, organ-grinders, rag-pickers, knife grinders, tinkers, beggars– in short, the whole indefinite, disintegrated mass, thrown hither and thither, which the French term *la boheme*.

Marx describes the methods Bonaparte used to "lure the masses" in the elections as the successful "speculation" on their "stupidity." Bonaparte's popular campaign promises consisted of the proposal to "increase the pay" of petty officers and to create a "loan bank for the workers" – "money as a gift and money as a loan." "Gifts and loans," he says, "these were the limits of the financial science

46 Fanon, *Wretched*, 11, 129–130; see also Michael Denning, "Wageless Life," *New Left Review* 66 (2010): 88.

of the lumpenproletariat, both the low and the exalted."[47] Some of the subtlety of this remarkable passage in the *Eighteenth Brumaire* is missed in translation; instead of "stupidity" read dullness or coarseness, "*Plattheit*"; instead of the low and the exalted read "vulgar and noble," "*des vornehmen und des gemeinen*"; instead of "money" as a "gift" and "loan," "*Geld geschenkt und Geld gepumpt*," "*Schenken und Pumpen*," read a much less formal meaning of "credit" such as shelling out or scrounging. Finally, "*Finanzwissenschaft*" was already becoming the German equivalent of political economy, so one could define the "financial science" of the lumpenproletariat as the political economy of promises of "pumped" – enthused and possibly fictitious – money.

Already in the prequel to the *Eighteenth Brumaire*, a compilation of journalistic articles eventually published as *The Class Struggles in France* in 1850, Marx begins the series with an analysis of the "finance aristocracy" that had supported the ruling July Monarchy between 1830 up to the revolution of 1848, with a grotesque rendering of them as promoting "the same prostitution, the same shameless cheating, the same mania to get rich" that was "repeated in every sphere, from the Court to the Cafe Borgne, to get rich not by production, but by pocketing the already available wealth of others." After providing graphic imagery of gambling and debauchery "where money, filth and blood commingle," he gives the dialectal formula of the "finance aristocracy" which "in its mode of acquisition as well as in its pleasures, is nothing but the rebirth of the lumpenproletariat on the heights of bourgeois society."

The appearance of the dialectical element at the "top" splits the financial arm of capital into two. As Marx says, this "mode of acquisition" does not apply to the "aristocracy of finance" as such, meaning "the great [government] loan promoters" and "holders of government securities," but rather the "series of speculations" promoted by a new "swarm of companies that have sprung up" trying to sell shares of "Californian gold" and other mining ventures, resulting in "sheer swindling which is characteristic of the French and Chinese alone."[48] I would thus subscribe to Hal Draper's notable but neglected emphasis that despite the weight and bent of the term, "it is not poverty that is the crux of the lumpenproletariat. It is the second meaning, suggested by 'knave,' which accounts for Stirner's usages, as well as Marx and Engels'." As Draper underscored, the same criteria applies at the dialectical "top": capital not directly based on profits of production but on "unproductive" and "parasitic" "speculation and

47 Marx, *The Eighteenth Brumaire*, 50, 57; for a different translation that renders it "Money as a gift and money on tick," "Donations and loans" see *MECW*, Vol. 11, 149, 143.
48 Marx, "Class Struggles in France," 51.

swindling," forged by the "near-criminal or extralegal excrescences" from both rich and poor, who, he adds in an orthodox vein, are as "dangerous to the long-range interests of the real capitalist class as the others are to the real proletariat."[49]

Any attempts to recover a "clean" logic of production, or separate a brazen "financial science" from the terms of colonial trade and exchange, fails, because of the characteristic lumpenproletarianization of the imperial economy itself, particularly in its "gold rush" moments. As Rosa Luxemburg says, when she first tried to note this, the "*Lumpen*" cannot be reduced to "merely a special section, a sort of social wastage which grows enormously when the walls of the social order are falling down," because it constitutes and is generated by the new and founding elements of an expanding commercial and colonial society. Luxemburg adds, in relation to the character of the capital flowing to the colonies for the sole reason to seek much higher and thus more volatile rates of return, that the

> gradations between commercial profiteering, fictitious deals, adulteration of foodstuffs, cheating, official embezzlement, theft, burglary, and robbery, flow into another in such fashion that the boundary lines between honorable citizenry and the penitentiary has disappeared. In this the same phenomenon is repeated as in the regular and rapid degeneration of bourgeois dignitaries when they are transplanted to an alien soil in an overseas colonial setting. With the stripping off of conventional barriers and props for morality and law, bourgeois society itself falls victim to direct and limitless *Verlumpung*.[50]

Here, Luxemburg remarkably extends the scope of the category for the analysis of colonialism itself. As she suggests in the *Accumulation of Capital*, the "emigration of capital from the old centres to the colonies" is then "followed" by economic migrants themselves, whether the "stream of people from Europe settling in North and South America, South Africa and Australia in the nineteenth century," or where "different modes of 'moderate' slavery and forced labour" was imposed by "European and North American capital" to "secure the necessary minimum of labour in the African colonies, in the West Indies, South America and the South Seas."[51]

---

49 Draper, *Lumpenproletariat*, 35; Hal Draper, *Karl Marx's Theory of Revolution Vol. II* (New York: NYU Press, 1977), 473.

50 Rosa Luxemburg, *The Russian Revolution and Leninism or Marxism?* (Ann Arbor: University of Michigan Press, 1961), 73–74.

51 Rosa Luxemburg and Nikolai Bukharin, *Imperialism and the Accumulation of Capital* (London: Allen Lane, 1972), 121.

If *lumpenproletarianization* is not given a more expansive and dynamic role in imperial capitalism, it will remain reduced to a lens which categorically renders them as "ghostly figures outside the domain of political economy" and economic analysis, as Marx wrote in his 1844 *Economic and Philosophical Manuscripts*, the text of his first encounters with political economy and written before he coined the term:

> political economy thus does not recognize the unoccupied worker, the working man so far as he is outside this work relationship. Swindlers, thieves, beggars, the unemployed, the starving, poverty-stricken and criminal working man, are figures which do not exist for political economy but only for other eyes. [The eyes of] criminal law, doctors, religion, statistical tables, politics, and the work-house beadle.[52]

In contrast to equilibrium-based concepts of exchange which converge on a generality, the recursive "mode of acquisition" or modality of payments in "gifts and loans" created an open-ended dynamic, every time an event. To capture this dialectic a third term must appear, one which deviates from the poles of a static opposition, whether that is between buyer and seller or between workers and employers. The term I have used, the "lumpen-broker," is simply the "broker" prefixed by the dialectical breakdown between two commercial positions or social classes arising, as Jeffrey Mehlman notes in his precise discussion of the meaning of the term, from the "decomposition" of each pole and resulting in the "strange irruption of something lower than the low . . . at the top."[53] The hyphen keeps the dual or equivocal nature of the "lumpen-broker" intact. Touts are almost by definition lumpen-brokers, engaging in *déclassé* or *Lazzaroni* brokerage operations. At the same time, the susceptible and temptable targets of recruitment where also largely drawn from the largest pools of the lumpenproletariat, as put forth by Worsley. What can be found through the concept, is not merely the inherent intrigue of their para-commercial techniques, but a fully historical understanding of how the colonial economy unfolded through its undercurrents. At times, the structure of accumulation was gained, allocated, and halted as a by-product of these techniques, almost completely.

52 Karl Marx and Erich Fromm, *Marx's Concept of Man: Including 'Economic and Philosophical Manuscripts'* (London: Bloomsbury Publishing, 1961), 91.
53 Jeffrey Mehlman, *Revolution and Repetition: Marx/Hugo/Balzac* (Berkeley: University of California Press, 2018), 13.

Conclusion: Making Colonial Labor Markets

> For the one dominating truth which overshadows everything else at this point is a political and economic one. The Industrial System, run by a small class of Capitalists on a theory of competitive contract, had been quite honestly established by the early Victorians and was one of the primary beliefs of Victorianism. The Industrial System, so run, had become another name for hell. By Morris's time and ever since, England has been divided into three classes: Knaves, Fools, and Revolutionists.
>
> – G. K. Chesterton, *The Victorian Age in Literature*

> the 'makers' of economic entities – of descriptions, of simulacra or provocations – are presented in a strangely anodyne, benevolent light, and all deceit, manipulation or negativity seems strangely drained out of worlds in which, at best, we see a kind of horizontal contest between practitioners. Economic reality is not just stripped of its forms of symbolic violence, power and exploitation, it also appears here largely shorn of dissimulation, malevolence, negativity – to remain in the dramatic language of performance, it largely lacks comedy, tragedy or farce, as though the sociologists of the performative turn were still too tied to a kind of value-free 'technical criticism', or straining too hard not to ... critique capitalism.
>
> – Alberto Toscano, *Structured by Cows*

This is what I have been able to uncover and piece together: starting in the 1930s, but with important earlier anchors, a surge of touts sweep through Nigeria generating an unexpected lifeline for a new generation of Calabar middlemen trying to recoup the fortunes lost to British monopoly-capital and plunging palm oil prices; these touts sometimes promised a *dash* as a wage advance, but they simply added it to their own commission once they could drop the workers off at the Spanish Labor Office; but after mounting the largest labor trafficking network on the African coast they are effectively replaced by resident touts, who harness and radically realign an existing labor force; employers flood the market with escalating offers of advances to adept workers finishing their first or second contract, but these amounts quickly become a pittance because of post-war inflation and the lagging revisions of official wage rates, which are certainly not considered enough to compensate their first largely unpaid contract; so re-contracted workers start outmaneuvering the stipulations on capped wages and the pass-laws to pocket advances, often deserting to other plantations and signing new contracts under false names, and are joined by new illegal recruits posing as experienced hands who also receive the always increasing *dash*. Guards, guards everywhere, yet they are unaware of the hide-outs and usurped identities of illegally recruited labor and deserters and are unable to trace back the forged initial permit that was the first step to legitimately acquire other permits, because there are a

https://doi.org/10.1515/9783110755923-010

dozen offices able to issue these and many more bribed functionaries who had been selling them to touts.

How to theorize this? In a first instance, it is remarkable how the historically present mediators have been mostly lost or not pursued in the study of free and forced labor markets, fading into a new background of vertically integrated "labor supply chains" or "communities." Not endowed with the capacity to act independently and lacking decent impulses, they were at best intermediary or passive instruments of other primary agents and forces. In histories of colonial labor regimes, recruiters have appeared as relatively simple, callous but hazy agents who somehow imposed, manipulated, and reordered the values of local societies to successfully extract labor from these. The absence of a specific theoretical engagement with this type of recruitment is even more surprising because recruiters are agents of singular historical consequence and also of profound conceptual importance, because through their techniques they set the parameters of the price and even the experience of labor.

Considered in this more encompassing way they are the fragmented mirror image of unions where syndicalism could not appear – they mediated entry and exit, deployed and cashed out on a kind of pseudo-political power arising from an artificial labor scarcity, were delegated the selection of the final place of work, and recursively managed to differentiate and pull the average working conditions in certain directions and push out other employers as a concomitant to the allocation of the advances of re-hired workers. Their deliberation and bargaining was done in extremely chaotic and in irreducibly excessively transactional ways. Their importance lies precisely in their power to affect and interfere in the organization of production and become antagonistic stumbling blocks at various junctures. They were far from a quasi-automatic stepping stone between workers and employers.

It is at the same time unnecessary but still instructive to recall how the techniques and characters of this historically emergent labor market already appear in Engels, if only to underline how distinct and accurate the schema proved to be. In *The Condition of the English Working Class*, Engels first noted the characteristics of "early stage" and "incipient" labor markets, with its "miserable wiles and subterfuges which are considered the acme of cleverness, and petty-devices of swindling and pilfering." For the England of the 1840s, he concluded that "those tricks do not pay any longer in a large market, where time is money, and where a certain standard of commercial morality is unavoidably developed, purely as a means of saving time and trouble. And it is the same with the relation between the manufacturer and his hands."[1] The ongoing existence of "incipient" labor markets, or as he says elsewhere, the creation of the division of labor involved four "means": "violence and robbery, trickery and fraud." This sequence is a precise characterization of the steps of colonial recruitment, "by fraud, by promises, threats, violence," as he says again, is unmistakably *ürsprungliche* or "primitive" accumulation.[2]

Engels starts his first *Outline of a Critique of Political Economy* with precisely this insight, written in 1843, a year before the *Condition:* "Political economy came into being as a natural result of the expansion of trade, and with its appearance elementary, unscientific huckstering was replaced by a developed system of licensed fraud, an entire science of enrichment." He describes trade relations, drawing from his own experience, as an antagonistic two-way struggle, that with the figure of the broker would constitute two separate and distinctively asymmetric relationships, to the buyer and seller, but operating with the same principles. In order to "become a direct source of gain for the trader," there is in "every purchase and sale" a "mutual mistrust," which leads to what he calls the two axioms or bluffs of trade: first its "secretiveness – the concealment of everything" and thus permitting one "to take the utmost advantage of the ignorance, the trust, of the opposing party," and second, to "impute qualities to one's commodity which it does not possess." Thus, exchange itself acquires tout-like and highly empirical characteristics: "legalised fraud. Any merchant who wants to give truth its due can bear me witness that actual practice conforms with this theory."[3]

With Engels' ethnographic account of a "real exchange," a more practical theory of labor exchanges and even trade can be found in this tradition. In Marx, the most elaborate characterization of trade which "multiplies money circulation" and "dissolves the old relationships" appears in Volume III of *Capital*, in particular the chapter "Historical Facts about Merchant's Capital." The way Marx delimits this type of non-equivalent exchange would characterize the recruiter as a mercantile agent well, as the recruiter "fixes the values of commodities," in this case of the commodity "labor," but also "appropriates an overwhelming portion of the surplus-product [as] a mediator" of "underdeveloped" communities. Here "commercial profit not only appears as out-bargaining and cheating, but also largely originates from them."[4] "Cheating"

1 Engels, *Condition*, 312.

2 Engels, "The Mark," 1892, available at https://www.marxists.org/archive/marx/works/1892/12/mark.htm; Engels, *Anti-Dühring*, 386.

3 Engels, "Outlines of a Critique of Political Economy," 418.

4 Marx, "Capital, Volume Three," 328–329.

workers directly out of their wages, but also the outbargaining of employers through upfront commissions and advances can only appear in a labor market when the primary form of payment is conducted with "gifts and loans."

A broad and insistent emphasis on lumpen-techniques is absent from the historically argued final section on "primitive accumulation" in Volume I of *Capital*, with its elaborate description of the early proletariat "forcibly expropriated from the soil, driven from their homes," which coincides with only one aspect of the lumpen: "turned en masse into beggars, robbers, vagabonds, partly from inclination, in most cases from stress of circumstances," "whipped, branded, tortured by laws grotesquely terrible, into the discipline necessary for the wage system." In this "historic genesis of capitalist production," capital "wants and uses the power of the state to 'regulate' wages, i.e., to force them within the limits suitable for surplus-value making," an "essential element of the so-called primitive accumulation." The "colonial system" here, figures along with "public debts, heavy taxes, protection, [and] commercial wars" as the state-birthed engendering of "industry," were labor, "like [for] the royal navy" was "recruited by means of the press-gang."[5]

Wages did not fall or rise with the market as they were pre-set by the labor legislation and were only irregularly revised upwards. This was the "essential element" of the indentured contract. Nevertheless, the commissions and advances moved rapidly and created the traps and bonanzas of the labor market in formation. These two extremes constantly crystallized in the Gulf of Guinea, and direct our attention to the actions of the mediators of these two systematic potentials. Precisely because wages were capped via top-down and state-regulated contracts, a necessary surplus of money emerged from it. This "pumped" money spread through the actions and visions of recruiters, who turned advances into a great many false promises or considered the rising *dash* of experienced workers as just another opportunity to seize a smaller but overall inflating share of labor costs being paid out by employers. This "surplus" is constitutive of the irrevocable and imposed contract, which releases a commission and the possibility of advances.

The "release" forged an almost century-long dynamic of recruitment in Fernando Po with its distinctly "peaceful" recruiting techniques. As Samita Sen says so precisely in relation to her study of indentured recruitment for Assam and elsewhere: "what was at issue was not so much the capacity of market penetration to loosen workers from the land but an excess of commercialized labor mobilization, over which neither the planters nor the state was able to establish ef-

5 Marx, *Capital*, 701, 537.

fective control."[6] Moulier Boutang refers to this as a "heightened" commodified character of labor in the mercantile sense of the term: "forms of unfree labor (workers under peonage, or workers tied to their employers through debt bondage) resembles more what economists and merchants have historically called a market than the very paradoxical market of free wage-labor."[7] The post-emancipation concern with the impermissibly excessive commercialization of labor was reflected on the surface of the new order of contracts which formally suppressed what it structurally generated – the continuing wholesale purchase of people and the possibility of workers treating themselves as their own speculative commodity. The measure of this "excess" is purely its price, achieved by a kind of arbitrage and speculation without entering the world of production. The price of labor was not based on a simple traffic of equivalents formalized in money, labor as just another barter-commodity, nor on any consistent or averaged labor theory of value-based exploitation. Contracts were not simply more or less opaque options of rational choice or market-mediated necessities backed by outward facing legal frameworks or the generalized monetization of social reproduction.

It was entirely historical forces that created the horizon in which new labor would be priced. The contract led directly to the clumping, bundling and intervals of wage payments, which drove the recruiter-driven labor market. Within this contract form, the search for the price in the search for labor involved the massive imprint of the brokers who created the social form of volatile new markets. Absolute windfalls and total failures were both common outcomes. It is the variations in the final price, and its subdivisions and allocations, that should preoccupy us because this price mechanism directly shows the extreme and unstable political power of the imperial order. The instability revealed by examining recruiting techniques is impossible to see if wage payments simply take place on the abstract economic "stage" of exchange without the context of the concrete roles and power relations within semi-anonymous and impersonal markets. Recruiters and their mediation of wage payments not only contradicted the colonial self-image of free or regulated contracts, but also exposed the contradictions of imperial capitalism itself, which is to say, they thwarted colonial ideology and permitted its economy to develop explosively towards its collapse.

Touts thus revealed the historical "truth" about the imperial mode of production and rendered any attempts at marrying liberal ideology and imperial capitalism fully incompatible. Touts also exposed the false consignment of unfree

6 Sen, "Commercial Recruiting," 11.
7 Moulier-Boutang, "Unfree Labor."

labor into an unpolitical history. They combined the wage contract and the labor question, its "scarcity" vis-à-vis an imperially propelled new demand, into a dramatic circulation and determination of the closing price of labor, where the location of the contradiction between capital and labor outside of the strike could take hold. They generated wealth on the move, at a distance from both capital and labor. Touts could confound and reroute imperial economics – they spotted gaps and pushed it and its principally paper-based surveillance apparatus to extremes. The political economy of contracts within a labor scarcity was weaved and laced with autonomous intermediaries that could contradict – add loopholes and shortcuts – and cause the entire "economic force" of the colony to, alternatingly, intensify or crumble. They compromised channels, found its weakest link, and made visible the foundations and inconsistency of a colonial capitalist mode of production that had tried to distance itself from slavery and issue the false inauguration of the era of free labor.

Recruiters appear between perpetual and punctuated labor, between the permanent and unpaid labor of the "slave" and the daily payments to casual, precarious and self-assembling "free labor." On either end of this theoretical and metaphorical spectrum there is no need for recruiters. However, only by considering the extreme distribution of the structure of payment within recruited labor is it possible to conceptually suspend the poles of the "free" and "unfree" labor spectrum and gain a closer insight into the variety of recruiter-driven labor markets. On both ends of this recruiter-only spectrum the wage suddenly disappears: the absolute commission, a fully parasitic owner, and the absolute advance, receiving payments before having done any work whatsoever. The way the wage of contract labor was consequently lumped and dispensed directly led to the expansion of commodified labor and the unfolding of the "real" price of labor, through the handling of the "excess" generated from the contract, the commissions and the *dash*.

It is remarkable how much of this volatility and political potential simply disappears when touts are considered to be merely a component of "high transaction costs." The now hegemonic new institutional economics of Douglass C. North considers contracts, formally enforced by external third parties or the state, as lowering uncertainty and liabilities and thus reducing transactions costs. In the labor market, all the extra steps and costs imposed by brokerage and their financial elements, such as advances and the imprecise calculations of returns, are usually said to be merely reflections of an intense scarcity or an artificial border, occurring only in booming sectors where labor was in great demand, where a business had a high labor turnover, or where work was remote and inhospitable – but without giving theoretical weight to the many possible and impermissible twists. As John Holt, Frederick Cooper and Rebecca

Scott say in *Beyond Slavery*, in relation to situations of "intimidation and deception" that "led the poor of Asia or Africa into boats headed, like the slave ships, for the West Indies or the sugar islands of the Indian Ocean-or, later, the cocoa islands off Central Africa," such movements arose simply where "labor was not readily available in the right place" or "at the right price."[8] All this is lost too when recruited labor is considered either an upgraded substitution of slavery or the imperfect new generalization of free labor; a dubious fog or blurry middle. The contract manufactured both the status of the worker and the dynamism that would make these appear via a new generation of recruiters. One can even speak of the contract or recruiter-contract mode of labor production, much like land was the underlying leverage in serfdom or property the ultimate tool in slavery. The base of this colonial economy was the contract, or beyond it but with the same effects, the configurations of sovereignty and money creation.

---

8 Frederick Cooper, Thomas C. Holt, and Rebecca J. Scott, *Beyond Slavery: Explorations of Race, Labor, and Citizenship in Postemancipation Societies* (Chapel Hill: University of North Carolina Press, 2000), 22–23. A related literature has considered "this kind of labor scarcity" to be "only a problem in the colonial agricultural periphery of an expanding capitalist universe," Steinfeld, *Coercion, Contract and Free Labor*, 5; where "only" designates a world being draped in enclaves of export and exploitation that exploded beyond the Caribbean heartlands with the formal abolition of slavery, an expansive implanting of an "immense accumulation of commodities" and the wholesale creation of new labor-intensive sectors, such as shipping and freight or logging and mineral extraction along new commodity frontiers requiring mass and medium-term relocation of workers and porterage, and the commercial farms and plantations growing all sorts of industrial and consumer crops such as cotton, palm oil, rubber, cocoa, coffee, etc., each employing from a few to several hundred workers, rarely if ever locally sourced, situated in a patchwork of slopes, valleys, islands across different imperial territories on various continents: i.e. what one may properly call the global economy.

Archives

AGA	Archivo General de la Administración, Alcalá de Henares, Spain
AMAE	Archivo General del Ministerio de Asuntos Exteriores y de Cooperación, Madrid, Spain (Closed in 2013, moved to AGA)
ANC	Archives Nationales du Cameroun, Yaoundé, Cameroon
BArch	Bundesarchiv Lichterfelde, Berlin, Germany
BNA	Buea National Archives, Buea, Cameroon
BNE	Biblioteca Nacional de España, Madrid, Spain
BNM	Biblioteca Nacional de Guinea Ecuatorial, Malabo, Equatorial Guinea
NAC	National Archives of Nigeria, Calabar
NAE	National Archives of Nigeria, Enugu
NAI	National Archives of Nigeria, Ibadan
TNA	The National Archives of the UK, London
SOAS	Archives & Special Collections, SOAS Library, London, UK
RHL	Rhodes House Library, Oxford, UK

https://doi.org/10.1515/9783110755923-011

Bibliography

Abdullah, Ibrahim. "Culture, Consciousness and Armed Conflict: Cabral's Déclassé/ (Lumpenproletariat?) in the Era of Globalization." *African Identities* 4, no. 1 (2006): 99 – 112.

Abdullah, Ibrahim. "Rethinking African Labour and Working-Class History: The Artisan Origins of the Sierra Leonean Working Class." *Social History* 23, no. 1 (1998): 80 – 96.

Abu-Manneh, Bashir. "Who Owns Frantz Fanon's Legacy?" *Jacobin*, October 12, 2021.

Acemoglu, Daron, and Alexander Wolitzky. "The Economics of Labor Coercion." *Econometrica* 79, no. 2 (2011): 555 – 600.

Adamu, Mahdi. *The Hausa Factor in West African History*. Ibadan: Oxford University Press Nigeria, 1979.

Aderinto, Saheed, and Paul Osifodunrin. "'500 Children Missing in Lagos': Child Kidnapping and Public Anxiety in Colonial Nigeria." In *Children and Childhood in Colonial Nigerian Histories*, edited by Saheed Aderinto, 97 – 121. New York: Palgrave Macmillan, 2015.

Afigbo, Adiele E. *The Abolition of the Slave Trade in Southeastern Nigeria, 1885 – 1950*. Rochester: University Rochester Press, 2006.

Agiri, B.A. "The Development of Wage Labour in Agriculture in Southern Yorubaland 1900 – 1940." *Journal of the Historical Society of Nigeria* 12, no. 1 (1983): 95 – 107.

Ahuja, Ravi. "Networks of Subordination–Networks of the Subordinated: The Ordered Spaces of South Asian Maritime Labour in an Age of Imperialism (C1890 – 1947)." In *The Limits of British Colonial Control in South Asia: Spaces of Disorder in the Indian Ocean Region*, edited by Ashwini Tambe and Harald Fischer-Tine, 13 – 48. London: Routledge, 2009.

Ahuja, Ravi. "Mobility and Containment: The Voyages of South Asian Seamen, c. 1900 – 1960." *International Review of Social History* 51, no. S14 (2006): 111 – 41.

Akerlof, George A., and Robert J. Shiller. *Phishing for Phools: The Economics of Manipulation and Deception*. Princeton: Princeton University Press, 2015.

Akinyemi, Bolaji. "Nigeria and Fernando Poo, 1958 – 1966: The Politics of Irridentism." *African Affairs* 69, no. 276 (1970): 236 – 49.

Akyeampong, Emmanuel K. *Between the Sea and the Lagoon: An Eco-Social History of the Anlo of Southeastern Ghana, c. 1850 to Recent Times*. Oxford: James Currey, 2001.

Alexander, Catherine. "Legal and Binding: Time, Change and Long-Term Transactions." *Journal of the Royal Anthropological Institute* 7, no. 3 (2001): 467 – 85.

Allen, Richard B. *Slaves, Freedmen and Indentured Laborers in Colonial Mauritius*. Cambridge: Cambridge University Press, 1999.

Allen, Richard B. "European Slave Trading, Abolitionism, and 'New Systems of Slavery' in the Indian Ocean." *PORTAL: Journal of Multidisciplinary International Studies* 9, no. 1 (2012): 1 – 21.

Allen, Richard B. "Re-Conceptualizing the 'New System of Slavery.'" *Man In India* 92, no. 2 (2012): 225 – 45.

Allen, Victor L. "The Meaning of the Working Class in Africa." *The Journal of Modern African Studies* 10, no. 2 (1972): 169 – 89.

Allen, William, and Thomas Richard Heywood Thomson. *A Narrative of the Expedition Sent by Her Majesty's Government to the River Niger, in 1841, Under the Command of Captain H. D. Trotter, R. N.: In Two Volumes*. Vol. 2. London: Bentley, 1848.

https://doi.org/10.1515/9783110755923-012

Allina, Eric. *Slavery by Any Other Name: African Life Under Company Rule in Colonial Mozambique.* Charlottesville: University of Virginia Press, 2012.

Allina, Eric. "Resistance and the Social History of Africa." *Journal of Social History* 37, no. 1 (2003): 187–98.

Almonte, Enrique de. *Los naturales de la Guinea española considerados bajo el aspecto de su condición de súbditos españoles.* Madrid: Real Sociedad Geográfica, 1910.

Alpes, Maybritt Jill. *Brokering High-Risk Migration and Illegality in West Africa: Abroad at Any Cost.* New York: Taylor & Francis, 2016.

Alpes, Maybritt Jill. "Why Aspiring Migrants Trust Migration Brokers: The Moral Economy of Departure in Anglophone Cameroon." *Africa* 87, no. 2 (2017): 304–21.

Althusser, Louis, and Etienne Balibar, eds. *Reading Capital.* London: Verso, 1998.

Álvarez Chillida, Gonzalo. "Claves de la historia colonial española de la Guinea Ecuatorial." In *Guinea Ecuatorial (des)conocida: lo que sabemos, ignoramos, inventamos y deformamos acerca de su pasado y su presente*, edited by Juan Aranzadi and Gonzalo Álvarez Chillida, 1: 247–411. Madrid: UNED, 2020.

Álvarez Chillida, Gonzalo, and Gustau Nerín. "Guinea Ecuatorial: El legado de la colonización española." *Ayer* 109, no. 1 (2018): 13–32.

Amin, Samir. "Les effets structurels de l'intégration internationale des économies précapitalistes: une étude théorique du mécanisme qui a engendré les économies dites sous-développées." PhD Thesis, Université de Paris, 1957.

Amin, Samir. "Modes of Production and Social Formations." *Ufahamu: A Journal of African Studies* 4, no. 3 (1974): 57–86.

Amin, Samir, and Catherine Coquery-Vidrovitch. *Histoire économique du Congo, 1880–1968: du Congo français à l'Union douanière et économique d'Afrique centrale.* Paris: Anthropos, 1969.

Amin, Samir, and Daryll Forde, eds. *Modern Migrations in Western Africa.* Oxford: International African Institute, Oxford University Press, 1974.

Amin, Shahid, and Marcel van der Linden, eds. *"Peripheral" Labour?: Studies in the History of Partial Proletarianization.* Cambridge: Cambridge University Press, 1997.

Amrith, Sunil S. *Crossing the Bay of Bengal: The Furies of Nature and the Fortunes of Migrants.* Cambridge: Harvard University Press, 2013.

Anderson, David M. "Master and Servant in Colonial Kenya, 1895–1939." *The Journal of African History* 1, no. 3 (2000): 459–85.

Anderson, Martha. "From Adumu to Mami Wata: Central Ijo Water Spirit Imagery." In *The Multi-Disciplinary Approach to African History: Essays in Honour of Ebiegberi Joe Alagoa*, edited by Ebiegberi J. Alagoa and Nkparom C. Ejituwu, 257–73. Port Harcourt: University of Port Harcourt Press, 1998.

Aranzadi, Juan. *Viviendo con Guinea Ecuatorial: aportaciones a una conversación antropológica.* Barcelona: Bellaterra, 2021.

Aranzadi, Juan. "Estudio introductorio. Hacia un replanteamiento radical de los estudios sobre Guinea Ecuatorial." In *Guinea Ecuatorial (des)conocida: lo que sabemos, ignoramos, inventamos y deformamos acerca de su pasado y su presente*, edited by Juan Aranzadi and Gonzalo Álvarez Chillida, 1: 41–246. Madrid: UNED, 2020.

Archer, Leonie, ed. "Introduction." In *Slavery and Other Forms of Unfree Labour*, 1–18. London: Routledge, 1988.

Ardener, Edwin, and Shirley Ardener. *Kingdom on Mount Cameroon: Studies in the History of the Cameroon Coast, 1500–1970*. New York: Berghahn Books, 1996.
Ardener, Edwin, Shirley Ardener, and W.A. Warmington. *Plantation and Village in the Cameroons: Some Economic and Social Studies*. London: Oxford University Press for the Nigerian Institute of Social and Economic Research, 1960.
Armas y Céspedes, Francisco de. *De la esclavitud en Cuba*. Madrid: Establecimiento Tipografico de T. Fortanet, 1866.
Arrighi, Giovanni. "Labour Supplies in Historical Perspective: A Study of the Proletarianization of the African Peasantry in Rhodesia." *Journal of Development Studies* 6, no. 3 (1970): 197–234.
Asiegbu, Johnson U.J. *Slavery and the Politics of Liberation 1787–1861: A Study of Liberated African Emigration and British Anti-Slavery Policy*. New York: Africana Pub. Corp., 1969.
Asiegbu, Johnson U.J. "British Slave Emancipation and 'Free' Labour Recruitment from West Africa, 1840–1861." *Sierra Leone Studies* 26 (1970): 37–47.
Asiwaju, A.I. "Migrations as Revolt: The Example of the Ivory Coast and the Upper Volta before 1945." *The Journal of African History* 17, no. 4 (1976): 577–94.
Atiyah, Patrick S. *The Rise and Fall of Freedom of Contract*. Oxford: Oxford University Press, 1979.
Atkins, Keletso E. *The Moon Is Dead! Give Us Our Money!: The Cultural Origins of an African Work Ethic, Natal, South Africa, 1843–1900*. Portsmouth: Heinemann, 1993.
Austen, Ralph A. "Social Bandits and Other Heroic Criminals: Western Models of Resistance and Their Relevance for Africa." In *Banditry, Rebellion and Social Protest in Africa*, edited by Donald Crummey, 89–108. London: James Currey, 1986.
Austen, Ralph A. "The Abolition of the Overseas Slave Trade: A Distorted Theme in West African History." *Journal of the Historical Society of Nigeria* 5, no. 2 (1970): 257–74.
Austen, Ralph A., and Jonathan Derrick. *Middlemen of the Cameroons Rivers: The Duala and their Hinterland, c.1600-c.1960*. Cambridge: Cambridge University Press, 1999.
Austin, Gareth. *Labour, Land, and Capital in Ghana: From Slavery to Free Labour in Asante, 1807–1956*. Rochester: University of Rochester Press, 2005.
Austin, Gareth. "Cash Crops and Freedom: Export Agriculture and the Decline of Slavery in Colonial West Africa." *International Review of Social History* 54, no. 1 (2009): 1–37.
Austin, Gareth. "Factor Markets in Nieboer Conditions: Pre-Colonial West Africa, c.1500–c.1900." *Continuity and Change* 24, no. 1 (2009): 23–53.
Austin, Gareth, and Stephen Broadberry. "Introduction: The Renaissance of African Economic History." *The Economic History Review* 67, no. 4 (2014): 893–906.
Authaler, Caroline. *Deutsche Plantagen in Britisch-Kamerun: Internationale Normen und lokale Realitäten 1925 bis 1940*. Köln: Böhlau Verlag, 2019.
Aworawo, David. "Decisive Thaw: The Changing Pattern of Relations between Nigeria and Equatorial Guinea, 1980–2005." *Journal of International and Global Studies* 1, no. 2 (2010): 89–109.
Aworawo, David. "Different Strokes: Spanish Policy toward Cuba and Equatorial Guinea during the Colonial Period." *Lagos Historical Review* 7 (2007): 57–72.
Aworawo, David. "Foreign Policy and the Travails of Nigerian Migrants in Equatorial Guinea, 1930–1980." *Nigerian Journal of International Affairs* 25, no. 2 (1999): 24–35.
Azikiwe, Ben N. "George Schuyler, Slaves Today, A Story of Liberia." *The Journal of Negro History* 17, no. 3 (1932): 382–83.

Azikiwe, Ben N. "In Defense of Liberia." *The Journal of Negro History* 17, no. 1 (1932): 30–50.

Azikiwe, Nnamdi. *Liberia in World Politics.* Westport, Conn.: Negro University Press, 1970.

Baak, Paul E. "About Enslaved Ex-Slaves, Uncaptured Contract Coolies and Unfreed Freedmen: Some Notes about 'Free' and 'Unfree' Labour in the Context of Plantation Development in Southwest India, Early Sixteenth Century-Mid 1990s." *Modern Asian Studies* 33, no. 1 (1999): 121–57.

Baguena Corella, Luis. *Manuales del Africa Española I: Guinea.* Madrid: Instituto de Estudios Africanos, 1951.

Bakunin, Mikhail. "The International and Karl Marx." In *Bakunin on Anarchy*, edited by Sam Dolgoff, 286–320. New York: Vintage Books, 1971.

Balachandran, Gopalan. "Making Coolies, (Un)Making Workers: 'Globalizing' Labour in the late-19th and early-20th Centuries." *Journal of Historical Sociology* 24, no. 3 (2011): 266–96.

Balachandran, Gopalan. "Recruitment and Control of Indian Seamen: Calcutta, 1880–1935." *International Journal of Maritime History* 9, no. 1 (1997): 1–18.

Balachandran, Gopalan. "Searching for the Sardar: The State, Pre-Capitalist Institutions, and Human Agency in the Maritime Labour Market, Calcutta, 1880–1935." In *Institutions and Economic Change in South Asia*, edited by Burton Stein and Sanjay Subrahmanyam, 206–36. Delhi: Oxford University Press, 1996.

Balandier, Georges. "The Colonial Situation: A Theoretical Approach." In *Social Change: The Colonial Situation*, edited by Immanuel Wallerstein, 34–61. New York: John Wiley & Sons, 1966.

Balandier, Georges. "La situation coloniale: Approche théorique." *Cahiers Internationaux de Sociologie* 11 (1951): 44–79.

Balboa Navarro, Imilcy. "Libertos, vagos y bandoleros: La reglamentación del trabajo tras la abolición de la esclavitud (Cuba 1886–1895)." *Relaciones* 32, no. 127 (2011): 87–116.

Balboa Navarro, Imilcy. *Los brazos necesarios: inmigración, colonización y trabajo libre en Cuba, 1878–1898.* Valencia: Centro Francisco Tomás y Valiente, 2000.

Ballano, Fernando. *Aquel negrito del África tropical: el colonialismo español en Guinea (1778–1968).* Madrid: Sial/Casa de África, 2014.

Banaji, Jairus. *A Brief History of Commercial Capitalism.* Chicago: Haymarket Books, 2020.

Banaji, Jairus. *Theory as History. Essays on Modes of Production and Exploitation.* Leiden: Brill, 2010.

Banaji, Jairus. *Agrarian Change in Late Antiquity Gold, Labour, and Aristocratic Dominance.* Oxford: Oxford University Press, 2007.

Banaji, Jairus. "Modernizing the Historiography of Rural Labour: An Unwritten Agenda." In *Companion to Historiography*, edited by Michael Bentley, 88–104. London: Routledge, 2006.

Banaji, Jairus. "The Fictions of Free Labour: Contract, Coercion, and So-Called Unfree Labour." *Historical Materialism* 11, no. 3 (2003): 69–95.

Banciella y Bárzana, José César. *Rutas de Imperio "Fernando Póo y Guinea" (su significación actual y potencial ante las necesidades económicas de España).* Madrid: Librería General de Victoriano Suárez, 1940.

Barchiesi, Franco. "Precarious Liberation: A Rejoinder." *South African Review of Sociology* 43, no. 1 (2012): 98–105.

Barnett, Randy E. "The Sound of Silence: Default Rules and Contractual Consent." *Virginia Law Review* 78 (1992): 821–911.

Barrow, Clyde. *The Dangerous Class: The Concept of the Lumpenproletariat.* Ann Arbor: University of Michigan Press, 2020.

Bastian, Misty L. "Fires, Tricksters and Poisoned Medicines: Popular Cultures of Rumor in Onitsha, Nigeria and its Markets." *Etnofoor* 11, no. 2 (1998): 111–32.

Bastian, Misty L. "Bloodhounds who have no Friends: Witchcraft and Locality in the Nigerian Popular Press." In *Modernity and its Malcontents: Ritual and Power in Postcolonial Africa*, edited by Jean Comaroff and John Comaroff, 129–66. Chicago: University of Chicago Press, 1993.

Bates, Crispin. "Some Thoughts on the Representation and Misrepresentation of the Colonial South Asian Labour Diaspora." *South Asian Studies* 33, no. 1 (2017): 7–22.

Bates, Crispin. "Coerced and Migrant Labourers in India: The Colonial Experience." *Edinburgh Papers In South Asian Studies* 13 (2000): 2–33.

Bates, Crispin, and Marina Carter. "Sirdars as Intermediaries in Nineteenth-Century Indian Ocean Indentured Labour Migration." *Modern Asian Studies* 51, no. 2 (2017): 462–84.

Bates, Crispin, and Marina Carter. "Tribal and Indentured Migrants in Colonial India: Modes of Recruitment and Forms of Incorporation." In *Dalit Movements and the Meanings of Labour in India*, edited by Peter Robb, 159–85. Delhi: Oxford University Press, 1993.

Bauer, Arnold J. "Rural Workers in Spanish America: Problems of Peonage and Oppression." *The Hispanic American Historical Review* 59, no. 1 (1979): 34–63.

Baumann, Oscar. *Eine Afrikanische Tropeninsel: Fernando Póo und die Bube.* Wien: Hölzel, 1888.

Beecroft, John, and J.B. King. "Details of Explorations of the Old Calabar River, in 1841 and 1842." *Journal of the Royal Geographical Society of London* 14 (1844): 260–83.

Behal, Rana. "Power Structure, Discipline, and Labour in Assam Tea Plantations under Colonial Rule." *International Review of Social History* 51, no. S14 (2006): 143–72.

Behal, Rana, and Prabhu Mohapatra. "'Tea and Money versus Human Life': The Rise and Fall of the Indenture System in the Assam Tea Plantations 1840–1908." *Journal of Peasant Studies* 19, no. 3–4 (1992): 142–72.

Beinart, William. "Joyini Inkomo: Cattle Advances and the Origins of Migrancy from Pondoland." *Journal of Southern African Studies* 5, no. 2 (1979): 199–219.

Bellucci, Stefano, and Andreas Eckert, eds. *General Labour History of Africa: Workers, Employers and Governments, 20th–21st Centuries.* Rochester: Boydell & Brewer, 2019.

Bellucci, Stefano, and Bill Freund. "Introduction. Work across Africa: Labour Exploitation and Mobility in Southern, Eastern and Western Africa." *Africa* 87, no. 1 (2017): 27–35.

Berg, Elliot J. "Backward-Sloping Labor Supply Functions in Dual Economies – the Africa Case." *The Quarterly Journal of Economics* 75, no. 3 (1961): 468–92.

Berlant, Lauren. *Cruel Optimism.* Durham: Duke University Press, 2012.

Berman, Bruce J., and John M. Lonsdale. "Crises of Accumulation, Coercion and the Colonial State: The Development of the Labor Control System in Kenya, 1919–1929." *Canadian Journal of African Studies* 14, no. 1 (1980): 55–81.

Bernault, Florence, ed. *Enfermement, prison et châtiments en Afrique du 19e siècle à nos jours.* Paris: Karthala, 1999.

Bernault, Florence. “The Shadow of Rule: Colonial Power and Modern Punishment in Africa.” In *Cultures of Confinement: A History of the Prison in Africa, Asia and Latin America*, edited by Frank Dikötter and Ian Brown, 55–94. London: Hurst, 2007.

Bernault, Florence, and Janet Roitman, eds. *A History of Prison and Confinement in Africa*. Portsmouth: Heinemann, 2003.

Bernstein, Henry. *Class Dynamics of Agrarian Change*. Sterling: Kumarian Press, 2010.

Berry, Sara. *No Condition Is Permanent: The Social Dynamics of Agrarian Change in Sub-Saharan Africa*. Ann Arbor: University of Wisconsin Press, 1993.

Berry, Sara. “Stable Prices, Unstable Values: Same Thoughts on Monetization and the Meaning of Transactions in West African Economies.” In *Money Matters: Instability, Values, and Social Payments in the Modern History of West African Communities*, edited by Jane Guyer, 299–313. Portsmouth: Heinemann, 1995.

Bersselaar, Dmitri van den. “‘Somebody must necessarily go to bring this Drink’: Gin Smugglers, Chiefs and the State in Colonial Ghana.” *Cultural and Social History* 11, no. 2 (2014): 243–61.

Bersselaar, Dmitri van den. “Creating ‘Union Ibo’: Missionaries and the Igbo Language.” *Africa: Journal of the International African Institute* 67, no. 2 (1997): 273–95.

Bescherer, Peter. *Vom Lumpenproletariat Zur Unterschicht: Produktivistische Theorie Und Politische Praxis*. Frankfurt am Main: Campus Verlag, 2013.

Bischof, Christopher. “Chinese Labourers, Free Blacks, and Social Engineering in the Post-Emancipation British West Indies.” *Past & Present* 231, no. 1 (2016): 129–68.

Blanchard, Peter. “Recruitment of Workers in the Peruvian Sierra at the Turn of the Century: the Enganche System.” *Inter-American Economic Affairs* 33, no. 3 (1979): 63–83.

Bolland, O. Nigel. “Labour Control and Resistance in Belize in the Century After 1838.” *Slavery & Abolition* 7, no. 2 (1986): 175–87.

Bolland, O. Nigel. “Systems of Domination after Slavery: The Control of Land and Labor in the British West Indies after 1838.” *Comparative Studies in Society and History* 23, no. 4 (1981): 591–619.

Bolt, Jutta, and Erik Green. “Was the Wage Burden Too Heavy? Settler Farming, Profitability, and Wage Shares of Settler Agriculture in Nyasaland, c. 1900–60.” *The Journal of African History* 56, no. 2 (2015): 217–38.

Bolt, Maxim. “Waged Entrepreneurs, Policed Informality: Work, the Regulation of Space and the Economy of the Zimbabwean–South African Border.” *Africa* 82, no. 1 (2012): 111–30.

Bonelli Rubio, Juan Maria. “Geografía económica de la Guinea Española.” In *España en Africa*, edited by José Diaz de Villegas y Bustamente, 193–204. Madrid: Instituto de Estudios Africanos, 1949.

Bosma, Ulbe, Elise van Nederveen Meerkerk, and Aditya Sarkar, eds. *Mediating Labour: Worldwide Labour Intermediation in the Nineteenth and Twentieth Centuries*. Cambridge: Cambridge University Press, 2012.

Brandon, Pepijn, and Aditya Sarkar. “Labour History and the Case against Colonialism.” *International Review of Social History* 64, no. 1 (2019): 73–109.

Brass, Tom. *Labour Regime Change in the Twenty-First Century: Unfreedom, Capitalism and Primitive Accumulation*. Leiden: Brill, 2011.

Brass, Tom. *Towards a Comparative Political Economy of Unfree Labour: Case Studies and Debates*. London: Routledge, 1999.

Brass, Tom. “Who these days is not a Subaltern? The Populist Drift of Global Labor History.” *Science & Society* 81, no. 1 (2017): 10–34.

Brass, Tom. “Why Unfree Labour is not ‘so-called’: The Fictions of Jairus Banaji.” *Journal of Peasant Studies* 31, no. 1 (2003): 101–36.

Brass, Tom, and Henry Bernstein. “Introduction: Proletarianisation and Deproletarianisation on the Colonial Plantation.” *The Journal of Peasant Studies* 19, no. 3–4 (1992): 1–40.

Braudel, Fernand. *Civilization and Capitalism, 15th–18th Century. Volume III. The Perspective of the World.* Berkeley: University of California Press, 1983.

Brauner, Christina. *Kompanien, Könige und* caboceers: *Interkulturelle Diplomatie an Gold- und Sklavenküste im 17. und 18. Jahrhundert.* Köln: Böhlau Verlag, 2015.

Brauner, Christina. “Connecting Things: Trading Companies and Diplomatic Gift-Giving on the Gold and Slave Coasts in the Seventeenth and Eighteenth Centuries.” *Journal of Early Modern History* 20, no. 4 (2016): 408–28.

Breckenridge, Keith. *Biometric State: The Global Politics of Identification and Surveillance in South Africa.* Cambridge: Cambridge University Press, 2014.

Breckenridge, Keith. “Flesh Made Words: Fingerprinting and the Fantasy of Documentary Panopticism, 1900–1930.” *Occasional Paper* 23 (2014): 76–96.

Breckenridge, Keith. “No Will to Know: The Rise and Fall of African Civil Registration in Twentieth-Century South Africa.” *Proceedings of the British Academy* 182 (2012): 357–83.

Breckenridge, Keith. “Power Without Knowledge: Three Nineteenth Century Colonialisms in South Africa.” *Journal of Natal and Zulu History* 26, no. 1 (2008): 3–30.

Breman, Jan. *Taming the Coolie Beast: Plantation Society and the Colonial Order in Southeast Asia.* Oxford: Oxford University Press, 1989.

Bright, Rachel K. *Chinese Labour in South Africa, 1902–10: Race, Violence, and Global Spectacle.* London: Palgrave Macmillan, 2013.

Brook, Ian. *The One-Eyed Man Is King.* London: Cassell, 1966.

Brooks, George E. *Eurafricans in Western Africa: Commerce, Social Status, Gender, and Religious Observance from the Sixteenth to the Eighteenth Century.* Athens: Ohio University Press, 2003.

Brooks, George E. *The Kru Mariner in the Nineteenth Century: An Historical Compendium.* Newark: Liberian Studies Association in America, 1972.

Brown, Carolyn A. *“We Were All Slaves”: African Miners, Culture, and Resistance at the Enugu Government Colliery.* Portsmouth: Heinemann, 2003.

Brown, Laurence. “‘A Most Irregular Traffic’: The Oceanic Passages of the Melanesian Labor Trade.” In *Many Middle Passages: Forced Migration and the Making of the Modern World*, edited by Emma Christopher, Marcus Rediker, and Cassandra Pybus, 184–203. Berkeley: University of California Press, 2007.

Bukharin, Nikolai. *Historical Materialism: A System of Sociology.* Cosmonaut Press, 2021.

Burton, Andrew. *African Underclass: Urbanisation, Crime & Colonial Order in Dar es Salaam.* Oxford: James Currey, 2005.

Bussard, Robert L. “The ‘Dangerous Class’ of Marx and Engels: The Rise of the Idea of the Lumpenproletariat.” *History of European Ideas* 8, no. 6 (1987): 675–92.

Cabanellas, Guillermo. *La selva siempre triunfa: novela del África española.* Buenos Aires: Editorial Ayacucho, 1944.

Cahen, Michel. "Slavery, Enslaved Labour and Forced Labour in Mozambique." *Portuguese Studies Review* 21, no. 1 (2013): 253–66.

Cahen, Michel. "*Indigenato* before Race? Some Proposals on Portuguese Forced Labour Law in Mozambique and the African Empire (1926–1962)." In *Racism and Ethnic Relations in the Portuguese-Speaking World*, edited by Francisco Bethencourt and Adrian Pearce, 149–71. Oxford: Oxford University Press, 2012.

Caldeira, Arlindo Manuel. "Learning the Ropes in the Tropics: Slavery and the Plantation System on the Island of São Tomé." *African Economic History* 39 (2011): 35–71.

Callebert, Ralph. "African Mobility and Labor in Global History." *History Compass* 14, no. 3 (2016): 116–27.

Callebert, Ralph. "Cleaning the Wharves: Pilferage, Bribery, and Social Connections on the Durban Docks in the 1950s." *Canadian Journal of African Studies* 46, no. 1 (2012): 23–38.

Callebert, Ralph. "Rethinking the Underclass: Future Directions in Southern African Labor History." *International Labor and Working-Class History* 82 (2012): 136–42.

Campbell, Gwyn. "Introduction: Slavery and Other Forms of Unfree Labour in the Indian Ocean World." *Slavery & Abolition* 24, no. 2 (2003): ix–xxxii.

Campos Serrano, Alicia. *De colonia a Estado: Guinea Ecuatorial, 1955–1968.* Madrid: Centro de Estudios Políticos y Constitucionales, 2002.

Campos Serrano, Alicia. "El régimen colonial franquista en el Golfo de Guinea." *Revista Jurídica UAM* 3 (2000): 79–108.

Campos Serrano, Alicia, and Plácido Micó Abogo. *Labour and Trade Union Freedom in Equatorial Guinea.* Madrid: Fundación Paz y Solidaridad Serafín Aliaga, 2006.

Canetti, Elias. *Crowds and Power.* London: Orion Publishing, 2000.

Carles, Emilio. *Misioneros, negreros y esclavos. Notas de un viaje a Fernando Poo.* Valencia: Cuadernos de Cultura, 1932.

Carlyle, Thomas. "Diderot." In *The Collected Works of Thomas Carlyle*, 4: 180–243. London: Chapman and Hall, 1871.

Carpenter, Bennett Dempsey. "Lumpen: Vagrancies of a Concept from Marx to Fanon (and On)." PhD Thesis, Duke University, 2019.

Carswell, Grace, and Geert De Neve. "From Field to Factory: Tracing Transformations in Bonded Labour in the Tiruppur Region, Tamil Nadu." *Economy and Society* 42, no. 3 (2013): 430–54.

Carter, Marina. *Servants, Sirdars, and Settlers: Indians in Mauritius, 1834–1874.* Oxford: Oxford University Press, 1995.

Carter, Marina. "The Transition from Slave to Indentured Labour in Mauritius." In *The Wages of Slavery: From Chattel Slavery to Wage Labour in Africa, the Caribbean, and England*, edited by Michael Twaddle, 115–36. London: Frank Cass, 1993.

Carter, Marina. "Strategies of Labour Mobilisation in Colonial India: The Recruitment of Indentured Workers for Mauritius." *Journal of Peasant Studies* 19, no. 3–4 (1992): 229–45.

Casey, Matthew. "From Haiti to Cuba and Back: Haitians' Experiences of Migration, Labor, and Return, 1900–1940." PhD Thesis, University of Pittsburgh, 2012.

Castel, Robert. *From Manual Workers to Wage Laborers: Transformation of the Social Question.* Translated by Richard Boyd. London: Transaction Publishers, 2002.

Castro Antolín, Mariano L. de. "Fernando Poo y los emancipados de La Habana." *Estudios Africanos* 8, no. 14 – 15 (1994): 7 – 19.

Castro Antolín, Mariano L. de, and Donato Ndongo-Bidyogo. *España en Guinea: Construcción del desencuentro: 1778 – 1968.* Toledo: Sequitur, 1998.

Castro Rodríguez, Mayca de. "¿Anticolonialismo colonial? Crítica y blanquitud en la obra de Guillermo Cabanellas sobre la colonización de Guinea Ecuatorial." *Journal of Spanish Cultural Studies* 21, no. 2 (2020): 187 – 204.

Cervantes-Rodriguez, Margarita. *International Migration in Cuba: Accumulation, Imperial Designs, and Transnational Social Fields.* University Park: Pennsylvania State University Press, 2011.

Chapdelaine, Robin P. "Marriage Certificates and Walker Cards: Nigerian Migrant Labor, Wives, and Prostitutes in Colonial Fernando Pó." *African Economic History* 48, no. 2 (2020): 1 – 36.

Chapdelaine, Robin P. *The Persistence of Slavery: An Economic History of Child Trafficking in Nigeria.* Boston: University of Massachusetts Press, 2021.

China and Commission to ascertain the condition of Chinese coolies in Cuba. *The Cuba Commission Report: A Hidden History of the Chinese in Cuba: The Original English-Language Text of 1876.* Baltimore: Johns Hopkins University Press, 1993.

Christophersen, Paul. "A Note on the Words *Dash* and *Ju-Ju* in West African English." In *Perspectives on Black English*, edited by Joey Lee Dillard, 212 – 15. Berlin: Walter de Gruyter, 1975.

Clarence-Smith, William G. *Cocoa and Chocolate, 1765 – 1914.* London: Routledge, 2000.

Clarence-Smith, William. G., and Steven Topik, eds. *The Global Coffee Economy in Africa, Asia and Latin America, 1500 – 1989.* Cambridge: Cambridge University Press, 2003.

Clarence-Smith, William G. "African and European Cocoa Producers on Fernando Poo, 1880s to 1910s." *The Journal of African History* 35, no. 2 (1994): 179 – 99.

Clarence-Smith, William G. "Cocoa Plantations and Coerced Labor in the Gulf of Guinea, 1870 – 1914." In *Breaking the Chains: Slavery, Bondage and Emancipation in Africa and Asia*, edited by Martin A. Klein, 150 – 70. Madison: University of Wisconsin Press, 1993.

Clarence-Smith, William G. "Labour Conditions in the Plantations of Sao Tomé and Principe, 1875 – 1914." *Slavery & Abolition* 14, no. 1 (1993): 149 – 67.

Clarence-Smith, William G. "The Economic Dynamics of Spanish Colonialism in the Nineteenth and Twentieth Centuries." *Itinerario* 15, no. 1 (1991): 71 – 90.

Clarence-Smith, William G. "Emigration from Western Africa, 1807 – 1940." *Itinerario* 14, no. 1 (1990): 45 – 60.

Clarence-Smith, William G. "Spanish Equatorial Guinea, 1898 – 1940." In *The Cambridge History of Africa: From 1905 to 1940*, edited by Arthur D. Roberts, 537 – 44. Cambridge: Cambridge University Press, 1986.

Clarence-Smith, William G. "The Impact of the Spanish Civil War and the Second World War on Portuguese and Spanish Africa." *The Journal of African History* 26, no. 4 (1985): 309 – 26.

Cohen, Gerald A. "Capitalism, Freedom and the Proletariat." In *The Idea of Freedom: Essays in Honour of Isaiah Berlin*, edited by Alan Ryan, 9 – 25. Oxford: Oxford University Press, 1979.

Cole, Teju. *Every Day Is for the Thief: Fiction.* New York: Random House, 2014.

Comaroff, Jean, and John Comaroff. *The Truth about Crime: Sovereignty, Knowledge, Social Order.* Chicago: University of Chicago Press, 2016.

Comisión para el Desarrollo Económico de Fernando Poo y Rio Muni. *Plan de desarrollo económico de la Guinea Ecuatorial: 1964–1967.* Madrid: Presidencia del Gobierno, 1963.

Cooper, Frederick, Thomas C. Holt, Rebecca J. Scott, and Frederick Cooper. *Beyond Slavery: Explorations of Race, Labor, and Citizenship in Postemancipation Societies.* Chapel Hill: University of North Carolina Press, 2000.

Cooper, Frederick. *Decolonization and African Society: The Labor Question in French and British Africa.* Cambridge: Cambridge University Press, 1996.

Cooper, Frederick. *From Slaves to Squatters: Plantation Labor and Agriculture in Zanzibar and Coastal Kenya, 1890–1925.* New Haven: Yale University Press, 1980.

Cooper, Frederick. "African Labor History." In *Global Labour History: A State of the Art*, edited by Jan Lucassen, 45–66. Bern: Peter Lang, 2006.

Cooper, Frederick. "Conditions Analogous to Slavery: Imperialism and Free Labor Ideology in Africa." In *Beyond Slavery: Explorations of Race, Labor, and Citizenship in Postemancipation Societies*, edited by Frederick Cooper, Thomas C. Holt, and Rebecca J. Scott, 107–49. Chapel Hill: University of North Carolina Press, 2000.

Cooper, Frederick. "Work, Class and Empire: An African Historian's Retrospective on E. P. Thompson." *Social History* 20, no. 2 (1995): 235–41.

Coquery-Vidrovitch, Catherine. "The Colonial Economy of the Former French, Belgian and Portuguese Zones." In *General History of Africa, Volume VII, Africa Under Colonial Domination 1880–1935*, edited by A. Adu Boahen, 351–82. Paris: UNESCO, 1985.

Coquery-Vidrovitch, Catherine. "Research on an African Mode of Production." *Critique of Anthropology* 2, no. 4–5 (1975): 38–71.

Cordero Torres, José María. *Política colonial.* Madrid: Ed. Cultura Hispánica, 1953.

Cordero Torres, José María. *Tratado elemental de derecho colonial español.* Madrid: Editora Nacional, 1941.

Costa Oliveira, Jorge Eduardo da. *A economia de São Tomé e Príncipe.* Lisboa: Instituto para a Cooperação Portuguesa, 1960.

Crespi, Liliana. "En busca de un enclave esclavista. La expedición colonizadora a las islas de Fernando Poo y Annobon, en el Golfo de Guinea (1778–1782)." *Revista Digital Estudios Históricos* 4 (2010).

Crisp, Jeff. "The Labour Question in the Gold Coast, 1870–1906." In *Proletarianisation in the Third World: Studies in the Creation of a Labour Force Under Dependent Capitalism*, edited by Barry Munslow and Martin H.J. Finch, 18–42. London: Croom Helm, 1984.

Crush, Jonathan. *The Struggle for Swazi Labour, 1890–1920.* McGill: Queen's Press, 1987.

Crush, Jonathan. "Swazi Migrant Workers and the Witwatersrand Gold Mines 1886–1920." *Journal of Historical Geography* 12, no. 1 (1986): 27–40.

Cuba. "Reglamento para la introducción de los trabajadores chinos de la Isla de Cuba." Havana: Imp. del Gobierno y Capitanía General, 1860.

Curtin, Philip D. *Cross-Cultural Trade in World History.* Cambridge: Cambridge University Press, 1984.

Da Col, Giovanni. "Preface." In *Fake: Anthropological Keywords*, edited by Jacob Copeman and Giovanni Da Col, ix–xi. Chicago: HAU, 2020.

Daimon, Anusa. "Settling in Motion as Consciousness: Nyasa (Malawian) Informal Transit across Southern Rhodesia towards South Africa from the 1910s to the 1950s." *African Studies* 80, no. 1 (2021): 1–20.

Daly, Samuel Fury Childs. *A History of the Republic of Biafra: Law, Crime, and the Nigerian Civil War.* Cambridge: Cambridge University Press, 2020.

Daly, Samuel Fury. "De trabajadores a soldados: trabajo forzado y conscripción en la Guinea Española y la Nigeria oriental, 1930–1970." *Millars. Espai i Història* 43 (2017): 219–41.

Daly, Samuel Fury Childs. "Dropped Subjects: Igbo Labor Migration to Fernando Po, 1940–1974." *Igbo Studies Review* 1, no. 1 (2013): 1–17.

Damir-Geilsdorf, Sabine, Ulrike Lindner, Gesine Müller, Oliver Tappe, and Michael Zeuske, eds. *Bonded Labour: Global and Comparative Perspectives.* Berlin: transcript, 2016.

Davidson, Basil. "Appendix Equatorial Guinea, c.1940 to 1975." In *The Cambridge History of Africa: From c. 1940 to c. 1975*, edited by Michael Crowder, 806–11. Cambridge: Cambridge University Press, 1984.

De Haas, Michiel. "Moving Beyond Colonial Control? Economic Forces and Shifting Migration from Ruanda-Urundi to Buganda, 1920–60." *The Journal of African History* 60, no. 3 (2019): 379–406.

De Neve, Geert. "Entrapped Entrepreneurship: Labour Contractors in the South Indian Garment Industry." *Modern Asian Studies* 48, no. 5 (2014): 1302–33.

De Neve, Geert. "Asking for and Giving Baki: Neo-Bondage, or the Interplay of Bondage and Resistance in the Tamilnadu Power-Loom Industry." *Contributions to Indian Sociology* 33, no. 1–2 (1999): 379–406.

De Vito, Christian G., Juliane Schiel, and Matthias van Rossum. "From Bondage to Precariousness? New Perspectives on Labor and Social History." *Journal of Social History* 54, no. 2 (2020): 644–62.

Di Nunzio, Marco. *The Act of Living: Street Life, Marginality, and Development in Urban Ethiopia.* Ithaca: Cornell University Press, 2019.

Deleuze, Gilles. *Difference and Repetition.* London: Continuum, 2004.

Denning, Michael. "Wageless Life." *New Left Review* 66, no. Nov/Dec (2010): 79–97.

Dike, Kenneth O. *Trade and Politics in the Niger Delta: 1830–1885.* Oxford: Clarendon Press, 1956.

Dike, Kenneth O., and Felicia Ifeoma Ekejiuba. *The Aro of South-Eastern Nigeria, 1650–1980: A Study of Socio-Economic Formation and Transformation in Nigeria.* Ibadan: Ibadan University Press, 1990.

Domar, Evsey D. "The Causes of Slavery or Serfdom: A Hypothesis." *The Journal of Economic History* 30, no. 1 (1970): 18–32.

Donoghue, John. "Kidnappers and Subcontractors: Historical Perspectives on Human Trafficking." In *Human Bondage and Abolition: New Histories of Past and Present Slaveries*, edited by Elizabeth Swanson and James B. Stewart, 123–53. Cambridge: Cambridge University Press, 2018.

Dore, Elizabeth. *Myths of Modernity: Peonage and Patriarchy in Nicaragua.* Durham: Duke University Press, 2006.

Dore, Elizabeth. "Patriarchy from Above, Patriarchy from Below, Debt Peonage on Nicaraguan Coffee Estates, 1870–1930." In *The Global Coffee Economy in Africa, Asia and Latin America, 1500–1989*, edited by William G. Clarence-Smith and Steven Topik, 209–35. Cambridge: Cambridge University Press, 2003.

Dougnon, Isaie. "Migration for 'White Man's Work': An Empirical Rebuttal to Marxist Theory." *African Identities* 7, no. 3 (2009): 353–71.

Draper, Hal. *Karl Marx's Theory of Revolution Vol. II*. New York: NYU Press, 1977.

Draper, Hal. *The Concept of the "Lumpenproletariat" in Marx and Engels*. Paris: Institut de Science économique appliquée, 1972.

Du Chaillu, Paul B. *Explorations & Adventures in Equatorial Africa: With Accounts of the Manners and Customs of the People, and of the Chace of the Gorilla, Crocodile, Leopard, Elephant, Hippopotamus, and Other Animals*. London: John Murray, 1861.

Dupré, Georges, and Pierre-Philippe Rey. "Reflections on the Pertinence of a Theory of the History of Exchange." In *The Articulation of Modes of Production*, edited by Harold Wolpe, 171–208. London: Routledge, 1980.

Eckert, Andeas. "Urbanization in Colonial & Post-Colonial West Africa." In *Themes in West Africa's History*, edited by Emmanuel Akyeampong, 208–25. Oxford: James Currey, 2006.

Eckert, Andreas. "African Rural Entrepreneurs and Labor in the Cameroon Littoral." *The Journal of African History* 40, no. 1 (1999): 109–26.

Einzig, Paul. *Primitive Money: In Its Ethnological, Historical and Economic Aspects*. Oxford: Pergamon Press, 1966.

Ejituwu, Nkparom C. "Old Calabar Rediscovered." In *The Multi-Disciplinary Approach to African History: Essays in Honour of Ebiegberi Joe Alagoa*, edited by Ebiegberi Joe Alagoa and Nkparom C Ejituwu, 133–51. Port Harcourt: University of Port Harcourt Press, 1998.

Ejituwu, Nkparom C. "Anglo-Spanish Employment Agency: Its Role in the Mobilization of Nigerian Labour for the Island of Fernando Po." In *The Nigeria-Equatorial Guinea Transborder Cooperation: Proceeding of the Nigeria-Equatorial Guinea Transborder Cooperation Workshop, Held at Metropolitan Hotel, Calabar, 21–28 November, 1992*, edited by Bawuro M. Barkindo, A. I. Asiwaju, and Ricardo Elo Mabale, 42–57. Lagos: Terminal Products, 1995.

Ekechi, Felix K. "Pawnship in Igbo Society." In *Pawnship, Slavery, and Colonialism in Africa*, edited by Paul E. Lovejoy and Toyin Falola, 165–87. Trenton: Africa World Press, 2003.

Ekechi, Felix K. *Pioneer, Patriot, and Nigerian Nationalist: A Biography of the Reverend M.D. Opara, 1915–1965*. Durham: Carolina Academic Press, 2010.

Ekechi, Felix K. *Tradition and Transformation in Eastern Nigeria: A Sociopolitical History of Owerri and Its Hinterland, 1902–1947*. Kent: Kent State University Press, 1989.

Ekejiuba, Felicia. "Currency Instability and Social Payments Among the Igbo of Eastern Nigeria, 1890–1990." In *Money Matters: Instability, Values, and Social Payments in the Modern History of West African Communities*, edited by Jane Guyer, 133–61. Portsmouth: Heinemann, 1995.

Ellis, Stephen. *This Present Darkness: A History of Nigerian Organized Crime*. Oxford: Oxford University Press, 2016.

Eltis, David, and Lawrence C. Jennings. "Trade between Western Africa and the Atlantic World in the Pre-Colonial Era." *The American Historical Review* 93, no. 4 (1988): 936–59.

Emenanjo, E. Nolue. "Slangs and Colloquialisms in Modern Igbo: A Preliminary Socio-Linguistic Study." *Ikenga: Journal of African Studies* 4, no. 2 (1980): 49–65.

Enahoro, Peter. *How to Be a Nigerian*. Ibadan: Daily Times of Nigeria, 1971.

Endemann, Wilhelm. *Handbuch des deutschen Handels-, See- und Wechselrechts*. Vol. 3. Berlin: Fues's Verlag, 1885.

Engels, Friedrich. *The Condition of the Working-Class in England in 1844*. London: Allen and Unwin, 1969.

Engels, Friedrich. *Anti-Dühring: Herr Eugen Dühring's Revolution in Science*. Moscow: Foreign Languages Publishing House, 1962.

Engels, Friedrich. "Supplement to Capital, Volume Three." In *Marx & Engels: Collected Works*, 37:873–900. London: Lawrence & Wishart, 1998.

Engels, Friedrich. "Preface to the 2nd Edition of 'The Peasant War in Germany.'" In *Marx & Engels: Collected Works*, 21: 93–101. London: Lawrence & Wishart, 1985.

Engels, Friedrich. "The Model Republic." In *Marx & Engels: Collected Works*, 9: 42–46. London: Lawrence & Wishart, 1979.

Engels, Friedrich. "The Peasant War in Germany." In *Marx & Engels: Collected Works*, 10: 397–482. London: Lawrence & Wishart, 1978.

Engels, Friedrich. "The Constitutional Question in Germany." In *Marx & Engels: Collected Works*, 6: 75–91. London: Lawrence & Wishart, 1976.

Engels, Friedrich. "Outlines of a Critique of Political Economy." In *Marx & Engels: Collected Works*, 3: 418–43. London: Lawrence & Wishart, 1975.

Engels, Friedrich. "The Condition of England. Past and Present by Thomas Carlyle." In *Marx & Engels: Collected Works*, 3: 444–69. London: Lawrence & Wishart, 1975.

Falola, Toyin. "The End of Slavery among the Yoruba." In *Slavery and Colonial Rule in Africa*, edited by Suzanne Miers and Martin A. Klein, 232–50. London: Frank Cass, 1999.

Fanon, Frantz. *The Wretched of the Earth*. New York: Grove Press, 1963.

Feierman, Steven. "African Histories and the Dissolution of World History." In *Africa and the Disciplines: The Contributions of Research in Africa to the Social Sciences and Humanities*, edited by Robert Bates and Valentin Y. Mudimbe, 167–212. Chicago: University of Chicago Press, 1993.

Fieldhouse, David K. *Merchant Capital and Economic Decolonization: The United Africa Company 1929–1987*. Oxford: Oxford University Press, 1994.

Finley, Moses. *The Ancient Economy*. Berkeley: University of California Press, 1973.

Finley, Moses. "Debt-Bondage and the Problem of Slavery." In *Economy and Society in Ancient Greece*, edited by Brent D. Shaw and Richard P. Saller, 150–66. New York: Viking Press, 1982.

Fischer, Michael H. "Working Across the Seas: Indian Maritime Labourers in India, Britain, and in Between, 1600–1852." In *Coolies, Capital, and Colonialism: Studies in Indian Labour History*, edited by Rana Behal and Marcel van der Linden, 21–46. Cambridge: Cambridge University Press, 2006.

Forde, Cyril D., and G.I. Jones. *The Ibo and Ibibio-Speaking Peoples of South-Eastern Nigeria*. London: Stone and Cox., 1967.

Fourchard, Laurent. *Trier, exclure et policer. Vies urbaines en Afrique du Sud et au Nigeria*. Paris: Les Presses de Sciences Po, 2018.

Fourchard, Laurent. "Crime and Illegal Work." In *General Labour History of Africa. Workers, Employers and Governments, 20th–21st Centuries*, edited by Stephano Bellucci and Andreas Eckert, 361–78. Rochester: Boydell & Brewer, 2019.

Fourchard, Laurent. "Urban Poverty, Urban Crime, and Crime Control: The Lagos and Ibadan Case, 1929–1945." In *African Urban Spaces in Historical Perspective*, edited by Toyin Falola, 291–320. Rochester: University Rochester Press, 2009.

Fourchard, Laurent. "Lagos and the Invention of Juvenile Delinquency in Nigeria, 1920–60." *The Journal of African History* 47, no. 1 (2006): 115–37.

Fradera, Josep M., and Christopher Schmidt-Nowara, eds. *Slavery and Antislavery in Spain's Atlantic Empire.* New York: Berghahn Books, 2013.

Fradera, Josep Maria. *Gobernar colonias.* Barcelona: Ediciones Península, 1999.

Frankema, Ewout, and Michiel de Haas. *Migration in Africa: Shifting Patterns of Mobility from the 19th to the 21st Century.* London: Routledge, 2022.

Freund, Bill. "Labor and Labor History in Africa: A Review of the Literature." *African Studies Review* 27, no. 2 (1984): 1–58.

Freund, Bill. "Labour Migration to the Northern Nigerian Tin Mines, 1903–1945." *The Journal of African History* 22, no. 1 (1981): 73–84.

Frost, Diane. *Work and Community among West African Migrant Workers since the Nineteenth Century.* Liverpool: Liverpool University Press, 1999.

Frykman, Niklas. "Impressment, Kidnapping, and Panyarring." In *The Princeton Companion to Atlantic History,* edited by Joseph C. Miller, 240–42. Princeton: Princeton University Press, 2015.

Frykman, Niklas. "Indentured Contracts." In *The Princeton Companion to Atlantic History,* edited by Joseph C. Miller, 242–44. Princeton: Princeton University Press, 2015.

Gabaccia, Donna R. "Aferword: Migration and Globalization: Bridging Three Eras in Modern World History." In *Connecting Seas and Connected Ocean Rims: Indian, Atlantic, and Pacific Oceans and China Seas Migrations from the 1830s to the 1930s,* edited by Dirk Hoerder and Donna R. Gabaccia, 8: 492–506. Leiden: Brill, 2011.

García Cantús, Dolores. "Fernando Poo: una aventura colonial española en el África occidental (1778–1900)." PhD Thesis, Universitat de València, 2004.

García Cantús, Dolores. "El tráfico de esclavos y la esclavitud a la base del surgimiento y desarrollo del sistema capitalista." *Anaquel de Estudios Árabes* 19 (2008): 53–65.

García Gimeno, Fernando. *Fernando el africano.* Barcelona: Arco Press, 2004.

Geertz, Clifford. *Peddlers and Princes: Social Change and Economic Modernization in Two Indonesian Towns.* Chicago: University of Chicago Press, 1963.

Ghosh, Kaushik. "A Market for Aboriginality: Primitivism and Race Classification in the Indentured Labour Market of Colonial India." In *Subaltern Studies X: Writings on South Asian History and Society,* edited by Gautam Bhadra, Gyan Prakash, and Susie Tharu, 10: 8–48. New Delhi: Oxford University Press, 1999.

Gibson, Charles. *The Aztecs under Spanish Rule: A History of the Indians of the Valley of Mexico, 1519–1810.* Stanford: Stanford University Press, 1964.

Ginés-Blasi, Mònica. "A Philippine 'Coolie Trade': Trade and Exploitation of Chinese Labour in Spanish Colonial Philippines, 1850–98." *Journal of Southeast Asian Studies* 51, no. 3 (2020): 457–83.

Ginés-Blasi, Mònica. "Exploiting Chinese Labour Emigration in Treaty Ports: The Role of Spanish Consulates in the 'Coolie Trade.'" *International Review of Social History* 66, no. 1 (2021): 1–24.

Godbout, Jacques, and Alain Caillé. *The World of the Gift.* Montreal: McGill-Queen's Press, 2000.

Goerg, Odile. "De la ségrégation colonial à la tentation sécessionniste: l'urbanisme sécuritaire." In *Security, Crime and Segregation in West African Cities since the 19th*

Century, edited by Laurent Fourchard and Isaac Olawale Albert, 245 – 63. Paris: Karthala, 2003.

Graeber, David. "Debt, Violence, and Impersonal Markets: Polanyian Meditations." In *Market and Society: The Great Transformation Today*, edited by Keith Hart and Chris Hann, 106 – 33. Cambridge: Cambridge University Press, 2009.

Granovetter, Mark. *Getting a Job: A Study of Contacts and Careers.* Chicago: University of Chicago press, 1974.

Granovetter, Mark S. "The Strength of Weak Ties." *American Journal of Sociology* 78, no. 6 (1973): 1360 – 80.

Graves, Adrian. "Truck and Gifts: Melanesian Immigrants and the Trade Box System in Colonial Queensland." *Past & Present* 101, no. 1 (1983): 87 – 124.

Great Britain. "Spanish Guinea." Historical Section of the Foreign Office. London: H.M. Stationery Office, 1920.

Green, Erik. "The Economics of Slavery in the Eighteenth-Century Cape Colony: Revising the Nieboer-Domar Hypothesis." *International Review of Social History* 59, no. 1 (2014): 39 – 70.

Green, Toby. *A Fistful of Shells: West Africa from the Rise of the Slave Trade to the Age of Revolution.* London: Penguin Books, 2020.

Gregory, Chris. *Gifts and Commodities.* London: Academic Press, 1982.

Gudeman, Stephen, and Alberto Rivera. *Conversations in Colombia: The Domestic Economy in Life and Text.* Cambridge: Cambridge University Press, 1990.

Gutkind, Peter C. W. "Trade and Labor in Early Precolonial African History: The Canoemen of Southern Ghana." In *The Workers of African Trade*, edited by Catherine Coquery-Vidrovitch and Paul E. Lovejoy, 25 – 50. London: Sage, 1985.

Guyer, Jane. *Marginal Gains: Monetary Transactions in Atlantic Africa.* Chicago: University of Chicago Press, 2004.

Guyer, Jane. "Labor." In *Critical Terms for the Study of Africa*, edited by Gaurav Desai and Adeline Masquelier, 190 – 201. Chicago: University of Chicago Press, 2018.

Guyer, Jane. "Gains and Losses in the Margins of Time: From West and Equatorial History to Present-Day South Africa, and Back." *Africa* 84, no. 1 (2014): 146 – 50.

Guyer, Jane. "Comparisons and Equivalencies in Africa and Melanesia." In *Money and Modernity: State and Local Currencies in Melanesia*, edited by David Akin and Joel Robbins, 232 – 46. Pittsburgh: University of Pittsburgh Press, 1999.

Han, Clara. "Precarity, Precariousness, and Vulnerability." *Annual Review of Anthropology* 47 (2018): 331 – 43.

Harries, Patrick. *Work, Culture, and Identity: Migrant Laborers in Mozambique and South Africa, c.1860 – 1910.* Portsmouth: Heinemann, 1993.

Hay, Douglas, and Paul Craven, eds. *Masters, Servants, and Magistrates in Britain and the Empire, 1562 – 1955.* Chapel Hill: University of North Carolina Press, 2004.

Heinrich, Michael. *Karl Marx and the Birth of Modern Society: The Life of Marx and the Development of His Work.* New York: NYU Press, 2019.

Henriet, Benoît. *Colonial Impotence: Virtue and Violence in a Congolese Concession (1911 – 1940).* Berlin: De Gruyter, 2021.

Herzog, Don. *Happy Slaves: A Critique of Consent Theory.* Chicago: University of Chicago Press, 1989.

Higginson, John. "The Making of an African Working Class: The Union Minière du Haut Katanga and the African Mine Workers, 1907 – 1945." PhD Thesis, University of Michigan, 1979.

Hobsbawm, Eric. *Bandits*. New York: Pantheon Books, 1981.

Hofmeester, Karin, and Pim Zwart, eds., *Colonialism, Institutional Change, and Shifts in Global Labour Relations*. Amsterdam: Amsterdam University Press, 2018.

Hollup, Oddvar. "Kinship and Marriage in the Construction of Identity and Group Boundaries among Indians in Mauritius." In *Culture, Creation, and Procreation: Concepts of Kinship in South Asian Practice*, edited by Monika Böck and Aparna Rao, 219 – 43. New York: Berghahn Books, 2000.

Hopkins, Anthony G. *An Economic History of West Africa*. London: Longman, 1973.

Hopkins, Anthony. "The Lagos Strike of 1897: An Exploration in Nigerian Labour History." *Past & Present* 35, no. 1 (1966): 133 – 55.

Hopkins, Anthony G. "The New Economic History of Africa." *The Journal of African History* 50, no. 2 (2009): 155 – 77.

Horne, Gerald. *The White Pacific: U.S. Imperialism and Black Slavery in the South Seas after the Civil War*. Honolulu: University of Hawaii Press, 2007.

Howard, Philip A. *Black Labor, White Sugar: Caribbean Braceros and their Struggle for Power in the Cuban Sugar Industry*. Baton Rouge: Louisiana State University Press, 2015.

Huard, Raymond. "Marx et Engels devant la marginalité: la découverte du lumpenproletariat." *Romantisme* 18, no. 59 (1988): 5 – 17.

Hu-DeHart, Evelyn. "La Trata Amarilla: The 'Yellow Trade' and the Middle Passage, 1847 – 1884." In *Many Middle Passages: Forced Migration and the Making of the Modern World*, edited by Emma Christopher, Marcus Rediker, and Cassandra Pybus, 166 – 83. Berkeley: University of California Press, 2007.

Huntley, Henry Vere. *Seven Years' Service on the Slave Coast of Western Africa*. London: T.C. Newby, 1850.

Hynd, Stacey. "'... a Weapon of Immense Value'? Convict Labour in British Colonial Africa, c. 1850 – 1950s." In *Global Convict Labour*, edited by Christian De Vito and Alexander Lichtenstein, 222 – 48. Leiden: Brill, 2015.

Igwe, Austine U., and Nwachukwu Obiakor. "The Effects of 'Permanent Migration' on the Economy of Owerri Province, Eastern Nigeria, 1950 – 1967." *Asian Journal of Social Sciences & Humanities* 4, no. 1 (2015): 177 – 85.

Iliffe, John. *Honour in African History*. Cambridge: Cambridge University Press, 2005.

Imbua, David L. *Intercourse and Crosscurrents in the Atlantic World: Calabar-British Experience, 17th–20th Centuries*. Durham: Carolina Academic Press, 2011.

India. "Proceedings of the Assam Labour Enquiry Committee in the Recruiting and Labour Districts, Vol. I (Evidence)." Calcutta: Government Priner, 1906.

International Commission of Inquiry into the Existence of Slavery and Forced Labor in the Republic of Liberia, and Cuthbert Christy. *Report of the International Commission of Inquiry into the Existence of Slavery and Forced Labor in the Republic of Liberia. Monrovia, Liberia, September 8, 1930*. [United States] Dept. of State. 147. Washington: U.S. Govt. print., 1931.

Irick, Robert L. *Ch'ing Policy toward the Coolie Trade, 1847 – 1878*. Taipei: Chinese Materials Center, 1982.

Jaiswal, Ritesh Kumar. "Ephemeral Mobility: Critical Appraisal of the Facets of Indian Migration and the *Maistry* Mediation in Burma (c. 1880–1940)." *Almanack* May-Aug (2018): 79–118.

Jaiswal, Ritesh Kumar. "Mediated (Im)Mobility: Indian Labour Migration to Ceylon under the Kangany System (c. 1850–1940)." In *The Palgrave Handbook of Bondage and Human Rights in Africa and Asia*, edited by Gwyn Campbell and Alessandro Stanziani, 227–54. New York: Palgrave Macmillan, 2020.

James, Deborah. "The Return of the Broker: Consensus, Hierarchy, and Choice in South African Land Reform." *Journal of the Royal Anthropological Institute* 17, no. 2 (2011): 318–38.

James, Deborah, and Dinah Rajak. "Credit Apartheid, Migrants, Mines and Money." *African Studies* 73, no. 3 (2014): 455–76.

Jeeves, Alan. *Migrant Labour in South Africa's Mining Economy: The Struggle for the Gold Mines' Labour Supply, 1890–1920*. Kingston: Queen's University Press, 1985.

Jeeves, Alan. "Migrant Labour in the Industrial Transformation of South Africa, 1920–1960." In *Studies in the Economic History of Southern Africa: Volume Two: South Africa, Lesotho and Swaziland*, edited by Z.A. Konczacki, Jane L. Parpart, and Timothy M. Shaw, 105–44. London: Routledge, 1990.

Jeeves, Alan. "Over-Reach: The South African Gold Mines and the Struggle for the Labour of Zambesia, 1890–1920." *Canadian Journal of African Studies* 17, no. 3 (1983): 393–412.

Jeeves, Alan, and Jonathan Crush, eds. *White Farms, Black Labor: The State and Agrarian Change in Southern Africa, 1910–50*. Portsmouth: Heinemann, 1997.

Jeffreys, M.D.W. "Review of Water Transport. Origins and Early Evolution." *African Studies* 8, no. 2 (1949): 104–6.

Johnson, Walter. "On Agency." *Journal of Social History* 37, no. 1 (2003): 113–24.

Jones, G.I. "Native and Trade Currencies in Southern Nigeria during the Eighteenth and Nineteenth Centuries." *Africa* 28, no. 1 (1958): 43–54.

Jones, G.I. *The Trading States of the Oil Rivers: A Study of Political Development in Eastern Nigeria*. London: James Currey, 1963.

Juif, Dácil, and Ewout Frankema. "From Coercion to Compensation: Institutional Responses to Labour Scarcity in the Central African Copperbelt." *Journal of Institutional Economics* 14, no. 2 (2018): 313–43.

Kagan Guthrie, Zachary. *Bound for Work: Labor, Mobility, and Colonial Rule in Central Mozambique, 1940–1965*. Charlottesville: University of Virginia Press, 2018.

Kahn, Victoria. *Wayward Contracts: The Crisis of Political Obligation in England, 1640–1674*. Princeton: Princeton University Press, 2009.

Kale, Madhavi. *Fragments of Empire: Capital, Slavery, and Indian Indentured Labor in the British Caribbean*. Pittsburgh: University of Pennsylvania Press, 2010.

Kalifa, Dominique. *Vice, Crime, and Poverty: How the Western Imagination Invented the Underworld*. New York: Columbia University Press, 2019.

Kautsky, Karl. *The Class Struggle (Erfurt Program)*. New York: Charles H. Kerr & Co., 1910.

Kessler, Friedrich. "Contracts of Adhesion–Some Thoughts About Freedom of Contract." *Columbia Law Review* 43 (1943): 629–42.

Klein, Martin A. *Historical Dictionary of Slavery and Abolition*. London: Rowman & Littlefield, 2014.

Kloosterboer, Willemina. *Involuntary Labour since the Abolition of Slavery: A Survey of Compulsory Labour throughout the World.* Leiden: Brill, 1960.

Knapp, Georg Friedrich. *Die Bauernbefreiung und der Ursprung der Landarbeiter in den älteren Theilen Preussens.* Leipzig: Duncker & Humblot, 1887.

Knight, Alan. "Debt Bondage in Latin America." In *Slavery and Other Forms of Unfree Labour*, edited by Leonie Archer, 102–17. London: Routledge, 1988.

Knight, Alan. "Mexican Peonage: What Was It and Why Was It?" *Journal of Latin American Studies* 18, no. 1 (1986): 41–74.

Knight, Franklin W. *Slave Society in Cuba during the Nineteenth Century.* Madison: University of Wisconsin Press, 1970.

Kobel, Armin. "La République de Guinée Equatoriale: ses ressources potentielles et virtuelles et les possibilités de son développement." PhD Thesis, Université de Neuchâtel, 1976.

Konings, Piet. *Labour Resistance in Cameroon: Managerial Strategies & Labour Resistance in the Agro-Industrial Plantations of the Cameroon Development Corporation.* London: James Currey, 1993.

Korieh, Chima. *Nigeria and World War II: Colonialism, Empire, and Global Conflict.* Cambridge: Cambridge University Press, 2020.

Korieh, Chima. *The Land Has Changed: History, Society and Gender in Colonial Eastern Nigeria.* Calgary: University of Calgary Press, 2010.

Krissman, Fred. "Sin Coyote Ni Patrón: Why the 'Migrant Network' Fails to Explain International Migration." *International Migration Review* 39, no. 1 (2005): 4–44.

Kubicek, Robert. "Mining: Patterns of Dependence and Development." In *Studies in the Economic History of Southern Africa: Volume Two: South Africa, Lesotho and Swaziland*, edited by Z.A. Konczacki, Jane L. Parpart, and Timothy M. Shaw, 64–87. London: Routledge, 1990.

Lamas, Bruno. *When Looms Begin to Weave by Themselves: The Decomposition of Capitalism, Automation and the Problem of "Modern Slavery."* Joseph C. Miller Memorial Lecture Series. Berlin: EB Verlag, 2021.

Lamounier, Lucia. "Between Slavery and Free Labour: Early Experiments with Free Labour and Patterns of Slave Emancipation in Brazil and Cuba." In *From Chattel Slaves to Wage Slaves: The Dynamics of Labour Bargaining in the Americas*, edited by Mary Turner, 185–201. Bloomington: Indiana University Press, 1995.

Lapavitsas, Costas. "Commodities and Gifts: Why Commodities Represent More than Market Relations." *Science & Society* 68, no. 1 (2004): 33–56.

Latour, Bruno. *An Inquiry into Modes of Existence: An Anthropology of the Moderns.* Harvard: Harvard University Press, 2013.

Latour, Bruno. *Reassembling the Social: An Introduction to Actor-Network-Theory.* Oxford: Oxford University Press, 2005.

Law, Robin. "Finance and Credit in Pre-Colonial Dahomey." In *Credit, Currencies, and Culture: African Financial Institutions in Historical Perspective*, edited by Endre Stiansen and Jane Guyer, 15–38. Uppsala: Nordic Africa Institute, 1999.

Law, Robin. "On Pawning and Enslavement for Debt in the Pre-Colonial Slave Coast." In *Pawnship in Africa: Debt Bondage in Historical Perspective*, edited by Toyin Falola and Paul E. Lovejoy, 55–69. Boulder: Westview Press, 1994.

Law, Robin. "Human Sacrifice in Pre-Colonial West Africa." *African Affairs* 84, no. 334 (1985): 53–87.

Lawrance, Benjamin Nicholas, Emily Lynn Osborn, and Richard L. Roberts, eds. *Intermediaries, Interpreters, and Clerks: African Employees in the Making of Colonial Africa.* Madison: University of Wisconsin Press, 2006.

Likuwa, Kletus. *Voices from the Kavango: A Study of the Contract Labour System in Namibia, 1925–1972.* Basel: Basler Afrika Bibliographien, 2020.

Likuwa, Kletus, and Napandulwe Shiweda. "Native Recruiters Activities along the Kavango River Boundary in North-East Namibia, 1925–1943." *Journal of Namibian Studies* 23 (2018): 87–100.

Lindner, Ulrike. "Indentured Labour in Sub-Saharan Africa (1880–1918): Circulation of Concepts between Imperial Powers." In *Bonded Labour: Global and Comparative Perspectives*, edited by Sabine Damir-Geilsdorf, Ulrike Lindner, Gesine Müller, Oliver Tappe, and Michael Zeuske, 49–72. Bielefeld: transcript, 2016.

Lindquist, Johan. "Brokers and Brokerage, Anthropology of." In *International Encyclopedia of Social and Behavioral Science*, 2nd ed., 870–74. Amsterdam: Elsevier, 2015.

Lindquist, Johan. "Beyond Anti-Anti-Trafficking." *Dialectical Anthropology* 37, no. 2 (2013): 319–23.

Lindquist, Johan, Biao Xiang, and Brenda S.A. Yeoh. "Opening the Black Box of Migration: Brokers, the Organization of Transnational Mobility and the Changing Political Economy in Asia." *Pacific Affairs* 85, no. 1 (2012): 7–19.

Linebaugh, Peter, and Marcus Rediker. *The Many-Headed Hydra: Sailors, Slaves, Commoners, and the Hidden History of the Revolutionary Atlantic.* New York: Verso, 2000.

Liniger-Goumaz, Max. *La Guinée équatoriale: un pays méconnu.* Paris: L'Harmattan, 1979.

Liniger-Goumaz, Max. "La cuestion bracera: 150 años de busqueda de mano de obra en Guinea Equatorial." *Estudios de Asia y Africa* 22, no. 74 (1987): 497–534.

Llompart Aulet, Sebastian. *Legislación del trabajo de los territorios españoles del Golfo de Guinea.* Madrid: Dirección General de Marruecos y Colonias, 1946.

Llompart Aulet, Sebastian. "Nigerianos en las provincias ecuatoriales." *Estadística española: revista del Instituto Nacional de Estadística* 10 (1961): 63–70.

Llompart Aulet, Sebastian, and Negociado de Estadistica del Gobierno General de los Territorios Españoles del Golfo de Guinea. "Anuario estadistico de los territorios españoles del Golfo de Guinea [1942–1945]." Madrid: Dirección General de Marruecos y Colonias, 1945.

Lonsdale, John, and Bruce Berman. "Coping with the Contradictions: The Development of the Colonial State in Kenya, 1895–1914." *The Journal of African History* 20, no. 4 (1979): 487–505.

Lovejoy, Paul E. *Transformations in Slavery: A History of Slavery in Africa.* Cambridge: Cambridge University Press, 2011.

Lovejoy, Paul E. "Pawnship, Debt, and 'Freedom' in Atlantic Africa During the Era of the Slave Trade: A Reassessment." *The Journal of African History* 55, no. 1 (2014): 55–78.

Lovejoy, Paul E., and David Richardson. "Trust, Pawnship, and Atlantic History: The Institutional Foundations of the Old Calabar Slave Trade." *American Historical Review* 104, no. 2 (1999): 333–55.

Lovejoy, Paul E., and David Richardson. "The Initial 'Crisis of Adaptation': The Impact of British Abolition on the Atlantic Slave Trade in West Africa, 1808–1820." In *From Slave Trade to "Legitimate" Commerce*, edited by Robin Law, 32–56. Cambridge: Cambridge University Press, 1995.

Lovejoy, Paul E, and Nicholas Rogers, eds. *Unfree Labour in the Development of the Atlantic World.* London: Frank Cass, 1994.

Lucassen, Jan, ed. *Global Labour History: A State of the Art.* Bern: Peter Lang, 2008.

Lucassen, Jan, and Leo Lucassen. *Migration, Migration History, History: Old Paradigms and New Perspectives.* Bern: Peter Lang, 1997.

Luxemburg, Rosa. *The Russian Revolution and Leninism or Marxism?* Ann Arbor: University of Michigan Press, 1961.

Luxemburg, Rosa, and Nikolai Bukharin. *Imperialism and the Accumulation of Capital.* London: Penguin Books, 1972.

Lynch, Hollis R. *K. O. Mbadiwe: A Nigerian Political Biography, 1915–1990.* New York: Palgrave Macmillan, 2012.

Lynn, Martin. "Commerce, Christianity and the Origins of the 'Creoles' of Fernando Po." *The Journal of African History* 25, no. 3 (1984): 257–78.

MacDonald, Andrew. "Colonial Trespassers in the Making of South Africa's International Borders 1900 to c. 1950." PhD Thesis, St John's College, Cambridge University, 2012.

MacDonald, Andrew. "Forging the Frontiers: Travellers and Documents on the South Africa-Mozambique Border, 1890s–1940s." *Kronos* 40, no. 1 (2014): 154–77.

MacDonald, Andrew. "The Identity Thieves of the Indian Ocean: Forgery, Fraud and the Origins of South African Immigration Control, 1890s–1920s." In *Registration and Recognition: Documenting the Person in World History,* edited by Keith Breckenridge and Simon Szreter, 253–76. Oxford: Oxford University Press, 2012.

MacGaffey, Janet, ed. *The Real Economy of Zaire: The Contribution of Smuggling & Other Unofficial Activities to National Wealth.* Philadelphia: University of Pennsylvania Press, 1991.

Macías Martín, Francisco J. *Cuba: Crisis política, crisis económica y emigración (1920–1935).* Tegueste: Ediciones de Baile del Sol, 2002.

Madrid, Francisco. *La Guinea incógnita: vergüenza y escándalo colonial.* Madrid: Editorial España, 1933.

Manchuelle, François. *Willing Migrants: Soninke Labor Diasporas, 1848–1960.* Athens: Ohio University Press, 1997.

Mann, Kristin. *Slavery and the Birth of an African City: Lagos, 1760–1900.* Bloomington: Indiana University Press, 2007.

Manning, Patrick. "Merchants, Porters and Canoemen in the Bight of Benin: Links in the West African Trade Network." In *The Workers of African Trade,* edited by Cathering Coquery-Vidrovitch and Paul E. Lovejoy, 51–74. Beverly Hills: Sage, 1985.

Manning, Patrick. "Slave Trade, 'Legitimate' Trade, and Imperialism Revisited: The Control of Wealth in the Bights of Benin and Biafra." In *Africans in Bondage Studies in Slavery and the Slave Trade,* edited by Philip D. Curtin and Paul E. Lovejoy, 203–33. Madison: University of Wisconsin Press, 1986.

Manning, Patrick. *Slavery and African Life: Occidental, Oriental, and African Slave Trades.* Cambridge: Cambridge University Press, 1990.

Marees, Pieter de. *Beschrijvinghe ende historische verhael vant gout koninckrijck van Guinea: anders de goutcuste de Mina genaemt leggende in het deel van Africa.* Amsterdam: Colijn, 1617.

Marees, Pieter de. *Description and Historical Account of the Gold Kingdom of Guinea (1602).* Edited by Albert van Dantzig and Adam Jones. Oxford: Oxford University Press, 1987.

Mark-Thiesen, Cassandra. *Mediators, Contract Men, and Colonial Capital: Mechanized Gold Mining in the Gold Coast Colony, 1879–1909*. Melton: Boydell & Brewer, 2018.

Mark-Thiesen, Cassandra. "The Dual Meaning of Debt: Political Considerations for the Mobilization of Mining Labour in Southwest Ghana, 1877–1911." In *The Vernacularization of Labour Politics*, edited by Rana Behal and Sabyasachi Bhattacharya, 252–66. New Delhi: Tulika Books, 2016.

Mark-Thiesen, Cassandra. "The 'Bargain' of Collaboration: African Intermediaries, Indirect Recruitment, and Indigenous Institutions in the Ghanaian Gold Mining Industry, 1900–1906." *International Review of Social History* 57, no. S20 (2012): 17–38.

Martin, Jane. "Krumen 'Down the Coast': Liberian Migrants on the West African Coast in the 19th and early 20th Centuries." *The International Journal of African Historical Studies* 18, no. 3 (1985): 401–23.

Martin, Susan M. *Palm Oil and Protest: An Economic History of the Ngwa Region, South-Eastern Nigeria, 1800–1980*. Cambridge: Cambridge University Press, 1988.

Martínez, Samuel. "From Hidden Hand to Heavy Hand: Sugar, the State, and Migrant Labor in Haiti and the Dominican Republic." *Latin American Research Review* 34, no. 1 (1999): 57–84.

Martino, Enrique. *How to Create a Labour Market in Colonial Situations: Spanish Guinea, Southern Cameroon, and Northern Gabon, 1890s–1940s*. Joseph C. Miller Memorial Lecture Series. Berlin: EB Verlag, 2021.

Martino, Enrique. "Touts and Despots: Recruiting Assemblages of Contract Labour in Fernando Pó and the Gulf of Guinea, 1858–1979." PhD Thesis, Humboldt-Universität zu Berlin, 2016.

Martino, Enrique. "Money, Indenture, and Neo-Slavery in the Spanish Gulf of Guinea, 1820s to 1890s." *Comparativ* 30, no. 5–6 (2020): 560–80.

Martino, Enrique. "Irrationality and Speculation in Finance." *HAU: Journal of Ethnographic Theory* 8, no. 3 (2018): 467–473.

Martino, Enrique. "Corrupción y contrabando: funcionarios españoles y traficantes nigerianos en la economía de Fernando Poo (1936–1968)." *Ayer* 109 (2018): 169–95.

Martino, Enrique. "*Dash*-Peonage: The Contradictions of Debt Bondage in the Colonial Plantations of Fernando Pó." *Africa* 87, no. 1 (2017): 53–78.

Martino, Enrique. "*Panya:* Economies of Deception and the Discontinuities of Indentured Labour Recruitment and the Slave Trade, Nigeria and Fernando Pó, 1890s–1940s." *African Economic History* 44, no. 1 (2016): 91–129.

Martino, Enrique. "Open Sourcing the Colonial Archive – A Digital Montage of the History of Fernando Pó and the Bight of Biafra." *History in Africa* 41 (2014): 387–415.

Martino, Enrique. "Clandestine Recruitment Networks in the Bight of Biafra: Fernando Pó's Answer to the Labour Question, 1926–1945." *International Review of Social History* 57, no. S20 (2012): 39–72.

Marx, Karl. *Capital*. London: Lawrence and Wishart, 1974.

Marx, Karl. "Capital, Volume Three." In *Marx & Engels: Collected Works*, Vol. 37. London: Lawrence & Wishart, 1998.

Marx, Karl. "Outlines of the Critique of Political Economy (Rough Draft of 1857–58) [First Instalment] (1857–58)." In *Marx & Engels: Collected Works*, 28: 49–540. London: Lawrence & Wishart, 1986.

Marx, Karl. "The Class Struggles in France, 1848 to 1850." In *Marx & Engels: Collected Works*, 10:45–239. London: Lawrence & Wishart, 1978.

Marx, Karl. "Das Kapital. Bd II." In *Marx-Engels-Gesamtausgabe*, 24: 7–507. Berlin/DDR: Dietz Verlag, 1963.

Marx, Karl. *The Eighteenth Brumaire of Louis Bonaparte*. Translated by Padover Saul K. Moscow: Progress Publishers, 1937.

Marx, Karl, and Friedrich Engels. "The German Ideology." In *Marx & Engels: Collected Works*, 5: 19–539. London: Lawrence & Wishart, 1976.

Marx, Karl, and Erich Fromm. *Marx's Concept of Man: Including "Economic and Philosophical Manuscripts."* London: Bloomsbury Publishing, 1961.

Mathew, Johan. *Margins of the Market: Trafficking and Capitalism across the Arabian Sea*. Oakland: University of California Press, 2016.

Mauss, Marcel. *The Gift: Forms and Function of Exchange in Archaic Society*. London: Routledge, 2002.

Mauss, Marcel. "Gift, gift." In *Gift: Marcel Mauss' Kulturtheorie der Gabe*, edited by Stephan Moebius, and Christian Papilloud, 13–17. Wiesbaden: VS Verlag für Sozialwissenschaften, 2006.

McClintock, Anne. *Imperial Leather: Race, Gender, and Sexuality in the Colonial Contest*. New York: Routledge, 1995.

McCreery, David. "Debt Servitude in Rural Guatemala, 1876–1936." *The Hispanic American Historical Review* 63, no. 4 (1983): 735–59.

McKeown, Adam. *Melancholy Order: Asian Migration and the Globalization of Borders*. New York: Columbia University Press, 2013.

McKeown, Adam. *Chinese Migrant Networks and Cultural Change: Peru, Chicago, and Hawaii 1900–1936*. Chicago: University of Chicago Press, 2001.

McKeown, Adam. "Global Migration, 1846–1940." *Journal of World History* 15, no. 2 (2004): 155–89.

McKeown, Adam. "How the Box Became Black: Brokers and the Creation of the Free Migrant." *Pacific Affairs* 85, no. 1 (2012): 21–45.

McKeown, Adam. "Conceptualizing Chinese Diasporas, 1842 to 1949." *The Journal of Asian Studies* 58, no. 2 (1999): 306–37.

McSheffrey, Gerald M. "Slavery, Indentured Servitude, Legitimate Trade and the Impact of Abolition in the Gold Coast, 1874–1901: A Reappraisal." *The Journal of African History* 24, no. 3 (1983): 349–68.

Mehlman, Jeffrey. *Revolution and Repetition: Marx/Hugo/Balzac*. Berkeley: University of California Press, 2018.

Meillassoux, Claude. *Anthropologie économique des Gouro de Côte d'Ivoire: de l'économie de subsistance à l'agriculture commerciale*. Paris: Éditions de l'École des hautes études en sciences sociales, 1964.

Melillo, Edward D. "The First Green Revolution: Debt Peonage and the Making of the Nitrogen Fertilizer Trade, 1840–1930." *The American Historical Review* 117, no. 4 (2012): 1028–60.

Mhone, Guy C.Z. *The Political Economy of a Dual Labor Market in Africa: The Copper Industry and Dependency in Zambia, 1929–1969*. Fairleigh: Dickinson University Press, 1982.

Middleton, John. "Merchants: An Essay in Historical Ethnography." *Journal of the Royal Anthropological Institute* 9, no. 3 (2003): 509–26.

Miers, Suzanne. "Slavery and the Slave Trade as International Issues 1890 – 1939." *Slavery and Abolition* 19, no. 2 (1998): 16 – 37.

Miers, Suzanne, and Martin A. Klein, eds. *Slavery and Colonial Rule in Africa.* London: Routledge, 1999.

Miers, Suzanne, and Igor Kopytoff, eds. *Slavery in Africa: Historical and Anthropological Perspectives.* Madison: University of Wisconsin Press, 1979.

Miers, Suzanne, and Richard Roberts, eds. *The End of Slavery in Africa.* Madison: University of Wisconsin Press, 1988.

Miller, Joseph C. *The Problem of Slavery as History: A Global Approach.* New Haven: Yale University Press, 2012.

Miller, Joseph C. *Way of Death: Merchant Capitalism and the Angolan Slave Trade, 1740 – 1830.* Madison: University of Wisconsin Press, 1988.

Miranda Junco, Agustín. *Leyes coloniales. Legislación de los territorios españoles del Golfo de Guinea.* Madrid: Imprenta Sucesores de Rivadeneyra, 1945.

Mishra, Amit Kumar. "Sardars, Kanganies and Maistries: Intermediaries in the Indian Labour Diaspora During the Colonial Period." In *The History of Labour Intermediation: Institutions and Finding Employment in the Nineteenth and Early Twentieth Centuries*, edited by Sigrid Wadauer, Thomas Buchner, and Alexander Mejstrik, 368 – 87. New York: Berghahn Books, 2015.

Mohabir, Nalini. "Servitude in the Shadow of Slavery? Towards a Relational Account of Indenture." In *Human Bondage in the Cultural Contact Zone. Transdisciplinary Perspectives on Slavery and Its Discourses*, edited by Raphael Hörmann and Gesa Mackenthun, 227 – 57. Münster: Waxmann Verlag, 2010.

Mohapatra, Prabhu. "From Contract to Status? Or How Law Shaped Labour Relations in Colonial India 1780 – 1920." In *India's Unfree Workforce: Of Bondage Old and New*, edited by Jan Breman, 96 – 125. New Delhi: Oxford University Press, 2009.

Mohapatra, Prabhu. "Eurocentrism, Forced Labour, and Global Migration: A Critical Assessment." *International Review of Social History* 52, no. 1 (2007): 110 – 15.

Monrad, Hans Christian. *Two Views from Christiansborg Castle: A Description of the Guinea Coast and Its Inhabitants.* Translated by Selena Axelrod Winsnes. Legon: Sub-Saharan Publishers, 2009.

Monteón, Michael. "The *Enganche* in the Chilean Nitrate Sector, 1880 – 1930." *Latin American Perspectives* 6, no. 3 (1979): 66 – 79.

Montgomery, James D. "Social Networks and Labor-Market Outcomes: Toward an Economic Analysis." *The American Economic Review* 81, no. 5 (1991): 1408 – 18.

Morrill, Warren T. "Two Urban Cultures of Calabar, Nigeria." PhD Thesis, University of Chicago, 1961.

Morris, Mike. "Social History and the Transition to Capitalism in the South African Countryside." *Review of African Political Economy*, no. 41 (1988): 60 – 72.

Moulier-Boutang, Yann. *De l'esclavage au salariat: économie historique du salariat bridé.* Paris: Presses universitaires de France, 1998.

Moulier-Boutang, Yann. "Forms of Unfree Labor: Primitive Accumulation, History or Prehistory of Capitalism?" *Viewpoint Magazine*, February 1, 2018. https://www.viewpointmag.com/2018/02/01/forms-unfree-labor-primitive-accumulation-history-prehistory-capitalism/.

Moya, Jose C. *Cousins and Strangers: Spanish Immigrants in Buenos Aires, 1850 – 1930.* Berkeley: University of California Press, 1998.

Muñoz Martínez, Celeste. "La ley contra la costumbre. Segregación, asimilación jurídica y castigo en la Guinea española bajo el franquismo (1936–1959)." PhD Thesis, Universitat de Barcelona, 2020.

Murray, Albert V. *The School in the Bush: A Critical Study of the Theory and Practice of Native Education in Africa.* New York: Routledge, 1967.

Murray, Martin J. "'Blackbirding' at 'Crooks' Corner': Illicit Labour Recruiting in the Northeastern Transvaal, 1910–1940." *Journal of Southern African Studies* 21, no. 3 (1995): 373–97.

Murray, Martin J. "The Triumph of Marxist Approaches in South African Social and Labour History." *Journal of Asian and African Studies* 23, no. 1–2 (1988): 79–101.

Naanen, Ben. "Economy within an Economy: The Manilla Currency, Exchange Rate Instability and Social Conditions in South-Eastern Nigeria, 1900–48." *The Journal of African History* 34, no. 3 (1993): 425–46.

Nair, Kannan K. *Politics and Society in South Eastern Nigeria, 1841–1906: A Study of Power, Diplomacy and Commerce in Old Calabar.* London: Routledge, 1972.

Nascimento, Augusto. "Escravatura, trabalho forçado e contrato em S. Tomé e Príncipe nos séculos XIX e XX: sujeição e ética laboral." *Africana Studia* 7 (2004): 183–217.

Navarro, Joaquín J. *Apuntes sobre el estado de la costa occidental de Africa y principalmente de las posesiones españoles en el Golfo de Guinea.* Madrid: Impr. Nacional, 1859.

Ndjio, Basile. "Mokoagne Moni: Sorcery and New Forms of Wealth in Cameroon." *Past & Present* 199, no. 3 (2008): 271–89.

Nerín, Gustau. *Traficants d'ànimes: els negrers espanyols a l'Àfrica.* Barcelona: Pòrtic, 2016.

Nerín, Gustau. *Corisco y el estuario del Muni: 1470–1931: del aislamiento a la globalización y de la globalización a la marginación.* Paris: L'Harmattan, 2015.

Nerín, Gustau. *La última selva de España: antropófagos, misioneros y guardias civiles: crónica de la conquista de los Fang de la Guinea Española, 1914–1930.* Madrid: Los Libros de la Catarata, 2010.

Nerín, Gustau, and Alfredo Bosch. *El imperio que nunca existió: La aventura colonial discutida en Hendaya.* Barcelona: Plaza & Janés, 2001.

Newell, Stephanie. *The Power to Name: A History of Anonymity in Colonial West Africa.* Athens: Ohio University Press, 2013.

Ngai, Sianne. *Theory of the Gimmick: Aesthetic Judgment and Capitalist Form.* Cambridge: Harvard University Press, 2020.

Nieboer, Herman J. *Slavery as an Industrial System: Ethnological Researches.* The Hague: M. Nijhoff, 1900.

Nietzsche, Friedrich. "On Truth and Lie in an Extra-Moral Sense." In *The Portable Nietzsche*, translated by Walter Kaufmann, 42–47. New York: Penguin Books, 1976.

Nigeria. "Annual Report on the Department of Labour and Resettlement of Ex-Servicemen 1949/50." Lagos: Government Printer, 1950.

Nigeria. "Annual Report of the Department of Labour, Nigeria, for the Year 1944." Lagos: Government Printer, 1945. CO 657/53.

Nigeria. "Annual Report on the Department of Labour, Nigeria, for the Year 1943." Lagos: Government Printer, 1945.

Nigeria and Aba Commission of Inquiry. "Notes of Evidence Taken by the Commission of Inquiry Appointed to Inquire into the Disturbance in the Calabar and Owerri Provinces, December, 1929." Lagos: Government Printer, 1930.

Nigeria, and Timothy Farley Smith. "Report on Employment of Nigerian Labour in Fernando Poo." Sessional paper (Nigeria). Lagos: Government Printer, 1939.

Nigerian Parliament. "Report of the Parliamentary Delegation to Fernando Poo & Rio Muni 1957." Lagos: Federation of Nigeria, 1958.

North-Coombes, M. D. "From Slavery to Indenture: Forced Labour in the Political Economy of Mauritius, 1834–1867." In *Indentured Labour in the British Empire, 1834–1920*, edited by Kay Saunders, 78–125. London: Croom Helm, 1984.

Northrup, David. *Indentured Labor in the Age of Imperialism, 1834–1922*. Cambridge: Cambridge University Press, 1995.

Northrup, David. *Beyond the Bend in the River: African Labor in Eastern Zaire, 1865–1940*. Athens: Ohio University Center for International Studies, 1988.

Northrup, David. *Trade Without Rulers: Pre-Colonial Economic Development in South-Eastern Nigeria*. Oxford: Clarendon Press, 1978.

Northrup, David. "Free and Unfree Labor Migration, 1600–1900: An Introduction." *Journal of World History* 14, no. 2 (2003): 125–30.

Northrup, David. "Freedom and Indentured Labor in the French Caribbean, 1848–1900." In *Coerced and Free Migration: Global Perspectives*, edited by David Eltis, 205–28. Stanford: Stanford University Press, 2002.

Northrup, David. "From Slavery to Neoslavery: The Bight of Biafra and Fernando Po in the Era of Abolition, 1827–1930." *Journal of Interdisciplinary History* 28, no. 1 (1997): 168–69.

Nwabughuogu, Anthony. "From Wealthy Entrepreneurs to Petty Traders: The Decline of African Middlemen in Eastern Nigeria, 1900–1950." *The Journal of African History* 23, no. 3 (1982): 365–79.

Nwokeji, G. Ugo. *The Slave Trade and Culture in the Bight of Biafra: An African Society in the Atlantic World*. New York: Cambridge University Press, 2010.

Nwokeji, G. Ugo. "The Slave Emancipation Problematic: Igbo Society and the Colonial Equation." *Comparative Studies in Society and History* 40, no. 2 (1998): 318–55.

Ocha'a Mve, Constantino. *Fuentes archivísticas y bibliotecarias de Guinea Ecuatorial. Guía general del administrativo, del investigador y del estudiante*. Madrid: Anzos, 1985.

Ocobock, Paul, and Andrew Burton. "The 'Travelling Native': Vagrancy and Colonial Control in British East Africa." In *Cast Out: Vagrancy and Homelessness in Global and Historical Perspective*, edited by A.L. Beier and Paul Ocobock, 270–301. Athens: Ohio University Press, 2008.

O'Connell Davidson, Julia. *Modern Slavery: The Margins of Freedom*. London: Palgrave Macmillan UK, 2015.

Ofonagoro, Walter. "An Aspect of British Colonial Policy in Southern Nigeria: The Problems of Forced Labour and Slavery, 1895–1928." In *Studies in Southern Nigerian History*, edited by Boniface Obichere, 219–44. London: Frank Cass, 1982.

Ofonagoro, Walter. "From Traditional to British Currency in Southern Nigeria: Analysis of a Currency Revolution, 1880–1948." *The Journal of Economic History* 39, no. 3 (1979): 623–54.

Oham, Anthony C. "Labor Migration from Southeastern Nigeria to Spanish Fernando Po, 1900–1968." MA Thesis, Central Michigan University, 2006.

Ojo, Olatunji. "The Southern Nigeria Native House Rule Ordinance (1901)." *African Economic History* 40 (2012): 127–36.

Okenve, Enrique N. "Equatorial Guinea 1927–1979: A New African Tradition." PhD Thesis, SOAS, 2007.

Okenve, Enrique N. "An Island in the Middle of Everywhere: Bioko under Colonial Domination." In *African Islands: Leading Edges of Empire and Globalization*, edited by Toyin Falola, R. Joseph Parrott, and Danielle Porter Sanchez, 125–56. Rochester: University of Rochester Press, 2019.

Okenve, Enrique N. "They Never Finished Their Journey: The Territorial Limits of Fang Ethnicity in Equatorial Guinea, 1930–1963." *International Journal of African Historical Studies* 47, no. 2 (2014): 259–85.

Okia, Opolot. *Labor in Colonial Kenya after the Forced Labor Convention, 1930–1963*. London: Palgrave Macmillan, 2019.

Okolie, Andrew C. "The Transformation of Eastern Nigeria: From Self Sufficiency to Social Crisis." In *The Foundations of Nigeria: Essays in Honor of Toyin Falola*, edited by Toyin Falola, 449–72. Trenton: Africa World Press, 2003.

Olukoju, Ayodeji. "Beyond a Footnote: Indigenous Scholars and the Writing of West African Economic History." In *Routledge Handbook of Global Economic History*, edited by Francesco Boldizzoni and Pat Hudson, 377–93. London: Routledge, 2015.

Olukoju, Ayodeji. "Self-Help Criminality as Resistance?: Currency Counterfeiting in Colonial Nigeria." *International Review of Social History* 45, no. 3 (2000): 385–407.

Olukoju, Ayodeji. "Social Prestige, Agency, and Criminality: Economic Depression and Currency Counterfeiting in Inter-War British West Africa." *International Journal of African Historical Studies* 54, no. 2 (2021): 149–73.

Orde-Browne, Granville St. John. *The African Labourer*. London: Routledge, 1967.

Orde-Browne, Granville St. John. *Labour Conditions in West Africa*. London: H.M. Stationary Office, 1941.

Osella, Filippo. "The (Im)Morality of Mediation and Patronage in South India and the Gulf." In *Patronage as Politics in South Asia*, edited by Anastasia Piliavsky, 365–94. Cambridge: Cambridge University Press, 2014.

Osoba, Segun. "The Phenomenon of Labour Migration in the Era of British Colonial Rule: A Neglected Aspect of Nigeria's Social History." *Journal of the Historical Society of Nigeria* 4, no. 4 (1969): 515–38.

Osterhammel, Jürgen. "Hierarchies and Connections: Aspects of a Global Social History." In *An Emerging Modern World, 1750–1870*, edited by Sebastian Conrad and Jürgen Osterhammel, 663–888. Cambridge: Harvard University Press, 2018.

Osuntokun, Akinjide. *Equatorial Guinea Nigerian Relations: The Diplomacy of Labour*. Lagos: Oxford University Press, 1978.

Osuntokun, Akinjide. "Relations Between Nigeria and Fernando Po from Colonial Times to the Present." In *Nigeria and the World: Readings in Nigerian Foreign Policy*, edited by Bolaji Akinyemi, 1–16. Ibadan: Ibadan University Press, 1978.

Ottenberg, Simon. *Igbo Religion, Social Life, and Other Essays*. Edited by Toyin Falola. Trenton: Africa World Press, 2006.

Oyono Sa Abegue, Valentin. "L'évolution Des Structures Productives et Sociales de l'économie de La Guinée Equatoriale 1858–1968." PhD Thesis, Université de Lyon II, 1985.

Pallaver, Karin. "Paying in Cents, Paying in Rupees: Colonial Currencies, Labour Relations, and the Payment of Wages in Early Colonial Kenya." In *Colonialism, Institutional Change, and Shifts in Global Labour Relations*, edited by Karin Hofmeester and Pim Zwart, 295–327. Amsterdam: Amsterdam University Press, 2018.

Pallaver, Karin, ed. *Monetary Transitions: Currencies, Colonialism and African Societies.* Basingstoke: Palgrave Macmillan, 2022.

Pardue, Jeff. "Antislavery and Imperialism: The British Suppression of the Slave Trade and the Opening of Fernando Po, 1827–1829." *Itinerario* 44, no. 1 (2020): 178–95.

Peck, Gunther. *Reinventing Free Labor: Padrones and Immigrant Workers in the North American West, 1880–1930.* Cambridge: Cambridge University Press, 2000.

Peebles, Gustav. "Rehabilitating the Hoard: The Social Dynamics of Unbanking in Africa and Beyond." *Africa* 84, no. 4 (2014): 595–613.

Pélissier, René. *Los territorios españoles de Africa.* Madrid: Consejo Superior de Investigaciones Científicas, 1964.

Peña y Goyoaga, José María de la. *Repertorio de legislación colonial (Territorios españoles del Golfo de Guinea). Años 1945–1954.* Madrid: Artes gráficas Fenix, 1955.

Perpiñá Grau, Román. *De colonización y economía en la Guinea española: investigación, sobre el terreno, de la estructura y sistema de colonización en la Guinea española, con referencia especial a lo económico, precedido de un estudio general de los territorios africanos.* Barcelona: Tall. Ibero Americanos, 1945.

Perpiñá Grau, Román. "Mano de obra africana, factor de coste colonial: investigación sobre el peso de los braceros contratados en Fernando Poo." *Cuadernos de Estudios Africanos* 3 (1947): 127–44.

Phillips, Anne. *The Enigma of Colonialism: British Policy in West Africa.* London: James Currey, 1989.

Pietz, William. "The Problem of the Fetish, II: The Origin of the Fetish." *RES: Anthropology and Aesthetics* 13 (1987): 23–45.

Piqueras, José Antonio, ed. *Azucar y esclavitud en el final del trabajo forzado. Homenaje a M. Moreno Fraginals.* Madrid: Fondo de Cultura Economica, 2002.

Plowman, Robert J. "The Voyage of the 'Coolie' Ship Kate Hooper October 3, 1857 – March 26, 1858." *Prologue Magazine*, 2001. https://www.archives.gov/publications/prologue/2001/summer/coolie-ship-kate-hooper-1.html.

Poincaré, Henri. *Science and Hypothesis.* London: Science Press, 1905.

Polanyi, Karl. *The Great Transformation: The Political and Economic Origins of Our Time.* Boston: Beacon Press, 1957.

Pozanco, Ángel M. *Guinea mártir: Narraciones, notas y comentarios de un condenado a muerte.* Barcelona: Colección Actualidad, 1937.

Prakash, Gyan. *Bonded Histories: Genealogies of Labor Servitude in Colonial India.* Cambridge: Cambridge University Press, 1990.

Pratten, David. *The Man-Leopard Murders: History and Society in Colonial Nigeria.* Edinburgh: Edinburgh University Press, 2007.

Quirk, Joel. *The Anti-Slavery Project: From the Slave Trade to Human Trafficking.* Philadelphia: University of Pennsylvania Press, 2011.

Quirk, Joel. "Defining Slavery in All Its Forms: Historical Inquiry as Contemporary Instruction." In *The Legal Understanding of Slavery*, edited by J. Allain, 253–78. Oxford: Oxford University Press, 2012.

Raman, Ravi. *Global Capital and Peripheral Labour: The History and Political Economy of Plantation Workers in India.* London: Routledge, 2010.

Ramos Izquierdo y Vivar, Luis, and Eduardo Navarro y Beltran del Rio. *Descripción geográfica y gobierno, administración y colonización de las colonias españolas del golfo de Guinea.* Madrid: Impr. de Felipe Peña Cruz, 1912.

Ranby, John. *Observations on the Evidence Given Before the Committees of the Privy Council and House of Commons in Support of the Bill for Abolishing the Slave Trade.* London: John Stockdale, 1791.

Rancière, Jacques. *The Flesh of Words: The Politics of Writing.* Stanford: Stanford University Press, 2004.

Rathbone, Richard. "West Africa, 1874–1948: Employment Legislation in a Nonsettler Peasant Economy." In *Masters, Servants, and Magistrates in Britain and the Empire, 1562–1955,* edited by Douglas Hay and Paul Craven, 481–98. Chapel Hill: University of North Carolina Press, 2004.

Renault, François. *Libération d'esclaves et nouvelle servitude: les rachats de captifs africains pour le compte des colonies françaises après l'abolition de l'esclavage.* Abidjan: Les Nouvelles Éditions Africaines, 1976.

Rey, Pierre-Philippe. *Colonialisme, néo-colonialisme et transition au capitalisme; exemple de la Comilog au Congo-Brazzaville.* Paris: F. Maspero, 1971.

Ribeiro da Silva, Filipa. *Dutch and Portuguese in Western Africa: Empires, Merchants and the Atlantic System, 1580–1674.* Leiden: Brill, 2011.

Richardson, Peter. *Chinese Mine Labour in the Transvaal.* London: Macmillan Press, 1982.

Ríos, Mateo. *La España ignorada.* Barcelona: Hispano Europea, 1959.

Robin, Cohen, and Michael David. "The Revolutionary Potential of the African Lumpenproletariat: A Sceptical View." *Institute of Development Studies Bulletin* 5, no. 2–3 (1973): 31–42.

Robins, Jonathan. *Oil Palm: A Global History.* Chapel Hill: University of North Carolina Press, 2021.

Rodríguez Barrera, Joaquín. *Manual del agricultor en Fernando Póo: El cacao.* Barcelona: Artes gráficas, 1924.

Roe, Henry. *West African Scenes: Descriptions of Fernando Po.* London: Elliot Stock, 1874.

Roitman, Janet. *Fiscal Disobedience: An Anthropology of Economic Regulation in Central Africa.* Princeton: Princeton University Press, 2004.

Roldán de Montaud, Inés. "On the Blurred Boundaries of Freedom Liberated Africans in Cuba, 1817–1870." In *New Frontiers of Slavery,* edited by Dale W. Tomich, 127–56. Albany: SUNY Press, 2016.

Roldán de Montaud, Inés. *Origen, evolución y supresión del grupo de negros "emancipados" en Cuba (1817–1870).* Madrid: Consejo Superior de Investigaciones Científicas, 1982.

Romero Moliner, Rafael. "Crónica de los territorios de Guinea." *Cuadernos de Estudios Africanos* 17 (1952): 90–92.

Romero Moliner, Rafael. "Apuntes sobre la estructura social de Fernando Poo." *Cuadernos de Estudios Africanos* 7 (1949): 23–52.

Rothman, E. Natalie. *Brokering Empire: Trans-Imperial Subjects between Venice and Istanbul.* Ithaca: Cornell University Press, 2015.

Roy, Tirthankar. "Sardars, Jobbers, Kanganies: The Labour Contractor and Indian Economic History." *Modern Asian Studies* 42, no. 5 (2008): 971–98.

Roy, Tirthankar. "Labour-Intensity and Industrialization in Colonial India." In *Labour-Intensive Industrialization in Global History*, edited by Gareth Austin and Kaoru Sugihara, 107–121. London: Routledge, 2013.

Ruiz Benitez, Demetrio. "Guinea española: su posición en África, economía de la colonia y estudio especial de su comercio exterior." MA Thesis, Escuela Central Superior de Comercio, 1970.

Sampedro, Benita. "¡Aquella mansión de desconsuelo y de horror!" In *Guinea Ecuatorial (des)conocida: lo que sabemos, ignoramos, inventamos y deformamos acerca de su pasado y su presente*, edited by Juan Aranzadi and Gonzalo Álvarez Chillida, 441–70. Madrid: UNED, 2020.

Sampedro, Benita. "Rethinking the Archive and the Colonial Library: Equatorial Guinea." *Journal of Spanish Cultural Studies* 9 (2008): 321–41.

Sandinot, Emmanuelle. "Guinea ecuatorial (española). Un territorio del que se habla poco." *Cuadernos de Ruedo Iberico* 13/14 (1967): 90–105.

Sant Gisbert, Jordi. "El comerç de cacau entre l'illa de Bioko i Barcelona: La Unión de Agricultores de la Guinea Española (1880–1941)." Ph.D. Thesis, Universitat Pompeu Fabra, 2017.

Sant Gisbert, Jordi. "El negocio del cacao: origen y evolución de la elite económica colonial en Fernando Poo (1880–1936)." *Ayer* 109, no. 1 (2018): 137–68.

Sant Gisbert, Jordi, and Eduard Gargallo Sariol. *El petit imperi: catalans en la colonització de la Guinea Espanyola*. Barcelona: Angle, 2021.

Sanz Casas, Gonzal. "Los finqueros y el uso del trabajo forzado en la agricultura colonial de la isla de Fernando Poo." *Arxiu d'Etnografia de Catalunya* 3 (1984): 123–36.

Sanz Casas, Gonzal. "Política colonial y organización del trabajo en la isla de Fernando Poo: 1880–1930." PhD Thesis, Universidad de Barcelona, 1983.

Sanz Casas, Gonzal. "Problemas de una agricultura colonial: Los territorios españolas del Golfo de Guinea, 1940–1960." MA Thesis, Universidad Autonoma Barcelona, 1975.

Schapera, Isaac. *Migrant Labour and Tribal Life. A Study of Conditions in the Bechuanaland Protectorate*. London: Oxford University Press, 1947.

Schuler, Monica. "Kru Emigration to British and French Guiana, 1841–1857." In *Africans in Bondage: Studies in Slavery and the Slave Trade*, edited by Philip D. Curtin and Paul E. Lovejoy, 155–201. Madison: University of Wisconsin Press, 1986.

Schuler, Monica. "The Recruitment of African Indentured Labourers for European Colonies in the Nineteenth Century." In *Colonialism and Migration: Indentured Labour Before and After Slavery*, edited by Peter Emmer, 125–60. New York: Springer, 1986.

Scott, Christopher D. "Peasants, Proletarianization and the Articulation of Modes of Production: The Case of Sugar Cane Cutters in Northern Peru, 1940–69." *Journal of Peasant Studies* 3, no. 3 (1976): 321–42.

Scott, Rebecca J. *Slave Emancipation in Cuba: The Transition to Free Labor, 1860–1899*. Princeton: Princeton University Press, 1985.

Scott, Rebecca J. "Defining the Boundaries of Freedom in the World of Cane: Cuba, Brazil, and Louisiana after Emancipation." *The American Historical Review* 99, no. 1 (1994): 70–102.

Seibert, Julia. *In die globale Wirtschaft gezwungen: Arbeit und kolonialer Kapitalismus im Kongo (1885–1960)*. Frankfurt am Main: Campus Verlag, 2016.

Sen, Samita. "Commercial Recruiting and Informal Intermediation: Debate over the Sardari System in Assam Tea Plantations, 1860–1900." *Modern Asian Studies* 44, no. 1 (2010): 3–28.

Sen, Samita. "Questions of Consent: Women's Recruitment for Assam Tea Gardens, 1859–1900." *Studies in History* 18, no. 2 (2002): 231–60.

Shepherd, Verene A. "The Other Middle Passage? Nineteenth-Century Bonded Labour Migration and the Legacy of the Slavery Debate in the British-Colonized Caribbean." In *Working Slavery, Pricing Freedom: Perspectives from the Caribbean, Africa and the African Diaspora*, edited by Verene A. Shepherd, 343–75. New York: Palgrave, 2002.

Siale Djangany, José Fernando. "Ësáasi Eweera: en el laberinto del Estado dual." *Éndoxa: Series Filosóficas* 37 (2016): 169–98.

Silva, S.B.D. de. *The Political Economy of Underdevelopment.* London: Routledge, 2012.

Silver, Morris. "The Role of Slave Markets in Migration from the Near East to Rome." *Klio* 98, no. 1 (2017): 184–202.

Silver, Morris. "Contractual Slavery in the Roman Economy." *Ancient History Bulletin* 25 (2011): 73–132.

Simmons, Donald C. "Analysis of the Reflection of Culture in Efik Folktales." PhD Thesis, Yale University, 1957.

Singha, Radhika. "Settle, Mobilize, Verify: Identification Practices in Colonial India." *Studies in History* 16, no. 2 (2000): 151–98.

Sinha, Nitin. "Contract, Work, and Resistance: Boatmen in Early Colonial Eastern India, 1760s–1850s." *International Review of Social History* 59, no. S22 (2014): 11–43.

Smith, Daniel Jordan. *A Culture of Corruption: Everyday Deception and Popular Discontent in Nigeria.* Princeton: Princeton University Press, 2008.

Smith, Robert. "The Canoe in West African History." *The Journal of African History* 11, no. 4 (1970): 515–33.

Smith, Robert. "The Lagos Consulate, 1851–1861: An Outline." *The Journal of African History* 15, no. 3 (1974): 393–416.

Spain and Gobierno General de los Territorios Españoles del Golfo de Guinea. *Memoria de la labor realizada en el período 1949–1955.* Madrid: Rama, 1955.

Spain, Ministerio de Trabajo, and Delegación Provincial del Golfo de Guinea. *Reglamentación del Trabajo de 9 de Noviembre de 1953.* Palma de Mallorca: Ministerio de Trabajo, 1958.

Stallybrass, Peter. "Marx and Heterogeneity: Thinking the Lumpenproletariat." *Representations* 31 (1990): 69–95.

Stanziani, Alessandro. *Labor on the Fringes of Empire: Voice, Exit and the Law.* Basingstoke: Palgrave Macmillan, 2019.

Stanziani, Alessandro. *Labour, Coercion, and Economic Growth in Eurasia, 17th–20th Centuries.* Leiden: Brill, 2012.

Stanziani, Alessandro. "Local Bondage in Global Economies: Servants, Wage Earners, and Indentured Migrants in Nineteenth-Century France, Great Britain, and the Mascarene Islands." *Modern Asian Studies* 47, no. 4 (2013): 1218–51.

Stanziani, Alessandro. "Beyond Colonialism: Servants, Wage Earners and Indentured Migrants in Rural France and on Reunion Island (c. 1750–1900)." *Labor History* 54, no. 1 (2013): 64–87.

Stedman Jones, Gareth. *Outcast London: A Study in the Relationship Between Classes in Victorian Society.* Oxford: Clarendon Press, 1971.

Steinfeld, Robert J. *Coercion, Contract, and Free Labor in the Nineteenth Century.* New York: Cambridge University Press, 2001.
Stevenson, J. "The London 'Crimp' Riots of 1794." *International Review of Social History* 16, no. 1 (1971): 40–58.
Stichter, Sharon. *African Society Today: Migrant Laborers.* Cambridge: Cambridge University Press, 1985.
Stirner, Max. *The Ego and Its Own: The Case of The Individual Against Authority.* Edited by David Leopold. Translated by Steven T. Byington. Cambridge: Cambridge University Press, 1995.
Sundiata, Ibrahim. *Brothers and Strangers: Black Zion, Black Slavery, 1914–1940.* Durham: Duke University Press, 2004.
Sundiata, Ibrahim. *From Slaving to Neoslavery: The Bight of Biafra and Fernando Po in the Era of Abolition, 1827–1930.* Wisconsin: University of Wisconsin Press, 1996.
Sundiata, Ibrahim. *Equatorial Guinea: Colonialism, State Terror, and the Search for Stability.* Oxford: Westview Press, 1990.
Sundiata, Ibrahim. "'Cuba Africana': Cuba and Spain in the Bight of Biafra, 1839–1869." *The Americas* 34, no. 1 (1977): 90–101.
Sundiata, Ibrahim. "The Rise and Decline of Kru Power: Fernando Po in the 19th Century." *Liberian Studies Journal* 6, no. 1 (1975): 25–43.
Sundiata, Ibrahim. "Prelude to Scandal: Liberia and Fernando Po, 1880–1930." *The Journal of African History* 15, no. 1 (1974): 97–112.
Talbot, Percy A. *Life in Southern Nigeria the Magic, Beliefs, and Customs of the Ibibio Tribe.* London: Macmillan and Co. limited, 1923.
Tapela, Henderson M. "The Cross River Basin: Colonial Labour Policies and Practices." In *A History of the Cross River Region of Nigeria*, edited by Monday B. Abasiattai, 198–214. Calabar: University of Calabar Press, 1990.
Tapela, Henderson M. "Nigerian Labour for Fernando Po." *The Calabar Historical Journal* 3, no. 1 (1985): 36–56.
Taussig, Michael. *Shamanism, Colonialism, and the Wild Man: A Study in Terror and Healing.* Chicago: University of Chicago Press, 1991.
Taylor, Harold R. *Jungle Trader.* London: Jarrolds, 1939.
Terán, Manuel de. *Síntesis geográfica de Fernando Poo.* Madrid: Consejo Superior de Investigaciones Científicas, 1962.
Testart, Alain. "What Is a Gift?" *HAU: Journal of Ethnographic Theory* 3, no. 1 (2013): 249–61.
Testart, Alain. "The Extent and Significance of Debt Slavery." *Revue Française de Sociologie* 43 (2002): 173–204.
Thornton, John K. *Africa and Africans in the Making of the Atlantic World, 1400–1680.* Cambridge: Cambridge University Press, 1992.
Tilly, Charles. "Transplanted Networks." In *Immigration Reconsidered: History, Sociology, and Politics*, edited by Virginia Yans-McLaughlin, 79–95. Oxford: Oxford University Press, 1990.
Tinker, Hugh. *A New System of Slavery: The Export of Indian Labour Overseas, 1830–1920.* London: Oxford University Press, 1974.
Tiquet, Romain. *Travail forcé et mobilisation de la main-d'œuvre au Sénégal: années 1920–1960.* Rennes: Presses universitaires de Rennes, 2019.

Tonkin, Elizabeth. "Creating Kroomen: Ethnic Diversity, Economic Specialism and Changing Demand." In *Africa and the Sea: Proceedings of a Colloquium at the University of Aberdeen, March 1984*, edited by Jeffrey C. Stone, 27–47. Aberdeen: University of Abderdeen, 1985.

Toscano, Alberto. "Structured by Cows." *Journal of Cultural Economy* 9, no. 3 (2016): 304–9.

Uchendu, Victor C. "Slaves and Slavery in Iboland, Nigeria." In *Slavery in Africa: Historical and Anthropological Perspectives*, edited by Suzanne Miers and Igor Kopytoff, 121–32. Wisconsin: University of Wisconsin Press, 1979.

United States Department of Labor. *Labor Digests on Countries in Africa.* Washington: Bureau of Labor Statistics, 1966.

Vahed, Goolam. "Power and Resistance: Indentured Labour In Colonial Natal, 1860–1911." In *Resistance and Indian Indenture Experience. Comparative Perspectives*, edited by Maurits S. Hassankhan, Brij V. Lal, and Doug Munro, 95–120. Delhi: Manohar, 2014.

Valenciano-Mañé, Alba. "When The Big Ones Abandon the Marketplace: Morals and Politics of Price in Equatorial Guinea." In *Research in Economic Anthropology*, edited by Peter Luetchford and Giovanni Orlando, 39: 49–70. London: Emerald Publishing Limited, 2019.

Valero y Belenguer, Jose. "La Guinea española. La isla de Fernando Póo." *Boletín de la Real Sociedad Geográfica* 32 (1892): 144–365.

van der Linden, Marcel. *Workers of the World: Essays Toward a Global Labor History.* Leiden: Brill, 2008.

van der Linden, Marcel, and Karin Hofmeester, eds. *Handbook Global History of Work. Handbook Global History of Work.* Berlin: De Gruyter, 2017.

van der Linden, Marcel, and Magaly Rodriguez Garcia, eds. *On Coerced Labor: Work and Compulsion After Chattel Slavery.* Leiden: Brill, 2016.

van der Linden, Marcel, and Karl Heinz Roth. "'Marxism' or Marx's Method? A Brief Response to Tom Brass." *Science & Society* 82, no. 1 (2018): 120–27.

van Onselen, Charles. *Chibaro: African Mine Labour in Southern Rhodesia, 1900–1933.* London: Pluto Press, 1976.

van Onselen, Charles. *New Babylon, New Nineveh: Everyday Life on the Witwatersrand 1886–1914.* Johannesburg: Jonathan Ball, 1982.

van Onselen, Charles. "Crime and Total Institutions in the Making of Modern South Africa: The Life of 'Nongoloza' Mathebula 1867–1948." *History Workshop Journal* 19, no. 1 (1985): 62–81.

van Onselen, Charles. "South Africa's Lumpenproletarian Army 'Umkosi Wa Ntaba – The Regiment of the Hills, 1890–1920." *Collected Seminar Papers. Institute of Commonwealth Studies* 21 (1977): 77–103.

van Rossum, Mathias. "Changing Tides: Maritime Labour Relations in Europe and Asia." In *Colonialism, Institutional Change, and Shifts in Global Labour Relations*, edited by Karin Hofmeester and Pim Zwart, 239–64. Amsterdam: Amsterdam University Press, 2018.

Varma, Nitin. *Coolies of Capitalism: Assam Tea and the Making of Coolie Labour.* Berlin: De Gruyter, 2017.

Varma, Nitin. "Coolie Acts and the Acting Coolies: Coolie, Planter and State in the Late Nineteenth and Early Twentieth Century Colonial Tea Plantations of Assam." *Social Scientist* 33, no. 5–6 (2005): 49–72.

Vaughan, Megan. *Creating the Creole Island: Slavery in Eighteenth-Century Mauritius.* Duke: Duke University Press, 2005.

Velarde Fuentes, Juan. "Perpiña Grau y el pensamiento estructuralista español." *Revista de Economía Política* 83 (1979): 41–58.

Velarde Fuentes, Juan. "Problemas de empleo en la Guinea Ecuatorial." *Revista de Trabajo* 2, no. 1 (1964): 141–77.

Vigneswaran, Darshan, and Joel Quirk, eds. *Mobility Makes States: Migration and Power in Africa.* Pittsburgh: University of Pennsylvania Press, 2015.

Vigneswaran, Darshan, and Joel Quirk, eds. *Slavery, Migration and Contemporary Bondage in Africa.* Trenton: Africa World Press, 2013.

Vincent, Joan. "Political Anthropology: Manipulative Strategies." *Annual Review of Anthropology* 7, no. 1 (1978): 175–94.

Vos, Jelmer. "'Without the Slave Trade, No Recruitment': From Slave Trading to 'Migrant Recruitment' in the Lower Congo, 1830–90." In *Trafficking in Slavery's Wake: Law and the Experience of Women and Children in Africa*, edited by Benjamin N. Lawrance and Richard L. Roberts, 45–64. Athens: Ohio University Press, 2012.

Walker, Harry. "Demonic Trade: Debt, Materiality, and Agency in Amazonia." *Journal of the Royal Anthropological Institute* 18, no. 1 (2012): 140–59.

Wareing, John. "'Violently Taken Away or Cheatingly Duckoyed'. The Illicit Recruitment in London of Indentured Servants for the American Colonies, 1645–1718." *The London Journal* 26, no. 2 (2001): 1–22.

Wariboko, Nimi. "A Theory of the Canoe House Corporation." *African Economic History* 26 (1998): 141–72.

Washbrook, Sarah. "*Enganche* and Exports in Chiapas, Mexico: A Comparison of Plantation Labour in the Districts of Soconusco and Palenque, 1876–1911." *Journal of Latin American Studies* 39, no. 4 (2007): 797–825.

Washbrook, Sarah. "'Una Esclavitud Simulada': Debt Peonage in the State of Chiapas, Mexico, 1876–1911." *The Journal of Peasant Studies* 33, no. 3 (2006): 367–412.

Watson, James L. "Transactions in People: The Chinese Market in Slaves, Servants and Heirs." In *Asian and African Systems of Slavery*, edited by James L. Watson, 223–51. Berkeley: University of California Press, 1980.

Weber, Max. *Economy and Society: an Outline of Interpretive Sociology.* New York: Bedminster Press, 1968.

Weber, Max. "Commerce on the Stock and Commodity Exchanges [Die Börsenverkehr]." *Theory and Society* 29, no. 3 (2000): 339–71.

Wedgwood, Hensleigh. *A Dictionary of English Etymology.* London: Macmillan, 1878.

Wieschhoff, Heinrich A. *Colonial Policies in Africa.* Philadelphia: University of Pennsylvania Press, 1944.

Wolf, Eric. *Europe and the People Without History.* Berkeley: University of California Press, 1982.

Wolf, Eric. "Aspects of Group Relations in a Complex Society: Mexico 1." *American Anthropologist* 58, no. 6 (1956): 1065–78.

Wolf, Eric, and Sidney Mintz. "Haciendas and Plantations in Middle America and the Antilles." *Social and Economic Studies* 6, no. 3 (1957): 380–412.

Wolff, Günther. "Ein Beitrag zur Wirtschaft von Fernando Poo." *Beiträge zur Kolonialforschung* 1 (1942): 93–110.

Worger, William H. *South Africa's City of Diamonds: Mine Workers and Monopoly Capitalism in Kimberley, 1867–1895.* New Haven: Yale University Press, 1987.

Worsley, Peter. "Frantz Fanon and the 'Lumpenproletariat.'" In *The Socialist Register 1972*, edited by Ralph Miliband and John Savile, Vol. 9. New York: Monthly Review Press, 1972.

Xavier, Adro. *España en Africa. Ayer y hoy.* Barcelona: Ferma, 1960.

Xiang, Biao. "Predatory Princes and Princely Peddlers: The State and International Labour Migration Intermediaries in China." *Pacific Affairs* 85, no. 1 (2012): 47–68.

Xiang, Biao, and Johan Lindquist. "Migration Infrastructure." *International Migration Review* 48 (2014): 122–48.

Yglesias de La Riva, Angel. *Politica indígena en Guinea.* Madrid: Instituto de Estudios Africanos, 1947.

Yun, Lisa. *The Coolie Speaks: Chinese Indentured Laborers and African Slaves in Cuba.* Philadelphia: Temple University Press, 2008.

Zavala, Silvio. "Origenes coloniales del peonaje en México." *El Trimestre Económico* 10, no. 40 (1944): 711–48.

Zedong, Mao. *Selected Works of Mao Tse-Tung.* London: Lawrence & Wishart, 1954.

Zeuske, Michael. *Handbuch Geschichte der Sklaverei: Eine Globalgeschichte von den Anfängen bis zur Gegenwart.* Berlin: Walter de Gruyter, 2013.

Zeuske, Michael. "Coolies – Asiáticos and Chinos: Global Dimensions of Second Slavery." In *Bonded Labour: Global and Comparative Perspectives*, edited by Sabine Damir-Geilsdorf, Ulrike Lindner, Gesine Müller, Oliver Tappe, and Michael Zeuske, 26–48. Bielefeld: transcript, 2016.

Index

https://doi.org/10.1515/9783110755923-013

Printed and bound by CPI Group (UK) Ltd, Croydon, CR0 4YY

13/09/2026

14961092-0002